THE IMPACT OF TECHNOLOGY AND INNOVATION ON THE WELLBEING OF THE LEGAL PROFESSION

THE IMPACT OF TECHNOLOGY AND INNOVATION ON THE WELLBEING OF THE LEGAL PROFESSION

Edited by
Michael LEGG
Prue VINES
Janet CHAN

INTERSENTIA
Cambridge – Antwerp – Chicago

Intersentia Ltd
8 Wellington Mews
Wellington Street | Cambridge
CB1 1HW | United Kingdom
Tel: +44 1223 736 170
Email: mail@intersentia.co.uk
www.intersentia.com | www.intersentia.co.uk

*Distribution for the UK and
Rest of the World (incl. Eastern Europe)*
NBN International
1 Deltic Avenue, Rooksley
Milton Keynes MK13 8LD
United Kingdom
Tel: +44 1752 202 301 | Fax: +44 1752 202 331
Email: orders@nbninternational.com

Distribution for Europe
Intersentia Publishing nv
Groenstraat 31
2640 Mortsel
Belgium
Tel: +32 3 680 15 50
Email: mail@intersentia.be

Distribution for the USA and Canada
Independent Publishers Group
Order Department
814 North Franklin Street
Chicago, IL 60610
USA
Tel: +1 800 888 4741 (toll free) | Fax: +1 312 337 5985
Email: orders@ipgbook.com

The Impact of Technology and Innovation on the Wellbeing of the Legal Profession

Artwork on cover: Wizemark / Stocksy

ISBN 978-1-78068-955-5
D/2020/7849/23
NUR 820

British Library Cataloguing in Publication Data. A catalogue record for this book is available from the British Library.

FOREWORD

There has been an explosion of concern about the impact of technology and innovation on the wellbeing of the legal profession, especially in Australia and the United Kingdom. Mention of 'wellbeing' itself signals something that is very new. The impact of stress and mental illness on the delivery of services, outside of the armed services, were not systemically studied before the twenty-first century. Such matters played no role in legal duties of care or professional regulation either, until the very recent past.

As a pointer to the modernity of the wellness issue, a cited text written in 2013 is described as pre-dating the 'current explosion of interest' in the United Kingdom (p. 314). Australian attention began earlier but it goes no further back than around the year 2000. For seeding the debate, much credit goes to the campaign of Marie and George Jepson and the Foundation they established following the death by suicide in 2004 of their lawyer son. The Tristan Jepson Memorial Foundation (now Minds Count) explored what is peculiarly toxic about the study and practice of law compared to other callings.

The chapters in this excellent compilation analyse key drivers that impact negatively upon the wellbeing of many legal practitioners. Some of them were changes in the nature of legal practice, others the stuff of modern life. The book's contributors strive to identify differential impacts on different classes of person. Students', teachers' and lawyers' own perceptions of their stress and anomie are surveyed as well. The paucity of practical solutions on offer confirms to this reader that little will improve under the dominant neoliberal ideology.

Change itself can bring dangerous levels of stress. This is so even if its innovations produce optimal outcomes in the careful hands of many users. (The same may be said about motor cars and circular saws.)

This book also highlights the recency of many key innovations on the technological front and in workplace practices. Word-processing computers arrived in the late 1970s. Cellular phones and the internet in the 1980s, with email quickly supplanting 'snail mail' and facsimiles. These changes allowed the upsides and downsides of 24/7 access to communication across the globe and the ambivalent benefits of 'work-place flexibility'. Aided by these developments and spurred on by the mindset of Neoliberalism, legal practice has transformed itself so totally that the 1970s (when I started in the profession) appear almost Dickensian. In the 1970s legal partnerships were severely limited in size and all of them functioned within a single jurisdiction, i.e. a single State or Territory in Australia. To canvass for legal work was unprofessional conduct. Barristers had no direct access to clients. Costs agreements were unheard of. If there were office diaries, they were to record work done, not used for detailed costing and aggressive management purposes. Anything approaching the notion of a "billable hour" was itself an undisclosed Alternative Fee Arrangement in those days. Brief fees were marked in advance on the briefs delivered to barristers. For briefs themselves, even a thin ring binder was exceptional. A mountain of documents or of cases to be researched, hidden in a tiny computer file, lay blessedly in the distant future.

Nationwide "Competition Principles" would be favoured by the larger over the smaller firms and generally resisted by the Bar. But they were promoted by government, which (rightly in my opinion) recognised that differences between professions, business and trades were marginal at best. With the curtailment of professional self-regulation, the exposure of unproductive restrictive practices, and key rulings such as *Street v Queensland Bar Association*, the practice and oversight of law would quickly cross state and national boundaries. This expansion in the size and horizons of legal firms would contribute to disconnectedness and stress.

Adding to the pressures upon lawyers of the 'old school', clients became less respectful of old school ties. Commercial and governmental entities called for tendering for such services as they were not beginning to manage in-house. Conveyancers and tax accountants nibbled on profitable corners of traditional legal businesses. The law's counterpart of "Dr Google" and the rise of consumerism touched the self-esteem and pocket books of lawyers, reminding them that their own 'wellbeing' was and is not an exclusive right. Economic busts may be inevitable but they tend to recur unexpectedly: seismic global economic downturns would bring their own shocks to 'normality' and income.

The law itself has changed markedly over this period, partly in response to all these phenomena, but certainly in ways that have made its practice more complex and stressful. Within the working life of today's senior practitioners, the fiction of the declaratory theory has been overtaken by a fast-evolving common law that functions inside burgeoning regimes of state regulation. An actionable duty of care in professional advice has been discovered, triggering a huge expansion of professional indemnity insurance and all that that entails. Liability for psychiatric injury unassociated with physical trauma has been recognised, leading to a tightening of the employer's duty to take reasonable care for a safe workplace. (There is still a long way to go in this pocket of tort law, in my opinion, and the task is made harder by what this book describes as the 'contractualisation' and 'uberisation' of legal practice.) Discrimination of various sorts has become actionable and bullying is no longer viewed as the peculiar risk of schoolboys. Students and teachers at universities have come to expect that care is taken for more than their physical safety.

These legal developments are, of course, to be welcomed. But navigating them has brought new levels of complexity and stress. The legal developments have in turn contributed to identifying problems ignored by previous generations, doubtless at the 'cost' of exposing the apparently rising levels of the problems needing to be faced. These changes in the law have at least recognised some of the harms that are now so clearly in view and palliated them to a degree.

Because one has to start and finish somewhere, the contributors to this work have addressed the impacts of technical change and innovation on the *legal* profession. But the surveys and studies discussed herein all recognise the impact of externalities. One that is only touched upon lightly is the recent entry of women in large numbers into the legal workplace. This entirely laudable development has undoubtedly added to the stress of many men and not a few women, for a range of reasons going beyond the added competition for advancement. One upside of this demographic has been some revaluation of the true worth of unpaid work in the home. But more than anything, it has promoted the discourse of 'work-life balance' that functions as both as an aspiration and one focus of expanding legal and moral duties of care of employers and professional organisations.

These last-mentioned phenomena remind us that the issues confronting the legal academy and the legal profession that are addressed in this book are really problems of living in the modern world. Great-grandparents and grandparents who endured global wars and the Great Depression led lives untouched by the technological and innovative changes addressed in this book. But the stories they could tell would remind us that each generation has to confront its own crises of change and innovation. The COVID-19 pandemic which has arrived as the book is about to be published has added its own severe disruptions, many of them likely to be long term. Hopefully it will seed some positive reassessments and adjustments.

Keith Mason AC, QC
May 2020

ACKNOWLEDGEMENTS

This book originated from a number of strands of thought arising from our different areas of scholarship over several years. As we had separately worked on different areas of focus on the legal profession and as concerns about mental health in the profession mounted, we decided to draw on expertise that we were aware of from around the world in order to organise a symposium to discuss the interaction of the changes in technology, the profession and its practices and how they might impact on wellbeing. The symposium, as all such symposia do, then allowed us to tease out further implications of the interactions discussed, resulting in this book.

We are grateful to a number of organisations for supporting our research endeavours: the Law Society of New South Wales Future of Law and Innovation in the Profession (FLIP) research stream at UNSW Law; Whittens & McKeough Lawyers (now Automic); the Allens Hub for Technology, Law and Innovation at UNSW Law; and the Law Council of Australia who kindly gave permission for Allison Wallace and Imogen D'Souza to use findings from their 'National Attrition and Re-Engagement Study (NARS) Report' 2013 in their chapter.

A number of people who have contributed to the book, including research assistants Lachlan McFarlane, Sharon Mo and Deborah Hartstein, we thank them.

We would also like to thank Ann-Christin Maak-Scherpe and Ahmed Hegazi of Intersentia for bringing the book into the world with such professionalism and attention to detail.

CONTENTS

Foreword v
Acknowledgements ix
List of Cases xvii
List of Authors xix
List of Tables and Figures xxi

PART I. INTRODUCTION

Chapter 1. The Changing Field of Lawyering and its Impact on Practice and Wellbeing
Michael LEGG, Prue VINES and Janet CHAN 3

1. Introduction 3
2. The Great Expansion: Law Firms, In-House Counsel, the Billable Hour and Budgets 6
3. Globalisation 8
4. Technology 11
5. The New Law Firm 15
6. The Sharing or Gig Economy 16
7. The Future of the Legal Profession 18
8. The Approach of this Book 20
9. Conclusion 27

PART II. CHANGE, STRESS AND WELLBEING

Chapter 2. Student Attitudes to Legal Education: Revisiting the Pointers to Depression and Anxiety?
Prue VINES and Alex STEEL 31

1. Introduction 32
2. The Prevalence of Depression in Lawyers and Law Students 33
3. Explanations for the Disproportionate Incidence of Depression and Anxiety 34

4. Aims of the 2018 Survey 39
5. Results 40
6. Limitations 52
7. Discussion 53
8. Conclusion 55

Chapter 3. The Paradox of Satisfaction and Distress Among Lawyers: Implications for a Changing Field
Suzanne POYNTON and Janet CHAN 57

1. Introduction: Satisfaction and Mental Health of Lawyers 58
2. Understanding Lawyering Stress 60
3. Research Method and Analysis 61
4. Results 65
5. Conclusions and Implications 73

Chapter 4. Stress, Bullying and Harassment in the Legal Profession: A Risky Business
Alison WALLACE and Imogen D'SOUZA 77

1. Introduction 77
2. Poor Mental Health in Legal Workplaces 78
3. Sexual Harassment in Legal Workplaces 80
4. Bullying in Legal Workplaces 82
5. Psychosocial Workplace Injury in Australia is on the Rise 83
6. Aims of the National Attrition Study 85
7. Methodology 86
8. Results 88

Chapter 5. Public Sector Lawyering Stress and Wellbeing: Neoliberalism at Work?
Janet CHAN and Holly BLACKMORE 105

1. Introduction: Neoliberalism and Lawyering 106
2. What is Neoliberalism? 108
3. Neoliberalisation of Lawyering and its Consequences in the Public Sector 112
4. Comparing Public/Community with Private Lawyering 116
5. Perceptions of 'Wellbeing Interventions' 124
6. Concluding Remarks 128

Chapter 6. Law Teachers Speak Out: What do Law Schools Need to Change?
Colin JAMES, Caroline STREVENS and Rachael FIELD 131

1. Introduction 131
2. The Neoliberal University and Legal Education.................. 133
3. An Ethical Imperative to Interrogate the Quality of Working Life for Law Teachers... 136
4. Methodology.. 137
5. Methodological Limitations 141
6. Demographics... 141
7. Satisfaction at Work 141
8. Qualitative Data in Response to: 'Please Explain What You Think your University Could do to Improve Staff Quality of Working Life'.. 143
9. A 'To-Do' List for Law School Leaders and Managers............. 150
10. Conclusion... 151

PART III. TECHNOLOGY, INNOVATION AND THE STRUCTURE OF LEGAL PRACTICE

Chapter 7. Behavioural Legal Ethics and Attorney Wellbeing in Contemporary Practice
Jennifer K. ROBBENNOLT 155

1. Introduction 155
2. Ethics and Wellbeing 156
3. Substance Abuse and Mental Health 163
4. Factors in the Modern Legal Profession that Influence Both Ethics and Wellbeing 165
5. Conclusion... 174

Chapter 8. Is 'Uberisation' the Path to Lawyer Wellbeing?
Margaret THORNTON 177

1. Introduction 177
2. The Psychological Distress of Lawyers........................ 180
3. Uber Lawyering.. 184
4. Flexible and Autonomous 187
5. The Debit Side of NewLaw 190
6. Conclusion.. 197

Chapter 9. Do Law Firm Structures Matter? Incorporated Legal Practices and the Health and Wellbeing of Lawyers
Tahlia GORDON 199

1. Introduction 200
2. The Unhealthy and Un-Well Profession: Legal Practitioners in Crisis 203
3. The Demands of Practising in the Traditional Law Firm Partnership Structure 205
4. Law Firm Practice Structures: A New Look but a Different Feel? . . . 218
5. Conclusion 236

Chapter 10. Artificial Intelligence and Lawyer Wellbeing
Felicity BELL, Justine ROGERS and Michael LEGG 239

1. Introduction 239
2. Definitions and Current Situation 242
3. Indicators of Wellbeing within a Wider Context 243
4. What does Artificial Intelligence Mean for Wellbeing? 250
5. Concluding Remarks 264

Chapter 11. Lawyers' Fee Arrangements and their Wellbeing
Michael LEGG and Justine ROGERS 267

1. Introduction 268
2. The Billable Hour and AFAs: The State of Play 270
3. Fees and Wellbeing 275
4. Billable Hours 284
5. Alternative Fee Arrangements 292
6. Conclusion 306

PART IV. CONCLUSION

Chapter 12. Reflections on the UK Experience of Legal Academic Wellbeing and the Legal Professions: Moving Across Silos
Richard COLLIER 313

1. Introduction 313
2. From Legal Practice to Law School: A Snapshot of Wellbeing and Mental Health in the UK Legal Community 315
3. Approaching (Legal) Academic Wellbeing 318

4. From Legal Practice to Law School, or Moving Across Silos: Shared Themes 322
5. The Potential and the Problems of Wellbeing: Identity, Resilience and Responsibility. 326
6. Concluding Remarks 330

Index. 335

LIST OF CASES

Anderson v. Cryovac 862 F.2d 910 (1st Cir. 1988) 297
British American Tobacco Australia Services Ltd v. Cowell
(2002) 7 VR 524 215
Da Silva Moore v. Publicis Groupe 287 FRD 182 (SDNY 2012) 13
Giannarelli v. Wraith (1988) 165 CLR 543 215
Hickie v. Hunt & Hunt (1998) EOC ¶92-137 [1998] HREOCA 8 184
Irish Bank Resolution Corporation Limited v. Quinn [2015] IEHC 175 13
Law Society of NSW v. Foreman (1994) 34 NSWLR 408 211
McCabe v. British American Tobacco Australia Ltd [2002] VSC 73 215
McConnell Dowell Constructors (Aust) Pty Ltd v. Santam Ltd (No. 1)
[2016] VSC 734 13
Pyrrho Investments Ltd v. MWB Property Ltd [2016] EWHC 256 (Ch) 13
Spence v. Gerard Malouf and Partners Pty Ltd [2010] NSWSC 764, [110] 295
Re Robb (1996) 134 FLR 294 295

LIST OF AUTHORS

Felicity Bell
Research Fellow for the Law Society of New South Wales Future of Law and Innovation in the Profession (FLIP) Research Stream at UNSW Law, Sydney, Australia

Holly Blackmore
Doctoral candidate and Research Officer at UNSW Law, Sydney, Australia

Janet Chan
Professor and leader of the Data Justice Stream for the Allens Hub for Technology, Law and Innovation at UNSW Law, Sydney, Australia

Richard Collier FAcSS FRSA
Professor of Law at Newcastle University, UK, and was recently a Leverhulme Trust Research Fellow engaged in studies of wellbeing and anxiety in law

Imogen D'Souza
Honours Student and Research Assistant at Urbis Pty Ltd, Sydney, Australia

Rachael Field
Professor of Law at Bond University, Australia

Tahlia Gordon
Doctoral candidate at UNSW Law and Director at Creative Consequences Pty Ltd.

Colin James
Senior Lecturer at the Australian National University College of Law, Canberra, Australia

Michael Legg
Professor of Law and Director, Law Society of New South Wales Future of Law and Innovation in the Profession (FLIP) Research Stream at UNSW Law, Sydney, Australia

Suzanne Poynton
Acting Director and Research Manager at the Bureau of Crime Statistics and Research at the Department of Communities and Justice NSW, Australia

Jennifer K. Robbennolt
Associate Dean for Research, Alice Curtis Campbell Professor of Law and Professor of Psychology, Co-Director of the Illinois Program on Law, Behavior and Social Science, University of Illinois, USA

Justine Rogers
Senior Lecturer and Deputy Director of the Law Society of New South Wales Future of Law and Innovation in the Profession (FLIP) Research Stream at UNSW Law, Sydney, Australia

Alex Steel
Professor of Law and Director of Teaching Strategy, Office of DVC Academic, UNSW, Sydney, Australia

Caroline Strevens
Reader in Legal Education and Head of Portsmouth Law School, UK

Margaret Thornton
Emerita Professor of Law, Australian National University, Canberra, Australia

Prue Vines
Professor of Law and Co-Director of Private Law and Policy Group at UNSW Law, Sydney, Australia

Alison Wallace
Public Policy Advisor and Program Evaluator with over thirty years' experience, previously worked as a Director in Urbis' Economic and Social Advisory Team, Sydney, Australia

LIST OF TABLES AND FIGURES

Tables

Chapter 2

Table 1. Bifurcated cultural backgrounds ... 42
Table 2. Students' self-rating of written English ... 42
Table 3. Students' self-rating of spoken English ... 43
Table 4. Parental education level ... 43
Table 5. Main reasons to do Law: Response count, percentage of total responses and mean rank (1 being highest rank, 5 lowest rank) ... 45
Table 6. Categories which >50% of students saw as essential ... 50

Chapter 3

Table 1. Characteristics of lawyers by severity level of reported mental health symptoms ... 66
Table 2. Logistic regression model comparing normal/mild/moderate vs severe/extremely severe depression (n = 746) ... 68
Table 3. Logistic regression model comparing normal/mild/moderate vs severe/extremely severe anxiety (n = 749) ... 69
Table 4. Logistic regression model comparing normal/mild/moderate vs severe/extremely severe stress (n = 749) ... 69
Table 5. Summary of the logistic regression models examining drivers of poor mental health ... 72

Chapter 4

Table 1. Participation in online surveys by lawyer cohort and gender ... 87
Table 2. Percentage of lawyers surveyed who had experienced bullying or intimidation in their current workplace ... 88
Table 3. Percentage of lawyers surveyed who had experienced sexual harassment in their *current* workplace ... 90

Chapter 5

Table 1. Depression Anxiety Stress Scores (DASS) by Workplace....... 117
Table 2. Ranking of Job Stressors by Workplace.................................. 118
Table 3. Median Job Satisfaction Scores by Workplace........................ 122

Figures

Chapter 2

Figure 1. Mean rankings of the importance of particular experiences by undergraduate law students in 2005 and 2018 (Average +/– SE).. 49
Figure 2. Most important aspects of degree... 49
Figure 3. Mean ratings of the importance of certain traits to employers by law students in 2005 and 2018 (Average +/– SE) 52

Chapter 4

Figure 1. Top ten causes of lawyers' dissatisfaction with current position, by gender.. 92
Figure 2. Top ten causes of women lawyers' dissatisfaction with current position, by legal sector/role................................ 93
Figure 3. Most common reasons for lawyers changing jobs in the previous five years, by sector... 95
Figure 4. Most important and most frequent reasons female lawyers changed jobs in last five years 96
Figure 5. Most important and most frequent reasons male lawyers changed jobs in last five years 97

Chapter 5

Figure 1. Perceived Effectiveness of Wellbeing Interventions................ 125

Chapter 11

Figure 1. Macquarie Bank 2017 Legal Benchmarking Results............... 273
Figure 2. Norton Rose Fulbright Litigation Trends Survey 2017 274

PART I

INTRODUCTION

CHAPTER 1

THE CHANGING FIELD OF LAWYERING AND ITS IMPACT ON PRACTICE AND WELLBEING

Michael LEGG, Prue VINES and Janet CHAN

1. Introduction 3
2. The Great Expansion: Law Firms, In-House Counsel, the Billable Hour and Budgets 6
3. Globalisation 8
4. Technology. 11
5. The New Law Firm 15
6. The Sharing or Gig Economy 16
7. The Future of the Legal Profession 18
8. The Approach of this Book 20
9. Conclusion 27

1. INTRODUCTION

The legal profession is facing a convergence of forces, most notably significant advances in the capabilities of technology, economic pressures challenging existing business models, and globalisation, that together herald a momentous change in the practice of law. From at least the 1970s the practice of law has experienced a number of changes which have impacted on the types of roles that lawyers play and the economics of lawyering, but they were more gradual as compared to the increased pace of change which is currently in play.

Around the world the legal profession has started to focus on these forces of 'disruption' and what they mean for lawyers, in their various roles, and the users of law, corporations, government, but especially the disadvantaged. For example in June 2013 the German Bar Association contracted with consulting firm PROGNOS to produce 'Der Rechtsdienstleistungsmarkt 2030' ('The Legal Services Market 2030') which outlines how the legal services market is expected to function in 2030.[1] The Law Society of England and Wales published its 'Future of Legal Services Report' in January 2016.[2] The American Bar Association (ABA) established a Commission on the Future of Legal Services which reported in August 2016 and has continued providing resources for the profession.[3] In Australia the lead in seeking to understand these developments and formulate responses has been taken by the Law Society of New South Wales and its report on the Future of Law and Innovation in the Profession (FLIP).[4] Academic attention has also been directed at these changes. A significant literature contributed to by both the profession and academics has developed on the changing legal profession and the impact of the various changes.[5] Richard Susskind[6] has predicted an increase in the use of technology, including without lawyers, commoditisation of legal work and a reconfiguration of the profession. Arguments about how the role of lawyers has changed and may change in the future have included both pessimistic accounts such as Susskind's, as well as more optimistic ones such as Trotter's, or Kronman's aspirational view of the lawyer-statesman.[7]

---

1 Deutscher Anwaltverein, 'Der Rechtsdienstleistungsmarkt 2030' (PROGNOS, 2013).

2 Law Society of England and Wales, *Future of Legal Services Report* (2016).

3 American Bar Association, Commission on the Future of Legal Services, *Report on the Future of Legal Services in the United States* (2016). Numerous State Bar associations in the US have also conducted inquiries and produced reports: https://www.americanbar.org/groups/bar_services/resources/resourcepages/future/.

4 The Law Society of New South Wales, Commission of Inquiry. *The Future of Law and Innovation in the Profession* (Sydney, 2017).

5 It is not possible to cover this whole literature, but see for example, L. Terry, S. Mark and T. Gordon, 'Trends and Challenges in Lawyer Regulation: The Impact of Globalisation and Technology' (2011–12) 80 *Fordham Law Review* 2661; R.W. Standt, 'All the Wild Possibilities: Technology that Attacks Barriers to Access to Justice' (2008) 42 *Loyola of L.A. Law Review* 1117; B. Simpson, 'Algorithm and Advocacy: Does the Legal Profession Have a Future in a Digital World?' (2016) 25(1) *Information and Communications Technology Law* 50–61; V. Waye, M.L. Verreynne and J. Knowler, 'Innovation in the Australian Legal Profession' (2018) 25(2) *International Journal of the Legal Profession* 213–42.

6 R. Susskind and D. Susskind, *The End of Lawyers* (Oxford University Press, 2008); R. Susskind. *The Future of the Professions* (Oxford University Press, 2015); R. Susskind, *Tomorrow's Lawyers* (2nd ed., Oxford University Press, 2017).

7 M. Trotter, *What's to Become of the Legal Profession?* (CreateSpace Independent Publishing Platform, 2017); A.T. Kronman, *The Lost Lawyer: Failing Ideals of the Legal Profession* (Belknap Press, Harvard University Press, 1993).

The legal profession has also recognised the need to focus on the wellbeing of its members. A major academic literature has emerged in recent years on issues concerning mental health in the legal profession.[8] Much of this concern has focused on mental health issues such as anxiety, stress, depression, substance abuse and suicide, which the practice of law may contribute to, or cause, given its demanding nature, including long hours, high pressure and exacting standards of performance. Many of these matters are longstanding, but as technological change and changes to the very structure and regulation of law firms impact on lawyers and users of law, we may face an increased incidence of mental health problems, or different kinds of mental health problems in the legal profession. Not least among these is a growing sense of anxiety about the ability to obtain and keep suitable employment, or to be promoted, and the demands of competence and ethics in a world which changes rapidly. These factors also affect law students.[9]

This edited collection, which grew out of a symposium at the University of New South Wales (UNSW) in 2018, brings the above two areas together by examining the impact of technology and innovation on lawyer wellbeing. In this chapter the editors set the stage for the discussion in later chapters by outlining the forces of change and the issues faced by the legal profession.

---

8 M. Seligman, P. Verkuil and T. Kang, 'Why Lawyers are Unhappy' (2001) 23 *Cardozo Law Review* 33; (2005) 10 *Deakin Law Review* 49; W. Eaton et al., 'Occupations and the Prevalence of Major Depressive Disorder' (1990) 32 *Journal of Occupational Medicine* 1079; G Benjamin, E. Darling and B. Sales, 'The Prevalence of Depression: Alcohol Abuse and Cocaine Abuse amongst United States Lawyers' (1990) 13 *International Journal of Law and Psychiatry* 233; S. Daicoff, 'Lawyer, Know Thyself: A Psychological Analysis of Personality Strengths and Weaknesses' (American Psychological Association, 2004); R.B. Allan, 'Alcoholism, Drug Abuse and Lawyers: Are We Ready to Address the Denial?' (1997) 31 *Creighton Law Review* 265; Beaton Consulting, *Annual Professions Survey 2007: Short Report* (BeyondBlue, 2007); N. Kelk et al., *Courting the Blues: Attitudes towards Depression in Australian Law Students and Legal Practitioners*, University of Sydney Brain and Mind Institute (2009). See also references in Chapter 11 of this volume, M. Legg and J. Rogers, 'Lawyers' Fee Arrangements and their Wellbeing'.

9 See P. Vines and A. Steel, Chapter 2 of this volume; and, inter alia, N. Kelk et al., above n. 8; R. Field, J. Duffy and C. James, *Promoting Law Student and Lawyer Well-being in Australia and Beyond* (London, Routledge, 2016); K.M. Sheldon and L. Krieger, 'Understanding the Negative Effects of Legal Education on Law Students: A Longitudinal Test of Self-Determination Theory' (2007) 33 *Personality and Social Psychology Bulletin* 883.

2. THE GREAT EXPANSION: LAW FIRMS, IN-HOUSE COUNSEL, THE BILLABLE HOUR AND BUDGETS

The 1970s saw two important developments in the practice of law in the United States which spread more or less contemporaneously to the rest of the common law world and indeed some of the civil law world.[10] First, in-house legal departments went from being a small number of lawyers to large undertakings. Legal departments became larger as corporations themselves grew, and regulations became more complex and profuse.[11] Secondly, time-based billing became the standard way to charge for legal services due to in-house legal departments wanting to be able to monitor external lawyers in the same way they were monitored within their corporations.[12]

As corporate clients grew, so did law firms and lawyers' pay. In the United States in 1968 annual remuneration for first-year associates stepped up from approximately US$10,000 to US$15,000. By the mid-1980s, lawyers' average starting salaries had risen to US$65,000 and continued to climb during the 1990s and 2000s, reaching approximately US$160,000 in 2007 (not including bonuses) – compared to average household income reported to be about US$50,000.[13]

As lawyer remuneration increased, so did the fees being charged and the budgets (billing targets) for lawyers. In the United States, during the period between 1985 and 2012, the fees lawyers charged for their services increased significantly. Nationwide, average hourly billing rates of law firm partners rose from about US$122 to US$536, or by approximately 339 per cent, while that of associates grew even more, from about

10 J. Flood, 'Megalawyering in the Global Order: The Cultural, Social and Economic Transformation of Global Legal Practice' (1996) 31(2) *International Journal of the Legal Profession* 169–213; G. Morgan and S. Quack, 'Institutional Legacies and Firm Dynamics: The Growth and Internationalization of UK and German Law Firms' (2005) 26(12) *Organization Studies* 1765–85; O. Mendelsohn and M. Lippman, 'The Emergence of the Corporate Law Firm in Australia' (1979) 3 *UNSW Law Journal* 78.

11 J. Choi, 'In Defense of the Billable Hour: A Monitoring Theory of Law Firm Fees' (2018) 70 *South Carolina Law Review* 297, 315–16.

12 H. Leblebici, 'Your Income' in L. Empson, *Managing the Modern Law Firm – New Challenges, New Perspectives* (Oxford University Press, 2007) 128; Choi, above n. 11, 314–16.

13 V. Marrero, 'The Cost of Rules, the Rule of Costs' (2018) 40 *Cardozo Law Review* 293, 305–6.

US$79 to US$370 per hour, or a rise of approximately 368 per cent. The increase was considerably more pronounced among big firms in major cities. In New York, for example, a sample of large law firms found that the average hourly billing rate for partners in 2013 was US$882 and for associates US$520.[14]

An ABA survey conducted in 1965 reported budgets of 1400 to 1600 hours per year for associates. In the 1970–80s budgets increased to between 1600 and 1800 hours. At the turn of the twenty-first century 1900 hours was expected of associates.[15] By 2010, the standard for major firms was 2000 hours.[16] Of course the budget is a minimum not a maximum. When these budgets are multiplied by the hourly rates above, then each 'fee-earner' (the term for lawyers in large law firms) was generating substantial revenue for the law firm. However, to meet their budget the time spent working must be billable, not undertaking administration, training or mentoring. The importance of billable hours is illustrated by the ABA's *Making Partner – A Guide for Law Firm Associates* from 2002, which listed a number of criteria for partnership. The first item was hard work – 'you devote a certain number of hours to the practice; that is, billable hours, practice development, training efforts, and management contribution, but particularly billable hours'.[17]

The rising legal fees, while able to be borne by large corporate clients, also created expectations as to what a lawyer should be paid in other areas of practice, including legal services provided to individuals. This had the effect that access to legal services became more expensive and out of reach for not just blue-collar workers, but also the middle-classes.[18] Before 2000 there were substantial increases in demand for lawyers and in lawyer compensation. The ABA has reported that the biggest jump in lawyer salaries came in 1997 to 2002 – up 45 per cent.[19] The 'business plan' for many corporate law firms was a combination of high billable hour budgets with high charge-out rates and numerous employed lawyers for each equity partner. However, this combination has been described as creating conditions 'that decrease opportunities for advancement and are hostile to

14 Ibid., 306–7.
15 Ibid., 307.
16 S. Harper, *The Lawyer Bubble – A Profession in Crisis* (Basic Books, New York, 2013) 79.
17 J. Sapp, *Making Partner – A Guide for Law Firm Associates* (ABA, 2nd ed., 2002) 8.
18 B. Barton and S. Bibas, *Rebooting Justice* (Encounter Books, New York 2017) 117.
19 American Bar Association, *ABA Profile of the Legal Profession* (2019) 15.

any attorney's search for a balanced life'.[20] Moreover, the law firm business model, which had been very successful in the latter part of the twentieth century, was bounded by the number of hours a lawyer could work and the fees that clients were willing to pay.

While the metrics of legal practice – budgets, charge-out rates and remuneration – have become a major focus of success they are often not the main driver for many lawyers. The ABA found that the most commonly cited reasons for people attending law school in the United States were: as a path to careers in politics, government or public service (44%); a passion for that type of work (42%); an opportunity to be helpful (35%), and to advocate for social change (32%). About one in three students (31%) said they were motivated by access to high-paying jobs.[21] A focus purely on the financial may ignore other important considerations for lawyer wellbeing, such as an alignment between the lawyer's values and the work they are undertaking. Australian surveys have shown similarly that students may study law for extremely idealistic reasons as well as being motivated by access to high-paying jobs.[22]

3. GLOBALISATION

Law firms started to globalise, or operate in jurisdictions outside their home country, in response to the needs of clients which were entering new markets and creating multi-national business enterprises.[23] In addition to establishing businesses overseas, there was also the rise of transnational disputes which required legal assistance in foreign courts or a resort to international arbitration. Further, expanding internationally was the logical next step for law firms looking to continue the expansion they had

---

20 S. Harper, *The Lawyer Bubble – A Profession in Crisis* (Basic Books, New York 2013), 90 (re United States); J. Garrick and A. Chan, 'Organisational Knowledge and the Effects of Billable Hours' (2006) 3(2) *International Journal of Learning and Intellectual Capital* 143 (re Australia and Hong Kong).

21 American Bar Association, n. 19 above, 26.

22 See M. Tani and P. Vines, 'Law Students' Attitudes to Education: A Pointer to Depression in the Legal Academy and the Profession?' (2009) 19(1) *Legal Education Review* 3–39; see also P. Vines and A. Steel, 'Student Attitudes to Legal Education: Revisiting the Pointers to Depression and Anxiety', Chapter 2 in this volume.

23 T. Angel, 'Your Challenge – Sustaining Partnership in the Twenty-First Century: The Global Law Form Experience' in L. Empson, *Managing the Modern Law Firm – New Challenges, New Perspectives* (Oxford University Press, Oxford 2007) 199–200.

undertaken domestically. Law firms have also responded to the global legal services market by outsourcing legal work to countries that have relatively low labour costs, such as India.

The dot-com boom of the 1990s spurred globalisation as telecommunications and computing advances allowed for affordable communication across borders and time zones. However, by 2000 the bubble had burst and this badly affected law firms closely linked to Silicon Valley in the United States (for example, the collapse of Cooley Godward, and Brobeck, Phleger & Harrison).[24] When combined with the terrorist attacks of 11 September 2001, global business generally slowed and with it the practice groups in law firms linked to corporate activity. When the economy is booming lawyers are needed to shepherd through mergers and assist in debt and capital raisings. When times are tight lawyers are needed to clean up the failures, through bankruptcy and insolvency work. In areas such as family law and wills there is no downtime. Divorce and death are not cyclical. Indeed, one of the factors in favour of law is that it is needed in both good and bad times.

The dot-com bust was soon made to look minor in contrast to the Global Financial Crisis (GFC) that grew out of the US sub-prime mortgage market. On 15 September 2008 the signature event of the GFC, the collapse of investment bank Lehman Brothers, occurred and the great recession commenced. In response, corporate users of legal services cut their budgets for legal expenditure. This decline in demand caused a reduction in legal positions and stagnation, or decline, in lawyer remuneration. Globalisation continued but in new directions. Australia, as one of the few jurisdictions that weathered the GFC relatively well, saw an influx of global law firms. Allen & Overy entered the Australian market in 2010 with a raid on national law firm Clayton Utz to establish a Sydney office. Clifford Chance and DLA Piper entered in 2011. However, the media reported: 'Corporate clients are looking afresh at their legal bills, and asking: "What's the risk? Do we really need a lawyer? Can we do it in-house?"'[25] The pressure to minimise 'legal spend' driven by the GFC has continued to the present day.

While law firm mergers begin in the mid-1990s, they have increased more recently. In 2015, there were 91 law firm mergers and acquisitions

---

24 D. Gross, 'The Dot-Firm's Dot-Bomb. How a Leading West Coast Law Firm Killed Itself', *Slate*, 31 January 2003.

25 N. McMahon, 'Law of the Jungle: Lawyers Now an Endangered Species', *Sydney Morning Herald*, 11 October 2014.

globally, a record high that included the largest law firm merger ever. Multinational law firm Dentons announced its merger with Chinese law firm Dacheng – firms of 2,500 and 3,500 lawyers, respectively.[26] Mergers have continued as law firms look for new markets and greater efficiencies. An example of law firm mergers building a global law firm is Norton Rose Fulbright. The UK-based Norton Rose combined with Australian firm Deacons in 2010. In 2011 it then combined with Canadian law firm Ogilvy Renault and South African firm Deneys Reitz to create a top 10 global legal practice with 38 offices and 2500 legal staff. Norton Rose then merged with US-based Fulbright & Jaworski in June 2013 to create a firm with 3800 lawyers. On 22 February 2017 the firm merged with another US firm, Chadbourne & Parke, and in December of the same year swallowed mid-tier Australian firm Henry Davis York.[27] Today Norton Rose Fulbright has more than 4,000 lawyers and other legal staff based in Europe, the United States, Canada, Latin America, Asia, Australia, the Middle East and Africa.[28]

A global law firm creates advantages and disadvantages. There can be greater opportunity for cross-selling to a global client who has operations in various jurisdictions where the firm operates. A client venturing into a new market may take comfort from the ability to use a well-known law firm. Equally, larger law firms can face more conflicts – ethical and business – where one arm of the firm represents adversaries or competitors of clients or potential clients of another arm of the firm. This can then limit some lawyers' ability to obtain or retain clients, which inhibits autonomy and control of the lawyer's practice. It can also create the need for a hierarchy in the firm as to which clients are more valuable, which can also affect the revenues generated by certain lawyers and in turn their remuneration.

Globalisation is not a spent force. The Law Society of England and Wales reported that the Economist Intelligence Unit's (EIU) long-term macroeconomic forecast, *Key Trends to 2050* (2015) predicts that emerging markets are expected to grow faster than developed economies, and 'as a result developing countries such as China and India are likely to overtake current global leaders such as the US, Japan and Western Europe'. The EIU also predicted that other emerging markets, such as Indonesia and Mexico will rank among the top ten global economies.[29] As a result

---

26 T. Replogle, 'The Business of Law: Evolution of the Legal Services Market' (2017) 6 *Michigan Business & Entrepreneurial Law Review* 287, 292.

27 https://www.nortonrosefulbright.com/en/global-statement/history.

28 https://www.nortonrosefulbright.com/en/about/our-firm.

29 Law Society of England and Wales, *Future of Legal Services Report* (2016) 36.

Anglo-American or global law firms may find new areas for growth and new clients looking to access capital and new markets. Multi-national corporations may also need in-house lawyers who can practise across borders in these new regions. Equally, as those emerging markets grow they may also give rise to new law firms and new competitors.

The significance of globalisation was starkly highlighted with the COVID-19 pandemic. COVID-19, emerged in China in December 2019 and then spread around the world. The World Health Organization characterised COVID-19 as a pandemic on 12 March 2020. National governments took various steps to try and slow the transmission of COVID-19, including closing borders, businesses and introducing 'social distancing' – reducing the number of close physical contacts a person has with other people.

For lawyers this meant working remotely from home with reliance on information and communications technology while dealing with financial pressures where clients cut back on spending, courts closed and transactions failed to complete, which in turn meant law firms reduced partnership draws and salaries.[30]

The response to the pandemic also created a range of additional non-financial stresses for lawyers, depending on their circumstances. These included social isolation due to loss of contact with their support network, needing to deal with their own or a family member's illness, providing support for older family members who were most at risk of fatality and children who may have had to adapt to online/home schooling, as well as dealing with the same fears and anxieties common to the entire population. The global pandemic led to widespread dislocation in the economy and in how lawyers needed to practice.

4. TECHNOLOGY

What we think of as technology now – namely, digital technology[31] – first impacted law through the back office of law firms and legal departments with applications such as word processing and accounting software. This

30 Clyde & Co, Covid-19 UK: Risk issues for law firms, 6 April 2020; D. Cassens Weiss, 'At least 19 more law firms cut pay and furlough employees; will partners ultimately benefit?', *ABA Journal*, 16 April 2020; M. Pelly, 'Big firms avoid pain but barristers suffer', *The Australian Financial Review*, 17 September 2020, 32.

31 We will use the term 'technology' in this way in this book, although, of course, technology just means 'tools'.

'new' technology was then employed to help lawyers capture and share their collective knowledge and experience through knowledge management databases and then interactive precedents.[32]

The dot-com boom from the mid-1990s to 2000 saw the internet transform business and the practice of law. Although the dot-com bubble burst, the internet continued. This became the backbone for introducing new ways for lawyers to communicate electronically such as through email, video-conferencing, and more recently social media.[33] Technology 'helps lawyers to work faster and more efficiently' but it also 'enables them to work constantly'.[34] The internet also facilitated sophisticated databases of case law, legislation and secondary materials. This was embraced by commercial providers such as Westlaw and LexisNexis who gave easy access to legal databases to lawyers who could pay. However, it also saw the founding of the Australasian Legal Information Institute (AustLII) in 1995 to provide free access to legal materials in Australia. In 2000 the British and Irish Legal Information Institute (BAILII) was established using AustLII software.[35] Free legal materials were available to both lawyers and non-lawyers. This assisted the lay person in accessing and de-mystifying the law. The internet also gave rise to the wider provision of commoditised legal services.[36]

However, the development of word processing, databases and email did not fundamentally transform legal practice. Rather it automated traditional practices and allowed for them to be done more efficiently. However, these efficiencies were not always obvious because the volume of available documents and case law also increased with the use of technology. Discovery in civil litigation is a prime example where technology substantially increased the work that lawyers needed to undertake, even as it increased efficiency in the production and dissemination of documents. Indeed, technology created more work to be done than the time that it saved through efficiencies.

More recently, artificial intelligence using both expert systems and machine learning for the provision of tailored legal information (some

---

32 R. Susskind, *A Guide to Strategy for Lawyers* (Canadian Bar Association, 2015) 52.

33 Ibid.

34 New York State Bar Association, *Report of the Task Force on the Future of the Legal Profession*, 2 April 2011, 3.

35 Australasian Legal Information Institute, *Celebrating 20 Years of Free Access to Law 1996–2015* (Austlii Annual Report 2015). The AUSTLII model has now expanded to Asia and Europe.

36 H. Mills, *The Rainmaker's Toolkit* (American Management Association, 2004) 4–6.

might say advice), technology-assisted review of documents, legal document creation, and prediction of legal outcomes has been achieving growing adoption.[37] For example, the technology-assisted review of documents for discovery has been accepted in court judgments in the United States, Ireland, England and Australia.[38]

As technology improves, more and more components of the legal service will have a technological aspect. It is important to note that legal and human skills will still be required and lawyers remain important to the delivery of many legal services (or products). Technology is a tool that the practising lawyer can employ to avoid some of the 'paper-shuffling' aspects of lawyering and allow them to focus on their core roles as advisor and advocate. New technology may present exciting opportunities for lawyers. The combination of machine learning and big data can provide insights that were not previously possible. Lawyers may be able to gain a deeper understanding of problems through new forms of analysis which in turn can lead to novel solutions. The lawyer with a keen desire to help others may find that technology provides a tool that assists in this endeavour; indeed it may magnify the lawyer's reach significantly.[39]

However, there are also reports that the increased use of technology to provide access to justice to consumers and to carry out routine legal services will result in fewer junior lawyers being needed for this work in the future. Technology such as interactive forms and 'chatbots' may replace the lawyer, and the client/consumer will deal with the technology directly. In other areas there may be increased opportunities for related roles such as legal technology professionals, legal data scientists, legal project managers and commoditised legal service assistants.[40] Changes to how work is undertaken can create increased uncertainty and apprehension, with ramifications for the wellbeing of individuals. Lawyers may find that they are doing a very different job from their predecessors.

---

37 M. Legg and F. Bell, *Artificial Intelligence and the Legal Profession: A Primer* (Law Society of NSW, 2019) 13–20. See also J.K. Robbennolt, 'Behavioural Legal Ethics and Attorney Wellbeing in Contemporary Practice', Chapter 7 of this volume.

38 *Da Silva Moore v. Publicis Groupe* 287 FRD 182 (SDNY 2012); *Irish Bank Resolution Corporation Limited v. Quinn* [2015] IEHC 175; *Pyrrho Investments Ltd v. MWB Property Ltd* [2016] EWHC 256 (Ch); *McConnell Dowell Constructors (Aust) Pty Ltd v. Santam Ltd (No. 1)* [2016] VSC 734.

39 T. Joseph, 'How Technology Can Help Legal Aid Services Run More Efficiently: A Technologist's View', *Law, Technology and Access to Justice Blog*, 21 June 2018.

40 R. Susskind, *Tomorrow's Lawyers* (2nd ed., Oxford University Press, 2017) Ch. 13; M. Legg, 'UNSW Law Mini-Curriculum Review Report on Technology and the Law School Curriculum' [2017] UNSW Law Research Series 90, p. 6.

The extent and speed of change from technological innovations remains unknown. In 2017 Macquarie Bank reported on the impact of technology on the legal profession and observed that while the adoption of new technologies was accelerating 'we have yet to see the full impact of potentially much more disruptive innovations, from data analytics to artificial intelligence'.[41] The forced reliance on technology as a result of COVID-19 is also likely to alter client and law firm expectations around the conduct of legal practice. Lawyers needed to engage in virtual meetings, mediations and court hearings, as well as rely on electronic signatures for transaction documents. These short-term fixes may become long term practices.

While the impacts of technology on the functioning of law and the legal profession are continuing, the ethical ramifications of technology for lawyers were highlighted by the American Bar Association when it approved changes to the Model Rules of Professional Conduct. Rule 1.1, Comment 8 was added to make clear that lawyers have a duty to be competent not only in the law and its practice, but also in technology.[42] Rule 1.1 states that 'A lawyer shall provide competent representation to a client' and further that 'competent representation requires the legal knowledge, skill, thoroughness and preparation reasonably necessary for the representation'. Comment 8 provides:

> To maintain the requisite knowledge and skill, a lawyer should keep abreast of changes in the law and its practice, including the benefits and risks associated with relevant technology, engage in continuing study and education and comply with all continuing legal education requirements to which the lawyer is subject.

In other jurisdictions, the general requirement of competence may be viewed as including competence with technology, without requiring any amendment to professional conduct rules.[43] The modern lawyer needs to possess a knowledge of the benefits and risks associated with technology for legal practice.

---

41 Macquarie Bank, *An Industry in Transition – 2017 Legal Benchmarking Results* (Macquarie Bank, 2017) 12.

42 R. Ambrogi, 'Make that 30 States, As another Adopts Ethical Duty of Technology Competence', *LawSites*: https://www.lawsitesblog.com/2018/03/make-30-states-another-adopts-ethical-duty-technology-competence.html.

43 M. Legg and F. Bell, 'Lawyers and the Black Box of Technology' (2020) 94 *Australian Law Journal* 107, 108.

5. THE NEW LAW FIRM

New business structures for practising law have been evolving for some time and include incorporated legal practices, listed law firms (such as Slater & Gordon and Shine Lawyers, which are listed on the Australian Securities Exchange, and Gately, which is listed on the London Stock Exchange) and multi-disciplinary practices.[44]

The GFC heralded a re-think of how law could be practised, with new business models and fee arrangements being adopted. The New York State Bar Association observed in 2011:

> The economic downturn of 2008–09 produced considerable economic fallout for law firms, including lower earnings, reduced hiring, more downsizing, and greater internal reorganization. As the economy recovers, it is apparent to many observers that the legal profession will not return to business as usual, and that to be successful in the post-recession era, law firms will need to engage in long-term restructuring to maintain sustainability and grow organically.
>
> Competition for legal work will be intense, not only within the legal profession, but also among law firms and nonlegal service providers, foreign law firms, pro se litigators [litigants in person] and self-help providers, as well as companies that use innovative delivery systems.[45]

The post-GFC world is also one where the time required to reach partnership has been extended, with a range of new titles and roles added to the law firm pyramid.[46] In the 1980s, it was 6–8 years to partnership, in the 1990s this became 10 years, until today when it is frequently 15 years, unless someone is in the right place at the right time, i.e. they have a skillset and/or client relationships that a law firm needs. There is also a greater willingness by those at senior levels in the profession to recruit and move laterally from one firm to another.[47] In short, for younger lawyers the road to partnership is longer and less certain than before.

More recently, a new business model allowing for a virtual law firm has developed as a result of advances in technology. The virtual law

---

44 See C. James, C. Strevens and R. Field, 'Law Teachers Speak Out: What do Law Schools Need to Change?', Chapter 6 of this volume.

45 New York State Bar Association, above n. 33, 2.

46 A. Yoon, 'Competition and the Evolution of Large Law Firms' (2014) 63 *DePaul Law Review* 697, 710–12.

47 Harper, above n. 16, 210.

firm provides access to a network of lawyers who can be located almost anywhere. The virtual firm allows a client (or another law firm) to access legal services as needed, which means the client can scale up or down the necessary expertise as required. Technology allows for those legal services to be delivered over the internet through specialist portals, email or voice/video conferencing. This is discussed further below in relation to the so-called sharing or 'gig' economy.

The commoditisation of routine legal services has also seen new businesses provided by lawyers and non-lawyers, including standard form contracts for a range of activities such as business formation and selling or buying products and services, as well as document review for due diligence and discovery. There is also a range of new ways to provide legal information, most notably through the smartphone app. The cost of some legal services is declining with ramifications for law firm profitability and access to justice.

An important component of these new ways of practising law is the Alternative Fee Arrangement (AFA), which is any form of billing other than time-based billing, such as fixed fees, capped fees and success fees. New forms of billing have been adopted to align economic incentives with new organisational forms and the use of technology.[48]

6. THE SHARING OR GIG ECONOMY

A month before the collapse of Lehman Brothers, a new business providing an online marketplace for offering and obtaining accommodation, called Airbnb, was founded. In March 2009 another online marketplace, but this time for transport, called Uber, launched in Chicago, Houston and San Francisco. These online marketplaces combined technology and business models to provide a new way of offering services, but also a new way of working for those who provided the underlying service. Commentators have identified a change in attitude from 'jobs' to 'work' in the economy. Today's workers take an average of more than 11 different jobs between the ages of 18 and 48.[49] The approach to work created by

---

[48] See M. Legg and J. Rogers, 'Lawyers' Fee Arrangements and their Wellbeing' Chapter 11 of this volume.

[49] A. Moore, 'California helped create and grow the sharing economy, hopefully it won't destroy it', *The Orange County Register*, 5 June 2018.

Airbnb and Uber has now been adopted as a way to link lawyers and potential clients, although to date in a much more decentralised manner.[50]

The virtual law firm, also called NewLaw, may take a number of forms in the sharing economy. It may be a dispersed law firm that assists individual lawyers conduct their individual practices by providing regulatory and administrative support, or it may be only a legal marketplace which provides an online platform to connect lawyers and clients.[51] In both situations the lawyers are usually more senior or established lawyers with well-honed skillsets, looking for a new way to practice. Alternatively the virtual firm may be a tech-enabled labour hire service, typically providing more junior or less experienced lawyers to law firms and corporate clients on an 'as needed' basis.[52] The contract or project lawyer allows firms and clients to minimise fixed costs and only pay for lawyers when they need them.[53] For the contract lawyer they gain flexibility in their work but also uncertainty and the loss of some statutory benefits.

Large law firms have incorporated the ideas of the gig economy into their offerings to clients. The Chicago-based firm McDermott, Will & Emery, for example, reportedly created a new tier of attorneys – called permanent contract associates – so as to provide lower cost (lower paid) lawyers to undertake more basic tasks such as document review.[54] Herbert Smith Freehills offers Alternative Legal Services teams, based in Australia, Belfast, London and Shanghai, which undertake e-discovery and due diligence.[55] King & Wood Mallesons created KWMConnexion to connect its alumni with in-house legal positions in corporations and government.[56]

Other approaches have included traditional law firms investing in NewLaw. Australian firm Gilbert + Tobin became the first investors in LegalVision, a commercial NewLaw firm that is built on AFAs

50 See M. Thornton, 'Is "Uberisation" the Path to Lawyer Wellbeing?' Chapter 8 of this volume.

51 J. Gonczi, *Tranforming the Legal Landscape: The NewLaw Philosophy* (LegalVision, 2016) 7.

52 Ibid.

53 J. Furlong, *Do Law Differently – Futures for Young Lawyers* (The Canada Bar Association, 2016) 13.

54 R. Marcus, 'The Impact of Digital Information on American Evidence-Gathering and Trial – The Straw That Breaks the Camel's Back?' in M. Kengyel and Z. Nemessányi (eds), *Electronic Technology and Civil Procedure* (Springer, 2012) 38, citing K. Schmitt, 'McDermott Plans to Fill Cheap Seats', *San Francisco Recorder*, 1 November 2007, 1.

55 https://careers.herbertsmithfreehills.com/au/alternative-legal-services/what-we-offer.

56 https://www.kwm.com/en/au/knowledge/hubs/kwm-alumni/kwm-connexion.

and technology.[57] DLA Piper partnered with Lawyers on Demand (labour hire virtual law firm)[58] and Norton Rose Fulbright formed a strategic alliance with LawPath (a legal marketplace).[59]

Much of this chapter has concerned itself with the modern large law firm, in which the lawyers are in Australia and the UK termed 'solicitors'. The large law firm is a relatively recent development, and it still does not employ all solicitors by any means. The legal profession also includes barristers in Australia and the UK who work as sole practitioners. There are three other sectors of solicitors who may also be impacted by these changes. These include small solicitor firms and sole practitioners, and community legal centre solicitors and government lawyers. Smaller firms and community legal centres may be unable to pay for sophisticated technology and may be disproportionately affected by law apps and chatbots.

7. THE FUTURE OF THE LEGAL PROFESSION

In the United States the GFC led to a decline in employment opportunities for law graduates who had hefty student loan repayment obligations due to the cost of an American legal education.[60] An oversupply of law graduates was also reported in Australia and the UK.[61] Yet despite the slow-down, a young lawyer described their employment experience in 2014 as follows:

> You're paid more than the average graduate but you work your arse off. You're flogged. You're married to the job. Start at 7am and finish at 10 to 10.30 at night. And there are times when they don't go home from work at all.[62]

---

57 https://www.afr.com/business/legal/gilbert--tobin-first-investors-in-disruptor-legalvision-20151109-gkuixn.

58 https://lodlaw.com/news_article/dla-piper-takes-flexible-resourcing-capability-global-with-lod-and-adventbalance/.

59 http://www.nortonrosefulbright.com/news/138783/norton-rose-fulbright-and-lawpath-have-formed-a-strategic-alliance-to-provide-start-ups-and-smes-with-greater.

60 B. Tamanaha, *Failing Law Schools* (University of Chicago Press, 2012); B. Barton, *Glass Half Full: The Decline and Rebirth of the Legal Profession* (Oxford University Press, 2015).

61 E. Tadros and K. Walsh, 'Too many law graduates and not enough jobs', *Australian Financial Review* (online), 22 October 2015.

62 McMahon, above n. 25.

Downturns in legal demand don't just result in fewer employment opportunities, but also those that do have a position are required to work harder. However, in 2018 global law firms in Australia could not hire sufficient junior lawyers.[63] Some have suggested this was a short-term respite due to the Royal Commission into Misconduct in the Banking, Superannuation and Financial Services Industry of 2018 and that even with greater regulatory requirements demand for legal services will decline.[64]

However, statistics on the legal profession suggest that the number of practising lawyers has not declined in countries such as the US, the UK and Australia. In the United States as of 1 January 2019, there were 1,352,027 active lawyers, which was a 12.4% increase since 2010. Over the same period, the population of the United States grew by only 6.3%.[65] In England and Wales as at 31 July 2018, there were 143,167 solicitors with practising certificates (PCs) and 188,868 individuals on the Roll of Solicitors. The number of solicitors with PCs was 2.5% higher than a year earlier.[66] The majority of solicitors are still employed in private practice firms; however the number of solicitors working in-house continues to grow.[67] In Australia, according to figures from the Australian Bureau of Statistics in 2002 solicitors constituted 84.5% and barristers 6.3% of the profession.[68] In 2018 there were 76,303 solicitors who were in practice.[69] Between 2011 and 2018, there has been a 33% increase in the number of solicitors practising in Australia.[70] The majority of solicitors in Australia were working in private practice (69%), followed by in-house positions with corporations (15%) and government (12%). However, growth since 2011 has been +61% in the corporate legal sector and +61% in the government legal sector, while private practice grew by +23%.[71] There were 18,748 private law firms. Of these, 79% were sole practitioner firms – that

63 A. Patrick, 'Juniors lawyer shortage drives Freehills to New Zealand', *Australian Financial Review* (online), 20 September 2018.

64 M. Pelly and E. Tadros, 'Lawyers fear slowdown after Hayne "sugar hit"', *Australian Financial Review* (online), 28 June 2019.

65 American Bar Association, above n. 19, 5.

66 Law Society of England & Wales, *Trends in the Solicitors' Profession: Annual Statistics Report 2018* (2019) 3–4.

67 Ibid., 11.

68 Australian Bureau of Statistics, *8667.0 Legal Practices Australia 2001–02*. These are the latest figures available as the ABS no longer collects these statistics.

69 Urbis Pty Ltd, *2018 National Profile of Solicitors* (2019) 1.

70 Ibid.

71 Ibid., 3.

is, the solicitor was the principal of their own firm; 8% had between two and 10 partners, less than 2% had 11–39 partners and less than 1% had 40 partners or more. Among private practice solicitors, more than one-third (38%) were sole practitioners.[72]

While the need for lawyers will continue, the type of work and the areas in which lawyers practise seem likely to change. As Dr. George Beaton and Imme Kaschner have written:

> New ways of doing legal work often rely on a reduction in fixed costs, through only paying for work on an as-needed basis, necessitating changes in financial planning and life planning for freelance legal professionals. Law firms also face significant emotional and financial cost in restructuring internal processes in ways that cause the loss of jobs held by long-term employees.[73]

Restructuring and retraining will bring with it uncertainty and strain, which can have detrimental effects.[74] This means that the changes wrought by technology and innovation in the legal profession, while often driven by the need for greater efficiency, may also create significant financial stress for legal businesses and the lawyers working for them. This significant financial stress adds to the stressors created by technological change to create a situation where lawyers' wellness can be significantly affected.

8. THE APPROACH OF THIS BOOK

The conditions outlined above provide the background which informs the chapters in this book. The book seeks to provoke a response in its readers to the situation in which the legal profession in much of the developed world finds itself. The interaction and stresses created by new technology and innovation in the legal system are complex and need to be considered in a sophisticated way. It is also not to be forgotten that the clients of the legal profession are necessarily subject to many of the same demands (and some of the same stresses) and that the structural and regulatory changes

---

72 Ibid., 26.

73 G. Beaton and I. Kaschner, *Remaking Law Firms: Why and How* (American Bar Association, 2016) 27.

74 The Law Society of New South Wales, above n. 4, 84.

to the profession may impact on clients or users of the legal system as well. The book seeks to tease out the interactions between all these factors, evaluating how the profession is travelling in its dealings with change, and discussing ways of enhancing lawyers' wellbeing that go beyond initiatives that treat the symptoms without addressing the fundamental issues. It also considers how these broader changes interact with the culture and ethics of legal practice. The book discusses how the changing practice environment affects lawyers at different career stages in different settings. In this book lawyers are defined broadly to include law students, legal practitioners and legal academics.

This section introduces the chapters in the book and describes how factors such as technological change, globalisation and corporatisation of legal practice create new stressors which lawyers seek to manage. The book is divided into four parts, of which the first comprises this chapter.

Part II is entitled 'Change, Stress and Wellbeing'. Taking the view that the interaction with legal practice and the legal system begins with law students, in Chapter 2 'Student Attitudes to Legal Education: Revisiting the Pointers to Depression and Anxiety', Prue Vines and Alex Steel draw on two surveys of law students 15 years apart, in order to find out whether the earlier findings – that law students were disproportionately competitive, lacking in autonomy and lacking in social connectedness compared with students from other faculties – continue to be borne out. The fact that law students have been disproportionately likely to suffer from depression and anxiety in many jurisdictions raises the question of whether legal education itself creates the problem or whether there are other factors at play. The early findings suggested that law students' own characteristics might contribute to this, in particular the tendency to use external rather than internal motivating factors. The later survey appears to show some reduction in competitiveness and a possible increase in autonomy which augurs well for future lawyers' ability to be resilient in the face of the inevitable stresses of professional life as a lawyer.

It is known that lawyers can suffer disproportionately from depression and anxiety compared with the rest of the population. However, it appears that they also have very high levels of job satisfaction. In Chapter 3 'The Paradox of Satisfaction and Distress amongst Lawyers: Implications for a Changing Field', Suzanne Poynton and Janet Chan report on a national survey of Australian lawyers to investigate the inter-relationships between distress, satisfaction and work-related variables. Using multivariate logistic regression, the analyses show that work-related variables such as perceived 'effort–reward imbalance', 'overcommitment' and 'work–family conflict' were significantly associated with severe symptoms of depression, stress and anxiety, when other variables were taken into account. Alcohol use was a significant predictor of severe depression and stress (but not anxiety), while career dissatisfaction was highly correlated with severe depression (but not anxiety and stress). The survey could not take into account changes to market structure or to structures of legal work which may have an impact on both job satisfaction and work stress.

Chapter 4 by Alison Wallace and Imogen D'Souza, 'Stress, Bullying and Harassment in the Legal Profession: A Risky Business', draws on data from a large national study of Australian lawyers to explore mental health issues and the extent of bullying and sexual harassment among lawyers. The results show that nearly half (46 per cent) of lawyers reported having been bullied or intimidated in their current workplace, with a significantly higher proportion of female lawyers, especially those working in large law firms and in major city locations, reporting such experience, compared with male lawyers. The survey also shows that one in five lawyers reported having experienced sexual harassment in their current workplace, with female lawyers three times more likely than male lawyers to have done so, and female barristers reporting the highest level of sexual harassment. In response to these findings, various initiatives are being canvassed by professional bodies to raise awareness, set standards, and manage the psychosocial risk factors in the workplace. The authors stress the importance of monitoring and evaluating these initiatives.

One major change in the field of lawyering not discussed in the previous sections was the impact of 'neoliberalism' (or 'new public management') on the structures and processes of public administration and on the legal profession. Chapters 5 and 6 discuss this development in relation to lawyers employed in the public and community sectors and law teachers in universities. The strongly neoliberal turn in public management has included extensive cuts to funding for users and providers of legal service (e.g. legal aid and community legal centres) as well as the promotion of market mechanisms, casualisation of the labour force and competition for resources among public institutions, including universities.

Public lawyers are the focus of Chapter 5 'Public Sector Lawyering Stress and Wellbeing: Neoliberalism at Work?' in which Janet Chan and Holly Blackmore discuss the impact of neoliberalism on public lawyers.

Chan and Blackmore draw on a national survey of lawyers to compare the emotional states, job stressors and job satisfaction between lawyers working in the public/community sectors and those working in the private sector. The results suggest that lawyers working in the public and community sectors were suffering similar levels of negative psychological symptoms as those working in the private sector and nominated a similar set of stressors in their job. However, while lawyers working in the private sector mentioned billable hours and lack of control over work as among their top stressors, lawyers working in the government and community sectors highlighted a different set of stressors: the lack of resources, funding uncertainty and job insecurity. In terms of job satisfaction, lawyers in the private sector were more satisfied with their remuneration and opportunities for advancement than those working in the public or community sectors, while the latter were more satisfied with the value of their work to society. In spite of the neoliberal environment which encourages individual responsibility for wellbeing, many lawyers continued to take seriously the discourse on wellbeing and welcomed both individual and structural interventions.

The university is the subject of Chapter 6, 'Law Teachers Speak Out: What do Law Schools Need to Change?', where Colin James, Caroline Strevens and Rachael Field present the qualitative results of national surveys conducted in the UK and in Australia on law teachers' experience of wellbeing and stress. The authors highlighted what respondents thought their university could do to improve law teachers' quality of working life. The results suggest that the UK and Australian experiences are similar: the majority of respondents were generally satisfied with their life (66 per cent in Australia and 59 per cent in the UK). However, respondents in both countries were critical of the 'neoliberal' changes in their universities, which they saw as detrimental not only to law teachers but also to the student experience and their university's performance. The areas highlighted include: increased workload as well as administrative burden, dissatisfaction with the level of teacher support, distrust of senior management, disagreement with the strategic priorities of universities (on enrolment numbers and income), the loss of professional autonomy, and inadequate communication between managers and teachers. The chapter concludes with a list of suggested structural and cultural reforms to address the stressors of law teachers

Part III incorporates those chapters with a stronger focus on 'Technology, Innovation and the Structure of Legal Practice'. In Chapter 7,

'Behavioural Legal Ethics and Attorney Wellbeing in Contemporary Practice', Jennifer K. Robbennolt examines the connection between the state of ethics and professionalism in legal practice and the wellbeing of legal practitioners. She suggests that these two concerns are related, with one influencing the other and vice versa. Moreover, she identifies many aspects of modern legal practice that impact on both ethics and wellbeing: e.g. the adversarial nature of legal practice, its time and financial pressures, and the leadership and culture of legal workplaces. The chapter concludes that these inter-connections must be taken seriously when reforms to address ethics or wellbeing are being considered.

One of the changes discussed in an earlier section of this chapter was the growth of the 'sharing economy' in legal practice – the use of digital platforms to assist clients to directly access lawyers. In Chapter 8, 'Is "Uberisation" the Path to Lawyer Wellbeing?' Margaret Thornton notes that this 'disruptive innovation' of NewLaw may raise significant questions for the meaning of the profession and law itself. 'Uberisation' is supposed to be cheaper, more accessible and offer autonomy and flexibility of work – is this a way to enhance lawyer wellbeing? Using interviews with lawyers working in this way, Thornton notes that NewLaw firms refuse to use the traditional hierarchical structures, and often do not use time-based billing, which is often regarded as a significant stressor in legal practice. Her interviewees often spoke of 'happiness', which is rare in other legal practice, but the negative side for lawyers practising this way included continuous connection and therefore an inability to switch off. The Utopia apparently offered may have its downside. Many of the innovations which make NewLaw possible and give relative autonomy and flexibility to the worker also put them in a position where they may effectively be working extraordinary hours. This cheaper way of practising is available to experienced lawyers who strike out on their own, but they then rarely employ junior staff, so that the traditional law firm role of training junior lawyers is lost, and the traditional track through to partnership is not possible and young lawyers may well be forced to stay in the gig economy, with all the negative factors that involves.

'The Corporatisation of the Legal Profession: The Impact of New Practice Structures on the Health and Wellbeing of Practitioners' is the subject of Chapter 9, by Tahlia Gordon. She discusses the changes created by legislation passed in New South Wales which allowed law firms to incorporate their practices and allowed for persons that are not legal practitioners to own or invest in law firms. This was the first time in the world that such legislation had been introduced and it was closely followed by England and Wales. Gordon examines the ramifications of these changes to the regulatory structure of law firms for the health and wellbeing of legal practitioners. Gordon argues that the benefits that are alleged to flow from non-lawyers owning or investing in law firms, such as access to external capital and limited liability, seem to suggest that non-lawyer law firm ownership or investment is likely to have a positive impact on the health and wellbeing of lawyers. Conversely, the costs of non-lawyer ownership such as threats to the professional and ethical obligations of lawyers and the impact of bureaucratisation suggest that the health and wellbeing of lawyers could be adversely impacted.

In Chapter 10 Felicity Bell, Justine Rogers and Michael Legg, members of the Law Society of NSW *Future of Law and Innovation in the Profession (FLIP)* Research Stream at UNSW Law, address 'Artificial Intelligence and Lawyer Wellbeing'. Recent improvements in artificial intelligence or AI have meant that it is capable of impacting professional work such as law. This chapter considers the impact of AI on wellbeing through focusing on professionalism from two conflicting perspectives: the traditional model of the profession as a calling and the more modern commercialistic focus of the profession as a business. Through these two models the authors explain that AI may enhance those aspects of professionalism that are associated with wellbeing, such as engagement in meaningful work and serving the community, through increased efficiency and being able to promote access to justice more widely. Yet it may also inflame existing pressures in the profession by heightening harmful elements: increasing competitive tensions in an already hyper-competitive occupation; giving rise to greater precarity of employment for newer members of the profession; potentially threatening the loss of lawyers' monopoly on legal work (where that monopoly still exists); and with associated loss of prestige and sense of purpose. The impact of AI on lawyer wellbeing will depend on the capabilities that AI obtains and the lawyer's ability to harness those capabilities for the benefit of the lawyer and their professional role.

'Lawyers' Fee Arrangements and their Wellbeing' is the title of Chapter 11. Michael Legg and Justine Rogers critically assess time-based billing, (also called 'the billable hour'), and alternative fee arrangements ('AFA's) such as contingency fees, fixed fees and value-based billing. Time-based billing is the starting point for this chapter, as this approach, despite its longevity and frequent use, has been subject to criticism because of its role in performance monitoring, including being linked to billing targets and promotion, with adverse effects for wellbeing. However, the chapter also considers AFAs, which have been promoted as the future for legal practice and an improvement on time-based billing. The chapter examines wellbeing through drawing on self-determination theory from the field of psychology and four overlapping dimensions of wellbeing: relatedness, autonomy, competence and motivation. Legg and Rogers argue that while time-based billing can have a negative effect on lawyer wellbeing, AFAs do not appear to be a panacea and can also have adverse effects. Much depends on context and how a particular billing method is employed. The billable hour as well as AFAs can be used in a positive manner. Fee arrangements are more likely to promote wellbeing if they support conditions and relationships that sustain lawyers' fundamental needs such as their motivations and relationships with others.

The connection between legal practice and the legal academy is addressed again in Chapter 12, which also constitutes our concluding Part IV. In 'Moving Across Silos: Legal Academic Wellbeing and the Legal Professions – Some Reflections on the UK Experience', Richard Collier moves the discussion to the UK, but also draws some conclusions pertinent to legal professionals across both private and public practice and also to law students and legal academics. He notes that there has been considerable attention paid in the UK recently to the mental health of lawyers. He seeks to extend this attention to legal academics by looking at factors that apply both to the legal profession and the legal academy and then to move beyond these silos. The UK, for example, has a dedicated University Mental Health Charter for students, and the profession has dedicated strategies to assist with problems with mental health, but the academy is often ignored. He notes that for both the professional and the academic lawyer the identification with a professional ideal can create enmeshment with practices that are harmful not only to the person but also the profession and academy themselves. An example is a culture of overwork. Both this and the recent identification of universities as 'anxiety-inducing factories', despite the increasing work on wellness for students, points to the fact that there remains a significant disconnection between the problems of mental health being caused in the profession and the academy and the various strategies that are being used to attempt to deal with the problem. It is a highly nuanced, difficult problem and its systemic nature must be recognised before the unintended complicity with harmful processes which academics and professionals may be engaging in is likely to be reduced.

9. CONCLUSION

This chapter has outlined the major changes in the *field* of lawyering.[75] Developments such as 'changes in the market structure for legal services in industrialised society and the attendant changes in the size, ownership, globalisation and management practices of law firms' have implications for workload, performance indicators, autonomy, what is valued in legal practice and how legal practitioners adapt to these demands.[76] Similarly, advances in digital technology have created both *resources* (e.g. efficiency, better communication, innovation) for and *constraints* (e.g. inflexibility, explainability, accountability) on legal practice.[77] The impact of these changes on the structures and processes of legal practice is only beginning to be monitored.[78]

Legal practice is complex and the last 25 years have exacerbated its complexity as technology has shifted and practice has changed. Change itself can be challenging and stressful, as it creates the need to learn new systems and methods. The legal profession has always changed in response to social change, but the rate of change has accelerated in a way which many lawyers find stressful. The stressors do not just arise out of the change; the changes to legal practice bring with them ethical challenges which must be addressed as well. Changes in technology drive, and are driven by, political and social change as well. The neoliberal turn's drive for efficiency has empowered some forms of digitisation which require outsourcing and the loss of jobs. Other aspects of technology can assist with efficiency but also run the risk of overwhelming the lawyers who are using them, and therefore sometimes undermining the efficiency goal. The modern law firm and modern lawyers are both challenged by these factors, but only the modern lawyer as a person can suffer stress and debilitation because of the impact of technology and change in the profession. The interaction

75 See J. Chan, 'Conceptualizing Legal Culture and Lawyering Stress' (2014–15) 21(2) *International Journal of the Legal Profession* 213–32. Chan uses a Bourdieusian framework to analyse legal practice, which postulates that 'professional practice emerges from the *interaction* between the professional *field* and the *habitus* of lawyers'.

76 Ibid.

77 For a similar analysis of the impact of technology on police practice, see J. Chan, 'Police and New Technologies' in T. Newburn (ed.), *Handbook of Policing* (Willan Publishing, 2003) pp. 655–79.

78 J. Rogers and F. Bell, 'Change Leadership for a Dynamic Profession' (2019) 60 *Law Society Journal* 86.

of technology and innovation creates an impact on the individual lawyer which the profession is only beginning to grapple with, and the evidence base on which the profession is making decisions about how to tackle this interaction is only beginning to exist. This edited volume provides the basis of further research and it is hoped, points to the need for ongoing monitoring and reflection on how these changing forces impact on legal practice.

PART II

CHANGE, STRESS AND WELLBEING

CHAPTER 2

STUDENT ATTITUDES TO LEGAL EDUCATION

Revisiting the Pointers to Depression and Anxiety?

Prue VINES and Alex STEEL*

1. Introduction 32
2. The Prevalence of Depression in Lawyers and Law Students 33
3. Explanations for the Disproportionate Incidence of Depression and Anxiety 34
4. Aims of the 2018 Survey 39
5. Results 40
   5.1. The Sample 40
   5.2. UNSW Law Student Demographics 41
   5.3. Age, Gender and Language 41
   5.4. Spoken and Written English 42
   5.5. Responses to Attitudinal Questions 44
      5.5.1. Reasons for Going to University 44
      5.5.2. Choosing Law School 45
      5.5.3. What were the Important Experiences at University? . . . 47
      5.5.4. Why are Good Grades Important? 48
      5.5.5. Most Important Skills and Knowledge Aspects of Degree 49
6. Limitations 52
7. Discussion 53
8. Conclusion 55

* We would like to thank Charlotte Brady for her superb research assistance and acknowledge the support of this research by the UNSW Scientia Education Academy.

1. INTRODUCTION

We are all now aware not only that there appears to be an epidemic of depression and anxiety in our society,[1] but that lawyers and law students also seem to be disproportionately affected. In 2014–15 11.2 per cent of the Australian population reported that they had an anxiety-related condition, and 9.3 per cent reported depression. The figures for lawyers and law students are greater and are discussed below. While we may accept that being in the legal profession creates large stressors which might contribute to depression or anxiety, it is not so obvious why law students might suffer this. One of the big issues is the extent to which their legal education contributes to this.[2] Seligman et al. have argued that pessimism is inherent in the nature of law and that this is a precipitating factor.[3] But is it? Could it be that law students self-select in some way and that the self-selection is the product of factors which might contribute to a greater likelihood of anxiety and depression developing?

This chapter considers the possible connections between aspects of student attitudes to learning and how they might affect wellbeing in those students. We argue that student wellbeing and its opposite are important indicators of the need to develop personal and professional identity that will enhance resilience throughout not only student days but also professional life. Most of this book focuses on how the wellbeing of legal

---

1 Australian Bureau of Statistics, 4364.0.55.001 – *National Health Survey: First Results*, 2014–15.

2 G.A. Benjamin et al., 'The Role of Legal Education in Producing Psychological Distress Among Law Students and Lawyers' (1986) 11(2) *American Bar Foundation Research Journal* 225; K.M. Sheldon and L.S. Krieger, 'Does Legal Education have Undermining Effects on Law Students? Evaluating Changes in Motivation, Values and Well-being' (2004) 22 *Behavioural Science & Law* 261; K.M. Sheldon and L.S. Krieger, 'Understanding the Negative Effects of Legal Education on Law Students: A Longitudinal Test of Self-Determination Theory' (2007) 33 *Personality and Social Psychology Bulletin* 833; A. Iijima, 'Lessons Learned: Legal Education and Law Student Dysfunction' (1998) 48(4) *Journal of Legal Education* 524; L.S. Krieger, 'What We're not Telling Law Students – and Lawyers – that they Really Need to Know: Some Thoughts-in-Action Toward Revitalizing the Profession from its Roots' (1998–99) 13 *Journal of Law and Health* 1; M. Dammeyer and N. Nunez, 'Anxiety and Depression Among Law Students: Current Knowledge and Future Directions' (1999) 23 *Law and Human Behaviour* 55; L.S. Krieger, 'Psychological Insights: Why Our Students and Graduates Suffer, and What We Might do About it' (2002) *Journal of the Association of Legal Writing Directors* 258.

3 M. Seligman, P. Verkuil and T. Kang, 'Why Lawyers are Unhappy' (2001) 23 *Cardozo Law Review* 33; (2005) 10 *Deakin Law Review* 49.

professionals may be affected by the changes to the way the legal profession is organised, and the changing use of technology in the legal profession. This chapter is intended to operate as a sort of baseline in which we examine the situation of the law student and whether we can predict students' likelihood of developing anxiety and depression from their early attitudes to legal education.

2. THE PREVALENCE OF DEPRESSION IN LAWYERS AND LAW STUDENTS

It has been clear for a long time that lawyers and law students are disproportionately affected by depression and anxiety. Early United States studies of lawyers showed a depressive illness rate of two to four times that of the general population.[4] Because there are major differences between Australian and United States legal education and indeed legal systems, it was problematic to assume that the United States research applied equally to Australian law students and lawyers. However, Australian studies, when eventually carried out, appear to have replicated US results.[5] The Brain and Mind Institute Report found 40 per cent of law students had symptoms of psychological distress at clinical levels, and that there

4 L.D. Eron and R.S. Redmount, 'The Effect of Legal Education on Attitudes' (1957) 9 *Journal of Legal Education* 431; W. Eaton et al., 'Occupations and the Prevalence of Major Depressive Disorder' (1990) 32 *Journal of Occupational Medicine* 1079; G.A. Benjamin, E. Darling and B. Sales, 'The Prevalence of Depression: Alcohol Abuse and Cocaine Abuse Amongst United States Lawyers' (1990) 13 *International Journal of Law and Psychiatry* 233; S.B. Shanfield and G.A. Benjamin, 'Psychiatric Distress in Law Students' (1985) 35 *Journal of Legal Education* 65; Seligman et al., above n. 3; M. Seligman, *Authentic Happiness* (Nicholas Brearley, 2004) 177; American Bar Association, *At the Breaking Point: The Report of a National Conference on the Emerging Crisis in the Quality of Lawyers' Health and Lives – Its Impact on Law Firms and Client Services* (1991). R.B. Allan, 'Alcoholism, Drug Abuse and Lawyers: Are We Ready to Address the Denial?' (1997) 31 *Creighton Law Review* 265.

5 Beaton Consulting, *Annual Professions Survey 2007: Short Report*; N. Kelk et al., *Courting the Blues: Attitudes towards Depression in Australian Law Students and Legal Practitioners*, University of Sydney Brain and Mind Institute, 2009; N. Skead and S.L. Rogers, 'Stress, Anxiety and Depression in Law Students: How Student Behaviours Affect Student Wellbeing' (2014) 40(2) *Monash University Law Review* 1–24; M.T. O'Brien, S. Tang and K. Hall, 'Changing Our Thinking: Empirical Thinking on Law Student Wellbeing, Thinking Styles and the Law Curriculum' (2011) 21 *Legal Education Review* 149; A. Lester, L. England and N. Antolak-Saper, 'Health and Wellbeing in the First Year: The Law School Experience' (2011) 36 *Alternative Law*

were high levels of anxiety and depression amongst lawyers in Australia. Studies of law students at ANU[6] and University of Melbourne also showed that approximately 30 per cent of law students experienced depression and anxiety. This was comparable to the United States data. A Beaton Consulting survey in 2011 found that lawyers were more likely than other professions to have symptoms of depression, but not the most likely to be diagnosed with depression.[7] This may have been because they were also most likely to think their employers would not be sympathetic and therefore did not present for diagnosis.

Other studies have continued to find that law students have high levels of psychological distress. Whether it is higher than other students' levels of distress has been difficult to determine because many studies have only looked at law students. A study by Larcombe et al. suggests that many students, not just law students, have very high levels of psychological distress compared with the general population.[8] A 2015 study found that law students' mean scores on anxiety and distress were significantly higher than those of psychology students.[9]

3. EXPLANATIONS FOR THE DISPROPORTIONATE INCIDENCE OF DEPRESSION AND ANXIETY

Before we consider the reason why law students and lawyers might be disproportionately affected, it is important to consider what are recognised as the causal or contributing factors to depression. A range of theories

---

Journal 47; W. Larcombe et al., 'Does an Improved Experience of Law School Protect Students against Depression, Anxiety and Stress? An Empirical Study of Wellbeing and the Law School Experience of LLB and JD Students' (2013) 35 *Sydney Law Review* 407.

6 O'Brien et al., above n. 5; Larcombe et al., above n. 5; W. Larcombe and K. Fethers, 'Schooling the Blues? An Investigation of Factors Associated with Psychological Distress Amongst Law Students' (2013) 36(2) *UNSW Law Journal* 390.

7 Beaton Consulting and BeyondBlue, 'Mental Health in the Workplace, 2011': http://www.beatonglobal.com/pdfs/Anxiety_and_depression_in_the_workplace.pdf.

8 W. Larcombe, S. Finch and R. Sore, 'Who's Distressed? Not Only Law Students: Psychological Distress Levels in University Students Across Diverse Fields of Studies' (2015) 37 *Sydney Law Review* 43.

9 N. Skead and S.L. Rogers, 'Do Law Students Stand Apart from other University Students in their Quest for Mental Health: A Comparative Study on Wellbeing and Associated Behaviours in Law and Psychology Students?' (2015) 42–43 *International Journal of Law and Psychiatry* 81–90.

are accepted in psychology as explanatory of depression. These include psychoanalytic theories through to cognitive behavioural theories. There are some common factors in these theories which are worth noting. Depression can arise out of life experiences including childhood events. Behavioural psychologists have developed various strategies based on cognitive style – in particular pessimism and optimism.[10] Despite the differences across psychological theories, an examination of a range of psychological literature showed that the dominant characteristics of depressed thinking were a loss of autonomy or learned helplessness. We investigated a range of psychological theories and concluded that attributional style (that is, the way one thinks about cause and effect in one's own life) is important for the development of depression. This view is consistent with both psychoanalytic and behavioural views of psychology.[11] Sheldon and others have set out what they consider to be the critical needs for wellbeing. These include 'self-esteem, competence, security (as an underlying requirement), social connection or relatedness to others, and autonomy'.[12]

Why lawyers and law students should be particularly subject to depression is difficult to discern. We know that law students have very high feelings of wellbeing when they enter law school and that this seems to dissipate within the first year to the point where many of them begin to suffer depression and anxiety.[13] Does this occur because of attributes of legal education or legal practice? Some have argued 'yes'. Paula Baron has argued that a Lacanian view of lawyer distress suggests that the individual is driven by an internalised demand (superego) which 'comments on the difference between how one is (ego) and how one could have been (ideal ego) ... [and] accentuates the subject's failures ... law students and lawyers are particularly subject to the demand of the Other.'[14] This is

10 For example, M. Seligman, *Learned Helplessness*, Ph.D. University of Philadelphia, 1972.

11 S.J. Blatt and C. Maroudas, 'Convergences among Psychoanalytic and Cognitive-Behavioural Theories of Depression' (1992) 9(2) *Psychoanalytic Psychology* 157.

12 M. Tani and P. Vines, 'Law Students' Attitudes to Education: A Pointer to Depression in the Legal Academy and the Profession?' (2009) 19(1) *Legal Education Review* 3–39 at 5 referring to K. Sheldon et al., 'What is Satisfying About Satisfying Events? Testing 10 Candidate Psychological Needs' (2001) 80 *Journal of Personality & Social Psychology* 325.

13 Iijima, above, n. 2, 526.

14 P. Baron, 'The Persistence of Distress' in R. Field, J. Duffy and C. James (eds), *Promoting Law Student and Lawyer Wellbeing in Australia and Beyond*, Routledge, 2016, p. 43.

consistent with the idea that people who choose law may have personality traits and dispositions which predispose them to depression and anxiety. Susan Daicoff argues strongly that people who choose law tend to have a particular personality profile.[15] She draws a complex picture, drawing on literature from the US and Australia, of a relationship between aspects of law school and this personality profile which leads to distress. She notes that law school tends to emphasise competitiveness which leads to social isolation; the workload is demanding which reduces social connectedness as well. This is exacerbated by law students' 'tendencies to ignore emotions, interpersonal concerns and warm interpersonal relations.'[16] She also argues that law schools foster the valuing of extrinsic rewards like marks and others' approval rather than intrinsic ones. Empirical studies have shown that this focus on extrinsic reward is likely to reduce emotional wellbeing. Daicoff also discusses issues of stress created by escalating financial debt which used not to be an issue for Australians but which have now begun to develop, although they have not yet reached the size of US student debt.

This literature suggests that empirical consideration of students' attitudes to their law studies and learning might tell us something about why distress is disproportionately common in law students.

In 2005 Tani, Vines and others conducted a survey of students' attitudes to education across the whole range of faculties of the University of New South Wales (UNSW).[17] Tani and Vines then re-analysed the data to look particularly at how law students' attitudes to their learning and education compared to all other faculties across the university.[18] Attitudes of students to their education are an important indicator of how they are likely to respond to particular methods of teaching. They can also be a strong indicator of when they feel empowered and disempowered and how they think about their social and educational connections including friends, teachers, employers and so on. The particular strength of this survey was that it examined attitudes across a number of faculties, rather than being confined to law students, so its findings allowed us to see patterns in particular areas of study compared with other areas. In particular we had

---

15 S.S. Daicoff, *Lawyer, Know Thyself: A Psychological Analysis of Personality Strengths and Weaknesses*, American Psychological Association, 2004.

16 Ibid. p. 144.

17 M. Tani (ed) with Armour, Ely, Kossew, Ho, Ramburith, Roberts, Scoufis, Vines and Vrcelj, 'On the Motivations, Expectations, and Experiences of Students in Tertiary Education: Findings from a Large Survey Carried Out at the University of New South Wales' Report, UNSW, 2006.

18 Tani and Vines, above, n. 12.

expected to see great similarities in attitude between students doing law and medicine.

The survey was administered by a paper questionnaire which was done in class. It was responded to by 2528 students across the 10 faculties of UNSW. These included 333 qualifying degree respondents from the Faculty of Law across the years from first to fifth year.

The attitudes students demonstrated were analysed in the light of the factors which are considered to be connected to depression and anxiety. We drew on Sheldon's work mentioned above, considering the critical needs for wellbeing as including 'self-esteem, competence, security (as an underlying requirement), social connection or relatedness to others, and autonomy'.[19] Of these, we decided that the important factors in the context of law school would be in particular the sense of autonomy, their level of social connectedness and their level of competitiveness.

This re-analysis of the questionnaire results established that law students were more likely than students in other disciplines to be doing their degree because other people (family and friends) wanted them to, were more driven by marks than other cohorts, were more likely to see their friends as possibly useful for professional reasons and more likely to see their employers as not interested in their values so much as their marks. They disliked group work and valued their own marks and the status of their university very highly.[20] For all these factors, there was a significant difference between law students and those from all other faculties, including medicine. These findings were analysed in terms of the corresponding contribution they would make to a sense of autonomy, social connectedness and competitiveness. For example, characteristics such as letting others decide whether they should go to university, or valuing marks or status of their university very highly were regarded as indicators of a lesser sense of autonomy. How friends were treated was regarded as a marker of the level of social connectedness. The dislike of group work appeared to be about social connectedness and competitiveness.

The findings of this survey were striking in that they showed that law students, compared with all other faculties in the university, were disproportionately more likely to have attitudes redolent of a lack of autonomy and authentic social connection. This is consistent with some of the work of the pioneers in the field in the US, Kennon M. Sheldon and Lawrence S. Krieger, who linked declining levels of wellbeing with declining

19 Tani and Vines, above, n. 12, 5, referring to Sheldon et al., n. 12.

20 Tani and Vines, n. 12.

intrinsic motivation.[21] What the study showed was that law students appeared to have a disproportionately low level of intrinsic motivation and a lesser sense of autonomy than other students; they were also less likely to be authentically socially connected, being disproportionately likely to think that friends were useful networks.

Later Australian studies have confirmed the view that law students were disproportionately extrinsically motivated. One question is whether this is a position that law students are likely to have before they get into law school (our study seemed to suggest this) or does it develop through their time in law school. Another question following on from this is to ask whether this is a characteristic which a disproportionate number of lawyers have, which contributes to their high levels of anxiety and depression.

A study by O'Brien et al.[22] suggested that law students' change in thinking style once they come to law school (which they characterised as reducing their experiential thinking) was associated with increases in depressive symptoms, again consistent with Sheldon and Krieger's findings. Larcombe, Malkin and Nicholson found that students' distress levels in law school appeared to be connected to the extent to which they learn to moderate their expectations.[23] If they did not moderate their expectations of results they were likely to become very distressed, and they found that law students did not take their own psychological distress into account in a way which would lead them to focus less on their marks. The students appeared to maintain their expectations of being in the top third of the cohort regardless of their experience. This study suggested that the continuing focus on marks by law students might be partly created by law school: 'that the experience of law school consolidates and emphasises non-intrinsic' motivation.

If this disproportionate proportion of law students has such characteristics which may be likely to make them more susceptible to anxiety and depression we need to know whether this is a stable situation for law students or was only a result of one particular cohort in 2005. To assist us with determining whether the findings of 2005 had validity over time we repeated the survey in 2018.

---

21 K.M. Sheldon and L.S. Krieger, 'Understanding the Negative Effects of Legal Education on Law Students: A Longitudinal Test of Self-Determination Theory' (2007) 33 *Personality and Social Psychology Bulletin* 883.

22 O'Brien et al., above, n. 5.

23 W. Larcombe, I. Malkin and P. Nicholson, 'Law Students' Motivations, Expectations and Level of Psychological Distress: Evidence of Connections' (2012) 22 *Legal Education Review* 71.

4. AIMS OF THE 2018 SURVEY

In 2018 we carried out another survey of first year UNSW law students. The aim of this project was to re-visit the findings in the Tani and Vines study about law students' attitudes to their legal education, although the comparator with students from other faculties was not available. It was felt it was timely to redo this survey in order to establish whether the various responses to the previous survey retain their validity.[24] We also wished to separate out the factors which might have confounded the earlier survey – which attitudes were held by beginning law students and which attitudes they might have developed in law school? For this reason we also did a separate survey of later year students which will only be peripherally commented on here.

One important difference between the 2005 and 2018 surveys is worth noting at the outset. This was the introduction of a new entry test for the undergraduate UNSW law degree. Applicants now have to sit the Law Admission Test[25] in addition to gaining a high matriculation score. That test requires students to submit essay-style answers to stimulus material and is designed to allow candidates to demonstrate their aptitude and skills for studying Law, and in particular their ability to write, draw conclusions and develop an argument. This additional hurdle to applying for UNSW Law might have had the effect of influencing the motivations of the students surveyed in 2018 in that it tended to reduce the number of students entering from high school who had done no or few humanities subjects.

The survey was offered to all students enrolled in the first semester intake of first year law (both LLB and JD), 492 students. Students were invited to complete the survey in class in *Introducing Law and Justice*, the foundational law course. The survey was completed in the second week of semester, prior to students taking classes about wellbeing which might have altered their responses to the questionnaire. It was administered online using Qualtrics survey software,[26] using a gateway in their course Moodle site to verify the student's enrolment in the law degree. Responses were all recorded anonymously. Ethics approval was obtained for the survey and for publication of results.[27]

---

24 The survey also included items drawn from a wide-ranging 2012 survey on student engagement. These results will be reported on separately.

25 https://www.law.unsw.edu.au/study/law-admission-test.

26 https://www.qualtrics.com/.

27 UNSW Ethics Approval HC180011.

Students were asked a range of questions, including the questions that had been asked in the Tani and Vines survey, about why they chose their course and how they feel about certain types of teaching such as group work. The survey was analysed in the same way as the previous survey, i.e. by administering Wilcoxon rank-sum and Kruskal-Wallis tests for each section of the survey. We did not attempt to measure rates of depression and anxiety.

5. RESULTS

5.1. THE SAMPLE

As the survey was undertaken in class the response rate was high. Of the 492 students enrolled, 378 partly completed the survey: 218 LLB (students coming to university for the first time after high school), 54 transfer students (students who did one year of university in another subject area and transferred to law in their second year) and 106 JD (JD students have done another degree before their law degree). Approximately 292 students completed all questions: 163 LLB, 37 transfer students and 92 JD.[28] There was thus a response rate, question by question, ranging from 60–77 per cent, a particularly high response rate for education surveys.

In this survey there were three cohorts – JD, LLB first year at university and LLB who were transferring into law from another subject. There were similar cohorts in the 2005 study although the JD was not available, but the equivalent was offered as a graduate LLB programme. In 2018, the LLB students doing the survey have had only one week of tertiary study and their responses are largely prior to any inculcation of tertiary education learning and lifestyle norms. The transfer students had previously enrolled in a non-law degree course and applied to transfer to a combined law degree at the end of their first year of study. These students therefore have adopted norms relevant to tertiary study *outside* of law school. Finally, the JD students also have negligible experience of law school study, but do have previous experience of fully completing a non-law degree. This cohort can also be split by age into those moving directly from one degree to

[28] The survey was long, and it was not compulsory to complete all questions. It appears some students did not answer questions that they did not consider relevant or easy to answer. Demographic questions, at the end of the survey were the least completed. 292 students completed the demographic question on their age.

another – and hence are experienced students; and those who have returned to study after life beyond university – and hence have a mature adult learner approach to study.

5.2. UNSW LAW STUDENT DEMOGRAPHICS

One significant limitation of any study of one student population is the extent to which the students are representative of the wider law student population. Many of the studies discussed above are based on populations of law students in highly sought-after urban law schools, and this is likely to influence student attitudes. To contextualise our findings, we begin by considering the sample's demographics.

5.3. AGE, GENDER AND LANGUAGE

292 students identified their age. The LLB students ranged in age from 17–20, with most being 18; the transfer students, from 18–21, with most being 19. In the JD cohort, 55 were aged 20–24, 23 were aged 25–29, and 14 were aged 30^{+}.

In terms of gender, the 2018 cohort was biased in favour of female students. University records indicate that enrolment was 55% female (193 female, 160 male), and for the JD 65% female (90 female, 49 male). Of those respondents (291) who indicated a gender 53% (105) of LLB and 66% (61) of JD identified as female. This overall gender balance remains consistent with the 2005 survey in which 54% of respondents were female.

Educational background was polarised between the 2018 cohorts. LLB students were overwhelmingly products of the Australian education system. 282 students identified the country that they had done most of their schooling in. Of the LLB students, 93% (182 of 195) had been educated in Australia. For the JDs however, 66% (56 of 86) had been educated outside of Australia, 60% (51) in China of which 50% (43) were under the age of 30.

Of the 286 students identifying a language mostly spoken with their families – either solely or in combination with another language, 52% (149) spoke English, 39% (112) 'Chinese' (most self-identified as Chinese, or Mandarin speakers, some identifying as Cantonese or Shanghainese) and 16% (45) identified other languages. Note that the high number of students identifying Chinese languages as those spoken with their family applies to both Australian-born Chinese who are products of the Australian education system (doing LLB) and International JD students from China who are not, and the latter may have a great deal more difficulty with English in their studies than the first group. This indicates the continuing bifurcation rather than spread of cultural backgrounds amongst the students.

Table 1. **Bifurcated cultural backgrounds**

	Bifurcated cultural backgrounds – First language (%)	
	2005	**2018**
English	61.8	52.1
Chinese/Mandarin/Cantonese	32.3	39.1
Other	5.9	15.7

2018 percentages include respondents who reported two languages 'mostly' spoken at home.

There is an increasing diversity of background since 2005, but the strong presence of Chinese-speaking students remains. It should also be noted that the cross-degree opt-in nature of the 2005 survey may have resulted in a slight overrepresentation of non-English speakers.

In 2009, 65% of students nominated English as a first language. In 2018, this was 61%.

5.4. SPOKEN AND WRITTEN ENGLISH

Similar results were reported for the standard of both spoken and written English between 2005 and 2018 for the LLB students, but a markedly different response was reported by JD students.

Table 2. **Students' self-rating of written English**

	Students' self-rating of written English (%)		
	2005	**LLB 2018**	**JD 2018**
Fair	7.0	2.5	43.5
Good	17.6	15.2	30.4
Excellent	74.1	82.2	26.1
No response	1.3	–	–

Table 3. Students' self-rating of spoken English

	Students' self-rating of spoken English (%)		
	2005	LLB 2018	JD 2018
Fair	6.0	2.0	34.8
Good	12.3	10.1	37.0
Excellent	81.1	87.8	28.3
No response	0.7	–	–

Of those reporting that English was not their first language only 8.6% of JD students considered their spoken English excellent and 12.5% that their written English was excellent.

In 2018, the same proportion of LLB students reported their mother having a university degree as reported their father having a university degree – over two thirds of students had two 'tertiary qualified' parents. JD students also had similar proportions but only half of students had a tertiary educated parent. Across the cohorts 74.9% of students reporting a mother with a university degree had done most of their schooling in Australia. For JD students, 51% of students educated in China had tertiary educated mothers, compared to 36% of those educated in Australia. For LLB students educated in Australia (the large majority) 67% had tertiary educated mothers – an increase from 46% in 2005. These figures suggest a growing rate of participation in higher education by women, in both Australia and China.

Table 4. Parental education level

	Parental education level (%)					
	2005		LLB 2018		JD 2018	
	Mother	Father	Mother	Father	Mother	Father
University degree	46	66	68.5	68.5	47.8	54.3
No university degree	50	30	29.4	27.9	50.0	42.4
Unknown	1	2	2.0	3.6	2.2	3.3
No response	3	2	–	–	–	–

Parental education levels appear to influence children's expectations and achievement in childhood.[29] Parental educational levels are

[29] P.E. Davis-Kean, 'The Influence of Parent Education and Family Income on Child Achievement: The Indirect Role of Parental Expectations and the Home Environment' (2005) 19 *Journal of Family Psychology* 294–304.

also a strong indicator of adult attainment in education and status of occupation.[30]

If university degrees can be seen as a proxy for social capital[31] this suggests that over the period of the two surveys the privileged nature of students entering UNSW has not fallen and is likely to have increased. It underlines the level of support for their study these students are likely to have – in contrast to cohorts of students where most are the first in their family to have undertaken tertiary study.[32]

5.5. RESPONSES TO ATTITUDINAL QUESTIONS

5.5.1. *Reasons for Going to University*

Students were asked to choose five statements about their reasons for going to university and rank them in importance.

Factors such as pleasing family, being like friends, finding a well-paying job and opening up a wider array of interesting job opportunities appear to be significantly less important reasons to go to university for undergraduate students in 2018 than 2005. Developing one's intellectual potential was significantly higher ranked in 2018 than 2005, and enjoying learning new things was ranked marginally higher, though this difference was not statistically significant. The lower ranking of 'opening up interesting job opportunities' in the 2018 cohort compared to the earlier one may reflect a new cynicism about the value of a university degree in the modern economy.

This is an interesting result, as the desire to please family and develop career prospects were characteristics that set law students apart from other faculties in 2005, and the 2018 cohort appear to be less motivated by those factors. It might indicate law students in 2018 experience a greater sense of autonomy than those in 2005 and are more intrinsically motivated. Is this a result of modern cognisance about wellbeing? Not worrying about

---

30 E.F. Dubow, P. Boxer and L.R. Huesmann, 'Long-term Effects of Parents' Education on Children's Educational and Occupational Success: Mediation by Family Interactions, Child Aggression, and Teenage Aspirations' (2009) 55(3) *Merrill Palmer Quarterly* 224–49: doi: 10.1353/mpq.0.0030.

31 J. Huang, H.M. Van Den Brink and W. Groot, 'A Meta-Analysis of the Effect of Education on Social Capital' (2009) 28(4) *Economics of Education Review* 454.

32 S. O'Shea et al., *First-in-Family Students, University Experience and Family Life: Motivations, Transitions and Participation*, Springer, 2017 ('*First-in-Family Students, University Experience and Family Life*').

money is a luxury. Do students who embark on a very expensive degree like law without worrying about career prospects come from privilege? Is the socio-economic background of law students in 2018 less diverse than in 2005?

The rankings for undertaking university studies because no quality jobs were available at a student's current level of education, or to achieve promotion in their current job, was similar between the two cohorts.

Overall, the difference between the two cohorts is significant and shows that the law students today appear to be more likely to have chosen for themselves or to have an intrinsic reason to do their university studies than law students were in 2005. The 2018 cohort may be more likely to do their studies because they enjoy learning new things, or because it will develop their intellectual potential (unless the 2005 sample was significantly skewed by later students).

5.5.2. *Choosing Law School*

Table 5. Main reasons to do Law: Response count, percentage of total responses and mean rank (1 being highest rank, 5 lowest rank)

	2005			2018		
	Count	**%**	**Mean**	**Count**	**%**	**Mean**
It was the program I qualified for.	132	8.7	2.86	92	8.9	3.2
I could not get into my first choice.	41	2.7	2.54	12	1.2	2.5
It was easy to manage in terms of time (i.e. allowed flexibility).	42	2.8	3.93	4	0.4	4
It was recommended to me by previous students.	125	8.2	3.43	52	5.0	3.66
It is personally interesting to me.	252	16.5	1.86	231	22.3	1.6
The faculty has a good reputation.	212	13.9	2.72	173	16.7	3.03
I like the methods of teaching.	139	9.1	3.3	82	7.9	3.61
I like the methods of assessment.	194	12.7	2.29	15	1.4	4.32
The program description was comprehensive and sounded interesting.	146	9.6	3.18	159	15.3	3.12
It is relevant to my present job or the career I envision for myself.	211	13.8	2.15	203	19.6	2.26
Other	32	2.1	2.88	14	1.4	3.06
Total Responses	1526			1037		
Total Respondents						

As can be seen by the means in Table 5, personal interest was a significantly more important reason for choosing law school for students in 2018 than 2005 while qualifying for the programme, and the reputation of the faculty, were significantly less important for students in 2018 than 2005. This may indicate that more students in 2018 are intrinsically motivated to be at law school, not superficially based on the prestige of the university, or out of not wanting to waste a good entrance score. It is also possible that the new entrance test, the LAT, has had some impact. Choosing law school because the programme description was comprehensive and interesting was ranked the same in 2005 and 2018, though by more students. Choosing UNSW Law because of preference for the teaching and assessment methods was ranked significantly lower by students in 2018 than in 2005. This is of interest because UNSW Law was long regarded as distinctive because of its excellence in teaching. The extent to which this is no longer as potent a factor may be due to either a decline in relative teaching prestige or a relative decline in teaching as a relevant factor in study and employment success. One other possible reason for this is that assessment based on class participation (which is a very important part of assessment at UNSW Law) is particularly intimidating. The majority of law students now also belong to the generation raised by the internet; more social communication is experienced in written formats than for previous students. Contributing in class might indeed be more anxiety provoking now than in 2005. Another possibility is that the students in 2018 were all first-year students. Comparing the average ratings given by 2018 students to each motivation, the Faculty's reputation had an overall score of 3.03, the teaching methods 3.61, and assessment 4.32. Personal interest was significantly more important to students, with an average score of 1.6.

Choosing law school as an alternative to another first programme choice had a higher average ranking in 2018 than 2005, though this was not statistically significant as there was substantial variation in rankings within the two groups. As entrance scores of law students are generally very high, relatively few programmes are closed off to students who are capable of entry into law. As Tani and Vines suggested,[33] this ranking is perhaps from students who did not get into their *university* of choice.

---

33 Tani and Vines, n. 12, 14.

Choosing law school because it was recommended by previous students was ranked significantly lower by students in 2018 than 2005. Perhaps students make the decision to go to law school more autonomously now, rather than on the recommendation of, or under pressure from, friends or family. Perhaps students entering law school now are less likely to know previous students, because they are now more likely to be coming from families and social groups with no previous contact with the legal profession.

Among cohorts in both 2005 and 2018, the majority of respondents reported they made their decision to go to law school independently. Of students who responded to this question in 2018, a far smaller proportion nominated their parents as the most influential factor in this decision than in 2005. This may indicate that students entering law school now have a greater sense of autonomy than students in 2005. Students who reported being influenced by their close friends were nearly equivalent in 2018 and 2005.

5.5.3. *What were the Important Experiences at University?*

Broadening one's knowledge while at university was ranked significantly higher by students in 2018 than 2005. This was followed by developing abilities to learn on one's own and broadening knowledge.

Getting good grades was ranked significantly lower in 2018 than 2005. This is extremely interesting since reliance on marks is based on a willingness to accept an external judgement. This might indicate that law students in 2018 are less reliant on extrinsic motivators for study than students in 2005. It might also indicate that students feel grades are less important because they are also perceived as less important to employers than other graduate qualities.[34] It may also be significant that in 2018 only commencing first years were surveyed. However, the individualist goal of good grades was still seen as generally more important than social goals.

Discovering what one really wants to do in the future was ranked marginally higher by students in 2018 than in 2005, and gaining knowledge

34 See discussion under Expectations of employers, below.

necessary for a future career was ranked marginally lower, though neither of these differences were statistically significant. This might indicate that law students in 2018 are studying law because of an intrinsic interest in it, less with specific career goals in mind but more as an exploratory exercise. Might a law degree be seen less as a professional degree and more as a liberal education, as students perceive the value of university degrees generally as inflated?

Similarly, gaining a network of friends to assist in one's future career was marginally less important to students in 2018 than 2005. This may indicate that beginning law students in 2018 are less likely to see friends as career assets, and more likely to look for authentic friendship. Does it indicate that law students now place a higher value on meaningful social connection? How students think about the value of their university friends could be more closely investigated in future surveys.

5.5.4. *Why are Good Grades Important?*

Nearly all respondents considered getting good grades was important. However, the reasons for this altered. Meeting family expectations as a reason why good grades are important was given a significantly lower ranking by students in 2018 than 2005. Getting a high-paying job as a reason why good grades were important was also given a marginally lower ranking by students in 2018 than 2005, though this difference was not statistically significant. This is interesting because it suggests that students are less affected by the extrinsic effects of marks. Perhaps while good grades are still important to students, law students are less motivated to achieve them by extrinsic pressures.

Reward for effort was given a significantly higher ranking by students in 2018 than 2005. To feel capable was also given a marginally higher ranking by the 2018 cohort, though this difference was not significant. Demonstrating that one has actually learned something, and prestige and honour had roughly the same mean rankings in 2005 and 2018. This might indicate that law students are now treating good grades as a pleasant addition to what they already recognise for themselves as hard work. However, this may be too good to be true. It probably indicates that law students still look extrinsically to grades to gauge their own competence. This may still suggest a lack of autonomy, or a low sense of competence.

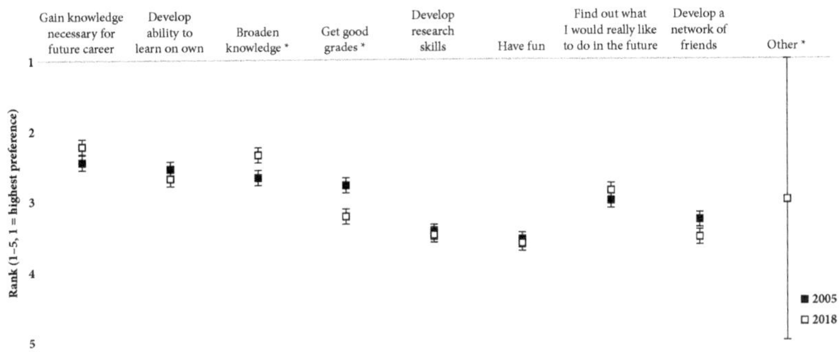

Figure 1. Mean rankings of the importance of particular experiences by undergraduate law students in 2005 and 2018 (Average +/– SE)

Statistically significant differences in cohort means are marked * (Kruskal-Wallis, df = 1, $p < 0.05$).

5.5.5. *Most Important Skills and Knowledge Aspects of Degree*

One set of questions asked students to rank on a Likert scale what they thought was most important about their law degree. Figure 2 below indicates the mean rankings given by law students in 2005 and 2018. The Likert scale ranged from Not Important (1) to Essential (5).

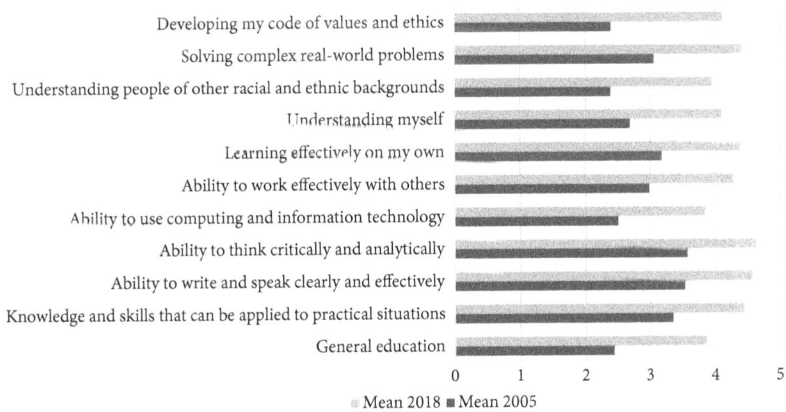

Figure 2. Most important aspects of degree

What is striking in these results is not only the overall similarity in comparative weight given to each outcome of a university degree, but the overall significant rise in each category's importance. It is even more striking that those categories where the mean has jumped the most are those with the lowest means – developing a personal code of ethics and understanding other cultures. It is unclear whether this is an increase in social awareness or just a product of the higher scores for the other categories. The other striking feature is the continued low level of ability to use computer technology as a desired outcome of university education – despite repeated government and industry commentary on its centrality to future work.

There are very high percentages of current first year law students entering university who believe that these outcomes are essential. Table 6 sets out the categories which over 50 per cent of students saw as essential to their degree.

Table 6. Categories which >50% of students saw as essential

Outcome	%
Knowledge and skills that can be applied to practical work situations	56.45%
Ability to write and speak clearly and effectively	66.24%
Ability to think critically and analytically	70.42%
Learning effectively on my own	51.13%
Solving complex real-world problems	54.84%

Related to these findings are students' views of employers' expectations. Students expected employers to attach a significantly higher value to graduates' personal code of values and ethics in 2018 than in 2005. It may be that students have intrinsic motivations for studying law, but beyond this, perceive that some internalised set of guiding values is essential to employment, and essential to lawyering in any capacity.

It was also apparent that students expected employers to value a graduate's ability to contribute to the welfare of their community far more in 2018 than 2005. This is an interesting finding. It may indicate that students are now more likely to view law as a noble profession, and to see giving back to the community as a capacity of lawyering in any form. This is in line with early research showing that first year students often come to law school intending to pursue a career in social justice.[35] Law students now might then experience a greater sense of intrinsic worth and social connectedness in studying it. However, this result may also be simply an artefact of the 2018 survey only sampling first year students, before they had time to develop cynicism.

Students in 2018 expected employers to value their capacity to understand people of racial and cultural backgrounds beyond their own significantly more than those in 2005. Could this be because interactions with people of other backgrounds are just more common? Because law school is generally more diverse? Because communicating across cultures is embedded in the curriculum? Interacting and cooperating with people of backgrounds beyond your own are an intrinsic part of university experience, internalised as of value at work too.

Students in 2018 expected employers to value their ability to solve quantitative problems significantly more than those in 2005. They also expected employers to value their job-ready skills and knowledge considerably more than those in 2005. This does not correspond to an increase in the ranking of the equivalent answer under question QO/16 ('What can students gain from studying?' question.) Could this be because this had a relatively high ranking anyway? Or because students do not feel job-ready skills are acquired at university, but experience greater pressure to acquire real-world skills outside of law school, i.e. internships, volunteering etc.?

Students in 2018 expected their overall marks/grades, and the university their law degree was from, to be significantly less important to employers than did students in 2005.This may indicate that students feel that the legal profession values graduates' intrinsic qualities – ethics, social conscience, personableness – more than mere grades.

The ability to solve complex real-world problems, think critically and analytically, write and speak clearly and effectively, work effectively with others and work effectively alone were considered somewhat more

---

35 For example, T. Nguyen, 'Affair to Forget: Law School's Deleterious Effect on Students' Public Interest Aspirations' (2008) 7(12) *Connecticut Public Interest Journal* 95; but note M.T. O'Brien, 'Connecting Law Students to Health' in Field et al., above n. 14, 168 says many go to law school because they just don't know what to do, which is also consistent with the findings of Tani and Vines, above n. 12.

valuable to employers in 2018 than 2005. A graduate's broad, general education was rated considerably more important to employers by students in 2018 than in 2005.

Maybe the rise in perceived value of these intrinsic qualities is the counterbalance to the drop in the perceived importance of extrinsic markers of achievement – grades/university reputation. Maybe this marks a shift in the expectations that this generation of lawyers will bring to the workforce, or again, just the naivete of first year students.

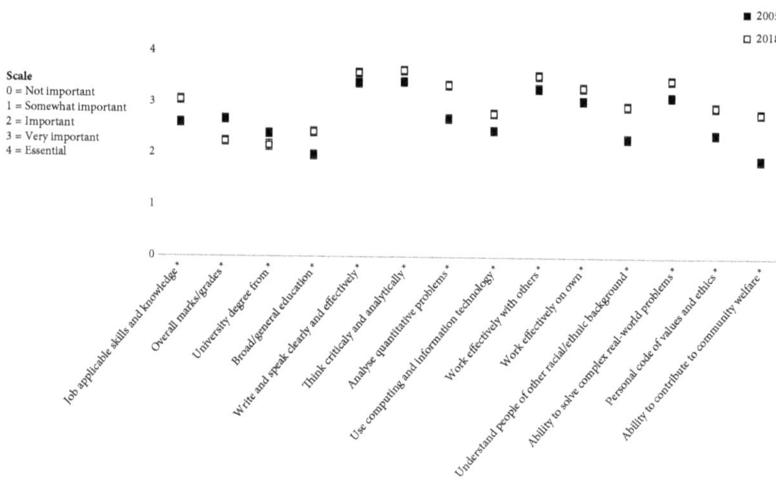

Figure 3. Mean ratings of the importance of certain traits to employers by law students in 2005 and 2018 (Average +/– SE)

Statistically significant differences between cohort means are marked * (Kruskal-Wallis, df = 1, $p < 0.05$).

6. LIMITATIONS

This study did not compare the law students with other groups within the university, so we cannot draw from it any conclusions about how law students compare with other cohorts. Because this part of the study drew only on students in their first two weeks of law school no inferences can be drawn at all about the effect of legal studies on students. We are currently surveying final year students and hope to be able to draw some conclusions about whether students increase in cynicism etc. during their degree. That is our hypothesis.

7. DISCUSSION

It will be recalled that law students appeared to be disproportionately likely to have attitudes to learning which indicated a lack of autonomy and social connectedness in the 2005 study. This was demonstrated, in particular, by the fact that students were disproportionately likely to be doing law for reasons not intrinsic to themselves – because someone else told them to, despite a lack of intrinsic interest and so on. They similarly seemed to be more likely to see friends in an instrumental way than other students. The picture that emerged appeared to emphasise extrinsic motivation over intrinsic motivation, so that marks, for example, had a very strong focus compared to the way students in other faculties thought about them. It was thought that this external motivation might provide a clue to the disproportionate level of distress that law students appeared to suffer. Obviously allowing other people to evaluate you is a dangerous strategy.

In this very draft report we can only make some preliminary suggestions about what we have found. The survey had quite a good response rate and there is no reason to be concerned about sample size.

There is some evidence in these results to support the inference that commencing law students in 2018 are unlikely to be as strongly affected by the same extrinsic motivators as their counterparts in 2005. In particular the data about why they chose their course suggests that students in law in 2018 have exhibited more autonomy than students in 2005. Although we could not compare law students with other students in different faculties in 2018, it may be that law students are still disproportionately lacking in autonomy compared with students in other faculties. A higher proportion of law students seem to demonstrate an intrinsic interest in their legal studies than did the law students in 2005. A surprising result was that the first year law students in 2018 did not expect their employers to be so concerned about their marks, and had a higher expectation that employers would be interested in their ethical values than we saw in the earlier study. Similarly there are big changes in the number of students who see the 'development of an ethical code' and 'general education' as major reasons for their study.

These results are very interesting as preliminary matters. We need to look at the results of the final year students before we decide that there has been a change in the attitudes of law students to their studies which is significant compared with 2005, and certainly whether that could have made any difference to their level of distress. It is worth noting that the majority of student responders in 2005 were in their first year, so the cohort may be more comparable to the 2018 cohort of first year students than we have feared. We also need to further pull apart responses from those students commencing straight from high school and those who are already graduates. If there have been changes to the way first year law students consider their law studies or degree, one thing which must be considered is the extent to which mental health and wellbeing has been taught in schools and discussed more openly in society in the last 15 years and whether that is a general factor. We still appear to have very high rates of anxiety and depression in our students, but we also know that rates of anxiety and depression have climbed in our society generally. It may be that law students and lawyers no longer stick out as much as they used to.

Those studies which have argued that law students' training may be a major factor in their levels of anxiety and depression have taken the view that the teaching of law has characteristics which may potentiate students' being motivated extrinsically. Such characteristics include the emphasis on marks, prizes, Dean's Lists etc. which exists in all law schools, and the emphasis in legal argument on removing emotion from the argument and using formalistic politeness instead. Law students typically have a large workload which may be isolating (and that workload continues into the legal profession and continues to be isolating).

Paula Baron has said: 'Law students and lawyers are particularly subject to the demand of the Other'.[36] This characteristic is typical of many professionals. Such people seek to please others, often to help others, both of these being opposite sides of the coin of allowing extrinsic markers to determine one's view of oneself. There is strong evidence that the focus on extrinsic reward is likely to damage wellbeing.

The evidence from our surveys and others suggests that law students and lawyers' propensity to suffer from anxiety and depression may well be sourced from two areas – first the personality profile of the person who appears disproportionately likely to be 'other-focused' or extrinsically rather than intrinsically motivated; and that this is likely to be exacerbated by what happens in law school, which emphasises competitiveness, marks, prizes, etc. and reduces focus on emotion. Social connection in law school is important, but if it is seen as mere networking it is unlikely to be protective against anxiety and depression. The problematic factors

---

36 Baron, above n. 14, 43.

in legal education appear to be further exacerbated by professional life as a lawyer. Most young lawyers are in situations where they have almost no autonomy – they are instructed by senior partners and are carrying out clients' instructions; they often work extremely hard and long hours, which prevents them from spending time on their personal relationships. Where they have billable hours, a partner may cross out all their work in a stroke on the basis that they did not really earn that money/the work was not good enough, etc. Extrinsic rewards and valuations continue to be the focus but are now characterised in terms of money and work brought into the firm etc. It is notable that, despite what are probably equivalent stressors in terms of workload, barristers' level of anxiety and depression is consistently less than that of solicitors. This may well reflect the greater level of autonomy that barristers exercise over their working life.

8. CONCLUSION

This report considering the two groups of law students in 2005 and 2018 cannot answer all the questions we have about why there is a disproportionate level of anxiety and depression amongst law students and lawyers. The evidence we have collected suggested that the very extreme levels of extrinsic motivation seen in law students may have reduced slightly in the 2018 cohort. It may be speculated whether this is partly attributable to the fact that schools and society have been emphasising wellness in the past 15 years, and students are more exposed to self-reflection than they were before; or that this is the view of first year students who are uncontaminated by their law studies yet (while the respondents in 2005 included some later year students). We will not be able to answer that particular question until after we analyse responses to a further survey of final year students.

What can be seen in the literature, however, is a fairly consistent set of factors which operate in law students and lawyers which do have some explanatory value in relation to anxiety and depression. These factors include personality traits or habits of focus on extrinsic factors as motivation, exacerbated by stressors in the legal education and professional environment which make people ill – focus on external reward or others' approval, endemic work overloading with little autonomy, a focus that is relentlessly unemotional, and a very high level of competition. Law schools and the legal profession have begun to see the damage done, but so far there is little attempt to change in meaningful ways. Work overload will not stop until employers hire enough employees; law is actually an emotional matter, as all life is, and the failure to recognise this simply exacerbates the artificiality and stress of professional life. This is only beginning to be broken down in the academy with the development of research areas in law and emotion, etc.[37] Giving some level of autonomy to students and lawyers, or at the very least explaining why you cannot, may be vital.

The law student becomes the lawyer. It seems clear that a proportion of students who enter law school may have characteristics which, if not handled carefully, might lead to anxiety or depression then or later. It behoves us to pay attention to these in the undergraduate law curriculum and in the profession. Too much stress will break any person. This is not a matter of survival of the fittest; it is a matter of removing barriers to good lawyering that are currently allowed to get in the way of complete and robust lives for people in the profession.

---

37 See, for example, H. Conway and J. Stannard, *Emotional Dynamics of Law and Legal Discourse*, Hart Publishing, 2016; S. Bandes and J. Blumenthal, 'Emotion and the Law' (2012) 8 *Annual Review of Law and Social Sciences* 161–81; *ARC Centre of Excellence on History of Law and Emotions*, http://www.historyofemotions.org.au/research/research-clusters/history-of-law-and-emotions/.

CHAPTER 3

THE PARADOX OF SATISFACTION AND DISTRESS AMONG LAWYERS

Implications for a Changing Field

Suzanne POYNTON and Janet CHAN*

1. Introduction: Satisfaction and Mental Health of Lawyers 58
2. Understanding Lawyering Stress 60
3. Research Method and Analysis 61
   3.1. Data Source and Sample 61
   3.2. Dependent Variables 62
   3.3. Independent Variables 63
   3.4. Statistical Analysis 64
4. Results 65
   4.1. Limitations 72
5. Conclusions and Implications 73

* This work was supported by an Australian Research Council Discovery Grant [DP110101000]. The authors would like to thank members of the research team: Sally Doran, Holly Blackmore, Rebecca Ananian-Welsh, Roland Alexander and Rabeatul Husna Abdull Rahman for their assistance with the research at various stages. We gratefully acknowledge the support of the legal professional community for publicising the survey. The project has benefited from the generous and expert advice of Peter Lovibond of the University of New South Wales and Ronit Dinovitzer of the University of Toronto. Colleagues at the Law Faculty, UNSW – David Dixon, Prue Vines, Michael Legg, Amrita Kapur, Keith Mason, and former Development Manager Hilary Blackman – all contributed to the development of this project. Finally, our very special thanks go to the hundreds of lawyers who took the time to complete the survey and those who participated in the interviews. Without their generous contributions this research would not have been possible.

1. INTRODUCTION: SATISFACTION AND MENTAL HEALTH OF LAWYERS

Surveys over the last 12 years have highlighted the prevalence of mental health and wellbeing issues among Australian lawyers. The 2006 annual survey of Australian professionals found that members of the legal profession were more likely than other similar professionals to report moderate to severe symptoms of depression (about 16% compared with 8% for engineering and 10% for accounting professionals) and to use alcohol and other drugs to manage feelings of sadness and depression (about 5% compared with 2% for engineering and 2.5% for accounting professionals).[1] A 2009 survey of over 2000 Australian law students, solicitors and barristers showed that nearly 60% of the respondents reported a moderate-to-very-high level of psychological distress.[2] Using a different scale, a 2013 national survey of Australian lawyers, Chan, Poynton and Bruce found a much higher proportion of respondents (26 to 32%) – compared with the population norm of 13% – reported experiencing moderate to extreme symptoms of depression, stress and anxiety.[3] Similar results were found in a smaller study of Australian lawyers, reporting an alarmingly high level (nearly 50%) of stress symptoms.[4]

Overseas research evidence on this issue is mixed. For example, Schiltz's review of the American empirical literature suggests that compared with the general population, lawyers were more likely to be depressed, to suffer from anxiety or other mental disorder, to abuse alcohol and drugs, and to commit suicide.[5] In contrast, Dinovitzer and Garth cite a number of systematic studies that show that lawyers reported a generally high level of job satisfaction.[6] It has been argued by Organ, who completed

1 Beaton Consulting, 'Annual Professions Survey Research Extract' (BeyondBlue 2007) <http://www.beyondblue.org.au>.

2 N. Kelk, G. Luscombe, S. Medlow and I. Hickie, *Courting the Blues: Attitudes towards Depression in Australian Law Students and Legal Practitioners*, Brain & Mind Research Institute, University of Sydney, 2009.

3 J. Chan, S. Poynton and J. Bruce, 'Lawyering stress and work culture: An Australian study' (2014) 37 *UNSW Law Journal* 1062.

4 A.J. Bergin and N.L. Jimmieson, 'Australian lawyer well-being: Workplace demands, resources and impact of time-billing targets' (2014) 21 *Psychiatry, Psychology and Law* 421.

5 P.J. Schiltz, 'On being a happy, healthy, and ethical member of an unhappy, unhealthy, and unethical profession' (1999) 52 *Vanderbilt Law Review* 871.

6 R. Dinovitzer and B.G. Garth, 'Lawyer satisfaction in the process of structuring legal careers' (2007) 41 *Law & Society Review* 1.

a comprehensive review of the North American research literature on lawyers in the past 25 years, that empirical studies have shown that 'on a fairly consistent basis – roughly 79–80 per cent of attorneys – indicate that they are positively satisfied with their jobs and/or careers'.[7] Organ found variations in satisfaction among subgroups of lawyers: experienced lawyers are more likely to report greater satisfaction compared with less experienced lawyers, and public sector (or public interest) lawyers show greater satisfaction than those in private (especially large firm) practice, but female lawyers are not less satisfied than male lawyers.[8]

These apparently contradictory results may be an artefact of the choice of variables, measurement scales or sampling methods. For example, in Kelk et al. (2009), Chan, Poynton and Bruce (2014) and Bergin and Jimmieson (2014), female lawyers were clearly over-represented.[9] Other studies relying on voluntary participation, such as Beaton Consulting,[10] provide very few details on response rates and representativeness of their survey samples. Given the self-selected nature of these surveys, estimates on the prevalence of mental health issues need to be used with caution: most likely these results only apply to the specific samples and should not be extrapolated to the population of legal practitioners.[11] In any case, even if the majority of lawyers were satisfied with their job, the presence of a sizeable minority suffering from depression or other mental health issues is still a problem that cannot be ignored. It is also obvious that positive ratings of job satisfaction or satisfaction about one's career choice as a lawyer are not the same as the absence of health and wellbeing issues. It is possible that prevailing assumptions and attitudes in legal practice (what may be loosely called 'legal culture') can play a large part in normalising certain lifestyles and responses to work stress.[12]

This chapter draws on a national survey of Australian lawyers conducted in 2012–2013 (the same sample as Chan et al.[13] but using multivariate

7 J.M. Organ, 'What do we know about the satisfaction/dissatisfaction of lawyers?: A meta-analysis of research on lawyer satisfaction and well-being' (2011) 8 *University of St. Thomas Law Journal* 225, 273.

8 Ibid.

9 N. Kelk et al., above n. 2; J. Chan et al., above n. 3; and A.J. Bergin and N.L. Jimmieson, above n. 4.

10 Beaton Consulting, above n. 1.

11 See C. Parker, 'The "moral panic" over psychological wellbeing in the legal profession: A personal or political ethical response?' (2014) 37 *UNSW Law Journal* 1103.

12 See J. Chan, 'Conceptualising legal culture and lawyering stress' (2015) 21 *International Journal of the Legal Profession* 213.

13 J. Chan, S. Poynton and J. Bruce, 'Lawyering stress and work culture: An Australian study' (2014) 37 *UNSW Law Journal* 1062.

rather than bivariate analysis) to investigate the inter-relationships between psychological measures such as depression, anxiety and stress; lawyers' expression of satisfaction with their chosen career; and variables relating to work demands and workplace culture. The chapter is organised as follows. The next section, drawing on previous studies, briefly describes how stress and wellbeing among members of the legal profession can be theorised. This is followed by a section on the research method and the basis of the multivariate analysis. The fourth section discusses the results and their limitations, while the final section extends the discussion to the implications of the research for lawyering in a changing world.

2. UNDERSTANDING LAWYERING STRESS

In her review of the literature on work stress, Chan has suggested that 'stress has been understood as a combination of physiological, psychological and social phenomena'.[14] For example, in science and medicine, theories such as the *demand–control model* (i.e., that job stress originates from work situations where demands are high but control is low),[15] the *effort–reward imbalance model* (i.e., that work that requires a great deal of effort but provides a low level of reward creates stress),[16] and the *organisational justice model* (i.e., that a lack of procedural justice or respect from a supervisor in a workplace is a form of stressor)[17] have found support in empirical research on work stress manifested in mental health outcomes.[18]

However, a more holistic view of stress – conceived by, for example, Pearlin and Bierman – describes it as a social process involving *sources of stress* (e.g., life events or chronic strains), *mediators of stress* (e.g., social support), and *manifestations of stress* (e.g. from physiological to emotion or behavioural expressions). This social process can depend on

---

14 J. Chan, above n. 12, 7.

15 See R. Karasek and T. Thorell, *Healthy Work: Stress, Productivity, and the Reconstruction of Working Life*, Basic Books, New York 1990.

16 See J. Siegrist, 'Adverse health effects of high effort – low reward conditions at work' (1996) 1 *Journal of Occupational Health Psychology* 27.

17 See M. Kivimaki, M. Elovainio, J. Vahtera, J. Ferrie and T. Theorell, 'Organizational justice and health of employees: Prospective cohort study' (2003) 60 *Occupational and Environmental Medicine* 27.

18 A.D. LaMontagne, T. Keegel, A.M. Louie and A. Ostry, 'Job stress as a preventable upstream determinant of common mental disorders: A review for practitioners and policy-makers' (2010) 9 *Advances in Mental Health* 17.

the social and economic status of individuals, so that 'the same objective stressor can and usually does evoke disparate stress responses in different individuals'.[19]

Citing research such as Lazarus and Folkman (1984), Peterson and Wilson (2002), and Idris et al. (2012), Chan extends these models to postulate that work stress is the result of a complex interaction between objective working conditions, workplace culture, and individual workers' psychological, physical and social characteristics which affect how workers perceive work demands in relation to their ability to cope with such demands.[20] This complex, interactional model has not been tested using empirical data. This chapter is a first attempt at using multivariate analysis to consider the interaction of various relevant variables applicable to the manifestation of work stress.

3. RESEARCH METHOD AND ANALYSIS

3.1. DATA SOURCE AND SAMPLE

The data used in this study come from a national cross-sectional survey of Australian legal practitioners, conducted in 2012–13.[21] A total of 1,008 responses were received to this survey. Only respondents who indicated that they were currently practising as a lawyer and were working on a full-time or part-time basis at the time of completing the questionnaire were included in the analysis (n = 877). The questionnaire, which most respondents completed online, consisted of 54 questions asking for demographic information and information about their professional background, career plan, current job, working conditions, and their mental health.

---

19 L.I. Pearlin and A. Bierman, 'Current issues and future directions in research into the stress process' in C.S. Aneshensel, J.C. Phelan and A. Bierman (eds), *Handbook of the Sociology of Mental Health*, Springer, Dordrecht 2013, p. 327.

20 R.S. Lazarus and S. Folkman, *Stress, Appraisal, and Coping*, Springer, New York 1984; M. Peterson and J.F. Wilson, 'The Culture–Work–Health Model and work stress' (2002) 26 *American Journal of Health Behavior* 16; and M.A. Idris, M.F. Dollard, J. Coward and C. Dormann, 'Psychosocial safety climate: Conceptual distinctiveness and effect on job demands and worker psychological health' (2012) 50 *Safety Science* 19; J. Chan, above n. 12.

21 For details, see J. Chan, S. Poynton and J. Bruce, above n. 3.

3.2. DEPENDENT VARIABLES

The primary outcome of interest was scores on the Depression Anxiety Stress Scales (DASS). The DASS is a well-validated measure of mental health and is specifically designed to differentiate between the emotional states of depression, anxiety and stress/tension.[22] The three scales are described as follows:

> [T]he Depression scale is characterised principally by a loss of self-esteem and incentive, and is associated with a low perceived probability of attaining life goals of significance for the individual as a person ... The DASS Anxiety scale emphasises the links between the relatively enduring state of anxiety and the acute response of fear ... the DASS Anxiety scale additionally addresses situational anxiety. The content of the Stress scale suggests that it is measuring a state of persistent arousal and tension with a low threshold for becoming upset or frustrated.[23]

The short version of DASS (DASS-21) was used here and includes 21 questions asking respondents to rate on a four-point severity scale whether certain statements (e.g. 'I felt I was close to panic') applied to them at all *over the past week*. It is important to note that these questions are not designed to diagnose clinical psychological disorders. However, DASS scores can be classified into five ranges to reflect the severity level of mental health symptoms: normal, mild, moderate, severe and extremely severe. These severity labels are used to categorise the degree of severity relative to the population. For example, a category of 'mild' means 'above the population mean but still well below dysfunctional levels'. The three binary dependent variables used in the multivariate analysis for this study were whether or not the respondent reported symptoms in the severe/extremely severe category on the depression scale (no = 0, yes = 1), anxiety scale (no = 0, yes = 1) and stress scale (no = 0, yes = 1). Of the 877 respondents who were included in the sample, 786 (89.6 per cent) completed all of the DASS-21 questions. Non-respondents were more likely to be aged under 30 years and on incomes lower than Au$60,000, but did not vary significantly from responders in terms of any other demographic or workplace characteristics.

---

22 P.F. Lovibond and S.H. Lovibond, 'The Structure of Negative Emotional States: Comparison of the Depression Anxiety Stress Scales (DASS) with the Beck Depression and Anxiety Inventories' (1995) 33 *Behaviour Research and Therapy* 335.

23 Ibid., 335.

3.3. INDEPENDENT VARIABLES

There were a large number of potential predictors drawn from the survey data. Most variables were entered into the model as categorical variables unless there was evidence of a linear relationship with the dependent variable. The predictors considered included the following:

Individual characteristics:

- **Age** (0 = under 30, 1 = 30–39, 2 = 40–49, 3 = 50^{+}).
- **Gender** (0 = male, 1 = female).
- **Children** (0 = no, 1 = yes).
- **Income** (0 = <Au$60,000, 1 = Au$60,001–90,000, 2 = Au$90,001–150,000, 3 = >$150,000).
- **Workplace type** (0 = small private law firm, 1 = chambers, 2 = community legal/other, 3 = corporate, 4 = government, 5 = large private law firm).
- **Workplace location** (0 = metropolitan, 1 = regional/remote).
- **Alcohol use** – alcohol consumption risk level derived from scores on the World Health Organization's Alcohol Use Disorders Identification Test (AUDIT).[24] (0 = never drink, 1 = low-risk drinker, 2 = medium risk drinker, 3 = high-risk drinker).

Perception of working conditions and workplace culture:

- **Effort and Reward Imbalance ratio** – ratio of Effort to Reward at work calculated from Siegrist's Effort–Reward Imbalance questionnaire.[25]

---

24 T.F. Babor, J.C. Higgins-Biddle, J.B. Saunders and M.G. Monteiro, *AUDIT: The Alcohol Use Disorders Identification Test Guidelines for Use in Primary Care*, World Health Organisation 2001, 2nd ed.

25 The Effort–Reward Ratio was calculated by dividing the average Effort score (over 3 items) by the average Reward score (over 7 items) for each respondent, reverse-coding where appropriate and multiplying by a correction factor (i.e. a factor accounting for the number of items used in each scale). Consistent with Niedhammer et al. (2004) several different formulations of the ERI score were tested in the logistic regression models including: a categorical variable defined by the quartiles of the distribution of the ratio, a continuous variable based on the ratio itself, a continuous variable based on the ratio logarithmically transformed and a categorical variable where exposed people are defined by a ratio over 1. The best-performing model (as indicated by the Akaike's Information Criterion (AIC) – see n. 29 below) was that which included a continuous variable based on the ratio itself. I. Niedhammer, M.L. Tek, D. Starke and J. Siegrist, 'Effort-reward imbalance model and self-reported health: Cross-sectional and prospective findings form the GAZEL cohort' (2004) 58 *Social Science & Medicine* 1531.

- **Overcommitment** – score on a 6-item scale from Siegrist's Effort–Reward Imbalance questionnaire measuring how people cope with the demands of work.[26]
- **Work–life balance** – score on the 5-item Work–Family Conflict (impact of work on family) scale developed by Netemeyer, Boles and McMurrian.[27]
- **Practice ethos** – average score on a 9-item scale called Practice Ethos.[28] A higher score represents a higher level of agreement with an ethos of legal practice characterised by long hours, combativeness, toughness and competitiveness. This variable was categorised based on the quartiles of the sample distribution.
- **Satisfaction with decision to become a lawyer** – respondents were asked 'overall how satisfied are you now with your decision to become a lawyer?' (0 = extremely/moderately satisfied, 1 = neither satisfied or dissatisfied, 2 = moderately/extremely dissatisfied).

3.4. STATISTICAL ANALYSIS

The first research question we addressed was whether there is a relationship between work-related factors (including career satisfaction) and mental health outcomes, after controlling for other sociodemographic and individual-level variables. Before developing the multivariate model, the bivariate relationships between each of the independent variables and the three outcome measures were examined using Pearson's Chi-square tests and t-tests. Binary logistic regression was then used to examine the effect of demographics, perceived job demands, job satisfaction and workplace characteristics on mental health outcomes, adjusting for confounding variables. Separate models were built for scores on the three different DASS scales; depression, anxiety and stress. Independent variables were entered as categorical variables unless there was evidence of a linear association with the outcome measure. Scores on the overcommitment scale were entered as a binary variable in the anxiety model to improve model fit.

---

26 J. Siegrist, above n. 16.

27 R.G. Netemeyer, J.S Boles and R. McMurrian, 'Development and Validation of Work-Family Conflict and Family-Work Conflict Scales' (1996) 81 *Journal of Applied Psychology* 400.

28 See J. Chan, S. Poynton and J. Bruce, above n. 3.

Each model was built using a manual backward elimination procedure. Initially, all independent variables showing a bivariate association with the dependent variable were included in the model and then variables with the highest p-value were sequentially removed. The Akaike's Information Criterion (AIC)[29] was used to select the final model which best fit the data. Model adequacy was also assessed using the Hosmer-Lemeshow Statistic and the area under the ROC curve (AUC).[30] Model misspecification was checked using STATA's linktest command.[31]

4. RESULTS

The vast majority of survey respondents reported experiencing normal, mild or moderate levels of depression (82.1%), anxiety (85.8%) and stress (84.6%) in the week preceding the survey. One in ten respondents reported symptoms in the extremely severe range for depression (10.9%) and anxiety (9.9%), while one in 20 reported extremely severe symptoms of stress (5.0%). Of those who reported experiencing severe/extremely severe symptoms on one of the three mental health outcomes measured, many also scored highly on one or more of the other scales. Of the total sample of 877 lawyers, 684 (78.0%) did not report any mental health symptoms in the severe/extremely severe range, 75 (8.6%) reported severe/extremely symptoms on one DASS measure, 55 (6.3%) reported severe/extremely severe symptoms on two DASS measures and 63 (7.2%) reported severe/extremely severe symptoms on all three DASS measures. Issues of comorbidity are not taken into account in this study.

29 AIC is a measure which rewards the goodness of fit and at the same time penalises the increasing number of parameters. The logistic regression model with the smallest AIC was chosen as the best model and used to estimate the effect of the independent variables on the outcome.

30 D.W. Hosmer and S. Lemeshow, *Applied Logistic Regression* (2nd ed.), John Wiley & Sons, NJ 2000. The Hosmer-Lemeshow Statistic compares observed and predicted values for groups of predictor values. The c-statistic, the area under the ROC curve, is a measure of concordance of the observed and predicted values; it ranges between 0.5 (no better than chance prediction) and 1.00 (perfect prediction).

31 This test uses the linear predicted value (e.g. y) and the linear predicted value squared (y^2) as predictors to rebuild the model. The test's assumption is that, if the model is properly specified, one should not be able to find any additional predictors that are statistically significant except by chance. Hence y should be a statistically significant predictor (because it is the predicted value from the model) but y^2 should not have much predictive power except by chance. Its significance would indicate a possible specification error.

Table 1. Characteristics of lawyers by severity level of reported mental health symptoms

	Depression		Anxiety		Stress	
	Normal/ mild/ moderate	Severe/ Ext. severe	Normal/ mild/ moderate	Severe/ Ext. severe	Normal/ mild/ moderate	Severe/ Ext. severe
	(n = 645)	(n = 141)	(n = 674)	(n = 112)	(n = 665)	(n = 121)
Gender (%)						
male	80.6	19.3	86.9	13.1	84.7	15.3
female	82.8	17.2	85.2	14.8	84.6	15.4
Age (%)						
under 30	81.9	18.1	83.1	16.9	83.5	16.5
30–39	84.2	15.8	86.7	13.3	85.1	14.9
40–49	76.7	23.3	82.2	17.8	79.5	20.6
50+	83.9	16.1	92.0	8.1	90.6	9.4
Children (%)						
no	80.3	19.7	84.6	15.4	83.1	16.9
yes	84.6	15.4	87.4	12.7	86.7	13.3
Income (%)						
<$60,000	77.8	22.2	83.7	16.3	83.0	17.0
$60,001–90,000	82.8	17.2	85.7	14.3	84.9	15.1
$90,001–150,000	81.1	18.9	83.4	16.6	82.0	18.0
>$150,000	86.1	13.9	90.8	9.3	89.0	11.0
Workplace type (%)						
small private law firm	78.1	21.9	82.9	17.1	81.4	18.6
chambers	85.3	14.7	89.0	11.0	88.1	11.9
community legal/other	81.8	18.2	86.4	13.6	81.8	18.2
corporate	79.6	20.4	89.8	10.2	77.6	22.5
government	82.7	17.3	86.4	13.6	85.2	14.8
large private law firm	84.3	15.7	85.5	14.5	88.0	12.1
Workplace location (%)						
metropolitan	82.7	17.3	86.3	13.7	85.8	14.2
regional/remote	79.0	21.0	83.3	16.7	79.0	21.0
Alcohol use (%)						
never	85.3	14.7	86.8	13.2	86.8	13.2
low risk	86.1	13.9	88.5	11.5	88.1	11.9

(continued)

Table 1 *continued*

	Depression		Anxiety		Stress	
	Normal/ mild/ moderate	**Severe/ Ext. severe**	**Normal/ mild/ moderate**	**Severe/ Ext. severe**	**Normal/ mild/ moderate**	**Severe/ Ext. severe**
	(n = 645)	**(n = 141)**	**(n = 674)**	**(n = 112)**	**(n = 665)**	**(n = 121)**
medium risk	80.5	19.5	82.6	17.4	81.1	19.0
high risk	54.9	45.1	72.6	27.5	60.8	39.2
Satisfaction with career (%)						
satisfied	89.0	11.0	89.2	10.8	88.5	11.5
neither	80.7	19.4	91.9	8.1	85.5	14.5
dissatisfied	55.7	44.3	69.8	30.2	69.1	30.9
Effort-reward ratio (%)						
ratio <=1	92.7	7.3	95.1	5.0	95.7	4.3
ratio >1	75.4	24.6	79.9	20.1	77.6	22.4
Overcommitment (%)						
low	91.1	8.9	95.5	4.5	96.2	3.8
high (upper tertile)	68.6	31.4	71.1	28.9	67.3	32.7
Work-family conflict scale (% median split)						
score <3.4	90.9	9.1	95.3	4.7	95.1	5.0
score >=3.4	74.4	25.6	77.5	22.5	75.6	24.4
Practice ethos (% median split)						
score <2.9	86.4	13.6	88.9	11.1	88.4	11.6
score >=2.9	77.7	22.3	82.6	17.4	80.8	19.2

Table 1 presents the characteristics of the survey respondents by whether or not they reported severe/extremely severe symptoms of depression, anxiety and stress. Overall there were very few differences at the bivariate level in terms of the demographic and workplace characteristics of lawyers reporting severe mental health symptoms compared with those reporting normal or only mild/moderate symptoms. Two exceptions are age and workplace location. A smaller proportion of lawyers aged over 50 reported severe symptoms of anxiety and stress compared with other age groups (although the difference on the stress scale was not significant at the 0.05 level), and a higher proportion of lawyers practising in regional/remote locations reported severe symptoms of stress.

There were, however, strong bivariate relationships between the severity of mental health symptoms and alcohol use, perceived job demands, career satisfaction and workplace culture. Lawyers reporting severe symptoms of depression, anxiety or stress were more likely than other lawyers to report consuming alcohol at high-risk levels, to be dissatisfied with their career decision to become a lawyer, to perceive their effort to reward imbalance at work as high, to report being less able to cope with the demands of work, to perceive greater work–family conflict in their working lives and to agree that the legal profession is characterised by an ethos of long hours, combativeness, toughness and competitiveness.

Table 2. Logistic regression model comparing normal/mild/moderate vs severe/extremely severe depression (n = 746)

Characteristic		Adjusted Odds Ratios	95% Confidence Interval	*p*-value
Age	30–39 vs under 30	0.98	[0.52, 1.84]	0.944
	40–49 vs under 30	2.49	[1.15, 5.40]	0.020
	50+ vs under 30	2.35	[1.03, 5.35]	0.042
Income	$60,001–90,000 vs <$60,000	0.61	[0.32, 1.17]	0.136
	$90,001–150,000 vs <$60,000	0.58	[0.30, 1.11]	0.098
	$150,000+ vs <$60,000	0.38	[0.17, 0.83]	0.015
Children	yes vs no	0.60	[0.34, 1.07]	0.082
Alcohol use	low risk vs never	1.20	[0.51, 2.81]	0.681
	medium risk vs never	1.71	[0.70, 4.22]	0.241
	high risk vs never	6.19	[2.19, 17.53]	0.001
Satisfaction with career	neither vs satisfied	1.94	[0.89, 4.24]	0.097
	dissatisfied vs satisfied	3.52	[2.13, 5.81]	<.001
Effort–Reward Imbalance		2.30	[1.35, 3.92]	0.002
Overcommitment		1.16	[1.07, 1.26]	<.001
Work–family conflict		1.39	[1.02, 1.89]	0.036

Note: Area under ROC curve = 0.845; Hosmer-Lemeshow test 720.49 (p = .582); AIC = 541.70.

Table 3. Logistic regression model comparing normal/mild/moderate vs severe/extremely severe anxiety (n = 749)

Characteristic		Adjusted Odds Ratios	95% Confidence Interval	*p*-value
Income	$60,001–90,000 vs <$60,000	0.68	[0.35, 1.35]	0.271
	$90,001–150,000 vs <$60,000	0.78	[0.40, 1.53]	0.472
	$150,000+ vs <$60,000	0.30	[0.14, 0.67]	0.003
Alcohol use	low risk vs never	0.89	[0.37, 2.11]	0.788
	medium risk vs never	1.52	[0.62, 3.75]	0.365
	high risk vs never	2.25	[0.77, 6.56]	0.139
Effort–Reward Imbalance		1.74	[1.03, 2.94]	0.038
Overcommitment	very high vs other	2.84	[1.56, 5.16]	0.001
Work–Family Conflict		2.43	[1.76, 3.37]	<.001

Note: Area under ROC curve = 0.834; Hosmer-Lemeshow test 742.4 ($p = .224$); AIC = 485.79.

Table 4. Logistic regression model comparing normal/mild/moderate vs severe/extremely severe stress (n = 749)

Characteristic		Adjusted Odds Ratios	95% Confidence Interval	*p*-value
Income	$60,001–90,000 vs <$60,000	0.58	[0.27, 1.25]	0.16 4
	$90,001–150,000 vs <$60,000	0.71	[0.33, 1.54]	0.389
	$150,000+ vs <$60,000	0.31	[0.13, 0.78]	0.013
Workplace type	chambers vs small private firm	1.08	[0.44, 2.61]	0.867
	community/other vs small private firm	1.56	[0.62, 3.89]	0.345
	corporate vs small private firm	3.17	[1.18, 8.57]	0.023
	government vs small private firm	2.03	[0.75, 5.47]	0.161

(continued)

Table 4 *continued*

Characteristic		Adjusted Odds Ratios	95% Confidence Interval	*p*-value
	large vs small private firm	0.65	[0.33, 1.27]	0.205
Alcohol use	low risk vs never	1.07	[0.42, 2.72]	0.880
	medium risk vs never	2.17	[0.82, 5.78]	0.119
	high risk vs never	4.98	[1.55, 15.99]	0.007
Effort–Reward Imbalance		3.21	[1.77, 5.82]	<.001
Overcommitment		1.35	[1.23, 1.49]	<.001
Work–Family Conflict		1.78	[1.24, 2.54]	0.002

Note: Area under ROC curve = 0.892; Hosmer-Lemeshow test 662.6 ($p = .968$); AIC = 446.57.

Tables 2 to 4 present the results of the three logistic regression models for depression, anxiety and stress (respectively). These models compare those who reported severe/extremely severe symptoms on these three measures with those who reported normal, mild or moderate symptoms. This comparison allows us to see whether a particular factor successfully discriminates between the two groups after other relevant factors have been controlled for. The magnitude of the association between the independent variables and mental health symptoms is expressed as an odds ratio.

The regression diagnostics for the three models shown in Tables 2 to 4 indicated that there were no significant differences between the predicted number of lawyers with severe mental health symptoms and the number observed. Furthermore, the three models estimated provided 'excellent' discrimination between groups, meaning that they were a very good fit to the data (with AUCs between .83 and .89).[32] Model fit was particularly good for the stress model.

Consistent with the bivariate analysis, very few demographic and workplace characteristics were significantly associated with severe symptoms of mental health amongst this cohort after adjusting for other

[32] See D.W. Hosmer and S. Lemeshow, above n. 30.

relevant factors. The exceptions are income level, age and workplace. Lawyers reporting low income levels (less than Au$60,000) were more likely to report severe symptoms of depression, stress and anxiety compared with lawyers receiving higher incomes (>Au$150,000$^+$), net of other factors. Age was significantly associated with severe depression. The odds of reporting severe symptoms of depression was 2.5 times higher for lawyers aged between 40 and 49 and 2.35 times higher for lawyers aged 50$^+$, compared with lawyers aged under 30. Workplace type was significantly associated only with severe stress. The odds of experiencing severe symptoms of stress were almost three times higher for lawyers working in corporate law firms compared with lawyers working in small private law firms, after controlling for other factors.

Alcohol use was highly significant in the depression and stress models, with the odds of experiencing severe symptoms of depression being six times higher for lawyers who drink at high-risk levels compared with lawyers who report never consuming alcohol and the odds of experiencing severe symptoms of stress being five times higher for lawyers who drink at high-risk levels compared with lawyers who report never consuming alcohol. Career satisfaction was significant only in the depression model, the odds of reporting severe depressive symptoms was 3.5 times higher for lawyers who reported being dissatisfied with their career choice compared with those who were satisfied.

On the other hand, perceived demands at work and the ability to cope with these demands were consistent independent predictors across all three measures of mental health. Lawyers who perceived greater imbalance between their efforts and rewards at work and a higher level of overcommitment were more likely to report severe symptoms of depression, anxiety and stress compared with lawyers who scored lower on these measures. Lawyers who reported severe levels of depression, anxiety and stress also perceived greater conflict between their work and family lives.

The results across the three logistic regression models are summarised in Table 5. A '–' sign indicates that the factor was associated with a decreased likelihood of severe symptomatology and a '+' indicates that the factor was associated with an increased likelihood of severe symptomatology. Where there is no significant independent association between the factor examined and the outcome an 'ns' has been entered into the relevant column.

Table 5. Summary of the logistic regression models examining drivers of poor mental health

Variable	Severe depression vs other	Severe anxiety vs other	Severe stress vs other
Age	+	ns	ns
Gender	ns	ns	ns
Children	ns	ns	ns
Income	–	–	–
Workplace type	ns	ns	+[a]
Workplace location	ns	ns	ns
Effort–Reward Imbalance	+	+	+
Overcommitment	+	+	+
Work–Family Conflict	+	+	+
Alcohol use	+	ns	+
Practice ethos	ns	ns	ns
Career dissatisfaction	+	ns	ns

[a] Severely stressed lawyers were more likely to be working in corporate legal firms compared to small law firms.

4.1. LIMITATIONS

It is important here to note that the cross-sectional design used in this study allows us to test the association between variables but limits our ability to make causal attributions. The strong relationship found here between risky alcohol consumption and severe DASS scores, for example, suggests co-occurrence of these two factors, but cannot tell us about the direction of the relationship. It is possible that high alcohol consumption leads to higher levels of stress, depression and anxiety but it is also possible that poorer mental health results in more risky drinking. Longitudinal data collected over multiple time points would need to be collected to better understand the causal nature of these relationships.

A further limitation of this study is the relatively low response rate to the online survey. Response rates varied across jurisdictions, ranging from one per cent to three per cent, but were generally higher in jurisdictions that had a smaller number of registered practitioners. The lowest response rates were mainly from jurisdictions that decided not to promote the research project to their members.[33] This, combined with the fact that the respondents self-selected into the survey, means that the sample is unlikely to be representative of the population of Australian legal practitioners. While a limitation, this is not a fatal flaw. Our study is not concerned with estimates of the percentage of Australian lawyers who are severely stressed, depressed or anxious (and should not be used as such) but is principally interested in the relationship between work conditions, coping styles, legal culture and poorer mental health outcomes amongst these legal professionals. There is no reason to suspect that the risk factors identified here would operate differently amongst a representative sample of solicitors, were it obtainable.

5. CONCLUSIONS AND IMPLICATIONS

This study set out to investigate the complex relationships between psychological measures (such as depression, anxiety and stress), lawyers' expression of satisfaction with their chosen career, and variables relating to perceived work demands and workplace culture, by drawing on the responses from a National survey of 877 Australian lawyers. Our results suggest that high-levels of self-rated stress, depression and anxiety are generally pervasive across age, gender, family structure, workplace type and locations. The factors that were found to be consistently associated with poorer mental health outcomes in this study were those related to perceived job demands. Specifically, respondents reporting severe levels of stress, anxiety and depression also reported high levels of work demands with few rewards, an inability to cope with these high levels of work demand and self-reported spill-over of work demands into family/home life. Income also appears to play an important role, particularly for those in the lowest income brackets. Independently of all other variables considered, respondents reporting low incomes were more likely to report severe mental health problems than respondents in the highest income range.

On the other hand, there was limited evidence from our analysis for the independent role of perceived workplace culture and career satisfaction

33 J. Chan, S. Poynton and J. Bruce, above n. 3.

in lawyers' mental health and wellbeing. The belief that a work culture of long hours, competitiveness and combativeness is contributing to higher stress and depression levels amongst practitioners was not borne out by the evidence presented here. Lower levels of perceived career satisfaction were found amongst more severely depressed respondents but not amongst those with high levels of self-rated anxiety and stress, suggesting that bad career choices only play a small part. Lawyers working in corporate legal firms appear to be at somewhat greater risk of severe stress than lawyers working in small law firms but are no more likely to report severe symptoms of depression or anxiety.

These results suggest that legal service organisations, institutions and professional bodies concerned with issues of stress and wellbeing amongst their constituents should focus on initiatives and strategies that operate to reduce workload and work demands that are placed on legal practitioners. Addressing underlying structural issues which contribute to these problems, such as billable target pressures, inflexible working arrangements and inadequate management systems may go some way to achieving this.[34] Increasing work rewards, in the form of greater opportunities or job security, and improving managerial style (e.g. greater respect and support) also have an important role to play. These initiatives are generally referred to in the literature as *primary interventions* and have the best evidence for successfully promoting good mental health in the workplace.[35] Our work also suggests that lawyers should be equipped with the personal skills necessary to manage these daily work pressures. Lawyers who reported that they found it hard to relax, switch off, or let go of work were generally doing more poorly than their colleagues in dealing with work stress and high demands. Training options such as workshops on building resilience or understanding mental illness may be beneficial in this regard, particularly where they provide real, practical strategies to help manage daily stressors.[36]

---

34 J. Briton, 'Lawyers, emotional distress and regulation' (2009), chapter presented at Bar Association of Queensland 2009 Annual Conference <http://www.lsc.qld.gov.au/__data/assets/pdf_file/0006/106197/lawyers-emotional-distress-and-regulation.pdf>; G. Davis, S. Owen, M. Coper, W. Ford and J. McKeough, 'Learning and Teaching in the Discipline of Law (Australian Learning and Teaching Council and Council of Australian Law Deans)' (2009) <www.olt.gov.au/system/files/resources/altc_LawReport.pdf>.

35 A.D. LaMontagne, T. Keegel, A.M. Louie and A. Ostry, above n. 18.

36 S. Poynton, J. Chan, M. Vogt, A. Grunseit and J. Bruce, 'Assessing the effectiveness of wellbeing initiatives for lawyers and support staff' (2018) 41 *UNSW Law Journal* 584.

These results from a cross-sectional study of individuals obviously do not take into account the effect of larger social, economic and technological changes in the field of legal practice, yet there is evidence to suggest that large changes can have a detrimental impact on the structural conditions of lawyering and indirectly on work stress among lawyers. For example, Campbell and Charlesworth's analysis of Melbourne solicitors in private practice has suggested that changes in the market structure of legal services have led to the rise of medium and large firms with a large proportion of salaried lawyers with little professional autonomy and intense workloads.[37] Similarly, Sommerlad's research on the changing conditions of legal aid services in the UK suggests that the introduction of New Public Management (NPM) and its focus on cost control, contractualisation and surveillance have led lawyers who were dedicated to servicing disadvantaged clients to feel demoralised and stressed.[38] Future research should examine systematically the longitudinal impact of major structural changes on lawyers' work stress and wellbeing.

---

37 I. Campbell and S. Charlesworth, 'Salaried lawyers and billable hours: A new perspective from the sociology of work' (2013) 19 *International Journal of the Legal Profession* 89.

38 H. Sommerlad, '"I've lost the plot": An everyday story of legal aid lawyers' (2001) 28 *Journal of Law and Society* 335.

CHAPTER 4

STRESS, BULLYING AND HARASSMENT IN THE LEGAL PROFESSION

A Risky Business

Alison WALLACE and Imogen D'SOUZA

1. Introduction 77
2. Poor Mental Health in Legal Workplaces 78
3. Sexual Harassment in Legal Workplaces 80
4. Bullying in Legal Workplaces 82
5. Psychosocial Workplace Injury in Australia is on the Rise 83
6. Aims of the National Attrition Study 85
7. Methodology 86
8. Results 88
   8.1. Bullying and Intimidation Experienced by Many 88
   8.2. Sexual Harassment Experienced by One in Five 89
   8.3. Poor Workplace Culture and Practises Driving Job Dissatisfaction 90
   8.4. Overwork the Main Cause of Attrition 93
   8.5. Discussion and Ways Forward 97
   8.6. Tackling Sexual Harassment and Bullying 98
   8.7. Managing Psychosocial Risk Factors 101

1. INTRODUCTION

This chapter discusses research on stress, bullying and harassment in the legal profession, with a particular focus on the results of a national study commissioned by the Law Council of Australia (the Law Council) and conducted by the independent research consultancy, Urbis.[1] One of the largest research projects of its kind undertaken in the Australian legal profession, the study involved almost 4,000 lawyers drawn from all States and Territories. The aim of the study was to explore the drivers of attrition from the legal profession (or sectors of the profession) and whether these drivers differed for female and male legal practitioners. The results of the study (published in 2014) are now being revisited, focusing on data that explored the extent of bullying and sexual harassment in the legal profession and other risk factors which are associated with poor mental health in the workplace.

We start by providing some context for the analysis. We draw on recent research which is adding to the mounting body of evidence that indicates that working in the legal sector can be a risky business. The results of the Law Council and other studies consistently show that certain negative behaviours and stress factors in legal workplaces are endemic, systemic and damaging to people's health and wellbeing. This raises serious questions about the level of commitment to work health and safety principles and practices within the legal sector, and about the willingness to take meaningful steps to ensure working in the legal profession is both safe and provides a sustainable career option for lawyers.

2. POOR MENTAL HEALTH IN LEGAL WORKPLACES

One in five Australians aged 16 to 85 years experiences a mental illness in any given year.[2] Almost one in two Australians (45 per cent) will experience a common mental disorder in their lifetime. It has been estimated that 8.6 million people in Australia will experience a common mental disorder in their lifetime (based on 2016 population).[3] The most common forms of mental illness are depression, anxiety and substance abuse disorder. Often these disorders occur in combination.[4] As our understanding of this major

1 Law Council of Australia, 'National Attrition and Re-engagement Study (NARS) Report', 2013, https://www.lawcouncil.asn.au/docs/a8bae9a1-9830-e711-80d2-005056be66b1/NARS%20Report.pdf.

2 Black Dog Institute, 'Facts & figures about mental health', https://www.blackdoginstitute.org.au/docs/default-source/factsheets/facts_figures.pdf?sfvrsn=8.

3 Ibid.

4 Black Dog Institute, above n. 2.

public health issue grows, there is an increasing spotlight on mental health and wellbeing in the workplace. Given the severe personal, organisational and economic costs of mental disorders, the imperatives for workplaces to foster psychologically positive environments have never been more critical.

As our knowledge of mental health in the workplace increases, there is growing evidence that certain types of jobs and professional groups experience above average levels of mental ill health, suicidal ideation and suicide. Lawyers are one of these groups.

Compared with other professions in Australia, lawyers experience the highest incidence of depressive symptoms.[5] Moreover, those working in law firms have been found to have the highest rate of depressive symptoms and are more likely than other lawyers to use alcohol and other drugs to manage these.[6] Research conducted by the Brain and Mind Institute found a high rate of suicide ideation among lawyers, and also that many lawyers do not seek help for mental health symptoms.[7] This study too found that abuse of alcohol as a coping mechanism is common amongst members of the legal profession.

A direct relationship has been found between certain workplace demands and pressures in the legal profession and levels of depression and anxiety amongst lawyers. These include constant time pressures, emotional demands, a relentless emphasis on profit-making, and a high level of competitiveness. Other pressures include lack of control over workloads and receiving limited praise or positive feedback for work efforts.[8] A Law Institute of Victoria study involving 965 lawyers found that certain types of legal workplaces – that is, large, metropolitan private law firms and Barristers' Chambers – were associated with high work family conflict scores.[9] In turn, these scores were strongly correlated with scores for depression, anxiety and stress. The study concluded that legal workplace culture plays an important part in moderating or aggravating depression,

---

5 Beaton Consulting, 'Annual Professions Survey', April 2007, 2–3, http://www.judicialcollege.vic.edu.au/sites/default/files/2007%20-%20Beyond%20Blue%20-%20Annual%20Professions%20Survey.pdf.

6 Ibid.

7 N. Kelk et al., 'Courting the Blues: Attitudes Towards Depression in Australian Law Students and Lawyers' Report (Brain and Mind Institute, University of Sydney, January 2009) 12.

8 Ibid.

9 J. Chan, S. Poynton and J. Bruce, 'Lawyering Stress and Work Culture: An Australian Study' (2014) 37 *University of New South Wales Law Journal* 1062–75.

anxiety and stress among lawyers. Yet another study found the great majority of lawyers surveyed who worked in small and medium sized law firms had either experienced anxiety in the workplace or knew someone close to them who had.[10] These studies evidence that poor mental health and wellbeing is common amongst legal practitioners and is a profession-wide issue, requiring action from professional associations, employers and universities.

3. SEXUAL HARASSMENT IN LEGAL WORKPLACES

Over the last year or so, sexual harassment in the workplace has received unprecedented attention in the media and in public discourse. Fuelled by the global MeToo movement, the issue has been met with timely and relevant concern from the general public, from government and certain industries.

Under the Sex Discrimination Act 1984 (Cth), sexual harassment in Australia is defined as

> any unwelcome sexual advance, request for sexual favours or conduct of a sexual nature in relation to the person harassed in circumstances where a reasonable person would have anticipated the possibility that the person harassed would be offended, humiliated or intimidated.[11]

The fourth National Survey on Sexual Harassment in Australian Workplaces was recently released by the Australian Human Rights Commission.[12] It confirmed that sexual harassment in Australian workplaces is widespread and pervasive, with as many as one in three people surveyed reporting they had been subjected to sexual harassment at work within

10 SWAAB, 'ANZ Meritas Wellness Survey 2019', 31 July 2019, https://www.swaab.com.au/news/breaking-anz-meritas-wellness-survey-2019.

11 Australian Human Rights Commission (AHRC), 'The Legal Definition of Sexual Harassment', 2018, https://www.humanrights.gov.au/our-work/sexual-harassment-workplace-legal-definition-sexual-harassment.

12 Australian Human Rights Commission (AHRC), 'Everyone's Business: Fourth National Survey on Sexual Harassment in Australian Workplaces', 2018, https://www.humanrights.gov.au/our-work/sex-discrimination/publications/everyones-business-fourth-national-survey-sexual.

the previous five years.[13] In June 2018, the Australian Human Rights Commission announced the National Inquiry into Sexual Harassment in Australian Workplaces, further evidence of the desire to raise public awareness of sexual harassment, to encourage reporting and to find ways to reduce the incidence of sexual harassment in the workplace. The focus of the National Inquiry is to explore the nature, prevalence and drivers of sexual harassment in Australian workplaces, as well as potential measures to address these.[14]

The legal profession is not immune from these trends. A study undertaken with members of the legal profession in Victoria found that as many as one in four women lawyers surveyed had experienced sexual harassment at work.[15] These incidents of sexual harassment were found to be under-reported and also contributing to women lawyers' decisions to leave the legal profession.[16] As part of its submission to the Australian Human Rights Commission Inquiry, the Women Lawyers Association of NSW presented the results of a survey of almost 250 women lawyers in NSW.[17] The study found that over 70 per cent of the women lawyers reported being sexually harassed at work, and in about half the cases, the harasser was their work manager. A major study recently commissioned by the International Bar Association involving almost 7,000 lawyers across 135 countries (937 from Australia) found similar high levels of sexual harassment.[18] More than one in three female lawyers (37 per cent) and one in 14 male lawyers (7 per cent) surveyed reported being subject to sexual harassment in the workplace during their legal career.

---

13 Ibid.

14 Australian Human Rights Commission (AHRC), 'National Inquiry into Sexual Harassment in Australian Workplaces', 20 June 2018, https://www.humanrights.gov.au/our-work/sex-discrimination/projects/national-inquiry-sexual-harassment-australian-workplaces.

15 Victorian Equal Opportunity And Human Rights Commission (VEOHRC), 'Changing the Rules: The Experiences of Female Lawyers in Victoria', December 2012, https://www.humanrightscommission.vic.gov.au/media/k2/attachments/Changing_the_Rules_Web.pdf_Final_1.pdf.

16 K. Toohey, 'Addressing sexual harassment in the workplace' (2013) 87 *Law Institute Journal* 9, 32.

17 Women Lawyers Association of NSW (WLANSW), 'Submission into the National Inquiry into Sexual Harassment in the Australian Workplace', 2019, p. 9, https://www.humanrights.gov.au/sites/default/files/2019-07/submission_340.1_-_women_lawyers_association_of_nsw.pdf.

18 International Bar Association (IBA), 'Us Too? Bullying and Sexual Harassment in the Legal Profession', 2019, pp. 8–9, https://www.ibanet.org/bullying-and-sexual-harassment.aspx.

Of particular concern was that the incidence of sexual harassment was considerably higher amongst Australian lawyers than their international counterparts.[19] The results of these important studies should be ringing alarm bells for the Australian legal profession.

The situation is particularly pressing given that, for a range of reasons, most incidents of workplace sexual harassment are not reported by lawyers. These reasons include fear of repercussions, fear that a report will have a negative impact on their career, and a fear that the complainant will be perceived as weak by colleagues or management. Self-employed lawyers worry about the impact of making a complaint on their business and possibly struggle to know who they can make a compliant to, for instance if the harasser is a client or a member of the judiciary.[20] In addition, some lawyers may think nothing will come of making a formal complaint. Research has shown that in cases where a report of sexual harassment has been made, most complainants found their workplace's response to the report 'insufficient' or 'negligible'.[21] A striking finding of the Women Lawyers Association of NSW study was that half the women lawyers surveyed said they were not confident their employer would deal with a sexual harassment complaint in a thorough, confidential or impartial manner.[22]

4. BULLYING IN LEGAL WORKPLACES

In Australia as in other countries in recent years, workplace bullying and harassment have been identified as some of the most significant risks to workers' health and wellbeing.[23] Under Section 789FD of the Fair Work Amendment Act 2013 (Cth), bullying in Australia is defined as when 'an individual or group of individuals repeatedly behave unreasonably towards a worker and that behaviour creates a risk to health and safety'.[24]

---

19 Ibid.

20 WLANSW, above n. 17, p. 13.

21 IBA, above n. 18, p. 65.

22 WLANSW, above n. 17, p. 15.

23 V. Edwards, 'Australian Workplace Bullying – Sixth Worst in the World', *The Australian*, 18 February 2014.

24 Fair Work Amendment Act 2013 (Cth) s. 789FD.

A growing number of studies have specifically examined the extent and nature of bullying within the legal profession. Most recently, the International Bar Association Report referred to above, found that more than half of women lawyers (55%) and 30% of male lawyers surveyed reported they had been bullied in their workplace.[25] Alarmingly, the incidence of bullying was relatively high in Australia. When comparing the results for Australia with those from eight other nations (including the United States and the United Kingdom), it was found that the gender weighted rate (61.4%) of bullying and sexual harassment for Australia was almost 50% higher than the global average rate (43%) and second only to Costa Rica.[26] These findings echo those of an Australian study, which found that over one in five (21%) lawyers surveyed reported that bullying occurred in their current workplace.[27]

It has been speculated that the culture of the legal workplace, with its emphasis on adversarial relationships and hierarchy, its professional mores and limited bureaucratic development, creates an environment that makes bullying behaviours more likely.[28] The legal profession has undergone significant change in the last decade. The growth of large legal firms, combined with the rapid pace and expanding complexity of legal work, has changed the way clients procure and use legal services. Furthermore, increased competition for legal positions has added to workplace pressure and competitiveness amongst lawyers.[29] Such a demanding and rapidly-changing workplace climate may increase the prospects of bullying behaviour.

5. PSYCHOSOCIAL WORKPLACE INJURY IN AUSTRALIA IS ON THE RISE

Traditionally, injury in the workplace has focussed on physical injuries. But this picture is rapidly changing with growing awareness and evidence

25 IBA, above n. 18, p. 8.

26 IBA, above n. 18, p. 86.

27 Law Society of Western Australia, 'Towards Dignity & Respect at Work: An Exploration of Work Behaviours in a Professional Environment', August 2010, 13, https://www.lawsocietywa.asn.au/wp-content/uploads/2015/10/Towards-Dignity-Respect-Work.pdf.

28 S. Le Mire and R. Owens, 'A Propitious Moment? Workplace Bullying and Regulation of the Legal Profession' (2014) 37(3) *UNSW Law Journal* 1030, 1031.

29 Ibid.

of the deleterious impacts that certain types of work and workplaces can have on people's psychological wellbeing. Psychosocial injury is now firmly embedded in work health and safety.

> The workplace, fundamental to a worker's physical, mental, economic and social wellbeing and in turn their family, has been recognised as a priority setting for health promotion by the World Health Organisation and Australian and State Governments.[30]

The changing nature of work and the workplace, the blurring of work and personal life, the globalisation of the economy, rapid technological change means 'it is now possible to be "online" and at work 24 hours a day 7 days a week, essentially anywhere any time'.[31] This is adding to stresses and pressures at work which are putting people's mental health at risk.

High level psychosocial risk factors in the workplace identified by SafeWork Australia include many that are prevalent in certain parts of the legal profession. These include high job demands involving long work hours: high workloads and levels of emotional effort; insufficient support from supervisors or peers; poor workplace relations and workplace culture; and isolation. Two in five (39 per cent) workers' compensation claims for mental health disorder in Australia are now caused by harassment, bullying or exposure to violence in the workplace.[32] As many as one in three mental health disorder compensation claims by women, and one in five by men, relate to harassment or bullying alone.[33]

Work-related psychological injury is expensive. It has been estimated that poor psychological health and safety costs Australian organisations Au$6 billion annually in lost productivity.[34] Moreover, workers' average compensation payments for claims involving mental health conditions are significantly higher than other claims (Au$24,500 compared with

---

30 Safework Australia (SWA), 'Work-related psychological health and safety: A systematic approach to meeting your duties', 2015, p. 2, https://www.safeworkaustralia.gov.au/doc/work-related-psychological-health-and-safety-systematic-approach-meeting-your-duties.

31 Ibid.

32 SWA, 'Work Related Mental Disorders Profile', 2015, p. 2, https://www.safeworkaustralia.gov.au/system/files/documents/1702/work-related-mental-disorders-profile.pdf.

33 Ibid.

34 SWA, above n. 30, p. 2.

Au$9,000) and involve three times the amount of time off work (15.3 weeks compared with 5.5 weeks).[35]

It is in this context that we now turn to the findings from the Law Council study, which speak to the level of sexual harassment, bullying and risk factors associated with psychosocial injuries in the legal workplace.

6. AIMS OF THE NATIONAL ATTRITION STUDY

The national study reported on here was commissioned by the Law Council of Australia and conducted by Urbis. The key aims of the research were to:

- Explore the drivers of attrition, retention, and re-engagement of women in the legal profession and how these compared to men.
- Explore the experiences and motivators of different cohorts of women lawyers including their age, number of years in practice, employment sector and regional location.
- Identify factors that may assist in retaining or re-engaging women lawyers in the legal profession, with a particular focus on those working in private practice and at the Bar.

The study explored a range of issues relating to lawyers' career intentions, career progression, job satisfaction, and reasons for career moves both within and out of the legal profession. In this context, lawyers were asked a number of questions relating to their experiences of bullying, intimidation and sexual harassment in their current workplace. It is the responses to these specific questions in the broader Law Council study that are the focus of discussion in this chapter. Also presented are findings relating to stressful or unhealthy aspects of working in the legal profession, identified as key drivers of both job dissatisfaction and decisions to change jobs or seek employment outside the legal profession altogether. Together, these findings provide an empirical basis and context to progress discussions about mental health risk factors for people working in the Australian legal profession.

35 SWA, 'Mental Health', 2019, https://www.safeworkaustralia.gov.au/topic/mental-health.

7. METHODOLOGY

The research comprised a combination of quantitative and qualitative methods Separate online surveys were conducted with three cohorts of lawyers, including those who:

- were currently practising law
- had left the legal profession in the previous five years
- had graduated in law in the previous five years but had made a decision not to practice law.

The rationale for this three-pronged approach was to explore the factors influencing lawyers' decisions to enter, remain in, or leave legal practice. The survey instruments were designed in close consultation with the Law Council's Executive Group, Equal Opportunity Committee, and Recruitment and Retention of Lawyers Working Group. Survey design was also informed by a review of the latest available literature and in-depth interviews with 18 key informants and stakeholders.

The study was widely promoted throughout the Australian legal profession and was supported by a communications strategy involving Law Council Directors, Working Groups and staff; State/Territory Law Societies and Bar Associations; government departments employing large numbers of lawyers; the Large Law Firm Group; Legal Aid Commissions; the National Association of Community Legal Centres; Aboriginal Legal Services; and the Council of Australian Law Deans. The online survey of currently practising lawyers was distributed by the Law Council of Australia to all State/Territory Law Societies and Bar Associations, who in turn distributed the survey to all their members. The lawyers surveyed online who in the last five years had been working in but had left the legal profession, or who had graduated in law but never practised law, were recruited from a research panel operated by Research Now.

In total, 3,960 lawyers responded to the surveys. The research generated a sufficiently large and robust sample to enable comparisons of survey responses by lawyer demographics, employment sector, and region. Most importantly, the number of survey responses received from both women and men enabled methodologically robust comparisons between male and female lawyers, something that has not been possible with surveys targeted at women only (See Table 1 for the split by lawyer cohort and respondent gender). Significance testing was conducted to determine significant differences between cohorts based on variables such as gender, age, work sector, years practising, parental status, etc. Only statistically significant differences in cohorts have been reported in relation to survey findings. Significance testing was conducted at a 95 per cent level of confidence.

Table 1. Participation in online surveys by lawyer cohort and gender

Lawyer cohort	Total number of respondents	Number of female lawyers	Number of male lawyers
Currently practising law	3,801	2,737	1,064
No longer practising law	84	71	13
Never practised law	75	53	22
Total	3,960	2,861	1,099

The profile of survey respondents was diverse in terms of length of time practising law: approximately a third each had been in practice for under five years, for six to 14 years, or for 15 years or more. In line with the profile of the legal profession, the majority of survey respondents worked in private legal practice, followed by those working as an in-house lawyer in the corporate or government sectors, or at the Bar.

In addition to the online survey, over 60 in-depth interviews were conducted with the three cohorts of lawyers: those who were currently practising law, those who had ceased practising law in the previous five years, and recent law graduates who had made a decision not to practise law. The main purpose of the in-depth interviews (conducted with women lawyers only, given the focus of the study) was to hear from the lawyers directly and in their own words about their experiences of working in the legal profession. The interviewees were drawn from a list of 1,315 respondents who, after completing the online survey, expressed an interest in being interviewed for the research. That so many lawyers did this suggests a high level of interest in the research and a desire to talk in more detail about their personal experiences. The lawyers interviewed were selected by the research team from Urbis to capture diversity in terms of lawyer characteristics including age, years since admission, employment sector, career intentions and progression. In-depth interviews were also conducted with Human Resource Managers of large law firms to obtain their views on drivers of attrition in the profession and potential solutions to encourage retention.

8. RESULTS

8.1. BULLYING AND INTIMIDATION EXPERIENCED BY MANY

The online survey asked respondents to indicate the extent to which they had experienced *bullying or intimidation in their current workplace.* Close to half of the lawyers (46 per cent) reported they had been bullied or intimidated in their current workplace (see Table 2 below). Bullying and intimidation were reported by both men and women, older and younger lawyers, newly admitted and more experienced practitioners, those working in private law firms and in in-house roles, and those located in urban and in rural settings. However, a higher incidence of bullying and intimidation was experienced amongst certain lawyers and workplace settings. Most notably:

- A significantly higher proportion of women than men reported being bullied or intimidated: 50% of the women lawyers surveyed indicated they had experienced bullying or intimidation in their current workplace, compared with 38% of their male counterparts.
- The incidence of bullying or intimidation was highest amongst those working in private legal practice, particularly in large law firms. As many as 50% of women lawyers working in large law firms reported being bullied or intimidated compared to 39% of those working in medium sized, and 38% in small firms.
- The incidence of bullying and intimidation was also significantly higher for women working in CBD locations (52%) compared to those working in a suburban location (41%) or in a major (40%) or small (44%) regional centre.

Table 2. Percentage of lawyers surveyed who had experienced bullying or intimidation in their current workplace

Experienced bullying or intimidation	**Total (%) (n = 3,733)**	**Male (%) (n = 1,037)**	**Female (%) (n = 2,696)**
Yes	46	38	50
Never	54	62	50
Not sure	<1	<1	<1

In the in-depth interviews, lawyers regularly reported that bullying, intimidation and aggression were in part an extension of the confrontational nature inherent in certain aspects of legal work:

> Just the way people like to write in letters and do the one-upmanship and bullying ... When lawyers behave badly to each other or confrontationally to each other, it's not a collaborative environment. Having worked in ones which are – the main way of working in health or social work or those kinds of things is in theory at least to actually start by assuming you can do win/win, as opposed to this sort of power over win/lose. It just infiltrates things. (Female lawyer who left legal practice)

> As much as I like law firms, I do dislike them as well. They are very aggressive and fear-mongering institutions. (Female lawyer now working in corporate legal)

> We have this adversarial system. It's almost the next step to make it that aggressive, go for the person, forget about the real resolution. If we can score points here, we'll do it. It's that sort of culture and fits very easily within an adversarial system. I think you tend to find a level of it in most firms. As to how far and how difficult it becomes, I think very much depends on the leadership in the firm. (Industry body)

> We are barristers. Our job is arguing, and sometimes debate gets pretty robust. I think there are lots of times when a male just thinks he's engaging in robust debate, but the female gets the message they're putting her down because she's female. (Barrister Chambers Manager)

8.2. SEXUAL HARASSMENT EXPERIENCED BY ONE IN FIVE

The online survey asked respondents to indicate the extent to which they had *experienced sexual harassment in their current workplace*. One in five lawyers surveyed reported experiencing sexual harassment at work. However, female members of the profession were three times more likely than males to have experienced sexual harassment at work: one in four women lawyers (24%) reported being sexually harassed in their current workplace compared with one in 12 men (8%) (see Table 3 below).

Table 3. Percentage of lawyers surveyed who had experienced sexual harassment in their *current* workplace

Experienced sexual harassment	Total (%) (n = 3,733)	Male (%) (n = 1,037)	Female (%) (n = 2,696)
Yes	19	8	24
No	81	92	76
Not sure	<1	<1	<1

Certain groups of women lawyers were found to be at particular risk of sexual harassment. Women barristers were twice as likely (55%) to have experienced sexual harassment than women lawyers working in private practice (22%) or in in-house roles in the corporate or government legal sectors (20%).

In the in-depth interviews, various women spoke of their experiences of receiving unwanted sexual advances, feeling objectified and being exposed to inappropriate sexual predation from male colleagues. The following responses provide two such examples:

> I was bemused by the fact that I was hit on quite aggressively by a number of male barristers … I mean, like, barristers attempted to kiss me. That happened twice with one silk and once with a contemporary who was married. I didn't think of it at the time, but both of these gentlemen were married. And that in and of itself doesn't really say anything about the kind of work that you get, but it does say something about how you are considered fair game. Things like that happen at the Bar that wouldn't happen in any other work environment. It happens all the time. (Female lawyer working in government legal)

> The sort of objectifying of women is a lot more blatant, which, you know, you may think 'no big deal'. But it's not. At the end of the day you realise, hey I'm just here to be a barrister I'm not here to be a woman. I'm just here to do my work. Just evaluate the merit of my work. You never know if you are being evaluated on your merit or on the size of your breasts or something else. (Female barrister)

8.3. POOR WORKPLACE CULTURE AND PRACTISES DRIVING JOB DISSATISFACTION

The survey explored drivers of both job satisfaction and job dissatisfaction amongst members of the legal profession. Most relevant to this chapter are the research findings relating to those elements of job dissatisfaction that pose the greatest risk for mental health. These include: poor work–life balance; insufficient support within the workplace for work–life balance; poor workplace culture overall; the stress of meeting billable hours; and excessive work hours.

Survey respondents were provided with 24 potential drivers of job satisfaction and dissatisfaction compiled from a review of relevant literature. They were then asked to rate the extent to which they were satisfied with each of these elements of their work and workplace, using a five-point scale ranging from very satisfied to very dissatisfied. Ten of these elements were then identified as the top drivers of job satisfaction and of job dissatisfaction, respectively.

The top 10 drivers of *job satisfaction* for both men and for women lawyers were identified. The major drivers of job satisfaction amongst those working in the legal profession relate to relationships (with peers and with managers); the degree of independence and control over their work; opportunities to do interesting and quality work using their skills; and the level of respect exhibited by clients. The top 10 drivers of job satisfaction proved to be the same for both male and female lawyers.

The top 10 drivers of *job dissatisfaction* for men and women lawyers are detailed in Figure 1 below. What is notable about this list is that five of the top ten sources of dissatisfaction relate to aspects of work that, according to the literature, are associated with a high risk of poor mental health in the workplace. These included, in descending order of frequency: the level of work–life balance; workplace culture; the requirement for billable hours; and the hours lawyers are required to work.

Similarly to the drivers of job satisfaction, the top 10 drivers of job dissatisfaction were the same for both men and women. However, some drivers of job dissatisfaction were more marked for women than for men. *Poor work–life balance* was a major source of job dissatisfaction amongst 30 per cent of women and 26 per cent of men, exacerbated by the view of around one in four lawyers that there was a *poor level of support for work–life balance* within their workplace. The *number of hours they were required to work* and the *requirements for billable hours* were major drivers of job dissatisfaction for both men and women (about one in five). Meanwhile, *unhappiness with workplace culture* was cited by one in four female and by one in seven male lawyers as a major source of job dissatisfaction.

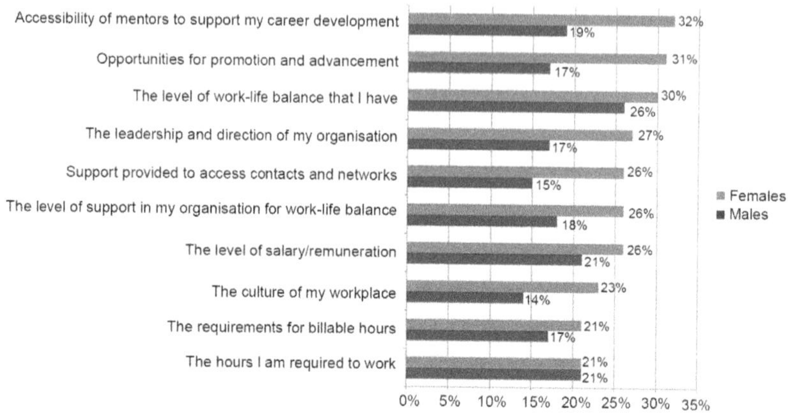

Figure 1. Top ten causes of lawyers' dissatisfaction with current position*, by gender

Notes. Base: All working respondents, n = 3,733; females, n = 2,696; males, n = 1,037
*Dissatisfied includes 'very dissatisfied' and 'dissatisfied' responses.

The level of dissatisfaction with the level of *work–life balance* and the *level of support provided for work life balance* was particularly marked for women employed in private practice and least evident amongst those employed in in-house roles (see Figure 2 below). Amongst women lawyers, dissatisfaction with work–life balance was also found to be significantly higher amongst those working in large rather than medium sized or small firms; those with no children in their care; those who worked full-time and those who reported working over 50 hours a week on average.

Confirming the results of the online survey, lawyers working in private practice who were interviewed in depth for the study expressed the greatest dissatisfaction with work life balance in their current workplace. These lawyers frequently referred to the ongoing pressure to meet billable targets, and to the expectation that they are available to their clients at any time, including late evenings and on weekends. The following comments illustrate these views:

> I think some of them are getting better, but there's no flexibility in terms of this idea that you have to be in the office at 7.30 and not leave before 7 and work ridiculous hours. I've just taken on a young lawyer from a large suburban

firm and as a norm she was working 12–14 hours a day. That is outrageous, and yes if you've got a big transaction on or something on that may be OK, but it should be the exception. It shouldn't be the norm and I'm sure she's not the only one. The hours that you have to work [in private practice] are just unsustainable. (Female lawyer now working in corporate legal)

The hours, the billing, the time recording the billing. The pressure of that sort of thing when I was working in private practice was just phenomenal. (Female lawyer now working in government legal)

Their client's expectation is for such quick turnaround. That's not ever really acknowledged with clients or not even in the office, that we're not available 24/7. That's not a message that in my experience was sent out to clients for obvious reasons, because it makes you uncompetitive. (Female lawyer who left legal practice)

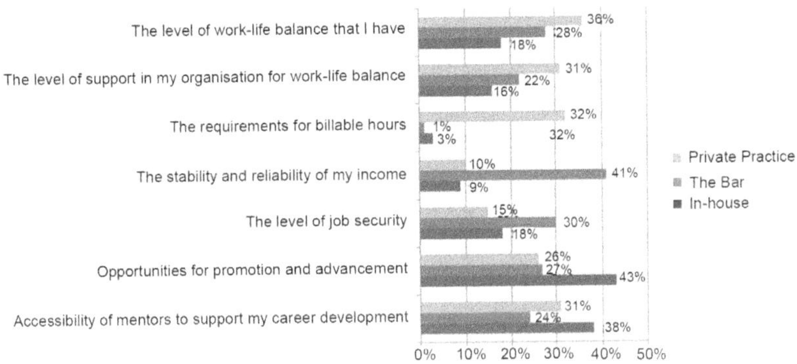

Figure 2. Top ten causes of women lawyers' dissatisfaction with current position, by legal sector/role

Note. Base: All female respondents working in private practice, at the Bar or in-house, n = 2,696; private practice, n = 1,686; the Bar, n = 201; in-house, n = 654.

8.4. OVERWORK THE MAIN CAUSE OF ATTRITION

The research study explored how frequently lawyers change jobs, involving moves within or across legal sectors, or outside the legal profession. We wanted to understand the main reasons for these moves and the extent to which they were primarily driven by 'push' or 'pull' factors': that is, by a desire to leave a job or by a desire to move to a better position. In particular, there was an interest in identifying factors driving attrition from certain sectors of the profession (in particular from private practice and the Bar to other legal sectors) or from legal practice altogether.

We found that a large proportion of lawyers had made recent career moves. As many as *60 per cent of female lawyers and 46 per cent of male lawyers had changed jobs in the previous five years.* The most common reasons for lawyers changing jobs were 'push' factors, i.e. aspects of their current employment they were unhappy with, rather than 'pull' factors; that is, better prospects or more interesting work in their new position.

With the exception of lawyers who moved from private practice to the Bar, the most common reasons lawyers gave for changing jobs in the previous five years were *poor work-life balance* and *unhappiness with workplace culture* (see Figure 3 below). These were in the top two or three reasons cited by lawyers who moved from private practice to corporate legal; from private practice to government legal; and from large private law firms to smaller firms. In addition, the *pressure of billable hours* and *reduced stress and pressure* were amongst the top five reasons lawyers gave for moving from private practice to corporate legal positions. Meanwhile, *mental or physical health* reasons were cited by one in five of lawyers leaving the Bar to take on another role.

Whilst 'pull' factors (such as *better salary and remuneration*, *more interesting or varied work* or a *change in practice area*) were also common reasons for career moves, these tended to be both *less frequent* and *less important* than the 'push' factors described above (see Figures 4 and 5 below). Importantly, despite some differences between male and female lawyers in the major reasons for their career moves, both cited *unhappiness with workplace culture* as the most important and the most frequent reason for their career move.

This finding is further supported when examining the main reasons given by lawyers who intended to change jobs in the next five years. Around a third (37 per cent of women and 31 per cent of men) of those surveyed were considering moving to a new position in the next five years, most within the next two years. For both men and women, the most important and most frequent reason for changing jobs was a desire for *better work-life balance.*

Large private firm → Small private firm

(n = 29)

1 Better work–life balance (41%)

Unhappy with the workplace culture (41%)

2 Unhappy with the leadership and direction of the organisation (34%)

Private firm → Government

(n = 89)

1 Better work–life balance (76%)

2 Unhappy with the workplace culture (53%)

3 Unhappy with the leadership and direction of the organisation (49%)

4 More flexibility to balance my work and personal responsibilities (48%)

5 Change in practice area/different type of work (45%)

Other roles → The Bar

(n = 72)

1 More independence/control in work (65%)

2 More interesting or varied work (61%)

3 Wanted to start a new firm/sole practice/work for myself (49%)

4 Unhappy with the workplace culture (44%)

It's part of my career plan (44%)

5 Better salary/remuneration (43%)

More scope for flexible working arrangements (43%)

Large private firm → Medium private firm

(n = 46)

1 Unhappy with the workplace culture (52%)

2 Unhappy with the leadership and direction of the organisation (48%)

3 Unhappy with the relationship I had with the person to whom I reported (39%)

Better work–life balance (39%)

The Bar → Other roles

(n = 36)

1 Taking time out from the profession (parental leave) (33%)

2 Better work–life balance (25%)

3 More flexibility to balance my work and personal responsibilities (19%)

Looking for a change/something new (19%)

Mental or physical health reasons (19%)

Private firm → Corporate legal

(n = 119)

1 Better work–life balance (65%)

2 More interesting or varied work (52%)

Unhappy with the workplace culture (52%)

3 Better salary/remuneration (45%)

4 Reduced stress and pressure (44%)

5 More flexibility to balance my work and personal responsibilities (40%)

Too much pressure on billable hours (40%)

Figure 3. Most common reasons for lawyers changing jobs in the previous five years, by sector

Similarly, a desire for *better work–life balance* was the most important and most frequent important reason for deciding to cease practising as a lawyer cited by the 85 former legal practitioners who took part in the research. Other major reasons for leaving legal practice included a desire to *reduce workplace stress and pressure* and have *more flexibility to balance work and family responsibilities*, and *unhappiness with workplace culture*.

The in-depth interviews with women lawyers who had given up legal practice reflected the findings of the online survey: work–life imbalance, workplace stress and pressure were common reasons for job dissatisfaction and were the key 'push' factors for leaving private practice or the Bar. Women lawyers (particularly those who had been working in private practice) said such stresses made their work unenjoyable, unsustainable and incompatible with other responsibilities and priorities:

> The stress and the pressure outweighed the good. So, there was a lot of good working in legal practice and that was satisfying, but the stress and the pressure overshadowed and diluted that. (Female lawyer who left legal practice)
>
> I was working three days a week and I was extremely busy – coming home and working most nights to midnight or later because I was in the middle of a big case, and it was just going on forever … It was too hard to work on my other responsibilities and interests to keep working on that basis. (Female lawyer who left legal practice)
>
> The workload was getting too high and it was just consuming my whole life. So, when an opportunity came up that was more money, less hours and gave me a nine-day fortnight, it was a win/win situation for me. (Female lawyer who left legal practice)

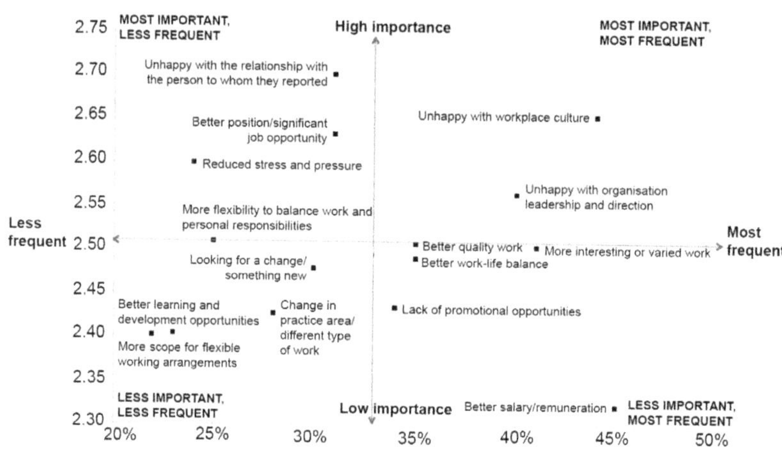

Figure 4. Most important and most frequent reasons female lawyers changed jobs in last five years

The **most frequent** axis refers to the percentage of lawyers who reported each reason as a factor in changing jobs.

The **most important** axis refers to how important each reason was in making the decision to change jobs – rated on a three point scale from 1 (minor importance) to 3 (major importance).

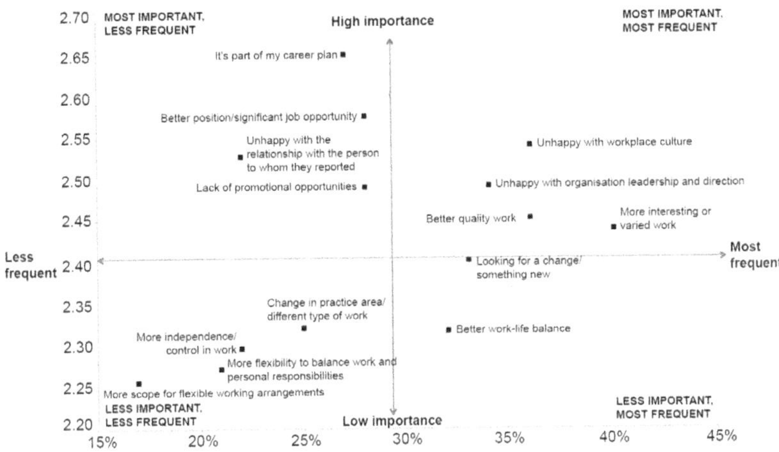

Figure 5. Most important and most frequent reasons male lawyers changed jobs in last five years

The **most frequent** axis refers to the percentage of lawyers who reported each reason as a factor in changing jobs.

The **most important** axis refers to how important each reason was in making the decision to change jobs – rated on a three point scale from 1 (minor importance) to 3 (major importance).

8.5. DISCUSSION AND WAYS FORWARD

The findings from the national research study conducted for the Law Council paint a worrying picture of the risks associated with working in the legal profession. Challenging, stimulating and satisfying though legal work may be, the results of the Law Council study and those of other recent studies consistently highlight some of the downsides of working in the legal sector. The Law Council study takes this further by demonstrating the implications for individual lawyers and the profession. It revealed many lawyers are electing to change jobs because they are unhappy with the stress, demands, work-life balance and workplace culture of their current employ. These negative 'push' factors are in many cases the most important and most frequent reasons for changing jobs, particularly amongst lawyers leaving private practice to work in another sector of the profession, and those leaving large law firms to work in a smaller firm. Private legal practice is where the great majority of lawyers are employed and the Law Council research findings highlight that this is where the greatest problems lie. Women at the Bar are also at significant risk. The research evidence is in: so what can be done?

There are renewed calls for the profession to take action that will result in real change. The personal, health and financial costs for individual lawyers and their families, and also for the profession more broadly, are too great to ignore. Although these issues are by no means confined to the Australian legal profession, Australia now has a strong evidence base which clearly establishes the prevalence of workplace risk factors in the legal sector. Through various mechanisms and initiatives, there is potential and the opportunity for the Australian legal sector to lead the way by showing it is committed to legislative, policy, procedural and cultural reforms, and most importantly, to ensuring that these changes are effectively implemented and monitored.

8.6. TACKLING SEXUAL HARASSMENT AND BULLYING

The Law Council study showed that as many as one in four Australian women lawyers have been sexually harassed in their current workplace. Male lawyers, too, have been sexually harassed at work, although three times less often than women lawyers. By far the highest level of sexual harassment is reported by women practising at the Bar. There is a certain irony that the legal sector has such a troubling record when it comes to reporting and dealing with unlawful behaviour in the form of sexual harassment in the workplace.

Bullying is also rife in the Australian legal profession. Both female and male lawyers experience intimidating and bullying behaviour in the workplace, albeit women more frequently than men. By far the highest level of bullying in the profession is reported by women working in private legal practice, particularly in large law firms. Steps need to be taken to raise awareness and understanding of what constitutes bullying behaviour in the legal profession and the negative impact it has on work culture, staff morale and wellbeing, professional practice and business.

The International Bar Association report on bullying and sexual harassment has made six key recommendations based on a review of the literature and consultations.[36] These include: *raising awareness* of these issues through wide dissemination of the report and encouraging dialogue between stakeholders; *implementing and revising policies and standards* including legislative and regulatory reforms; *introducing regular and customised training* for management and staff, sponsored by leaders, addressing all negative behaviours, and moving beyond a compliance

---

36 IBA, above n. 18, p. 99.

frame; *increasing dialogue and best practice sharing* across workplaces, professional associations, working groups, and regulators; *taking ownership* of driving cultural change from the top and role modelling; *data gathering and more transparency* to improve the quality of data available at macro and micro levels and looking to other professions to see how they have successfully done this.

Attempts at adopting a systemic approach to addressing bullying and sexual harassment in the legal sector are emerging. One joint initiative, announced in early 2019, involves the Victorian Legal Services Board and the Victorian Legal Services Commissioner.[37] A key aim of the project is to foster partnerships between WorkSafe Victoria, the Victorian Human Rights and Equal Opportunities Commission and other authorities to deal with sexual harassment at both the individual and organisational levels. Another recent initiative has been announced by the Chief Justice in Victoria in response to a report that highlighted a high level of bullying of barristers in the courtroom.[38] A written protocol has been developed for members of the Bar to raise sexual harassment concerns directly with the Chief Justice or the Chief Judge as a safer option to raise a concern than a formal complaint to the Legal Services Commissioner.[39] The Judicial College, Victorian Civil and Administrative Tribunal and the Victorian Bar Council have also pledged support for reform in relation to bullying, intimidation and harassment, including new education programmes.[40]

The New Zealand Law Society established a working group in early 2019 to consider what improvements can be made to enable reporting of sexual harassment. Its plan of action includes a dedicated helpline to enable reporting of concerns related to workplace harassment, which it is hoped will make it easier 'for people to raise and discuss sensitive matters in their workplace'.[41] It is also planning to establish an online facility whereby lawyers can report unacceptable conduct, potentially anonymously. Various information resources and strategies will be introduced to

37 For more information about this programme, see here: Victorian Legal Services Commissioner (VLSC), 'Sexual harassment in the legal profession', 6 February 2019, https://lsbc.vic.gov.au/?p=6319.

38 The Victorian Bar, 'Quality of Working Life Survey Final Report and Analysis', October 2018, pp. 1–40, https://www.vicbar.com.au/sites/default/files/Wellbeing%20of%20the%20Victorian%20Bar%20report%20final%20Oct%202018.pdf.

39 Ibid.

40 Ibid.

41 New Zealand Law Society, 'Bullying and Harassment in the Legal Profession', 8 February 2019, https://www.lawsociety.org.nz/practice-resources/the-business-of-law/workplace-environment/bullying-and-harassment.

raise awareness and provide practical assistance to report and manage harassment and bullying within the profession.

The Australian Human Rights Commission Inquiry may be a catalyst for reform on sexual harassment in the workplace. At the time of writing, the Commission had received a number of submissions from national and State-based legal professional bodies containing recommendations on addressing workplace sexual harassment. Amongst other things, these recommendations include changes to the legislation that would legally require employers to maintain a workplace free of sexual harassment; the introduction of an obligation upon employees or bystanders who witness sexual harassment to report such behaviours; clarification or simplification of the definition of sexual harassment within the Sex Discrimination Act; strengthening protections for whistle-blowers; and shifting the onus of proof for complainants.[42] There have also been calls to lift the veil of secrecy around sexual harassment in the legal sector by increasing transparency and accountability for the way complaints of sexual harassment are handled, as well establishing an independent industry body to which complaints can be made.[43]

Many legal professional bodies have convened committees or working groups to find ways of reducing bullying and sexual harassment in the profession. These bodies provide ready-made forums for considering the research evidence and helping to drive change in the profession. The Law Council has made statements of commitment to eliminating sexual harassment and bullying and sharing information about policies, guidelines and other initiatives of its member constituents.[44] Having a national dialogue about strategic initiatives and what works and what doesn't is important. Enlisting advice and support from external advisors with experience in addressing similar behaviour in other professional service sectors and from those bodies charged with educating, supporting and/or regulating workplace health and safety, may assist with devising approaches that are based on evidence and best practice.

---

42 L. Knowles, 'Sexual harassment of women rife in Australian legal profession, survey finds', *ABC News*, 8 March 2019.

43 WLANSW, above n. 17, p. 20.

44 Law Council of Australia, 'Law reform, cultural change and honesty critical to combat sexual harassment in the legal profession', https://www.lawcouncil.asn.au/media/media-releases/law-reform-cultural-change-and-honesty-critical-to-combat-sexual-harassment-in-the-legal-profession.

8.7. MANAGING PSYCHOSOCIAL RISK FACTORS

Finally, in addressing other common psychosocial risk factors in legal workplaces, SafeWork Australia and its State equivalents advise a multi-pronged approach. SafeWork Australia has recently released a new Guide to Work-related Psychological Health and Safety.[45] This provides guidance on a systematic approach involving prevention, early intervention, effective leadership and management commitment, identifying and eliminating psychosocial risk factors, and supporting recovery. These guidelines provide a framework for developing strategies tailored to legal workplaces.

Mental health initiatives specifically targeting legal practitioners are beginning to emerge. One example is the *Resilience@Law Legal Profession Mental Health Toolkit* which has been produced by resilience@law (a joint initiative of Reslience@Law members and other law firms and the Black Dog Institute).[46] This takes the form of a Mental Health Toolkit containing practical guidance and resources, including-information sheets, research, videos, depression self-tests, pathways to sources of help, rights and responsibilities.

In recent years, there has been growing attention given to providing supports to members of the legal profession experiencing, or at risk of, poor mental health. The Law Council constituent bodies have a range of initiatives in place.[47] These include: employee assistance programmes; specialist 'Lifeline for Lawyers' crisis support hotlines; LawCare professional and confidential referral service for solicitors seeking psychological support; BarCare counselling service for barristers; wellbeing and resilience guides, programmes; and activities; peer mental health and suicide awareness programmes and stress management seminars; peer support and mentoring groups; factsheets and videos, and self-assessment and stress management tools. These are important initiatives, but it is nevertheless interesting to note that there seems to be a far greater focus on supporting individuals rather than organisations,

45 See aforementioned report here: SWA, 'Work-related psychological health and safety: A systematic approach to meeting your duties', 2015, https://www.safeworkaustralia.gov.au/doc/work-related-psychological-health-and-safety-systematic-approach-meeting-your-duties.

46 Black Dog Institute, 'Resilience@Law Legal Profession Mental Health Toolkit', https://blackdoginstitute.org.au/docs/default-source/education-resources/black-dog-institute-mental-health-toolkit---resilience@law.pdf?sfvrsn=2&sfvrsn=2.

47 Law Council of Australia, above n. 44.

and on managing rather than preventing workplace-related mental health issues. In addition, there seems to be little if any research or evaluation available to assess to what extent these initiatives are being utilised and are effective.

On the positive side, there seems to be a growing recognition at the national level of the need to take a more holistic view of mental health and stress in the legal profession.[48] Such an approach would need to address not only cultural and historical practices, financial and business pressures, but also broader resourcing issues to do with the level of government funding of the courts and legal services that are placing significant pressures upon people who work in the legal profession, putting their health at risk. In addition, the Law Council's submission to the Productivity Commission Inquiry into Mental Health emphasised the social and economic benefits of improving mental health in the general workplace including the legal profession.[49] Meanwhile the issue of vicarious trauma through continual exposure of some members of the profession, including judges, to deeply upsetting and disturbing evidence and material, is also being more widely discussed.

In conclusion, it is important to monitor new initiatives to measure reach, response and impact so that learnings can be developed to improve and strengthen existing models and support the development of new approaches. Based on recent research and developments, some common themes are emerging as to how best to tackle harassment, bullying and other psychosocial risk factors in the legal profession. These include:

- Alignment of strategies with Work Health and Safety legislation and the latest evidence on identifying and managing psychosocial risk factors in the workplace;
- Adoption of a systemic approach to reform, involving different parts of the legal sector and profession;

48 Law Council of Australia, 'Healthy lawyers, justice critical focus of Law Week 2019', https://www.lawcouncil.asn.au/media/media-releases/healthy-lawyers-justice-critical-focus-of-law-week-2019.

49 Law Council of Australia, 'Social and economic benefits of improving mental health', submission to the Productivity Commission Inquiry into Mental Health, 24 April 2019, https://www.lawcouncil.asn.au/media/news/the-social-and-economic-benefits-of-improving-mental-health.

- Driving cultural change from the top, especially in large law firms;
- Education targeting all levels of the legal profession;
- Forging partnerships with external experts and relevant legal agencies and bodies to develop effective strategies;
- Increased accountability and transparency through meaningful monitoring and reporting;
- Development of a strong evidence base about what works and what doesn't and sharing learnings.

CHAPTER 5

PUBLIC SECTOR LAWYERING STRESS AND WELLBEING

Neoliberalism at Work?

Janet CHAN and Holly BLACKMORE*

1. Introduction: Neoliberalism and Lawyering. 106
2. What is Neoliberalism? 108
3. Neoliberalisation of Lawyering and its Consequences in the Public Sector. 112
    3.1. Evidence in the UK 112
    3.2. Evidence in Australia. 114
4. Comparing Public/Community with Private Lawyering 116
    4.1. Level of Depression, Anxiety and Stress 117
    4.2. Top Job Stressors 117
    4.3. Job Satisfaction 120
5. Perceptions of 'Wellbeing Interventions' 124
6. Concluding Remarks 128

* This work was supported by an Australian Research Council Discovery Grant [DP110101000]. The authors would like to thank members of the research team: Sally Doran, Rebecca Ananian-Welsh, Roland Alexander and Rabeatul Husna Abdull Rahman for their assistance with the research at various stages. We gratefully acknowledge the support of the legal professional community for publicising the survey. Finally, our very special thanks go to the hundreds of lawyers who took the time to complete the survey and those who participated in the interviews. Without their generous contributions this research would not have been possible.

1. INTRODUCTION: NEOLIBERALISM AND LAWYERING

The consequences of neoliberalism for lawyering in the private sector have been discussed extensively in the literature.[1] In her 2016 paper Margaret Thornton eloquently identifies the central role of neoliberalism in shaping society and, by extension, the field of legal practice:

> Neoliberalism is the dominant ideology of our time and shows no sign of abating. The undue deference accorded the economy and capital accumulation means that comparatively little attention is paid to the pressures this involves for workers. Although conventionally viewed as privileged professionals, lawyers in corporate law firms have been profoundly affected by the neoliberal turn as firms have expanded from local to national, to global entities, with the aim of maximising profits and making themselves competitive on the world stage.[2]

Thornton has identified some key features of neoliberal practices in law, such as: global competition, bureaucratisation, cost cutting and profit maximisation. This has led to the 'erosion of the autonomy of employed lawyers in private law firms'.[3] The erosion is made possible by 'disciplinary' technologies such as billable hours, giving rise to the culture of working long hours, which 'represent the crucial source of profitability for law firms'.[4] With an abundance of law graduates ready to replace them, the salaried lawyers fit the image of the 'disposable workers of neoliberalism'.[5] By extrapolating from a 2015 study by Schrecker and Bambra which 'shows compellingly that neoliberalism has eroded the conditions conducive to a healthy life and has given rise to four identifiable "epidemics": obesity, stress, austerity and inequality', Thornton concludes that 'neoliberal technologies, such as billable hours, have engendered high rates of stress and depression in the legal profession in Australia in the twenty-first century'.[6]

---

1 See, for example, M. Thornton, 'Squeezing the Life Out of Lawyers: Legal Practice in the Market Embrace' (2016) 25 *Griffith Law Review* 471; C. Parker, 'The "Moral Panic" over Psychological Wellbeing in the Legal Profession: A Personal or Political Ethical Response?' (2014) 37 *UNSW Law Journal* 1103.

2 M. Thornton, above n. 1, 471.

3 Ibid., 474.

4 Ibid., 476.

5 D. Harvey, *A Brief History of Neoliberalism*, Oxford University Press 2005, p. 169, cited in M. Thornton, above n. 1, 477.

6 M. Thornton, above n. 1, 479.

Thornton's critique goes further to examine the 'counter discourse' of wellbeing and work–life balance which has emerged in recent years. Instead of a discourse of resistance, Thornton argues that it is in fact further evidence that it is part of the neoliberal project. This is because: programmes are directed to *individual* wellbeing; they often fail to address structural and cultural causes of stress; they maintain the myth of the autonomous lawyer; they focus on individual self-care (responsibilisation); they expect lawyers to maintain resilience in spite of excessive workload. Thornton points out that in spite of good intentions, flexible work (which is an ambiguous concept) can have negative effects on lawyers' careers. As a result, many women lawyers in search of work–life balance have left private firms for government jobs or quit lawyering altogether.[7]

However, few studies have analysed the impact of neoliberalism on public sector lawyers. This chapter examines how lawyering in the public and community sectors in Australia has been affected by the neoliberal turn in public management. Neoliberal strategies pursued in Australia include

> extensive cuts in the overall amounts of funding available to the users and providers of legal services; changes to the types of legal assistance, programmes and services that remain eligible for government funding; and alterations to the ways in which providers can access or apply for funding.[8]

The impact of such cost cutting on public sector lawyering has been explored in terms of problematic access to justice, challenges to the provision of legal services, decreased capacity of community legal centres to engage in systemic advocacy, and the increased adoption of technology and other resources. Drawing on data from a 2012–13 national survey of Australian lawyers (hereafter 'the National Survey')[9] and a 2011–15 study of a public sector legal service organisation (hereafter 'the Public Legal

7 Law Council of Australia, *National Attrition and Re-engagement Study (NARS) Report*, Urbis 2014.

8 A. Flynn and J. Hodgson, 'Access to Justice and Legal Aid Cuts: A Mismatch of Concepts in the Contemporary Australian and British Legal Landscapes' in A. Flynn and J. Hodgson (eds), *Access to Justice & Legal Aid: Comparative Perspectives on Unmet Legal Need*, Hart Publishing, Oxford 2017, p. 1.

9 J. Chan, S. Poynton and J. Bruce, 'Lawyering Stress and Work Culture: An Australian Study' (2014) 37 *UNSW Law Journal* 1062.

Service Study'),[10] this chapter describes the specific vulnerabilities and levels of job satisfaction among public and community sector lawyers, and the perceived effectiveness of wellbeing initiatives introduced by their workplaces.

The chapter is organised as follows. It begins by examining more closely neoliberalism as a concept (Section 2) and how lawyering in the public and community sectors has been affected by the neoliberal turn (Section 3). The next section compares self-reported levels of depression, anxiety and stress, top stressors and job satisfaction among lawyers working in the community and government sectors with those working in the private sector (Section 4). To understand how the discourse of wellbeing and work-life balance is received, Section 5 examines lawyers' perceptions of the effectiveness of wellbeing initiatives. The last section discusses the implications of the findings for improving the wellbeing of lawyers.

2. WHAT IS NEOLIBERALISM?

The word 'neoliberalism' has only become popular in academic discourse since the turn of the twenty-first century.[11] The word – often used in its adjectival form – referred to 'the general shift from the social-democratic and progressive-liberal era to policies and institutions that were more concerned to promote market mechanisms and were more friendly to business and capital'.[12] By 2016, however, the term neoliberalism had become extremely widely used in academic work[13] and its conceptual usefulness is beginning to be debated.[14]

---

10 S. Poynton, J. Chan, M. Vogt, A. Grunseit and J. Bruce, 'Assessing the Effectiveness of Wellbeing Initiatives for Lawyers and Support Staff' (2018) 41 *UNSW Law Journal* 584.

11 See D. Harvey, *A Brief History of Neoliberalism*, Oxford University Press 2005; D. Cahill and M. Konings, *Neoliberalism*, Polity Press 2017.

12 D. Cahill and M. Konings, *Neoliberalism*, Polity Press 2017, p. 13.

13 B. Dunn, 'Against Neoliberalism as a Concept' (2017) 41 *Capital & Class* 435, 436, found over 400,000 academic publications have used this term.

14 See, for example, ibid.; D. Cahill and M. Konings, 'Neoliberalism: A Useful Concept?' (2017) <http://ppesydney.net/neoliberalism-useful-concept/>; R. Prince, 'Is Neoliberalism still a Useful Term?' (2015) <http://www.esocsci.org.nz/is-neoliberalism-still-a-useful-term/>, no longer available; R. Venugopal, 'Neoliberalism as Concept' (2015) 44 *Economy and Society* 165.

Dunn has argued that the concept has two weaknesses: first, it is too imprecise for contributing to our understanding of social practices; and second, it has become too 'self-referential' among the academic 'left' for it to be useful for informing political strategies.[15] The argument that the term neoliberalism has been used to characterise a broad range of phenomena is not new. Dunn cites a range of authors and examples to make the case that the term has been 'over-stretched', 'ill-defined', 'unstable', 'ambiguous', 'baggy', 'unclear' and used in such 'different and contradictory ways' that 'it means almost nothing'.[16] While the 'conceptual breadth' of neoliberalism can be defended along two lines – first, that the diversity of interpretations simply reflects the fact that social practices take many forms; and second, that many social science concepts are often contested – Dunn argues that in fact there have not been any meaningful contests, nor is there evidence of any 'movement towards shared understandings'.[17]

In relation to the second weakness, Dunn has argued that neoliberalism is a term that is used predominantly by the political left, and 'much more widely in academic discourse than within social movements themselves'.[18] His 2016 online searches of leading UK and US newspapers demonstrate 'rather starkly' that while the term was used 285,000 times in *The Guardian*, it rarely appeared in other newspapers.[19] The fact that the term is used mostly by the left elite and ignored by the alleged neoliberals themselves has meant that it 'becomes an obstacle rather than bridge to engagement with our intellectual adversaries'.[20] Even if this is not regarded as a problem, Dunn has argued that the term is still 'unhelpful, providing little guide to left practice'.[21] He asks what the specific reform proposals might be. for example, are the 'evils' specifically neoliberal or more generally capitalist ones?[22] He argues that for political practice to be effective, there needs to be more 'strategic thinking' in identifying what action is required in specific contexts; the

15 B. Dunn, above n. 13, 435.
16 B. Dunn, above n. 13, 437.
17 Ibid., 440–42.
18 Ibid., 442.
19 The term appeared from 8 to 155 times in the other newspapers – see Table 1, ibid., 443.
20 Ibid., 444.
21 Ibid., 445.
22 Ibid., 449.

danger of relying on a general, vague discourse such as neoliberalism may be that actions are focused on misplaced targets:

> The discourse of neoliberalism is inherently oppositional, but the term is used to encompass such diverse practices that without addition it provides little help identifying what exactly the user is against and provides at best a blunt instrument for practical politics.[23]

While advocating a more sparing and a more careful use of the term, Russell Prince has argued that neoliberalism remains a useful term 'for understanding contemporary culture' for three reasons: (1) neoliberalism has 'survived' because it is 'both vague and specific', i.e. it can be linked to a broad range of phenomena; (2) neoliberalism has 'always been a political project', not simply a set of policies; and (3) neoliberalism is 'historically significant' as it has transformed our political, economic and social 'settings in ways that have not been changed back'.[24]

In their book *Neoliberalism*, Cahill and Konings maintain the 'conviction that neoliberalism is a key concept for understanding the era we live in'.[25] They do not see 'a strict correspondence of concept and reality' as an appropriate basis for evaluating the usefulness of concepts, instead, they argue that:

> A label such as neoliberalism is of course not by itself capable of capturing the messy, complex dynamics and variegated details of social formations. The question is rather whether it provides a useful entry point, a way of looking at these processes that can subsequently be enriched with empirical detail. … The labels we use are in many respects less important than our description of the political economic processes to which the label refers.[26]

Their formulation of a critique of neoliberalism involves a 'critical synthesis' of a range of scholarly approaches. They argue that neoliberalism 'should not be separated from a more general understanding of capitalism':

> [Neoliberalism] represents an attempt to reconstruct capitalism in a way that registers some of the limitations of classic liberalism. Unlike the latter,

---

23 B. Dunn, above n. 13, 451.

24 R. Prince, 'Is Neoliberalism still a Useful Term?' (2015) <http://www.esocsci.org.nz/is-neoliberalism-still-a-useful-term/> no longer available.

25 D. Cahill and M. Konings, above n. 12, p. 20.

26 Ibid., p. 12.

> neoliberalism does not take the existence or reproduction of capitalism for granted. It is keenly aware that markets are not natural phenomena that simply emerge when institutional obstacles are removed. This constructivist impulse lies at the heart of neoliberal reason, and it is why neoliberalism involves much more than simple deregulation. Nevertheless, the notion that free markets are the most efficient and desirable basis of human organization, and the claim that states are inherently inefficient, remain central to the logic and appeal of neoliberalism ... This resulted in a new institutional architecture for managing capitalist social relations, at both domestic and global levels, even if there was, and is, a deep temporal and geographical unevenness to this process.[27]

While Dunn's critique has highlighted the imprecision and diversity of ways in which the concept of neoliberalism has been used, he has left the door open for greater contestations of the concept and perhaps a movement towards shared understandings. His argument that the concept is itself a barrier to political resistance may have been overdrawn: there has in fact been strong resistance or protest from divergent directions – from the Occupy Wall Street movement to the Tea Party in the US, Cahill and Konings have argued that the resilience of neoliberal policy and discourses, in spite of the global financial crisis and movements of resistance and protests, suggests that neoliberalism 'has been capable of producing its sources of legitimacy'.[28] They advocate that '[t]hose who have an interest in unmaking neoliberalism have much to gain from a clear perspective on its sources of durability and weakness, and on its recurrent and emerging contradictions'.[29]

In order to broaden our understanding of neoliberalism's impact on the legal profession, this chapter seeks to examine the neoliberal construction of lawyering in the public and community sectors and its consequences for the wellbeing of lawyers, its sources of durability and how resistance is possible.

---

27 Ibid., p. 20.
28 D. Cahill and M. Konings, above n. 12, p. 99.
29 Ibid., p. 102.

3. NEOLIBERALISATION OF LAWYERING AND ITS CONSEQUENCES IN THE PUBLIC SECTOR

3.1. EVIDENCE IN THE UK

A shift in the mode of the provision of legal services is one manifestation of the neoliberal turn in governments. In the UK, the strategies of New Public Management (or NPM, a form of neoliberal governance), as applied to the legal aid sector, have been summarised as follows:

> [T]he application of NPM to the legal aid sector has been characterised by a dual strategy of managerial control and financial retrenchment ... thereby operationalising the stated aim of cultural change in order to achieve both value for money for the tax payer, and improved quality for the consumer. Such a strategy has encompassed the broad range of measures applied to other sectors, including strict cost control ..., the contractualisation of relations between agencies and service providers and between clients and professionals ..., the generation of explicit performance indicators ..., delegated budgets and increased accountability through external audit.[30]

However, very little research has been published on the impact of neoliberalism on lawyers working in the public and community sectors. Hilary Sommerlad's research provides some insights into the impact of NPM on the legal aid sector in the UK in the mid-to-late 1990s.[31] Most practitioners Sommerlad interviewed perceived 'some change across the board in working practices and ethos, accompanied by significant decreases in practitioners' autonomy'.[32] There was a perception among practitioners that as a result of the introduction of various 'quality initiatives' and a predominantly 'managerial' approach, the 'transformation of the profession

30 H. Sommerlad, 'The Implementation of Quality Initiatives and the New Public Management in the Legal Aid Sector in England and Wales: Bureaucratisation, Stratification and Surveillance' (1999) 6 *International Journal of the Legal Profession* 311, 317.

31 H. Sommerlad, 'Managerialism and the Legal Profession: A New Professional Paradigm' (1995) 2 *International Journal of the Legal Profession* 159; H. Sommerlad, above n. 30; H. Sommerlad, '"I've Lost the Plot": An Everyday Story of Legal Aid Lawyers' (2001) 28 *Journal of Law and Society* 335.

32 H. Sommerlad, above n. 30, 336. This paper was based on 89 interviews, including 50 clients, 39 solicitors and some managers.

into a business' was accelerated.[33] Some respondents described a 'culture of fear' and a new professional ideology characterised by conformity, competitiveness, mistrust, alienation, and prioritising cost effectiveness over service to clients.[34]

In a later study, Sommerlad interviewed legal aid lawyers who were driven by social or political commitment to serve disadvantaged clients, and found that because of 'increased bureaucracy, declining income and autonomy and a discourse of contempt', many became demoralised, disillusioned, even embittered, because they were 'constantly being rubbished' by the 'political rhetoric'.[35] The discursive and material degradation of the legal aid professional exacerbated these feelings of stress and disillusionment:

> The contradictions confronting political lawyers working within mainstream professionalism have been exploited and exacerbated by a discourse which simultaneously demonizes sections of the clientele (and therefore all lawyers who work with them) whilst at the same time mobilizing the image of poverty lawyers as extracting riches from the misfortunes of the poor. Thus the degradation of the legal aid professional is achieved at the discursive level as well as a result of the material processes which, together, are eroding what are regarded as traditional professional traits. The result is the decline in income, greatly increased work burdens, high stress and low morale, which thereby accentuate the already existing tendency to 'burn out' and disillusion amongst welfare professionals. For some firms which are wholly legal aid practices the strain on both psychological and material resources seem to be very great.[36]

Sommerlad's research – based on self-reports among self-selected samples – suggests that the neoliberalisation of publicly funded legal services may have increased work stress among lawyers, especially those committed to the service of disadvantaged clients.

---

33 H. Sommerlad, above n. 30, 329.

34 Ibid., 331–32.

35 H. Sommerlad, '"I've Lost the Plot": An Everyday Story of Legal Aid Lawyers' (2001) 28 *Journal of Law and Society* 335, 350–56. This paper was based on interviews with 30 solicitors in 18 firms in England, drawn from 'that self-selecting group which entered the legal aid sector precisely because of a commitment to using the law to fulfil the promise of expanded citizenship' (p. 342).

36 Ibid., 359–60.

3.2. EVIDENCE IN AUSTRALIA

Similar developments have occurred in Australia since the mid-1980s.[37] More recent analysis of legal aid in both Australia and the UK shows that for nearly two decades

> there have been extensive cuts in the overall amounts of funding available to the users and providers of legal services; changes to the types of legal assistance, programmes and services that remain eligible for government funding; and alterations to the ways in which providers can access or apply for funding.[38]

The impact of such cost cutting on public sector lawyering has been explored in terms of problematic access to justice, challenges to the provision of legal services, decreased capacity of community legal centres to engage in systemic advocacy, and the increased adoption of technology and other resources.[39] However, data from the Public Legal Service Study[40] also suggests that a number of neoliberal features such as cost cutting, contractualisation and increased bureaucratisation have led to work stress among lawyers. As one lawyer pointed out, cuts in public funding for legal services over 10 years have led to increased job stress:

> The last ten years or so have seen more and more demands on the way we work and the number of court matters and other daily obligations and service delivery initiatives we have without any recognition that there is the need for more staff or better ways to work. There seems to be a lack of awareness by Govt that the public sector can only be pushed to work longer hours and on more

---

37 See S. Tomsen, 'Legal Services and Neo-liberalism in an Unequal Legal Order' (2007–08) 10 *Flinders Journal of Law Reform* 609; M.A. Noone and S.A. Tomsen, *Lawyers in Conflict: Australian Lawyers and Legal Aid*, Federation Press, Sydney 2006. Australia's legal aid system is a mixed model, comprising 'salaried lawyers working in statutory LACs [Legal Aid Commissions]; independent CLCs [Community Legal Centres] and Indigenous Legal Services; and private lawyers providing services under a "judicare" scheme, as well as on a pro bono basis', as well as 'a large volunteer base that provides services in CLCs' (M.A. Noone, 'Challenges Facing the Australian Legal Aid System' in A. Flynn and J. Hodgson (eds), *Access to Justice & Legal Aid: Comparative Perspectives on Unmet Legal Need*, Hart Publishing, Oxford 2017, p. 816).

38 A. Flynn and J. Hodgson, above n. 8, p. 1.

39 See chapters in A. Flynn and J. Hodgson, above n. 8.

40 This study consists of three waves of staff surveys, interviews with management and staff, and field observation. See S. Poynton et al., above n. 10, for full details of the research methods.

> stressful work for so long without something giving. (2013 survey respondent, Public Legal Service Study)

The lack of control over workload was seen as a contributor to the 'lack of wellbeing':

> [T]he worst stressor is having absolutely no control over the volume of work coming in as against staffing constraints in a climate where we are expected to maintain existing services. … Having no control over your work processes other than at a very local micro level creates a lack of wellbeing. (2013 survey respondent, Public Legal Service Study)

The stress brought on by an unrealistic workload was exacerbated by the fear of not meeting performance indictors:

> Well there is not enough time to do all of the work, physically do all the work, so I have to put in long hours – and this isn't just me, this is most of us – have to put in quite long hours and even then we're not getting all the work done. So it's hugely stressful because you're worried that you're not performing. Like for me personally I get stressed out because I'm not performing as well as I know I can. I'm worried about my reputation because I'm not acting properly on things, and that's because I'm in court and I get back and I might have 40 emails, telephone calls and then I might be in court the next day. (Interview participant, Public Legal Service Study)

Staff on contracts experienced additional stress as a result of the lack of job security:

> My major issue however stems from being employed as a temporary staff member, for in excess of 4 years, and facing contract renewal and associated uncertainty every 12 months. The stress I face is generally in relation to job security … I am currently applying for permanent positions, but hold concerns due to the current cost cutting and budget cuts. (2013 survey respondent, Public Legal Service Study)

> This job has long-term mental health impacts. I have developed depression due to working in this job but because I am on a contract, and don't have job security, I do not have the ability to take time off and also because I am not permanent, I am scared to tell my employers that I need time off for mental health reasons. I think if they knew this, it would adversely affect my future prospects within this organisation. And the sad thing about that is, I really love this organisation and I enjoy my job. (2011 survey respondent, Public Legal Service Study)

Increased bureaucratisation was another factor that affected service delivery and staff morale:

> It's just becoming more bureaucratic than it ever was and the emphasis is less on providing a good service than it is on filling out forms properly. I don't mean forms for stats, I mean forms and just internal things that are meant to work a particular way and they don't work a particular way but you haven't filled it in so you get a rude memo from someone about you haven't done this properly. It's just really patronising sometimes. (Interview participant, Public Legal Service Study)

These excerpts from survey respondents and interview participants in the Public Legal Service Study suggest that cost cutting, contractualisation and lack of job security, together with increased bureaucratisation, were regarded as significant factors that caused work stress among lawyers. What is not certain, however, is the extent to which public sector lawyers were differentially affected by neoliberalism compared with those who work in the private sector. This will be explored in the next section.

4. COMPARING PUBLIC/COMMUNITY WITH PRIVATE LAWYERING

In the absence of historical comparative data, it is obviously difficult to draw any firm conclusions about the impact of neoliberalism on stress and wellbeing among lawyers. Assuming that neoliberalism has had a pervasive influence on Australian lawyering, cross-sectional data can be used to investigate whether lawyers working in public or community sector experience different levels of stress and wellbeing compared with those working in private firms. This analysis will help to develop a more nuanced understanding of how different workplaces and regimes of practice can mitigate or aggravate the impact of these changes. This section draws on data from the National Survey conducted in 2012–13 to compare the emotional states, job stressors and job satisfaction among lawyers working in the public/community and private sectors.[41]

---

41 Note that the sample – a valid sample size of 965 with response rates ranging from one to three per cent depending on the State – is not representative of the population of Australian lawyers but it provides comparative information not previously available. See J. Chan et al., above n. 9, for full details of the questionnaire, recruitment methods and response rates.

4.1. LEVEL OF DEPRESSION, ANXIETY AND STRESS

Table 1 below provides a comparison of a measure of negative emotional states among lawyers working in these different sectors. The measure being used is a total of the depression, anxiety and stress scores on the Depression Anxiety Stress Scales (DASS). The DASS are well-validated measures and Australian normative data are available in order to compare raw scores with population percentiles. The short version of this scale includes 21 questions on a four-point severity scale and asks respondents to indicate whether these items applied to them at all over the past week. It is important to note that these questions are not designed to diagnose clinical psychological disorders.[42]

The results[43] show that the median DASS scores did not differ significantly among lawyers practising in the private, public and community sectors. In other words, lawyers working in the public and community sectors were suffering similar levels of negative psychological symptoms.

Table 1. Depression Anxiety Stress Scores (DASS) by Workplace

	Median DASS scores
Private firm (n = 459)	24
Community legal (n = 81)	24
Government legal (n = 81)	22

No significant differences (Kruskal-Wallis H test, p = .799).
Source: National Survey.

4.2. TOP JOB STRESSORS

To find out the major sources of stress among these lawyers, the National Survey participants were asked to identify in free text the three most

42 For further details on the DASS see P.F. Lovibond and S.H. Lovibond, 'The Structure of Negative Emotional States: Comparison of the Depression Anxiety Stress Scales (DASS) with the Beck Depression and Anxiety Inventories' (1995) 33 *Behaviour Research and Therapy* 335. Note that the total DASS scores used were produced by adding scores for each item and then multiplying the total by two to reflect the use of the 21-item scale, not the full 42-item scale.

43 For this analysis, only respondents who stated that they worked in a private firm, a government legal department, or a community legal centre are included; respondents

stressful things they encountered in their job. A total of 733 respondents (76 per cent of the sample) provided 2,226 aspects of their job that were regarded as stressful. These answers were coded into 51 categories reflecting seven broad areas: working conditions, working relationships, the client, the culture of the workplace, the nature of the work, personal issues, and other issues.

Table 2 below shows the rankings in the frequency with which different areas of stress were mentioned, broken down by workplace. The pattern is remarkably similar across groups, with 'working conditions' consistently being the top (most frequently nominated) area of stress, and with 'colleagues and other professionals' and 'clients' occupying the second or third spot. Within 'working conditions', 'time constraints and deadlines' and 'excessive workload' were mentioned by all three groups. However, there are variations between the groups: lawyers who work in private firms also mentioned 'billable hours', 'other financial issues' and 'lack of control over work' as stressors; 'interruptions' was mentioned by government lawyers; and 'lack of resources', 'lack of support staff' and 'job security' were mentioned by community lawyers. Within 'colleagues and other professionals', 'management and superiors' and 'working relationships' were nominated by lawyers working in all three sectors.

Table 2. Ranking of Job Stressors by Workplace

	Working conditions	Colleagues & other professionals	Clients	Nature of work	Culture	Personal issues	Other
Private firm (n = 422)	1	2	3	5	4	6	7
Community legal (n = 78)	1	3	2	4	7	5	6
Government legal (n = 76)	1	2	3	4	=5	=5	7

Source: National Survey.

In their responses, some community and government lawyers described stressors such as a lack of resources, funding uncertainty, a

who were barristers or those who worked in corporate legal departments and other workplaces are excluded.

shortage of support staff, budget restraints, and job security concerns. For example:

> Lack of resources to adequately advocate for our clients. Number of clients in need who cannot afford private lawyers. (Female, Community)[44]
>
> Not being able to assist people due to resource constraints and inadequacies of the law ... Current funding by Government as a CLC and lack of certainty over continued funding. (Female, Community)
>
> Difficult clients. Under-resourcing of CLC sector in relation to administration support. Threat of funding cuts to our CLC which would potentially impact upon my position (Female, Community)
>
> Time constraints. Staff constraints. Financial constraints. (Female, Community)
>
> Worry about losing my job due to lack of funding or funding cuts. Telephone advice line – people expecting immediate answers when I don't have resources to provide them. Worry about not being able to progress in my career in a community legal centre. (Female, Community)
>
> Decisions that are made by higher management that affect how I do my job (including budget restraints and restrictions on promotion/higher duty opportunities) ... Juggling my responsibility to the court and managing my litigation matters while keeping up to date with administrative reporting obligations as well as day-to-day administration tasks (I do not have any admin/support staff). (Female, Government)
>
> 1. Impending job cuts to legal aid due to lack of government funding. 2. Frustrating experiences with poor people-managers in management roles. 3. High pressures from clients and court users. (Female, Government)
>
> Lack of supervision because of the time pressures on principal lawyers. Lack of job security because jobs are often driven by time-limited grants in the CLC sector. Lack of part-time jobs on offer makes this problem even more pronounced. (Female, Community)
>
> My case load is made up of clients who are seriously traumatised with difficult histories, which frequently requires long exhausting conferences. Lack of acknowledgement of the good work we do. As our organisation is funded by the [Attorney-General's] department we are only offered short term employment contract which does not offer security. (Female, Community)

---

44 Note that some comments have been shortened to focus on the relevant content, and typos have been removed. Respondents are identified by their gender and their workplace type only.

These comments are consistent with those from the Public Legal Service Study cited in Section 3 above: they emphasised the under-resourcing, cost cutting, and lack of job security aspects of neoliberal policies.

4.3. JOB SATISFACTION

Research has shown that lawyers have consistently reported very high level of satisfaction with their job.[45] To measure their level of job satisfaction, in the National Survey respondents were asked to rate their satisfaction with their current job along 17 dimensions on a scale of 1 to 7, where 1 equals 'extremely satisfied' and 7 equals 'extremely dissatisfied'. These questions were adopted from a large US study examining the levels of job satisfaction among law graduates.[46] To simplify the analysis, four new factors were created by grouping several job satisfaction dimensions:[47]

- **Job Substance** – total of the following scores (maximum = 28):
  - Substantive area of your work
  - Tasks you perform
  - Intellectual challenge
  - Opportunities to build skills
- **Job Setting** – total of the following scores (maximum = 49):
  - Level of responsibility
  - Recognition for your work

[45] Empirical studies have consistently found that around eight in ten lawyers reported that they were satisfied with their job or career – see J.M. Organ, 'What do we Know about the Satisfaction/Dissatisfaction of Lawyers? A Meta-Analysis of Research on Lawyer Satisfaction and Well-being' (2011) 8 *University of St. Thomas Law Journal* 225, for a review of the North American research literature over 25 years.

[46] See R. Dinovitzer, B.G. Garth, R. Sander, J. Sterling and G.Z. Wilder, *After the JD: First Results of a National Study of Legal Careers*, American Bar Foundation and NALP Foundation 2004; R. Dinovitzer and B.G. Garth, 'Lawyer Satisfaction in the Process of Structuring Legal Careers' (2007) 41 *Law & Society Review* 1.

[47] These were derived from a factor analysis conducted by Dinovitzer and colleagues (Dinovitzer, Personal correspondence with author, 29 October 2013). The variable 'amount of travel' was excluded as it did not 'load well' with the factors. The score for each factor in the current analysis was simply the sum of the scores of the relevant variables, i.e. no factor loadings were used.

  - Control over amount of work
  - Control over how you work
  - Relationships with colleagues
  - Job security
  - Performance evaluation process
- **Job Social Value** – total of the following scores (maximum = 21):
  - Diversity
  - Opportunities for pro bono
  - Value of work to society
- **Job Power Track** – total of the following scores (maximum = 14):
  - Remuneration
  - Opportunities for advancement

Table 3 below compares the median job satisfaction scores among the three groups of lawyers. The results show that differences between the three groups were not statistically significant for Job Substance and Job Setting. However, lawyers working in community organisations were significantly *more satisfied*[48] with their Job Social Value (diversity, opportunities for pro bono work, value of work to society) than those working in government and private firms (a median of 6.0 among community lawyers, compared with 9.0 among government lawyers and 11.0 among private lawyers). In contrast, lawyers who worked in private firms were significantly *more satisfied* with their Job Power Track (remuneration, opportunities for advancement) than those who worked in the community sector.[49] These results suggest that private, community and government lawyers were satisfied with different aspects of their job.

---

48 A higher median indicates a higher level of dissatisfaction. The differences were statistically significant ($p < .001$) according to the Kruskal-Wallis H test and pairwise comparisons between community and private, and community and government.

49 A higher median indicates a higher level of dissatisfaction. The differences were statistically significant ($p < .001$) according to the Kruskal-Wallis H test and pairwise comparisons between private and community lawyers. However, the difference between private and government lawyers was not statistically significant.

Table 3. Median Job Satisfaction Scores by Workplace

JOB SUBSTANCE (Not Significant)	
Private firm (n = 482)	10.0
Community legal (n = 80)	9.0
Government legal (n = 83)	10.0
JOB SETTING (Not Significant)	
Private firm (n = 480)	22.0
Community legal (n = 79)	19.0
Government legal (n = 83)	22.0
JOB SOCIAL VALUE (p < .001)	
Private firm (n = 476)	11.0
Community legal (n = 79)	6.0
Government legal (n = 81)	9.0
JOB POWER TRACK (p < .001)	
Private firm (n = 480)	7.0
Community legal (n = 83)	9.0
Government legal (n = 84)	8.0

Kruskal-Wallis H test + pairwise comparisons.
Source: National Survey.

These results are consistent with some of the comments offered by survey respondents. For example, two community lawyers expressed high job satisfaction in spite of high demand and lack of resources:

> My supervisor and workplace are generally supportive of me. However, the level of demand for the work I undertake in the community legal sector and the lack of resources create the greatest level of stress. My job satisfaction is very high. I experienced burnout 12 months after entering full-time work because I had not taken time for a break since beginning study. Burnout is a very big issue in the community sector. Lack of job satisfaction seems to be a significant issue for corporate colleagues. My experience of practising law is different to corporate city colleagues who face a great deal of stress which has been created from within their workplace, generally by other people in their workplace. (Female, Community)

> My salary is ordinary and the legal work is just as demanding. I no longer have to do billing, although continuation of Government funding is a continual concern. But I work in a sector in which social justice is a priority, where disadvantaged people are assisted, and where I find the work to be more

> personally and professionally fulfilling than most of the work I did when in private practice. (Male, Community)

The precariousness of employment security, low remuneration and the lack of career advancement opportunities in the community sector were the downsides to the supportive environment of community legal centres, as one community lawyer explained:

> I feel very fortunate to work in a highly supportive, family friendly environment at a CLC. However, the payoff for these bonuses is twofold: a lack of job security due to the nature of short-term funding which pays my wages; and the low wages paid to solicitors working in the community sector, when compared even to wages for Legal Aid solicitors. Career advancement is also problematic, especially for community solicitors working in regional areas, who don't wish to move to a city area. (Female, Community)

As pointed out by another respondent, government lawyers similarly work under poor conditions and are only sustained by their personal commitment to serve the public interest:

> Government lawyers' conditions are often average to poor (offices are often utterly depressing for those fortunate to have an office as opposed to a workstation), and remuneration low despite long hours. … Government lawyers often work extremely long hours for little incentive other than a personal commitment to serving the public interest and personal professionalism. Although a drop in remuneration relative to private sector salaries is an acceptable concession on the part of any lawyer who truly wishes to work in the public interest, it is arguable that the drop is often too great. A sustained legal career in government is also undermined by the need for government lawyers who reach the top of their classification to transfer to a legal management position (which is inevitably bereft of a truly legal character) to secure higher remuneration. (Male, Government)

Yet there is a real fear that the work environment of government lawyers will become as competitive and 'cut throat' as the private sector:

> The legal profession is in reality overly competitive and obsessed with reputation and status … This reality prevents senior practitioners mentoring juniors for fear of enabling new competitors. Junior practitioners are afraid of revealing weakness or exposing themselves to liability, or hurting their own reputation, and therefore are also less willing to seek mentoring help. In addition, lawyers regularly snipe [at] other lawyers and use this negative feedback to bolster

> their own credentials. Further, it is very common now for lawyers to sue other lawyers or make complaints against them. All this means that practice can become isolating and depressing. If you have a difficult client workload on top the result is often catastrophic. I think these issues are amplified immensely in private practice contexts. This is why I will not work privately (unless it is with a friend who I would literally trust with my life), and thus will either tend to stay in governmental practice, or alternately work for myself at the Bar, if I have any choice. The result is that the only real source of comfort for many lawyers are avenues of relief outside their work context, and self-evidently, these avenues are not open if the lawyer happens to be working long hours. Fortunately for me I am in a less competitive arena [government], although this is slowly changing. I expect as governmental agencies move employees from permanency to contracts, there will be no job security, and the work will become just as cut-throat as private practice. (Male, Government)

These results suggest that job satisfaction for public and community lawyers was often a trade-off: a supportive and friendly work environment and the social value of the work could be sufficient compensation for low status and poor working conditions. But with the increasing trend to turn government legal services into managerialist and competitive workplaces, even this meagre trade-off could be wearing thin.

5. PERCEPTIONS OF 'WELLBEING INTERVENTIONS'

In Australia, there has been an increased awareness of the mental health and wellbeing issues in the legal profession since the publication of the 2006 Beaton Consulting survey[50] and the 2009 Brain and Mind Research Institute Study.[51] As a result, numerous interventions, including educational modules, awareness-raising strategies, counselling services, training in resilience and 'best practice' guidelines, have been initiated by law firms, law schools, professional associations and workplaces.[52] To understand

---

50 Beaton Consulting, 'Annual Professions Survey' (2007)<http://www.judicialcollege.vic.edu.au/sites/default/files/2007%20-%20Beyond%20Blue%20-%20Annual%20Professions%20Survey.pdf>.

51 N. Kelk, G. Luscombe, S. Medlow and I. Hickie, *Courting the Blues: Attitudes towards Depression in Australian Law Students and Lawyers*, Brain & Mind Research Institute: University of Sydney 2009.

52 See C. Parker, 'The "Moral Panic" over Psychological Wellbeing in the Legal Profession: A Personal or Political Ethical Response?' (2014) 37 *UNSW Law Journal* 1103,

how lawyers perceive the effectiveness of various types of interventions, respondents in the National Survey were asked about their experience with health and wellbeing initiatives available to legal practitioners. Respondents were also asked to rate the effectiveness of these for dealing with stress.

Figure 1 summarises the combined responses of the three groups of lawyers.[53] The initiatives included in the survey were: 'Offered breaks from working with clients', 'Extra time to complete work', 'Redistribution of work to other colleagues', 'Time off work', 'Time management training', 'Stress management training', 'Sport/exercise classes', 'Mentoring', 'Medical/health check-ups', 'Employee Assistance Programme' (EAP), and 'Counselling'.

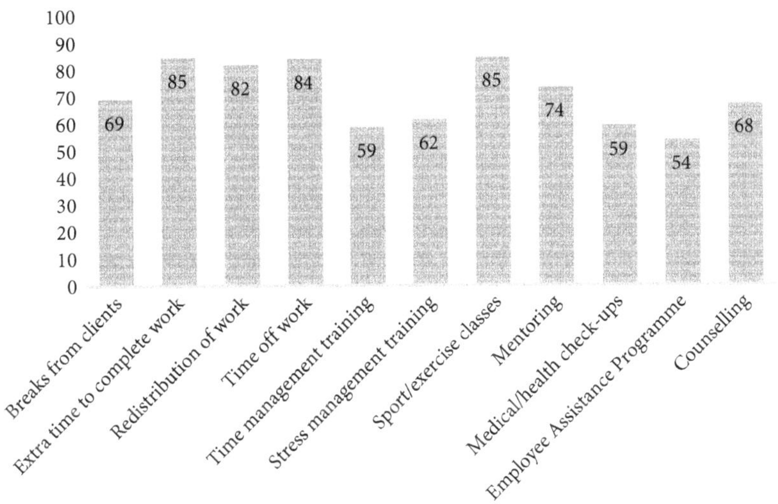

Figure 1. Perceived Effectiveness of Wellbeing Interventions

Percentage of respondents who rated the intervention as highly effective or quite effective.

Source: National Survey (includes all lawyers who worked in a private firm, a government legal department, or a community legal centre).

Appendix 2: (Practical and Policy Responses on Law Student and Lawyer Wellbeing) for a list of nearly 30 national or State-based programmes including the work of law schools, the Law Institute of Victoria, the Tristan Jepson Memorial Foundation, and the Wellness Network for Law.

53 Tests of significance show that there are only two interventions where differences between the three groups were statistically significant. The first relates to 'breaks from working with clients' ($X^2 = 21.8$, df = 2, $p < .001$, Cramer's V = .233): this is

LaMontagne et al. have classified work stress interventions into three categories: *primary* (to reduce risk factors or stressors), *secondary* (to change individual workers' response to stress) and *tertiary* (to treat or rehabilitate workers with job-related illness).[54] Using this classification, 'breaks from clients', 'extra time', 'redistribution' and 'time off' can be loosely defined as primary interventions addressing working conditions; 'time management', 'stress management', 'sport' and 'mentoring' as secondary interventions focusing on building individual resilience; and 'medical', 'EAP' and 'counselling' as tertiary interventions aiming at remedial measures to treat illness.[55] Figure 1 above shows that respondents were most likely to rate primary interventions as highly or quite effective (81%), less likely to rate secondary interventions (70%) and least likely to rate tertiary interventions (60%) as effective.

Some of the qualitative comments provided by respondents helped shed light on why primary interventions were highly valued:

> I am aware that others who have previously held my position have burnt out and left the role at around the 2-year mark. I purposefully take it a little easy as ongoing self-care. All the work gets done. I've spoken to my supervisor about it and there is no issue. I take multiple breaks during the day to check Facebook, or to read articles around social justice topics. (Female, Community)

> I am currently a CLC lawyer but worked previously in private practice. I found private practice extremely stressful due to the demands of making budget, and that I was not valued as a person apart from what I achieved for the firm; nor were my activities outside of work valued (it was difficult to even vary my lunch break – for example if I wanted to move my lunch break to a different time to

rated as highly effective or quite effective by 89% of community lawyers and 83% of government lawyers, but only 63% of private lawyers. The second relates to 'extra time to complete work' ($X^2 = 8.223$, df = 2, $p = .016$, Cramer's V = .125). Here the difference is less pronounced: this is rated as highly effective or quite effective by 94% of community lawyers and 90% of government lawyers, and 82% of private lawyers. This suggests that while flexible work arrangements – such as having breaks from working with clients and being given extra time to complete work – were highly valued, they were less frequently regarded as effective by lawyers who worked in private firms.

54 A.D. LaMontagne, T. Keegel and D. Vallance, 'Protecting and Promoting Mental Health in the Workplace: Developing a Systems Approach to Job Stress' (2007) 18 *Health Promotion Journal of Australia* 221.

55 Our classification here is not definitive. It is possible that counselling can be regarded as both a secondary and a tertiary intervention as it can both build resilience to stress and treat stress-related illness.

> enable me to attend a personal appointment, I was not treated with kindness!) I am much happier working as a CLC lawyer where none of these issues exist and I am valued as a person – They make the extra effort to give you work/life balance and flexibility, perhaps in part to make up for the pay being much less! I am a much happier lawyer working at a CLC. (Female, Community)

> The focus is on 'sink or swim', with partners often critical of lawyers rather than seeking to train and develop them. Mental issues would be perceived as demonstrating that you are not suited to the job. Resilience is seen as a key personality trait. With no flexibility in working hours to allow for social sports, lawyers often resort to isolated competitive physical exercise such as the gym, running or cycling. This creates further lack of interpersonal skills, with people isolated from others at work, at home and in their recreational activities. (Female, Private)

> My work expects that I am at work early (7.30–8am) and that I leave late (7.30–8pm). I have difficulty getting time to exercise during the day, even where I do not take a lunch break, and am expected to come in on the weekend to work, with no real compensation. I feel I do not have enough time to live a life outside of work, and am very dissatisfied with this. As a result I am looking to leave the private sector and find a job with stricter requirements as to hours employees can work (i.e. government) that rewards you where you are required to work extra hours (for example flexi-time). I am more than happy to take a large pay cut to achieve this. My current role is driving me away from law, as I do not enjoy my life and do not look forward to going to work; indeed, even the weekend is not something to look forward to as I will be expected to come in at least one, if not both days. (Male, Private)

A number of respondents commented on secondary interventions, but in a dismissive way:

> 'Resilience' in the workplace is tokenistic. (It also describes a method of coping which encourages 'toughening up' rather than getting better). It is only ever discussed briefly and there are very few real options for people who are struggling to pursue within the workplace. There is a sense of shame if you do not cope because it is still a man's world in a commercial law firm and you need to be 'hard' to keep up. Personal issues are only dealt superficially. Mental health initiatives are raised every now and then so it looks like firms are doing something about this, but it seems that this is all for show. The important thing is that you get your work done and whatever issues you experience doing this are irrelevant to the final outcome. (Female, Private)

> Although the firm I work for has addressed depression through seminars etc. with a view to helping overcome the high rate in legal firms, I believe that it would strongly prejudice my promotion chances if I admitted that I took

> anti-depressants. I think this is particularly the case for women, as we are already perceived by our male colleagues as having less tolerance to stress and so it is fatal to your career chances to reveal any such 'weakness'. (Female, Private)

These results suggest that – in spite of some of the cultural issues related to flexible working conditions pointed out by Thornton and others regarding women lawyers returning to work – lawyers still prefer interventions that are more 'structural' than 'responsibilising'.

In summary, the National Survey responses suggest that a very high percentage of lawyers perceived wellbeing interventions that address *working conditions* as effective. Interventions aimed at *training workers to be more resilient* and those aimed at *providing remedial services* were less frequently rated as effective. The only statistically significant differences between public/community and private lawyers' perceptions of wellbeing interventions were in relation to the fact that while flexible work arrangements – such as having breaks from working with clients and being given extra time to complete work – were highly valued, they were less frequently regarded as effective by lawyers who worked in private firms. These results show that while neoliberalism may have fundamentally altered the conditions of lawyering, lawyers themselves take seriously the discourse of stress and wellbeing, and are in favour of both structural and individual interventions.

6. CONCLUDING REMARKS

Many years ago the sociologist Stan Cohen[56] told the story of a fisherman who rescued a person found floating down a river; then he rescued another, and another. Here lies the dilemma: should he continue to rescue people downstream or go 'upstream' to deal with the source of the problem? When dealing with lawyering stress and wellbeing, while we may think that structural problems need to be addressed first, we should not undervalue the achievements of those in law firms, in the public sector and in the community, who have worked against all odds to raise consciousness and resources to implement wellbeing initiatives. Many are genuinely well intentioned and going beyond their normal duty to try to make a difference.

[56] S. Cohen, *Visions of Social Control*, Polity Press, Glasgow 1985.

This is not to deny the pernicious effects of neoliberal domination and the tokenistic nature of some of these initiatives (e.g. having such programmes can increase the reputational capital of firms and organisations).

As researchers and as advocates of reform, the authors may be equally well intentioned and eager to make a difference. While researchers cannot escape the domination of neoliberalism (it is particularly evident in universities), they are in a more independent position than law firm partners, legal service executives, managers, and lawyers who may have corporate and organisational interests to protect, so they are in a better position to speak truth to power. Changing entrenched structures and cultures is a mammoth task and requires a lot of effort, multiple strategies, and a great deal of persistence. There is no magic wand that will get us there. It will be left to those with more expertise and experience in social movements to discuss strategies and possibilities. There is no doubt, however, that one has to work both upstream and downstream in order to make dramatic changes as well as prevent individual casualties.

CHAPTER 6

LAW TEACHERS SPEAK OUT

What do Law Schools Need to Change?

Colin JAMES, Caroline STREVENS and Rachael FIELD

1. Introduction 131
2. The Neoliberal University and Legal Education.................. 133
3. An Ethical Imperative to Interrogate the Quality of Working Life for Law Teachers 136
4. Methodology.. 137
5. Methodological Limitations 141
6. Demographics... 141
7. Satisfaction at Work 141
8. Qualitative Data in Response to: 'Please Explain What You Think your University Could do to Improve Staff Quality of Working Life'.. 143
   8.1. Administrative Burden 144
   8.2. Teacher Support 145
   8.3. Workload.. 145
   8.4. Management Styles, Consultation and Transparency.......... 146
   8.5. Strategic Priorities 148
   8.6. Autonomy 148
   8.7. Communication and Respect................................. 149
9. A 'To-Do' List for Law School Leaders and Managers............. 150
10. Conclusion.. 151

1. INTRODUCTION

A significant body of empirical research in Australia and internationally has established that law students' wellbeing may significantly decrease during their legal education. Law teachers who interface with students are in a position to contribute to addressing this situation through intentionally designing, enacting and reforming law curricula – at the least to prevent the decline of law student wellbeing, if not positively to promote and support the wellbeing of law students. However, there is a paucity of research on the wellbeing of legal academics and their capacity to support student wellbeing. Indeed, few studies have explored the particular stressors experienced by legal academics in the contemporary neoliberal university, or how legal academics perceive their own wellbeing.

This chapter presents the qualitative results of national surveys of UK and Australian legal academics conducted in 2017, and explores law teachers' perceptions of their wellbeing and of their experience of stress at work. First, the authors consider the neoliberal landscape of higher education in the twenty-first century, a landscape that provides the context and framework for how law teachers experience law school as a work environment. Second, the methodology and results of the studies conducted in the UK and Australia in 2017 are explained.[1] Third, the authors discuss the themes presenting from the law teachers' responses to the open question: Please explain what you think your university could do to improve staff quality of working life?[2] The chapter concludes with a suggested to-do list for law school leaders to provide a work environment that better supports the wellbeing of their academics which, in turn, should enhance the capacity of law teachers to support the wellbeing of law students.[3]

---

1 Caroline Strevens, Colin James and Rachael Field, 'Fit Your Own Oxygen Mask First: The Contemporary Neoliberal University and the Well-Being of Legal Academics', Invited Keynote Presentation at the 2019 Wellness for Law Forum, Melbourne: https://law.unimelb.edu.au/wellness-for-law-forum.

2 The quantitative results from the surveys in both countries are still under analysis and will be released in a subsequent publication.

3 As the authors note later in the chapter their emphasis is on what law schools and universities can do structurally and culturally for their academic staff to improve the quality of working life, as opposed to suggestions for how individual staff might build their resilience and self-management skills. See for example on this important distinction: Henry A. Giroux, *Impure Acts*, Taylor and Francis, 2000.

2. THE NEOLIBERAL UNIVERSITY AND LEGAL EDUCATION

The modern neoliberal global context presents many economic, cultural and sociological challenges for the contemporary world.[4] Neoliberalism is a 'socio-economic theory that rejects governmental intervention in the domestic economy and promulgates materialism, consumerism, and the commodification of many public goods'.[5] Neoliberalism and its impact on contemporary society and workplaces is the subject of a significant body of critical scholarly literature.[6] Noted as developing out of approaches to politics and the free-market in the 1980s, neoliberalism has at its core concepts such as reduced government spending, privatisation and an increased role for the private sector; along with austerity, increased market productivity, output and production efficiencies and free trade.[7] It is uncontroversial that neoliberalism is rapidly changing labour markets and workplaces around the world.[8] In the context of this new labour market, concepts of wellbeing, resilience and self-management skills take on a new importance both in terms of the future sustainability of diverse industries and professions, and also in terms of the potential for societies, industries

---

4 Henry A. Giroux, *Against the Terror of Neoliberalism: Politics Beyond the Age of Greed*, Routledge, 2015; Henry A. Giroux, *Terror of Neoliberalism: Authoritarianism and the Eclipse of Democracy*, Routledge, 2018.

5 Daniel Saunders, 'The Impact of Neoliberalism on College Students' (2007) 8(5) *Journal of College and Character* 1, 1.

6 Key publications include Giroux, above n. 3; Alfredo Saad-Filho, 'Crisis in Neoliberalism or Crisis of Neoliberalism?' in Alfredo Saad-Filho (ed), *Value and Crisis: Essays on Labour, Money and Contemporary Capitalism*, Brill, 2019, 302–18; Simon Springer, Kean Birch and Julie MacLeavy (eds), *Handbook of Neoliberalism*, Routledge, 2016; William Davies, *The Limits of Neoliberalism. Authority, Sovereignty and the Logic of Competition*, Sage, 2016; Stuart Hall, Doreen Massey and Michael Rustin, *After Neoliberalism?: The Kilburn Manifesto*, Lawrence & Wishart, 2015; David Harvey, *A Brief History of Neoliberalism*, Oxford University Press, 2007; Alfredo Saad-Filho and Deborah Johnston, *Neoliberalism: A Critical Reader*, University of Chicago Press, 2005; Noam Chomsky, *Profit Over People: Neoliberalism and Global Order*, Seven Stories Press, 1999.

7 Natalie Goldstein, *Globalization and Free Trade*, Infobase Publishing, 2007.

8 Andrew Beer, Rebecca Bentley, Emma Baker, Kate Mason, Shelley Mallett, Anne Kavanagh and Tony LaMontagne, 'Neoliberalism, Economic Restructuring and Policy Change: Precarious Housing and Precarious Employment in Australia' (2016) 53(8) *Urban Studies* 1542–58.

and professions to resist the negative impacts of neoliberalism.[9] In this sense, creating positive and healthy workplaces that support the wellbeing of individual workers in the workplace takes on significance at a macro-global level.

Within the neoliberal discourse, the neoliberal university has also come under significant scholarly scrutiny,[10] as has the impact of this contemporary paradigm on law schools.[11] The corporatisation of universities and the commodification of knowledge are central criticisms, alongside the treatment of students as consumers and increased workload pressures for academics to 'do more with less'.[12] Universities are held to account on the basis of league tables of relative and questionable validity, and funding is linked to evidence of excellence in performance and quantities of outputs.[13] There has been significant growth in higher education with

---

9 Dennis K. Mumby, Robyn Thomas, Ignasi Martí and David Seidl, 'Resistance Redux' (2017) 38(9) *Organization Studies* 1157–83.

10 Richard Hil, *Whackademia: An Insider's Account of the Troubled University*, NewSouth Publishing, 2012; Richard Hil, *Selling Students Short: Why You Won't Get the University Education You Deserve*, Allen & Unwin, 2015; Catherine Manathunga and Dorothy Bottrell (eds), *Resisting Neoliberalism in Higher Education Volume II*, Palgrave Macmillan, 2019; Ivar Bleiklie, 'New Public Management or Neoliberalism, Higher Education' in J.C. Shin and P. Teixeira (eds), *Encyclopedia of International Higher Education Systems and Institutions*, Springer, 2018.

11 Paula Baron, 'Working the Clock: The Academic Body on Neoliberal Time' (2014) 4(2) *Somatechnics* 253–71; Paula Baron, 'A Dangerous Cult: Response to the Effect of the Market on Legal Education' (2013) 23 *Legal Education Review* 273; Nikki Sullivan and Jane Simon, 'Academic Work Cultures: Somatic Crisis in the Enterprise University' (2014) 4(2) *Somatechnics* 205–18; Richard Collier, '"Love Law, Love Life": Neoliberalism, Well-being and Gender in the Legal Profession – The Case of Law School' (2014) 17(2) *Legal Ethics* 202–30; Margaret Thornton, 'Neoliberal Melancholia: The Case of Feminist Legal Scholarship' (2004) 20(1) *Australian Feminist Law Journal* 7–22; Margaret Thornton, 'Among the Ruins: Law in the Neo-Liberal Academy' (2001) 20 *Windsor Year Book of Access to Justice* 3; Margaret Thornton, 'The Law School, the Market and the New Knowledge Economy' (2007) 17 *Legal Education Review* 1; Margaret Thornton, *Privatising the Public University: The Case of Law*, Routledge, 2011.

12 Gail Kinman, 'Doing More with Less? Work and Well-being in Academics' (2014) 4(2) Somatechnics 219–35; Judy Szekeres, 'General Staff Experiences in the Corporate University' (2006) 28(2) *Journal of Higher Education Policy and Management* 133–45.

13 F. King Alexander, 'The Changing Face of Accountability: Monitoring and Assessing Institutional Performance in Higher Education' (2000) 71(4) *The Journal*

the 'massification' of tertiary education, resulting in increased numbers of both students and institutions;[14] higher education systems are increasingly complex, costly and subject to political agendas;[15] controlling management and micro-management result in a loss of autonomy; and more and more importance is attributed to higher education in terms of the employability of individuals and the economic prosperity of societies.[16] A focus on the 'productivity, efficiency, and relevance of academic activities' has diminished the perceived value of the activities of higher education. The modern university is no longer a 'republic of scholars' but rather a 'corporate enterprise',[17] with some commentators acknowledging such developments by referring to the 'McDonaldization of higher education'.[18] Others assert that the neoliberal university is 'antithetical to traditional conceptualisations of academic autonomy and collegiality'.[19]

---

of Higher Education 411–31; Kevin J. Dougherty and Rebecca S. Natow, *The Politics of Performance Funding for Higher Education: Origins, Discontinuations, and Transformations*, Johns Hopkins University Press, 2015.

14 Ulrich Teichler, 'Massification: A Challenge for Institutions of Higher Education' (1998) 4(1) *Tertiary Education & Management* 17–27; Ka Ho Mok and Deane Neubauer, 'Higher Education Governance in Crisis: A Critical Reflection on the Massification of Higher Education, Graduate Employment and Social Mobility' (2016) 26(1) *Journal of Education and Work* 1–12; David J. Hornsby and Ruksana Osman, 'Massification in Higher Education: Large Classes and Student Learning' (2014) 67(6) *Higher Education* 711–19; Malcolm Tight, 'Mass Higher Education and Massification' (2019) 32(1) *Higher Education Policy* 93–108.

15 Sheila Slaughter and Larry L. Leslie, *Academic Capitalism: Politics, Policies, and the Entrepreneurial University*, The Johns Hopkins University Press, 1997; Jeffrey R. Di Leo, *Academe Degree Zero: Reconsidering the Politics of Higher Education*, Routledge, 2015.

16 Bleiklie, above n. 10, 1. See also John W. Meyer and Francisco Ramírez, 'The World Institutionalization of Education' in Jürgen Schriewer (ed), *Discourse Formation in Comparative Education*, Peter Lang Publishers, 2000, 111–32.

17 Nils Brunsson and Kerstin Sahlin-Andersson, 'Constructing Organizations: The Example of the Public Sector Reform' (2000) 21 *Organization Studies* 721–46; Christine Musselin, 'Are Universities Specific Organizations?' in Georg Krücken, Anna Kosmützky and Marc Torka (eds), *Towards a Multiversity? Universities Between Global Trends and National Traditions*, Transcript Verlag, 2007; Guy Neave, 'The Evaluative State Reconsidered' (1998) 33(3) *European Journal of Education* 265–84.

18 The term 'McDonaldization' was coined by George Ritzer in his 1998 work *The McDonaldization of Society*, Pine Forge Press. See also Dennis Hayes and Robin Wynyard, *The McDonaldization of Higher Education*, Bergin & Garvey, 2002.

19 Kinman, above n. 12, 219.

3. AN ETHICAL IMPERATIVE TO INTERROGATE THE QUALITY OF WORKING LIFE FOR LAW TEACHERS

In this contemporary neoliberal environment, universities as employers have legal and ethical duties to their staff in relation to the experience of the workplace and the reduction of stressors and negative impacts on the psychological wellbeing of those staff. Parker defines an ethic in terms of 'what is the good or right thing to do in particular circumstances'.[20] In tertiary education institutions, ethics are the principles and values which regulate the moral behaviour and choices of leaders and managers. The ethical question of what universities should do, given what is becoming known about the impact of neoliberalism on the university as a workplace, is clear. The ethical and moral thing to do – what universities and law schools 'ought to do' – is actively to seek to better understand the nature of the quality of working life in the neoliberal law school, and strategise and consult with staff about how issues of poor working life quality can constructively be addressed. This study is one step in such a process that hopefully can inform workplace reform in law schools in Australia and the UK, and perhaps beyond.

As noted above, universities have both ethical and legal duties in relation to the issue of law teacher wellbeing. The law of torts, and its subset the law of negligence, are relevant here. Legally, negligence can be established where a duty of care is owed and breached, and where the breach results in the causation of harm. It would be a complex evidentiary matter to prove such a tort, but nevertheless it is a possibility.[21] Whilst risk assessment in relation to potential tortious liability for law schools is a less admirable reason for reformative action than ethical drivers, it nevertheless may be one way to ensure that institutional leaders take issues of wellbeing in the neoliberal university seriously, and is at least deserving of further analytical attention – although this is outside the scope of the present chapter.

---

20 Christine Parker, 'A Critical Morality for Lawyers: Four Approaches to Lawyers' Ethics' (2004) 30 *Monash University Law Review* 49, 51.

21 Our Wellness Network for Law colleague Dr. Lloyd England has made a persuasive case for such a tort in the context of law student experience of psychological distress through legal education: Lloyd England, 'Buttercup Sues Her Law School – Tertiary Legal Education Providers' Liability in the Tort of Negligence Not to Cause Pure Mental Harm: Duty of Care', Paper presented to the Wellness for Law Forum, 15–16 February 2018, Bond University, Gold Coast, Australia.

The next sections discuss the authors' research methodology and results and present the thematic analysis of the qualitative narratives that law teachers provided in response to the open question: 'Please explain what you think your university could do to improve staff quality of working life.'

4. METHODOLOGY

This project has been designed to identify the perceptions of stress among Australian legal educators and to enable comparisons with results of a similar project in the UK which began with a survey of UK law teachers in 2015.[22] While there has been significant research conducted in Australia on the stress levels and wellbeing of law students,[23] there has been relatively little on those of legal educators.[24] This project assumes that legal educators have a role to play in the psychological wellbeing of their students, so it is important that law schools implement strategies to support the wellbeing of law teachers themselves, not only to enable the legal educators to manage their own psychological health and to thrive in the contemporary law school paradigm, but also for them to have the capacity to promote psychological wellbeing in their students.

The UK project was led by Dr. Clare Wilson and Caroline Strevens at the University of Portsmouth, following a pilot UK project in 2014 which involved 30 in-depth interviews with legal educators on topics that included their perceptions of wellbeing of law students and of law teachers.

---

22 See further, Clare J. Wilson and Caroline Strevens, 'Perceptions of Psychological Well-Being in UK Law Academics' (2018) 52(3) *The Law Teacher* 335–49.

23 Norm Kelk et al., *Courting the Blues: Attitudes towards Depression: Australian Law Students and Legal Practitioners*, Brain and Mind Research Institute, 2009; Catherine Leahy et al., 'Distress Levels and Self-Reported Treatment Rates for Medicine, Law, Psychology and Mechanical Engineering Tertiary Students: Cross-Sectional Study' (2010) 44 *Australian and New Zealand Journal of Psychiatry* 608; Beaton and Beyondblue, *Mental Health in the Workplace: A Joint Initiative between Beaton Research & Consulting and beyondblue* (2011); Molly Townes O'Brien et al., 'Changing Our Thinking: Empirical Research on Law Student Well-being, Thinking Styles and the Law Curriculum' (2011) 21 *Legal Education Review* 149–82. In 2015, Pauline Collins led a team of researchers in a multidisciplinary pilot study into stress and anxiety of law teachers at the University of Southern Queensland and the data are currently being analysed.

24 We are not aware of any other national survey of Australian and UK law teachers specifically.

The UK pilot results suggested that while legal educators were concerned about their students' wellbeing, they were less willing to discuss their own experiences or share their own levels of stress.[25] The researchers suggested one reason for this reluctance might be the presence of unresolved issues (that is, a lack of action on the part of management when issues had been raised in the past). A subsequent questionnaire was developed and distributed with the help of the UK Law Learned Societies and resulted in 185 completed responses in 2015.[26]

Subsequently an international collaboration was formed in order to widen the scope of the population sample and increase rigour and significance, and a second UK survey took place in 2017 contemporaneously with an Australian survey. A total of 132 completed UK questionnaires were collected. The two surveys were not identical, but the comparisons made in this chapter are drawn from several questions that were alike.

The Australian study was conducted in 2017 by Colin James from the Australian National University and Rachael Field from Bond University. They adapted the UK questionnaire for the Australian legal education context and with the help of Law Deans and Heads of Schools the survey was distributed by email to teaching academics in all Australian law schools and the College of Law. A total of 161 completed questionnaires were collected using a Qualtrics programme and returned for analysis.

The survey included open and closed questions. The narratives found in the survey data of open questions are a snap-shot of a small sample of self-selecting law teachers. Qualitative methods accommodate small sample sizes because the aim is not to prove theory but rather to explore phenomena and perceptions. A sample size of more than 20 participants is a standard-to-large sample size for a thematic, phenomenographical analysis and when analysed alongside the pertinent literature, the responses provide some illuminating preliminary insights which can inform the development of the authors' further research in this area.

It is important to highlight that the key focus of the study reported in this chapter – which the authors plan to continue to implement to achieve longitudinal data in both jurisdictions – was to develop a deeper understanding of the experience of the stressors of the contemporary

---

25 LERN (Legal Education Research Network) funded part of this work and the findings are reported here: https://ials.sas.ac.uk/sites/default/files/files/About%20us/Leadership%20%26%20Collaboration/LERN/LERN_Final_Report(CS)_Perceptions_of_wellbeing_in_Law_Teachers.pdf.

26 Wilson and Strevens, above n. 22.

law school as a workplace. Emphatically no claim is made that the data necessarily proves these perceptions, neither are generalisable claims made. Rather, in adopting a phenomenographical conceptual framework for the study, the authors received a snap-shot of the perceptions of a good number of legal educators across both jurisdictions. This snap-shot, when considered in the light of the scholarly literature and critique of the impact of neoliberalism on modern universities and law schools, offers insights into the experience of common stressors at law school.

Phenomenography is a qualitative, interpretivist research methodology that explores the different ways in which people understand the same concept or phenomenon.[27] This research methodology originated in the late 1970s in education research;[28] however it is now used extensively across a range of diverse disciplines such as guidance and counselling research,[29] health care,[30] physics and economics.[31] Phenomenographical approaches to the gathering and analysis of data are anchored in the understanding that lived experience is subjective, and individuals experience the world differently through different lenses.

> Phenomenography is focused on the ways of experiencing different phenomena, ways of seeing them, knowing about them and having skills related to them. The aim is, however, not to find the singular essence, but the

27 See for example, John A. Bowden and Eleanor Walsh (eds), *Phenomenography*, RMIT University Press, 2000; Gerlese Åkerlind, 'Variation and Commonality in Phenomenographic Research Methods' (2005) 24(4) *Higher Education Research & Development* 321; Ference Marton, 'Phenomenography – Describing Conceptions of the World Around Us' (1981) 10 *Instructional Science* 177; Ference Marton, 'Phenomenography – A Research Approach Investigating Different Understandings of Reality' (1986) 21(2) *Journal of Thought* 28; Lennart Svensson, 'Theoretical Foundations of Phenomenography' (1997) 16(2) *Higher Education Research & Development* 159.

28 See for example, Michal Prosser and Keith Trigwell, 'Using Phenomenography in the Design of Programs for Teachers in Higher Education' (1997) 16(1) *Higher Education Research & Development* 41.

29 Jaana Kettunen and Päivi Tynjälä, 'Applying Phenomenography in Guidance and Counselling Research' (2018) 46(1) *British Journal of Guidance & Counselling* 1–11.

30 Alan Barnard, Heather Mccosker and Rod Gerber, 'Phenomenography: A Qualitative Research Approach for Exploring Understanding in Health Care' (1999) 9(2) *Qualitative Health Research* 212–26.

31 Ming-Fai Pang and Ference Marton, 'Learning Theory as Teaching Resource: Enhancing Students' Understanding of Economic Concepts' (2005) 33(2) *Instructional Science* 159; Eleanor Walsh et al., 'Physics Students' Understanding of Relative Speed: A Phenomenographic Study' (1993) 30(9) *Journal of Research in Science Teaching* 1133.

variation and the architecture of this variation by different aspects that define the phenomena.[32]

The remainder of the chapter focuses on the qualitative data obtained in answer to the open question: 'Please explain what you think your university could do to improve staff quality of working life.' The extensive and detailed written narratives provided through the question were coded by the research team through a triangulated process, and the dominant themes were identified quite quickly. The authors nevertheless acknowledge that in future work a stronger alignment with phenomenographical methods is likely to involve the use of in-depth interviews in addition to the survey instrument.[33]

In analysing the data, the research team has drawn on the principles of self-determination theory (SDT) which include the importance of intrinsic over extrinsic motivation and the 'psychological needs triad' of autonomy, competence and relatedness.[34] The SDT model provides a good filter for critical analysis of experience in qualitative research. In a law school context, it holds that both students and teachers would benefit from a focus on intrinsic motivation and the three psychological needs being addressed. Many of the participants' comments below suggest that the drift towards neoliberal management and control in law schools aligns with extrinsic motivations and is not consistent with meeting the psychological needs of either staff or students.

---

32 Ference Marton and Shirley Booth, *Learning and Awareness*, Routledge, 2013; Caroline Walker, 'Learning to Learn, Phenomenography and Children's Learning' (1998) 15 *Educational and Child Psychology* 25–33.

33 Jörgen Sandbergh, 'Are Phenomenographic Results Reliable?' (1997) 16(2) *Higher Education Research & Development* 203. For some critical perspectives on phenomenography and its theory see for example, John Te Richardson, 'The Concepts and Methods of Phenomenographic Research' (1999) 69(1) *Review of Educational Research* 53; Graham Webb, 'Deconstructing Deep and Surface: Towards a Critique of Phenomenography' (1997) 33(2) *Higher Education* 195.

34 Richard M. Ryan and Edward L. Deci, 'Self-Determination Theory and the Facilitation of Intrinsic Motivation, Social Development, and Well-Being' (2000) 55(1) *American Psychologist* 68–78; Gordon B. Spence and Edward L. Deci, 'Self-Determination Theory Within Coaching Contexts: Supporting Motives and Goals that Promote Optimal Functioning and Well-Being' in David Clutterbuck, David Megginson and Susan David (eds), *Beyond Goals: Effective Strategies for Coaching and Mentoring*, Gower Publishing, 2013; Christopher B. Niemiec and Richard M. Ryan, 'Autonomy, Competence and Relatedness in the Classroom: Applying Self-Determination Theory to Educational Practice' (2009) 7(2) *Theory and Research in Education* 133–44.

5. METHODOLOGICAL LIMITATIONS

In terms of methodological limitations, one question was duplicated in the first release of the Australian questionnaire and another question was not included. The error was corrected by amending the questionnaire on 1 March 2017, removing the duplication and adding the missing 'question' which was '3. I have the opportunity to use my abilities at work'. Consequently, that question was answered by only 96 participants. One participant suggested that a question about opportunities for upward mobility could have been included as this was regarded as a possible factor in the job satisfaction of many law teachers. Finally, whilst the law teacher narratives about the quality of their working life constitute a rich and indicative data set, the number of responses compared to the overall number of law teachers invited to participate in both countries is low, and statistically significant conclusions cannot be claimed.

6. DEMOGRAPHICS

Respondents in the Australian study included 105 women, 50 men, two transgender and three people who chose not to disclose their gender. Most were employed full-time (75%); most had worked in legal practice before becoming an academic (73%); and most currently worked at a law school in a publicly funded university (83%).

The demographics of the UK study included 83 women, 48 men, and one person who chose not to disclose their gender. Most did not have a second job (78%) and unlike Australia, there were equal numbers of participants who had worked in legal practice prior to becoming an academic compared with those who had not. Over 90% of the UK participants worked in a publicly-funded university.

7. SATISFACTION AT WORK[35]

Whilst the key aim was to explore the perception of workplace stress experienced by law teachers, as evidenced by the discussion below of the

35 Unless otherwise specified 'agree' in this chapter includes 'strongly agree' and 'disagree' includes 'strongly disagree'.

thematic analysis of qualitative responses, the authors did seek to gain an overall understanding of law teacher satisfaction at work. More detailed quantitative results are still under analysis and will be released in a later publication. In brief, on the survey questions regarding their experience in the work place, most Australian respondents claimed to be satisfied in their role, with more than two-thirds agreeing to having a clear set of goals to enable them to do their job (72%), claiming to be happy with their working hours (66%), and satisfied in general with their life (66%). On the other hand, less than half agreed that they could voice their opinions and influence changes in their area of work (45%), or that their line manager acknowledged their work when they did a good job (42%). In response to the statement that their employer provides what they need to do their job effectively, a significant minority (32%) disagreed, with only 51% agreeing.

Time is an important resource, and while only 43% agreed that their line manager promoted flexible work hours effectively, half of the respondents agreed they were pressured to work long hours and 38% believed they had unachievable deadlines. It seems that most could manage their work on time, although a significant majority (61%) either disagreed with or were neutral about the statement they had unachievable deadlines. Other recent developments include the neoliberal shift in language towards viewing students as customers, with 78% of respondents finding having to do that stressful.

The UK quantitative data reveals law teachers experience a similar level of satisfaction in their role. The proportion of academics that agreed that they had a clear set of goals was 60%, and 63% confirmed that their current working hours suited their personal circumstances. A slightly lower proportion (59%) were satisfied in general with their life. A similar proportion of UK academics (45%) agreed that they could voice opinions and influence change.

As far as perceptions of time management and workload are concerned, only 35% of the UK academics thought that their line manager actively promoted flexible working hours, but there was a similar percentage who were neutral and only 29% who disagreed. Similarly, there was a reasonably even spread of opinion about whether law teachers were pressured to work long hours, with 40% agreeing and 34% disagreeing. This spread of response was similar to the numbers agreeing that they had unachievable deadlines, with 41% agreeing and 34% disagreeing. Unlike the Australian law teacher results, a larger proportion of participants were neutral on these issues and this also included the response of 50% (compared to the 78% of Australian academics) who found the concept of students as consumers as opposed to learners stressful. One possible explanation for these differences is that the preponderance of staff working in a public university in the UK was far higher. Note, again, that the overall numbers are relatively low and not statistically significant, so caution must be exercised in drawing conclusions from these results.

8. QUALITATIVE DATA IN RESPONSE TO: 'PLEASE EXPLAIN WHAT YOU THINK YOUR UNIVERSITY COULD DO TO IMPROVE STAFF QUALITY OF WORKING LIFE'

Law teachers in both the UK and Australian studies gave wide-ranging responses to this question. The key themes identified from the coding of those responses concerned: administrative burden, teacher support, workload, management styles, transparency, strategic priorities, autonomy, communication and respect.

An important outcome is how similar the experiences are between UK and Australian law teachers, based on the priorities for change they identified for their respective university employers. While the question specifically referred to the quality of law teachers' working life, most of the responses in both countries were directly related to the law teachers' capacity to sustain the quality of their work or to improve. Many of the comments were critical of university management and systems; however, in general the respondents showed what could be described as a selfless professionalism by offering ideas oriented to improve the institution with an ultimate focus on benefiting the student experience of wellbeing, learning and development. While some comments related to the need for improved security of employment, relatively few referred to improved experiences or benefits for law teachers themselves.

Many participants in both countries critiqued the neoliberal changes to the structures and functions of their universities that commenced late in the last century, as discussed above. Most had experienced the changes as detrimental, not just to their experience as law teachers, but impacting negatively on institutional performance and the student experience. For example, several law teachers referred to the importance of language in creating expectations:

> Stop treating students like consumers, which is raising their expectations of staff to unattainable levels of 'customer service'.

Many claimed the over-use of expressions such as 'excellence' as a performance goal in both volume and quality of teaching and research to be unreasonable and illogical, which for one (Australian) respondent 'makes me feel that I am not good enough, no matter how hard I try'. A suggestion from another (UK) respondent was 'we all have individual strengths that should be praised rather than expect[ing] all domains to be excellent'.

8.1. ADMINISTRATIVE BURDEN

Many academics in both countries emphasised a need to reduce the amount of bureaucracy imposed on teachers. Increased bureaucratic demands were emphasised by many as an aspect of neoliberal changes moving in the 'wrong' direction because they are experienced as shifting teachers' time, energy and focus away from the core function of student education and development. One result of the 'obsession about centralising services' is that teachers in both countries felt 'micro-managed' with 'conflicting messages about priorities', which another described as 'knee-jerk contradictory'. There is, according to many in the UK, an 'admin drift of administrative tasks being devolved to academic staff'; 'tedious and unnecessary administrative changes and requirements'; managers are 'obsessed with statistics and REF [Research Excellence Framework] work'; flexible arrangements are difficult to negotiate; and management's consultation with law teachers is often experienced as superficial. A common theme here was:

> Get administrators to do administration and academics to do academic work.

Similarly, in Australia, significant numbers of law teachers noted a growing pressure from managers to report on their teaching activities 'based on metrics that [are] … not clearly linked to student learning', adding 'considerable stress and time without clear gains'. Teachers felt the same 'admin drift' caused by managers 'pushing administrative duties from administrators to academics'.

> Academics are increasingly performing large administrative tasks whilst simultaneously being required to deliver increasingly higher research and teaching outputs.

Many teachers are required to manage metrics through data entry and spread-sheet completion, form-filling duties that are time-consuming and detract from teaching preparations and quality interactions with students. Law teachers in both countries indicated a perception that much of the administrative burden imposed on teachers serves the interests of senior management and the university executive rather than benefiting students' learning and development in a meaningful way.

8.2. TEACHER SUPPORT

Law teachers in both countries used the qualitative question as an opportunity to express their disappointment and in some cases frustration at the level of support provided by their universities. Their experience of being unsupported is consistent with the previous theme of being required to do increasing amounts of administrative work without relief from teaching or research obligations in response.

> Most of the time the permanent academics are doing admin while the actual teaching is being done by hired casuals.

The results are also consistent with the often-expressed perception that the university does not value teaching or student development, except for the student-feedback processes which, under the veil of student anonymity, are considered by many law teachers to be unfair and containing misinformed or mischievous critiques. Common suggestions for improved teaching support included: creating smaller classes by employing more teachers, reducing workload to enable teaching preparation and feedback on assessments, valuing teaching as much as research, providing support for dealing with difficult students and students with mental health issues, adopting the wellness guidelines for students and staff, and consulting better on teaching changes including explanations for executive decisions.

8.3. WORKLOAD

Related to both the call for better teaching support and the increased administrative burden on teachers is the identification by many participants in both countries of increased workloads that are becoming unmanageable.

> The risk of burn-out is extreme; it takes me some 30 minutes to wind down after a tutorial or lecture, and if it didn't, I know I wouldn't have given that session to the best of my ability.

While some reflect that working in legal practice was worse than teaching due to the demands of clients being more relentless than those of students, others observed that at least lawyers were paid appropriately: 'I'd be paid twice as much, or more'. UK teachers in particular claimed to have work overloads and several indicated they were at the point of resignation: 'in recent years I feel choked that it never seems to be enough', 'I work late into the evening and most weekends purely to keep on top of my workload', and more directly:

> My colleagues and I are exhausted. I cannot continue to perform or live this way and am actively looking to leave.
>
> Probably best to move somewhere else while [management] do whatever they want to rather than make further attempts to be listened to.
>
> We lose so many good colleagues due to their not being recognised.

Several respondents noted that workload reviews need to be done 'openly' and fairly, and with the process agreed. One teacher claimed to be working longer hours than before in commercial practice, whilst receiving only half the pay. Several in both countries claimed the lack of commercial sense in having highly-trained academics doing administrative 'form-filling' tasks that detracted from their core role as they understood it – teaching and student development.

8.4. MANAGEMENT STYLES, CONSULTATION AND TRANSPARENCY

Consistent with critiques of the neoliberal shift at the university level, many academics in both countries expressed a sense of distrust towards senior management and a belief the distrust was mutual. One respondent described this as a 'gulf' between the values of the university, focusing on extrinsic values 'such as the size of an atrium' being indicative of an institution having a world-class reputation and teachers who focus on the student experience of education and development.

Many teachers in both countries called for better line management within the law school. Specifically, several participants mentioned the importance of reducing bullying of teachers by managers or Heads of Faculty, and the failure to respond or adequately investigate when bullying allegations are raised. One respondent suggested that line managers should be capable and willing to engage in collaborative management rather than issuing decrees. Others suggested a tendency of universities to employ 'sociopaths' in management positions, as if that personality delivered more efficiency or speedier outcomes. On the other hand, some law teachers claimed their school needed stronger leadership, able to stand up for teachers and the quality of teaching against the unreasonable demands of university management.

An Australian law teacher observed that often 'mediocre academics' see transferring into management as a way forward. Others agreed that many managers were not good at management, as they failed to understand the importance of nurturing and mentoring staff to bring out their strengths. One example provided was a supervisor telling teachers 'to care less, be less thorough and be less efficient' in order to get through the increased workload, while this law teacher felt such an approach was contrary to their training as a legal professional.

Many observed that significant resources and management hours are spent justifying the latest 'restructure' that is driven more by university priorities and rankings instead of teachers' experiences of what policies and practices succeed in enhancing student education and development. Several teachers commented on how the frequency of change in university priorities impacts on academics, and not least through the increased administration burden of new forms and procedures.

> I am over restructuring. I cannot see the point.
>
> Do not re-invent everything every September.
>
> I find change fatigue one of the most challenging aspects of my working life.

Due possibly to inadequate transparency and lack of consultation, some teachers considered restructures as 'massive overhauls of structures for the sake of massive overhauls', which, since imposed from above, diminished the independence of law schools and risked damaging performance and morale.

8.5. STRATEGIC PRIORITIES

Consistent with critiques about management practices, responding academics were very critical of the changes attributed to neoliberal agendas. Central to these arrangements was the view that universities are no longer institutions for professional transformation and learning. Instead, like other businesses, universities now focus on selling their product and judge their success in the form of enrolment numbers. Some academics felt their university had no other option.

> The university is responding to global neoliberal competitiveness narratives in the same way as many other universities: students are consumers, decreasing public funding.

The end-effect for some academics has been to feel deflated and professionally compromised; no longer professionals in their own right, but workers subjected to evaluation and critique by consumer students who have increasing influence over what and how they are taught and how they are assessed:

> Anything a student wants, the student gets – people are scared to take the hard line because this will be undermined at faculty and university level.
>
> The university is too scared to be sued by students.

One consequence is that law teachers focus more on low-performing students to avoid complaints and appeals, leaving less time to nurture top performers, some of whom will lose focus and not achieve their best. Thus, law teachers feel academic standards are dropping while management see only a need to increase enrolment numbers and generate income.

> The university is driven by the money they make from bums on seats and this is particularly so with the glaring increase in international students for whom English is not their first language.

8.6. AUTONOMY

One example of neoliberal change has been to centralise administration by reducing staff in law schools and increasing numbers at university or faculty levels. As discussed above this change has increased the administrative burden on law teachers, which participants in this study say has consequently reduced their autonomy and time available for teaching preparation and student interactions.

Many academics indicated a lack of trust and confidence in university management, with some respondents recognising these feelings as probably mutual.

> [The university] could try acting with integrity rather than making statements about integrity and values while turning this place into somewhere I am no longer proud to work.

Increasing managers' level of trust could help reduce academics' experience of being micro-managed, which in turn could improve teachers' wellbeing. Some teachers indicated that the shift of power to the student through an institutional focus on student feedback and complaints undermined the autonomy of law teachers by accepting that 'students know better than lecturers about how and what they should be taught'.

8.7. COMMUNICATION AND RESPECT

Some academics report inadequate communication, being unsure of the structures and strategies in their organisation and, as a consequence, feeling unable to meaningfully contribute to decisions, changes or improvements. As a result, some teachers feel alienated from their university which in turn impacts their performance and wellbeing.

> For me, it all comes down to communication.
>
> The 'us' and 'them' culture can be extremely damaging for everybody, including students.

Several respondents felt consultation could be improved to make changes more effective and relevant to those impacted by new procedures:

> Managers [should be] listening to those who have to implement [changes], so as to appreciate the consequences on those who are directly affected.

9. A 'TO-DO' LIST FOR LAW SCHOOL LEADERS AND MANAGERS

Amongst those scholars who advocate for wellbeing in the law in Australia and the UK there is clear recognition that responsibility for addressing the mal-effects of neoliberalism on law schools as healthy workplaces lies predominantly with law school leaders and those with management decision-making power. This includes the Deans and Heads of School, the Executive of law faculties and schools, and the professoriate. Certainly, individual academics should also aim, as a part of a life well-lived, to optimise their wellbeing so as to 'flourish' in the academy.[36] As the authors have noted, a further motivation for structural and cultural reform in law schools is to create a working environment in which law teachers have capacity to adequately support the wellbeing of their students, and thereby support student learning and development success. For this reason, the 'to-do' list here draws on the structural and cultural reforms which the data has indicated are necessary to address the key stressors that law teachers are managing in contemporary times.

- Workload: Rethink how workloads are calculated for transparency and fairness.
- Management styles: Compulsory communication and dispute resolution and leadership training for all staff entering management positions.
- Administrative burden: Seek creative solutions for managing the administrative burden; acknowledge this burden in the workload; analyse the efficiency costs of appointing additional administrative staff to relieve academics of some tasks.
- Confusion about strategic priorities (research and teaching): Clarify Faculty strategic priorities and how they impact on staff workload management; develop policies through collegial and collaborative processes combined with leadership decision-making.
- Reduced autonomy: Acknowledge the autonomy that does exist, acknowledge staff concerns about reduction in autonomy, support staff to maximise their sense of autonomy.

---

36 Martin E. Seligman, *Authentic Happiness: Using the New Positive Psychology to Realize Your Potential for Lasting Fulfillment*, Simon and Schuster, 2002; Martin E. Seligman, *Flourish: A Visionary New Understanding of Happiness and Well-Being*, Simon and Schuster, 2012.

- Lack of communication: Improve communication across the law school – between academic and administrative staff, between management and staff 'on the ground'.
- Lack of transparency: Develop approaches to fairly increase transparency in decision-making (see also Workload above).
- Lack of respect: Instil an ethic of service leadership in management and the professoriate, thus modelling respect, and explicit encouragement and support of staff.

10. CONCLUSION

The fact that so many law teachers took the opportunity through the qualitative question to express frustration about their working conditions and their impact on their wellbeing, suggests that universities have not succeeded in recognising these issues as constituting legitimate concerns.

Many participants critiqued their universities' selling of education as a commodity in a market transaction, rather than offering students a supported process of learning and professional transformation. One teacher succinctly captured a range of concerns impacting the wellbeing of many participants:

> I feel as if I am being pulled in too many directions: admin, teaching, research partnership working, increased pastoral support for students.

As we noted at the outset of this chapter, a central motivation in understanding the experience of work stress in law schools is concern for the support and promotion of law students' learning success. Academics who are well will not only be able to flourish in their professional lives; they will also have capacity to support student wellbeing and thereby student learning.

PART III

TECHNOLOGY, INNOVATION AND THE STRUCTURE OF LEGAL PRACTICE

CHAPTER 7

BEHAVIOURAL LEGAL ETHICS AND ATTORNEY WELLBEING IN CONTEMPORARY PRACTICE

Jennifer K. ROBBENNOLT*

1. Introduction ... 155
2. Ethics and Wellbeing ... 156
   2.1. Ethics and Professionalism ... 156
   2.2. Wellbeing ... 159
   2.3. The Relationship between Ethics and Wellbeing ... 161
3. Substance Abuse and Mental Health ... 163
4. Factors in the Modern Legal Profession that Influence Both Ethics and Wellbeing ... 165
   4.1. Adversarialism ... 166
   4.2. Time and Financial Pressure ... 167
   4.3. Leadership and Culture ... 172
5. Conclusion ... 174

1. INTRODUCTION

Contemporary legal practice has much to recommend it. The practice of law can involve intellectually stimulating work, engagement with issues that are important to society and to individual clients, opportunities for problem solving, career-long learning and development, and much more.

* My thanks go to NICOLE DIORIO for her outstanding research assistance and to MATT BRAUN of the University of Illinois College of Law Library.

But legal practice also has its challenges. Aspects of the work can be repetitive, structural changes in the profession have put pressure on firms and attorneys, and new technologies are changing the ways law is practised. While most lawyers report being satisfied in their work, others are dissatisfied. And many, while satisfied overall, are unhappy with particular aspects of the profession. Some are concerned in particular about the effects of the modern practice environment on attorney wellbeing. Others are concerned about the state of ethics and professionalism in the practice of law. These two concerns are related – attorney wellbeing has implications for legal ethics, ethics have implications for attorney wellbeing, and there are a number of aspects of the profession that have implications for both.

2. ETHICS AND WELLBEING

2.1. ETHICS AND PROFESSIONALISM

Legal practice can present difficult ethical challenges for lawyers. The legal environment in which these challenges are faced is often defined by complex and ambiguous ethical rules and standards, agency relationships, and the ethos of an adversarial system.[1] Modern lawyers, moreover, practise in a world of financial and temporal pressures, new billing models, changing firm structures, increasing globalisation, and advances in technology. Issues of appropriate disclosure, confidentiality, conflicts of interest, candour and deception, communication, billing, competence, and more come up across practice settings. Whether a lawyer is in private practice or public service, a member of a large firm or in solo practice, doing litigation or transactional work, practising in the civil or criminal arena, or working as a judge, ethical issues pervade the work of lawyers.

Some ethical issues involve violations of the formal disciplinary rules of the profession and may or may not manifest in formal complaints. A survey by the American Bar Association found that 108,902 ethics complaints were made against US lawyers in 2016.[2] Charges were brought

---

1 J.K. Robbennolt and J.R. Sternlight, 'Behavioral Legal Ethics' (2013) 45 *Arizona State Law Journal* 1107. See generally P.J. Schiltz, 'On Being a Happy, Healthy, and Ethical Member of an Unhappy, Unhealthy, and Unethical Profession' (1999) 52 *Vanderbilt Law Review* 871, 874.

2 *Survey on Lawyer Discipline Systems (S.O.L.D.)*, American Bar Association Center for Professional Responsibility, Chicago 2016, p. 7.

against 3,017 lawyers after probable cause hearings.[3] In addition to ethical issues that involve violation of the formal disciplinary rules, ethics are also implicated in situations not addressed by the formal rules or where the rules themselves are ambiguous. As former Supreme Court Justice Potter Stewart said: 'Ethics is knowing the difference between what you have a right to do and what is right to do.' An assessment of lawyer behaviour might also include issues of professionalism and civility, discrimination, harassment or bullying, or taking credit where credit is not due, whether or not they are regulated by the rules of ethics or rise to the level of being actionable under some other body of law.[4] Studies, for example, have found that lawyers report relatively high rates of bullying, harassment, or intimidation in their workplaces.[5]

Some lawyers may be 'bad apples' – knowingly engaging in unethical or unprofessional conduct to benefit themselves or their clients. Recent research by psychologists, however, suggests a more complex range of cognitive, situational, and social influences on ethical behaviour. These influences can mean that ethical missteps are easier to take than lawyers might realise, can nudge lawyers into acting in ways that are counter to their own ideals, and can contribute to the other pressures to act unethically that come from clients, colleagues, and self-interest.[6] Ethical 'blind spots', for example, can hamper our ability to identify and effectively manage

---

3 Ibid., p. 11. See also T. Sklar, Y. Taouk, D. Studdert, M. Spittal, R. Paterson and M. Bismark, 'Characteristics of Lawyers Who Are Subject to Complaints and Misconduct Findings' (2019) 16 *Journal of Empirical Legal Studies* 318.

4 'Ethics' in this context includes all of these issues of ethics and professionalism.

5 Acritas, 'What's Preventing Women Progressing to the Top Levels in Law?' <https://www.acritas.com/video-script-what%E2%80%99s-preventing-women-progressing-top-levels-law>. P. Baron, 'The Elephant in the Room: Lawyer Wellbeing and Impact of Unethical Behaviors' (2015) 41 *Australian Feminist Law Journal* 87, 96–97 (reviewing studies). L.S. Rikleen, *Survey of Workplace Conduct and Behaviors in Law Firms* (Womens Bar Association of Massachussetts 2019). S. Skolnik, 'More Than Third of Female Lawyers Harassed at Work, Survey Shows' [29.11.2018] Bloomberg Law <https://news.bloomberglaw.com/us-law-week/more-than-third-of-female-lawyers-harassed-at-work-survey-shows>. See also M. Omari and M. Paull, '"Shut Up and Bill": Workplace Bullying Challenges for the Legal Profession' (2013) 20 *International Journal of the Legal Profession* 141.

6 Robbennolt and Sternlight, above n. 1. J.K. Robbennolt, 'Behavioral Ethics Meets Legal Ethics' (2015) 11 *Annual Review of Law and Social Sciences* 75. M.H. Bazerman and F. Gino, 'Behavioral Ethics: Toward a Deeper Understanding of Moral Judgment and Dishonesty' (2012) 8 *Annual Review of Law and Social Science* 85. M.H. Bazerman and A.E. Tenbrunsel, *Blind Spots: Why We Fail To Do What's Right and What To Do About It*, Princeton University Press, Princeton, NJ 2011. D. De Cremer and A.E. Tenbrunsel, *Behavioral Business Ethics: Shaping an Emerging Field*, Routledge Academic, New York 2011. G. Giegerenzer, 'Moral Satisficing: Rethinking

ethical issues.[7] The ways in which behaviour changes gradually over time can make it difficult to recognise when that behaviour has crossed ethical lines.[8] It can be easy to mobilise justifications for unethical behaviour[9] or to distance or dissociate ourselves from the ethical implications of decisions.[10] How decisions are framed can influence ethical decision making.[11]

Morality as Bounded Rationality' (2010) 2 *Topics in Cognitive Science* 528. J.J. Kish-Gephart et al., 'Bad Apples, Bad Cases, and Bad Barrels: Meta-Analytic Evidence About Sources of Unethical Conduct at Work' (2010) 95 *Journal of Applied Psychology* 1. B. Monin and A.H. Jordan, 'The Dynamic Moral Self: A Social Psychological Perspective' in D. Narvaez (ed), *Personality, Identity, and Character: Explorations in Moral Psychology*, Cambridge University Press, New York, 2009, p. 341. L.K. Trevino, 'Ethical Decision Making in Organizations: A Person-Situation Interactionist Model' (1986) 11 *Academy of Management Review* 601. L.K. Trevino et al., 'Behavioral Ethics in Organizations: A Review' (2006) 32 *Journal of Management* 961.

7 D. Chugh et al., 'Bounded Ethicality as a Psychological Barrier to Recognizing Conflicts of Interest' in D.A. Moore et al. (eds), *Conflicts of Interest: Challenges and Solutions in Business, Law, Medicine, and Public Policy*, Cambridge University Press, New York 2005, pp. 74, 80. See also E. Pronin et al., 'Objectivity in the Eye of the Beholder: Divergent Perceptions of Bias in Self Versus Others' (2004) 111 *Psychological Review* 781; R.F. West et al., 'Cognitive Sophistication Does Not Attenuate the Bias Blind Spot' (2012) 103 *Journal of Personality and Social Psychology* 506.

8 F. Gino and M.H. Bazerman, 'When Misconduct Goes Unnoticed: The Acceptability of Gradual Erosion on Others' Unethical Behavior' (2009) 45 *Journal of Experimental Social Psychology* 708. A.E. Tenbrunsel and D.M. Messick, 'Ethical Fading: The Role of Self-Deception in Unethical Behavior' (2004) 17 *Social Justice Research* 223, 224.

9 A. Pittarello, M. Leib, T. Gordon-Hecker and S. Shalvi, 'Justifications Shape Ethical Blind Spots' (2015) 26 *Psychological Science* 794, 804. M.E. Schweitzer and C.K. Hsee, 'Stretching the Truth: Elastic Justification and Motivated Communication of Uncertain Information' (2002) 25 *Journal of Risk and Uncertainty* 185, 201. S. Shalvi, J. Dana, M.J.J. Handgraaf and C.K.W. Dreu, 'Justified Ethicality: Observing Desired Counterfactuals Modifies Ethical Perceptions and Behavior' (2011) 115 *Organization Behavior and Human Decision Processes* 181, 190. S. Shalvi, O. Eldar and Y. Bereby-Meyer, 'Honesty Requires Time and Lack of Justifications' (2012) 23 *Psychological Science* 1264, 1270. S. Shalvi, F. Gino, R. Barkan and S. Ayal, 'Self-Serving Justifications: Doing Wrong and Feeling Moral' (2015) 24 *Current Directions in Psychological Science* 125, 130. E.L. Uhlmann, D.A. Pizarro, D. Tannenbaum and P.H. Ditto, 'The Motivated Use of Moral Principles' (2009) 4 *Judgment and Decision Making* 479, 491.

10 A. Bandura, 'Moral Disengagement in the Perpetuation of Inhumanities' (1999) 3 *Personality and Social Psychology* 193, 209. D.M. Bersoff, 'Why Good People Sometimes Do Bad Things: Motivated Reasoning and Unethical Behavior' (1999) 25 *Personality and Social Psychology Bulletin* 28, 29. J.R. Detert et al., 'Moral Disengagement in Ethical Decision Making: A Study of Antecedents and Outcomes' (2008) 93 Journal of Applied Psychology 374.

11 J.S. Cameron and D.T. Miller, 'Ethical Standards in Gain Versus Loss Frames' in D. De Cremer (ed), *Psychological Perspectives on Ethical Behavior and Decision Making*, Information Age Publishing, Charlotte, NC 2009, p. 91. C.P.R. Folmer and

Social norms influence people's sense of what behaviour is appropriate.[12] And it can be difficult to make good predictions about how ethically we will act in a particular moment.[13]

2.2. WELLBEING

Many lawyers report being relatively satisfied with both their jobs and their lives in general.[14] At the same time, however, lawyers experience varying degrees of satisfaction and dissatisfaction, a significant minority of lawyers are notably distressed, and dissatisfaction can originate from a range of sources. Attorneys, for example, tend to be more satisfied with some aspects of their jobs than others. They tend to be relatively satisfied with the level of responsibility they are afforded, the degree of control they

---

D. De Cramer, 'Bad for Me or Bad for us? Interpersonal Orientations and the Impact of Losses on Unethical Behavior' (2012) 38 *Personality Social Psychology Bulletin* 760. M.C. Kern and D. Chugh, 'Bounded Ethicality: The Perils of Loss Framing' (2009) 20 *Psychological Science* 387.

12 F. Gino et al., 'Contagion and Differentiation in Unethical Behavior: The Effect of One Bad Apple on the Barrel' (2009) *Psychological Science* 393. F. Gino et al., 'Contagion or Restitution? When Bad Apples Can Motivate Good Behavior' (2009) 45 *Journal of Experimental Social Psychology* 1299. M.J. O'Fallon and K.D. Butterfield, 'The Influence of Unethical Peer Behavior on Observers' Unethical Behavior: A Social Cognitive Perspective' (2012) 109 *Journal of Business Ethics* 117. A.M. Perlman, 'Unethical Obedience by Subordinate Attorneys: Lessons from Social Psychology' (2007) 36 *Hofstra Law Review* 451.

13 Y. Kivetz and T.R. Tyler, 'Tomorrow I'll Be Me: The Effects of Time Perspective on the Activation of Idealistic Versus Pragmatic Selves' (2007) 102 *Organizational Behavioral and Human Decision Processes* 193. See also H.E. Hershfield et al., 'Short Horizons and Tempting Solutions: Lack of Continuity to Our Future Selves Leads to Unethical Decision Making and Behavior' (2012) 117 *Organizational Behavioral and Human Decision Processes* 298; D. Read et al., 'Mixing Virtue and Vice: Combining the Immediacy Effect and Diversification Heuristic' (1999) 12 *Journal of Behavioral Decision Making* 257.

14 R. Dinovitzer and B. Garth, 'Lawyer Satisfaction in the Process of Structuring Legal Careers' (2007) 41 *Law and Society Review* 1. T.W. Smith, 'Job Satisfaction in the United States' [17.04.2007] National Opinion Research Center, University of Chicago <http://www-news.uchicago.edu/releases/07/pdf/070417.jobs.pdf>. J. Monahan and J. Swanson, 'Lawyers at Mid-Career: A 20-Year Longitudinal Study of Job and Life Satisfaction' (2009) 6 *Journal of Empirical Legal Studies* 451, 469–75. J. Monahan and J. Swanson, 'Lawyers at the Peak of Their Careers: A 30-Year Longitudinal Study of Job and Life Satisfaction' (2019) 16 *Journal of Empirical Legal Studies* 4. J.E. Wallace, *Juggling It All: A Study of Lawyers' Work, Home, and Family Demands and Coping Strategies: Report of Stage Two Findings*, Law School Admission Council, Newton, PA 2004.

have over *how* they engage in their work, the intellectual challenge and problem-solving aspects of their work, and their relationships with their colleagues. In contrast, attorneys tend to be less satisfied with how they are evaluated, the (lack of) opportunities they have to engage in pro bono work, their (lack of) control over the *amount* of work that they have to do, and the degree to which they perceive their work as being of value to society.[15]

Even these findings can vary by practice setting and many practice settings may be characterised by a mix of high positives and high negatives. When it comes to the social value of their work or their work–life balance, lawyers in private practice tend to be less satisfied than lawyers working in government settings. On the other hand, lawyers in private practice tend to be more satisfied with the opportunities they have for intellectual challenge than lawyers in other practice settings. Attorneys in large private firms tend to be less satisfied overall and with their ability to control their workloads, but more satisfied with their income, prestige and opportunities for advancement.[16] One recent study of lawyers in the United States and

---

15 R. Dinovitzer and B. Garth, above n. 14, at 9. See also A.J. Bergin and A.J. Jimmieson, 'Australian Lawyer Well-Being: Workplace Demands, Resources, and Impact of Time Billing Targets' (2014) 21 *Psychiatry, Psychology and Law* 427 (18% dissatisfied). J. Chan, S. Poynton and J. Bruce, 'Lawyering Stress and Work Culture: An Australian Study' (2014) 37 *University of New South Wales Law Journal* 1062. J. Chan and H. Blackmore, 'Public Sector Lawyering Stress and Wellbeing: Neoliberalism at Work?' (2020) Chapter 5 of this volume; The Law Society, 'Resilience and Wellbeing Survey Report (Junior Lawyers Division)' [04.2018] <http://communities.lawsociety.org.uk/Uploads/p/d/i/jld-resilience-and-wellbeing-survey-report-2018.pdf>.

16 R.O. Lempert et al., 'Michigan's Minority Graduates in Practice: The River Runs Through Law School' (2000) 25 *Law & Social Inquiry* 395, 446. See K.G. Dau-Schmidt and K. Mukhopadhaya, 'The Fruits of Our Labors: An Empirical Study of the Distribution of Income and Job Satisfaction Across the Legal Profession' (1999) 49 *Journal of Legal Education* 342, 360–62. R. Dinovitzer and B. Garth, above n. 14, p. 22; K.E. Hull, 'Cross-Examining the Myth of Lawyers' Misery' (1999) 52 *Vanderbilt Law Review* 971. J. Monahan and J. Swanson, Lawyers at Mid-Career, above n. 14, p. 477. See generally L.S. Krieger and K.M. Sheldon, 'What Makes Lawyers Happy? A Data-Driven Prescription to Redefine Professional Success' (2015) 83 *George Washington Law Review* 554. J.M. Organ, 'What Do We Know About the Satisfaction/Dissatisfaction of Lawyers? A Meta-Analysis of Research on Lawyer Satisfaction and Well-Being' (2011) 8 *University of St. Thomas Law Journal* 225. For research on law students and wellbeing, see M. Dammeyer and N. Nunez, 'Anxiety and Depression Among Law Students: Current Knowledge and Future Directions' (1999) 23 *Law and Human Behavior* 55, 61. J.M. Organ, 'Suffering in Silence: The Survey of Law Student Well-Being and the Reluctance of Law Students to Seek Help for Substance Use and Mental Health Concerns' (2016) 66 *Journal of Legal Education* 116. T.D. Peterson and E.W. Peterson, 'Stemming the Tide of Law Student Depression: What Law

Canada found that higher status lawyers tend to have more mental health symptoms and no better physical health compared to lower status lawyers – a 'status-health paradox'.[17] This pattern is complicated by the fact that higher income and higher workplace stressors tend to co-occur.[18] Thus, while workplace stressors are associated with depression, high income tends to suppress those effects, making the gap between high and low status lawyers smaller than it might otherwise be. Conversely, while high income tends to be associated with better health outcomes, workplace stressors tend to suppress those benefits.[19]

Attorneys, therefore, may simultaneously be relatively satisfied overall, dissatisfied with particular aspects of their practice, and experiencing impaired levels of wellbeing. Many lawyers have problems with mental health, including depression, anxiety, feelings of inadequacy, loneliness, and other psychological problems; difficulties with substance abuse; and physical problems such as heart disease.[20] These problems can have harmful consequences for attorneys' health, relationships, personal life, job satisfaction, and ability to practise effectively and well.

2.3. THE RELATIONSHIP BETWEEN ETHICS AND WELLBEING

Commentators have begun to argue that attorney wellbeing and legal ethics and professionalism are 'inextricably tied together'[21] or 'inseparable'.[22]

Schools Need to Learn from the Science of Positive Psychology' (2009) 9 *Yale Journal of Health Policy, Law and Ethics* 357, 358. K.M. Sheldon and L.S. Krieger, 'Does Legal Education Have Undermining Effects on Law Students? Evaluating Changes in Motivation, Values, and Well-Being' (2004) 22 *Behavioral Sciences & the Law* 261.

17 J. Koltai, S. Scheiman and R. Dinovitzer, 'The Status-Health Paradox: Organizational Context, Stress Exposure, and Well-Being in the Legal Profession' (2018) 59 *Journal of Health and Social Behavior* 20.

18 Ibid.

19 Ibid.

20 See generally J. Chan, S. Poynton and J. Bruce, above n. 15. P.R. Krill, R. Johnson and L. Albert, 'The Prevalence of Substance Use and Other Mental Health Concerns Among American Attorneys' (2016) 10 *Journal of Addiction Medicine* 46, 48. S. Poynton and J. Chan, 'The Paradox of Satisfaction and Distress Amongst Lawyers: Implications for a Changing Field' (2020) Chapter 3 of this volume.

21 L.S. Krieger, 'The Most Ethical of People, the Least Ethical of People: Proposing Self-Determination Theory to Measure Professional Character Formation' (2011) 8 *University of St. Thomas Law Journal* 168.

22 L.S. Krieger, 'The Inseparability of Professionalism and Personal Satisfaction: Perspectives on Values, Integrity and Happiness' (2005) 11 *Clinical Law Review* 425.

These ties run in both directions – with ethics influencing wellbeing and wellbeing influencing ethics.

First, consider that attorneys' unethical behaviour has implications for wellbeing. Experiencing ethical conflict, for instance, can produce 'emotional exhaustion' and job dissatisfaction.[23] More broadly, unethical behaviour can affect the wellbeing of the direct target or victim, but also the wellbeing of the perpetrator, those who observe or learn about the behaviour, and others.[24] Each of these groups may experience increased workplace stress as a result of unethical behaviour, and may, variously, experience guilt, anger, shock, empathy, feelings of vulnerability, or other emotional reactions.[25] Anxiety and depression can result.[26] In addition, unethical behaviour can impact physical health – increasing unhealthy behaviours such as smoking or the over-consumption of alcohol, impacting sleep patterns, and negatively impacting cardiovascular health.[27] Not all unethical acts will produce decrements in wellbeing or decrease wellbeing to the same degree. Much will depend on the specifics of the behaviour, the extent to which it is perceived as unethical, its perceived severity, how the individual is situated as to the behaviour (for example, as perpetrator, victim, or observer), and a variety of individual differences.[28]

In the other direction, aspects of attorney wellbeing have implications for unethical behaviour. Dissatisfaction, lack of wellbeing, and related problems can result in basic ethical difficulties, including a lack of

---

R.R. Sims and W.I. Sauser, Jr., 'The Relationship Between Business Ethics and Job-Related Well-Being' in S. Valentine (ed), *Organizational Ethics and Stakeholder Well-Being in the Business Environment*, Information Age Publishing, Charlotte, N.C. 2014, p. 39. See generally M.H. Weresh, 'The Chicken or the Egg? Public Service Orientation and Lawyer Well-Being' (2014) 36 *University of Arkansas at Little Rock Law Review* 463 (arguing a link between wellbeing and professionalism/service).

23 J.D. Kammeyer-Muller, L.S. Simon and B.L. Rich, 'The Psychic Cost of Doing Wrong: Ethical Conflict, Divestiture Socialization, and Emotional Exhaustion' (2012) 38 *Journal of Management* 784, 785.

24 R.A. Giacalone and M.D. Promislo, 'Unethical and Unwell: Decrements in Well-Being and Unethical Activity at Work' (2010) 91 *Journal of Business Ethics* 275. P. Baron, above n. 5.

25 R.A. Giacalone and M.D. Promislo, above n. 24, p. 280.

26 Ibid., p. 285.

27 Ibid., p. 282.

28 Ibid., pp. 282–85. See also R.A. Giacalone, C.L. Jurkiewicz and M. Promislo, 'Ethics and Wellbeing: The Paradoxical Implications of Individual Differences in Ethical Orientation' (2016) 137 *Journal of Business Ethics* 491.

competence and diligence, and a lack of professionalism.[29] One recent report, for example, noted that, '[t]roubled lawyers can struggle with even minimum competence.'[30]

In addition, a variety of factors that we think of as impacting wellbeing may also impact ethics, and factors typically thought of as influencing ethics also have implications for wellbeing. And as we shall see, many aspects of modern legal practice have implications for both wellbeing and ethics or professionalism.

3. SUBSTANCE ABUSE AND MENTAL HEALTH

One way that a lack of wellbeing among lawyers manifests is through high rates of substance abuse, depression, and anxiety.[31] And, in turn, substance abuse is likely to diminish wellbeing, impair functioning, and contribute to ethical problems.

A recent study of US lawyers found that many lawyers (between 21% and 36%) reported engaging in problematic drinking behaviours.[32] These rates of problematic drinking are higher than those found for other highly-educated workers or for physicians.[33] One in five attorneys reported

29 A.J. Bergin and N.L. Jimmieson, above n. 15, p. 428 (distress can lead to ethical problems due to 'working more slowly, making more errors, being unable to concentrate and absenteeism'). *The Path to Lawyer Well-Being: Practical Recommendations for Positive Change*, American Bar Association, Chicago 2017, pp. 8–9. See also *Model Rules of Professional Conduct*, 2016 ed., American Bar Association, Chicago 2016 (rule 1.1 (Competence) and rule 1.3 (Diligence)).

30 *The Path to Lawyer Well-Being*, above n. 29.

31 See *At the Breaking Point: A National Conference on the Emerging Crisis in the Quality of Lawyers' Health and Its Impact on Law Firms and Client Services*, American Bar Association, Chicago 1991. A.J. Bergin and N.L. Jimmieson, above n. 29. L.S. Krieger and K.M. Sheldon, above n. 16; P.J. Schiltz, above n. 1, p. 874. For reviews, see N. Levit and D.O. Linder, *The Happy Lawyer: Making A Good Life In The Law*, Oxford University Press, New York 2010, pp. 3–7; J.M. Organ, 'What Do We Know About the Satisfaction/Dissatisfaction of Lawyers?', above n. 16.

32 P.R. Krill, R. Johnson and L. Albert, above n. 20, p. 48. For older studies, see C.J.A. Beck et al., 'Lawyer Distress: Alcohol-Related Problems and Other Psychological Concerns Among a Sample of Practicing Lawyers' (1995–96) 10 *Journal of Law and Health* 1; G.A.H. Benjamin et al., 'The Prevalence of Depression, Alcohol Abuse, and Cocaine Abuse Among United States Lawyers' (1990) 13 *International Journal of Law and Psychiatry* 233. See also P. Krill, 'ALM Survey on Mental Health and Substance Abuse: Big Law's Pervasive Problem' [14.09.2018] Law.com.

33 P.R. Krill, R. Johnson and L. Albert, above n. 20, p. 51 (reviewing studies).

behaviours that raised an intermediate level of concern for drug abuse and with another 3% raising substantial concern.[34] The study also found significant rates of mental health problems. Nineteen per cent reported symptoms of anxiety and 28% reported symptoms of depression.[35] Approximately one-quarter (23%) reported elevated levels of stress.[36] Lawyers also reported experiencing social anxiety (16%), attention deficit hyperactivity disorder (13%), panic disorder (8%), and bipolar disorder (2%).[37] Other studies have found that many lawyers use drugs or alcohol to manage stress.[38] Those who do so tend to report being 'more stressed and less in control'.[39]

Similarly, a recent study of Australian lawyers found that many lawyers reported symptoms of moderate to extremely severe depression (32%), anxiety (28%), and stress (26%).[40] Higher levels of depression, anxiety, and stress were associated with dissatisfaction with the nature of the job, the job setting, the social value of the job, the potential for advancement in the job, more over-commitment and work–family conflict, and practice settings characterised by competitiveness and long hours.[41] Almost one-third (32%) were at medium or high risk of problem drinking.[42] And mental health problems and problem drinking had some tendency to co-occur.[43]

A number of studies have shown that a high percentage of lawyers who become defendants in disciplinary cases have problems with drugs or alcohol or suffer from psychological problems such as depression.[44]

---

34 Ibid., p. 49.

35 Ibid., p. 50. See also W.W. Eaton et al., 'Occupations and the Prevalence of Major Depressive Disorder' (1990) 32 *Journal of Occupational Medicine* 1079.

36 P.R. Krill, R. Johnson and L. Albert, above n. 20, p. 50.

37 Ibid.

38 P.B. Pierson, A. Hamilton, M. Pepper and M. Root, 'Stress Hardiness and Lawyers' (2017) 42 *Journal of the Legal Profession* 1, 59.

39 Ibid.

40 J. Chan, S. Poynton and J. Bruce, above n. 15. See also A.J. Bergin and N.L. Jimmieson, above n. 15 (finding that 37% of the Australian lawyers in their sample showed symptoms of moderate to extremely severe depression and that 35% were positive for problem drinking).

41 J. Chan, S. Poynton and J. Bruce, above n. 15, pp. 1084–85.

42 Ibid., p. 1087.

43 Ibid. See also N. Kelk, G. Luscombe, S. Medlow and I. Hickie, *Courting the Blues: Attitudes towards Depression in Australian Law Students and Legal Practitioners*, Brain & Mind Research Institute, University of Sydney, Sydney 2009.

44 See e.g., Supreme Court of Illinois, Attorney Registration & Disciplinary Commission, 'Annual Report of 2017' [28.04.2018], p. 39 (Chart 21D) (finding that 29% of disciplined lawyers had at least one substance abuse or mental impairment issue); M. Seto, 'Killing Ourselves: Depression as an Institutional, Workplace, and Professionalism

This may not be surprising given that both depression and substance abuse are connected with impaired cognitive functioning – including effects on memory, attention, and problem solving.[45] A study that examined attorneys who were placed on probation for violations between 1981 and 2014 found that 24% had a mental health issue, 30% had a substance issue, 6% suffered from both mental health and substance abuse issues, and 4% had either a mental health or substance abuse problem in conjunction with other 'non-impairment' issues.[46]

Despite these problems, lawyers are often hesitant to seek treatment. Studies have found that not wanting others to know that they need help and concerns for privacy were the most commonly reported barriers to getting treatment.[47] Lawyers' disinclination to seek help for substance abuse and mental health difficulties can make wellbeing improvements elusive and can compound the potential for ethical missteps.

4. FACTORS IN THE MODERN LEGAL PROFESSION THAT INFLUENCE BOTH ETHICS AND WELLBEING

Not only do wellbeing and ethics influence each other, but there are many aspects of modern legal practice that have implications for *both* wellbeing and ethics or professionalism. In particular, the adversarial nature of legal practice, the time and financial pressures of modern practice, and the culture of legal workplaces can all have consequences for lawyer wellbeing and legal ethics.

Problem' (2012) 2 Western Journal of Western Studies 1 (describing Canadian data). See generally A. Elwork, *Stress Management for Lawyers*, 3rd edn., Vorkell Group, North Wales, P.A. 2007, p. 17. S. Daicoff, *Lawyer, Know Thyself: A Psychological Analysis of Personality Strengths and Weaknesses*, American Psychological Association, Washington D.C. 2004, p. 13.

45 *The Path to Lawyer Well-Being*, above n. 29, pp. 8–9.

46 Supreme Court of Illinois, Attorney Registration & Disciplinary Commission, 'Annual Report of 2014' [30.04.2015], p. 35.

47 P.R. Krill, R. Johnson and L. Albert, above n. 20, pp. 46, 48. P.B. Pierson, A. Hamilton, M. Pepper and M. Root, above n. 38, p. 13 (citing studies). See also D. Water, 'South Carolina Attorneys Look Inward to Address High Rates of Substance Abuse and Mental Illness' [26.09.2018] *Charleston City Paper* <https://www.charlestoncitypaper.com/charleston/south-carolina-attorneys-look-inward-to-address-high-rates-of-substance-abuse-and-mental-illness/Content?oid=22867135>.

4.1. ADVERSARIALISM

Lawyers represent parties' interests in litigation and transactions in which their clients' positions are, to varying degrees, in conflict with those of other parties, regulators, and other actors. This is, perhaps, most starkly seen in the litigation context, where parties are set in clear adversarial relationship to each other. But even in situations in which clients seek to cooperate in service of mutually beneficial deals, their interests will not always perfectly align.

Adversarial situations are, by their nature, rife with the potential for ethical questions to arise. Questions about appropriate disclosure, the temptation to dissemble or exaggerate, disinclination to sufficiently question one's own position or assumptions, the bounds of zealous advocacy, and other ethical matters inevitably come up in this context. And being in an adversarial posture is also one situational factor that can influence the tendency to act unethically.[48]

As a preliminary matter, psychological research has found that unethical behaviour is more likely to occur when situations are simply framed as 'competitive' as compared to those framed as 'cooperative'.[49] Moreover, people tend to judge behaviour as more ethical and find it easier to justify when that behaviour is a response to perceived unfair or unethical behaviour on the other side.[50] Indeed, attorneys who were asked to evaluate a set of questionable negotiation tactics found the tactics to be more acceptable when they were used in response to a questionable tactic used by the other side than when they were evaluated in isolation.[51] These sorts of effects can be magnified to the extent that adversaries more easily attribute bias or unfairness to those on the other side – simply because they are on the other side,[52] or because adverse interests are more salient than interests held in common.[53]

---

48 See generally J.K. Robbennolt and J.R. Sternlight, above n. 1, pp. 871, 874.

49 M.E. Schweitzer et al., 'Conflict Frames and the Use of Deception: Are Competitive Negotiators Less Ethical?' (2005) 35 *Journal of Applied Social Psychology* 2123, 2140.

50 M. Garcia et al., 'Morally Questionable Tactics: Negotiations Between District Attorneys and Public Defenders' (2001) 27 *Personality and Social Psychology Bulletin* 731.

51 Ibid.

52 K.A. Kennedy and E. Pronin, 'When Disagreement Gets Ugly: Perceptions of Bias and the Escalation of Conflict' (2008) 34 *Personality and Social Psychology Bulletin* 833. E. Pronin et al., above n. 7, p. 793. See also N. Epley and E.M. Caruso, 'Perspective Taking: Misstepping Into Others' Shoes' in K.D. Markman et al. (eds), *Handbook of Imagination and Mental Simulation*, Psychology Press, New York 2009, p. 295.

53 See J.R. Pierce, G.J. Kilduff, A.D. Galinski and N. Sivanathan, 'From Glue to Gasoline: How Competition Turns Perspective Takers Unethical' (2013) 24 *Psychological Science* 1986, 1994 (perspective taking as 'rational amplifier').

The adversarial system also has implications for wellbeing. Adversarialism often involves 'zero-sum' situations or thinking – that is, that when one side gains, the other must lose. Psychologist Martin Seligman and colleagues have argued that a focus on zero-sum outcomes results in predictable, and negative, emotional consequences for lawyers – including anxiety, anger, and sadness.[54] Given other countervailing benefits of the adversarial system, they suggest that efforts ought to be made to distinguish an adversary framework for resolving legal questions from zero-sum implications by emphasising the cooperative aspects of legal practice, looking for possibilities for joint gain, and refraining from personal or overly combative behaviour.[55]

4.2. TIME AND FINANCIAL PRESSURE

Modern legal practice can involve long hours, high billable-hours requirements, lack of control over workflows, heavy caseloads, and tight deadlines.[56] Lawyers may face pressure to develop new billing structures and to be cost efficient, increased competition for business, the fast pace that comes from new technology,[57] and pressure to bring in clients. Hierarchical firm structures, lateral partner hiring and 'free agents',[58] competition from alternative legal services providers,[59] and the related instability in employment[60] can all contribute to the pressures and uncertainties. Law school debt can result in financial pressures.[61]

54 M.E.P. Seligman et al., 'Why Lawyers are Unhappy' (2001) 23 *Cardozo Law Review* 33.

55 Ibid.

56 See, e.g., P.B. Pierson, A. Hamilton, M. Pepper and M. Root, above n. 38, pp. 13–14, 42. J. Chan, S. Poynton and J. Bruce, above n. 15.

57 For an in-depth look at the wellbeing implications of artificial intelligence, see F. Bell, J. Rogers and M. Legg, 'Artificial Intelligence and Lawyer Wellbeing' (2020) Chapter 10 of this volume. See also A. McPeak, 'Disruptive Technology and the Ethical Lawyer' (2019) 50 *University of Toledo Law Review* 457.

58 P.B. Pierson, A. Hamilton, M. Pepper and M. Root, above n. 38, pp. 15, 36–37.

59 J. Tashea, 'Alternative Legal Services Providers Come Into Their Own As Major Players, Says New Report' [30.01.2019] *ABA Journal* <http://www.abajournal.com/news/article/alternative-legal-service-providers-worth-over-10-billion-come-into-their-own-says-new-report/?utm_source=maestro&utm_medium=email&utm_campaign=weekly_email>.

60 See generally H. De Witte, J. Pienaar and N. De Cuyper, 'Review of 30 Years of Longitudinal Studies on the Association Between Job Insecurity and Health and Well-Being: Is There Causal Evidence?' (2016) 51 *Australian Psychologist* 18.

61 P.B. Pierson, A. Hamilton, M. Pepper and M. Root, above n. 38, pp. 18–19.

Many lawyers are concerned that the practice of law has become more of a business and less of a profession.[62]

These pressures have implications for lawyer wellbeing. Time pressure is a key contributor to a lack of wellbeing at work.[63] Indeed, many lawyers identify time and workload pressures as among the most frustrating aspects of their jobs.[64] Billing one's time can lead to the tendency to see time as money.[65] Thinking of time in economic terms leads to the sense that any time not spent at work is lost compensation, more difficulty savouring non-work activities, increased impatience, and a more central role for economic factors in evaluating life satisfaction.[66] And those who bill the most time tend to experience more pressure, role ambiguity and conflict, anxiety,

---

62 See generally A.O. Adedira, J. Hagan, P. Parker and G. Plickert, 'Making the Best of a Bad Beginning: Young New York Lawyers Confronting the Great Recession' (2017) 9 *Northeastern University Law Review* 259; A.J. Bergin and N.L. Jimmieson, above n. 15; R. Collier, 'Wellbeing in the Legal Profession: Reflections on Recent Developments (Or, What Do We Talking About, When We Talk About Wellbeing?)' (2016) 23 *International Journal of the Legal Profession* 41; W.D. Henderson, 'From Big Law to Lean Law' (2014) 38 *International Review of Law and Economics* 5; W.D. Henderson, 'The Legal Profession and Legal Services: Nature and Evolution' (§1-1.1) in *Legal Ethics, Professional Responsibility, and the Legal Profession*, West Academic Publishing, St. Paul, MN 2018, p. 1; D.J. Merritt, 'What Happened to the Class of 2010? Empirical Evidence of Structural Change in the Legal Profession' [2015] *Michigan State Law Review* 1043. See also H.M. Kritzer, 'The Professions Are Dead, Long Live the Professions: Legal Practice in a Postprofessional World' (1999) 33 *Law & Society Review* 713.

63 D. Kahneman et al., 'A Survey Method of Characterizing Daily Life Experience: The Day Reconstruction Method,' (2004) 306 *Science* 1776; D.L. Rhode, 'Balanced Lives For Lawyers' (2002) 70 *Fordham Law Review* 2207. See also B.S. McCann et al., 'Hostility, Social Support, and Perceptions of Work' (1997) 2 *Journal of Occupational Health Psychology* 175, 179 (finding that time pressure was associated with job dissatisfaction in a sample that included attorneys).

64 See, e.g., J. Robben, 'Burnout: Cautionary Tales' [10.2008] *Oregon State Bar Bulletin* <http://www.osbar.org/publications/bulletin/08oct/burnout.html>.

65 J.A. Evans et al., 'Beach Time, Bridge Time, and Billable Hours: The Temporal Structure of Technical Contracting' (2004) 49 *Administrative Science Quarterly* 1.

66 S.E. DeVoe and J. House, 'Time, Money, and Happiness: How Does Putting a Price on Time Affect Our Ability to Smell the Roses?' (2012) 48 *Journal of Experimental Social Psychology* 466. S. DeVoe and J. Pfeffer, 'When is Happiness About How Much You Earn? The Effect of Hourly Payment on the Money-Happiness Connection' (2009) 35 *Personality and Social Psychology Bulletin* 1602. S.E. DeVoe and J. Pfeffer, 'Hourly Payment and Volunteering: The Effect of Organizational Practices on Decisions About Time Use' (2007) 50 *Academy of Management Journal* 783. S.E. DeVoe and J. Pfeffer, 'When Time is Money: The Effect of Hourly Payment on the Evaluation of Time' (2007) 104 *Organizational Behavior and Human Decision Processes* 1.

job dissatisfaction, and dissatisfaction with the interaction between work and their rest of their lives.[67]

These pressures also have implications for legal ethics. Time pressures, for example, can influence ethical decision-making.[68] Similarly, lack of sleep[69] and cognitive fatigue[70] can lead to more unethical decisions. When people are fatigued – by lack of sleep, the load of making decisions, or economic pressure[71] – they are more likely to put themselves in ethically precarious situations and more likely to resolve those questions less ethically.[72] Lack of sleep has also been linked to more intense anger reactions.[73] In addition, financial pressure,[74] feelings of financial deprivation,[75] and perceptions of unfairness with regard to income[76]

---

67 A.J. Bergin and N.L. Jimmieson, above n. 15. See M. Legg and J. Rogers, 'Lawyers' Fee Arrangements and their Wellbeing' (2020) Chapter 11 of this volume.

68 S. Shalvi, O. Eldar, and Y. Bereby-Meyer, above n. 9. See also J.M. Darley and C.D. Batson, 'From Jerusalem to Jericho: A Study of Situational and Dispositional Variables in Helping Behavior' (1973) 27 *Journal of Personality and Social Psychology* 100.

69 See, e.g., C.M. Barnes et al., 'Lack of Sleep and Unethical Conduct (2011) 115 *Organizational Behavior and Human Decision Processes* 169, 178; M.S. Christian and A.P.J. Ellis, 'Examining the Effects of Sleep Deprivation on Workplace Deviance: A Self-Regulatory Perspective' (2011) 54 *Academy of Management Journal* 913, 926. See also W.D.S. Kilgore et al., 'The Effects of 53 Hours of Sleep Deprivation on Moral Judgment' (2007) 30 *Sleep* 345, 350.

70 F. Gino et al., 'Unable to Resist Temptation: How Self-Control Depletion Promotes Unethical Behavior' (2011) 115 *Organizational Behavior and Human Decision Processes* 191, 199. N.L. Mead et al., 'Too Tired to Tell the Truth: Self-Control Resource Depletion and Dishonesty' (2009) 45 *Journal of Experimental Social Psychology* 594, 596.

71 S. Mullainathan and E. Shafir, *Scarcity: The New Science of Having Less and How It Defines Our Lives*, Picador, New York 2014. K.D. Vohs et al., 'Making Choices Impairs Subsequent Self-Control: A Limited-Resource Account of Decision Making, Self-Regulation, and Active Initiative' (2008) 94 *Journal of Personality and Social Psychology* 883, 897.

72 N.L. Mead et al., above n. 70, p. 596.

73 Z. Krizan and G. Hisler, 'Sleepy Anger: Restricted Sleep Amplifies Angry Feelings' (2019) 148 *Journal of Experimental Psychology* 1239.

74 See, e.g., New York State Bar Association, Committee on Legal Education and Admission to the Bar, 'Law School Debt and the Practice of Law', p. 2 <http://www.nycbar.org/pdf/report/lawSchoolDebt.pdf>. ('Financial pressures have been identified as contributing to transgressions of ethical proscriptions and as contributing to the disturbing erosion of professionalism in the practice of law.')

75 E. Sharma, N. Mazar, A.L. Alter and D. Ariely, 'Financial Deprivation Selectively Shifts Moral Standards and Compromises Moral Decisions' (2014) 123 *Organizational Behavior and Human Decision Processes* 90–100.

76 L.K. John, G. Loewenstein, and S.I. Rick, 'Cheating More for Less: Upward Social Comparisons Motivate the Poorly Compensated to Cheat' (2014) 123 *Organizational Behavior and Human Decision Processes* 101–9.

have all been linked to ethical missteps. Focusing on the business aspects of a decision (rather than its ethical contours) can result in ethical missteps.[77] Unrelenting pressure to meet difficult targets can sap the strength to resist temptation.[78] Being shy of one's goals increases the likelihood that one will act unethically[79] and unethical behaviour has been linked to attempts to maintain high levels of performance.[80] And when performing capably is harder than expected, unethical behaviour is more likely.[81]

Uncertainty and instability, too, have implications for ethics. 'A lawyer secure in her environment and with stability around her will … know that a mistake won't necessarily result in a job loss, but instead an opportunity to grow ….'[82]

Recent research also finds that anxiety more generally can play an important role in ethical decision-making. Anxiety is associated with a tendency to identify, pay attention to, and remember actual and perceived threats.[83] Responding to this state of threat can increase an inclination toward self-interest, focus attention on external goals, and decrease attention to core ethical principles.[84] Accordingly, research has found that anxiety can lead to more self-interested unethical behaviour and that people in a state of anxiety tend to perceive their own self-interested unethical behaviour as less questionable.[85]

Time and financial pressures also implicate the difference between extrinsic and intrinsic goals, a distinction that has implications for both

---

77 M. Kouchaki, K. Smith-Crowe, A.P. Brief and C. Sousa, 'Seeing Green: Mere Exposure to Money Triggers a Business Decision Frame and Unethical Outcomes' (2013) 121 *Organizational Behavior and Human Decision Processes* 53–61; A.E. Tenbrunsel and D.M. Messick, 'Ethical Fading: The Role of Self-Deception in Unethical Behavior' (2004) 17 *Social Justice Research* 223–36.

78 D.T. Welsh and L.D. Ordóñez, 'The Dark Side of Consecutive High Performance Goals: Linking Goal Setting, Depletion, and Unethical Behavior' (2014) 123 *Organizational Behavior and Human Decision Processes* 79–89.

79 Ibid. M.E. Schweitzer, L. Ordóñez and B. Douma, 'Goal Setting as a Motivator of Unethical Behavior' (2004) 47 *Academy of Management Journal* 422–32.

80 C. Moore, S.W. Wakeman and F. Gino, 'Dangerous Expectations: Breaking Rules to Resolve Cognitive Dissonance' (2014) *Harvard Business School Working Paper 15-012*.

81 Ibid.

82 J.W. Richter, 'What Do Associates Want From Their Firms? You May Be Surprised' [02.05.2018] *ABA Journal*.

83 M. Kouchaki and S.D. Desai, 'Anxious, Threatened, and Also Unethical: How Anxiety Makes Individuals Feel Threatened and Commit Unethical Acts' (2014) 100 *Journal of Applied Psychology* 360, 361.

84 Ibid., p. 362.

85 Ibid. (reporting a series of studies using different methods and noting some possible boundary conditions).

wellbeing and ethics. Extrinsic goals and motivations relate to external rewards or outcomes, such as money, honours, power, or achieving better outcomes as compared to others.[86] Intrinsic motivations, in contrast, arise from the inherent enjoyment or stimulation of an activity – and identified motivation occurs '[w]hen the activity expresses or furthers … core beliefs or values.' Intrinsic values include self-understanding and growth, meaning in life, helping others, and intimacy with others and community.[87]

Law Professor Larry Krieger argues that that these differences in motivations have implications for both wellbeing and ethics or professionalism. He notes that the '(intrinsic) values and motivations that promote happiness are by their very nature likely to produce professional behavior, while those (extrinsic) values and motivations that produce frustration and angst are often associated with the loss of lawyer professionalism.'[88] He notes that intrinsic values are associated with wellbeing and that internally motivated work that expresses those values is more satisfying.[89] Indeed, positive wellbeing has been associated with the 'successful pursuit of life goals that are intrinsic in content; concordant with a person's interests, motives, and values; and internally consistent.'[90] In contrast, a sense of meaninglessness tends to be associated with distress.[91]

So, too, are there implications for ethics. Professional rules of ethics, for example, require competence.[92] When people are intrinsically motivated, they tend to be more engaged, focused, diligent, and thorough, which can

---

86 L.S. Kreiger, above. n. 21, p. 180; L.S. Krieger, above n. 22, p. 429.

87 L.S. Kreiger, above n. 21, pp. 175–76.

88 L.S. Krieger, above n. 22, p. 429.

89 L.S. Kreiger, above n. 21, pp. 176–77.

90 S. Lyubomirsky et al., 'Pursuing Happiness: The Architecture of Sustainable Change' (2005) 9 *Review of General Psychology* 111, 114.

91 See, e.g., K.M. Sheldon and L. Houser-Marko, 'Self Concordance, Goal-Attainment, and the Pursuit of Happiness: Can There Be an Upward Spiral?' (2001) 80 *Journal of Personality and Social Psychology* 152; R.A. Emmons, 'Personal Goals, Life Meaning, and Virtue: Wellsprings of a Positive Life' in C.L.M. Keyes and J. Haidt (eds), *Flourishing: Positive Psychology and the Life Well-Lived*, American Psychological Association, Washington, D.C. 2003, pp. 105, 113; T. Kasse and R.M. Ryan, 'Further Examining the American Dream: Differential Correlates of Intrinsic and Extrinsic Goals' (1996) 22 *Personality and Social Psychology Bulletin* 280; K.M. Sheldon et al., 'The Independent Effects of Goal Contents and Motives on Well-Being: It's Both What You Pursue and Why You Pursue It' (2004) 30 *Personality and Social Psychology Bulletin* 475 (2004). See also L.S. Krieger, above n. 22; M.E.P. Seligman, *Flourish: A Visionary New Understanding of Happiness and Well-Being*, Free Press, New York 2011, p. 17.

92 See, e.g., American Bar Association, 'Model Rules of Professional Conduct,' above n. 29, R. 1.1.

result in greater persistence at the task and a better quality work product.[93] Krieger argues, further, that intrinsic values contribute to civility in the profession and that extrinsic values contribute to ethical problems:

> [I]f a person does not care about relating positively to others, she is more likely to be abrasive, abusive, inconsiderate, or untrustworthy. When distracted from self-awareness and authenticity by external aspirations, she is less aware of critical internal checks on behavior … and thus more prone to dishonesty, lack of candor, manipulation of facts, and (again) untrustworthy behavior. When not focused on serving her client, profession, or society, she is more likely to exhibit selfish or self-serving behaviors, and less likely to be well prepared or to keep her caseload within limits that assure her full attention and best work product. … An attorney driven by a desire for power, popularity, image, or influence may seek to manipulate or dominate others to achieve those goals. If driven to 'win,' she will experience pressure and angst, and tend to 'do what it takes' to achieve victory … When extrinsic goals dominate, such 'ends' ultimately can justify aberrant 'means' in many forms – such as withholding information during discovery, filing frivolous or excessive pleadings or motions to gain advantage unwarranted by the merits, making false representations in or out of court, or exhibiting abusive behavior toward the opposing client or counsel. … And of course, if maximizing earnings and gaining affluence primarily drives a lawyer, she again may part from honesty, integrity, and decency to reach her goals. Clearly, these results can, and often do, entirely undermine attorney ethics, professionalism, health, and satisfaction along the way.[94]

4.3. LEADERSHIP AND CULTURE

The nature of the leadership and culture of an organisation like a law firm or other legal practice setting also has implications for both ethical behaviour and wellbeing.[95] Ethical leaders model, promote, communicate about,

---

93 L.S. Kreiger, above n. 21, p. 177.

94 Ibid., pp. 182–83. Krieger notes that empirical studies are lacking in this area.

95 See e.g., M. Kaptein, 'Developing and Testing a Measures for the Ethical Culture of Organizations: The Corporate Ethical Virtues Model' (2008) 29 *Journal of Organizational Behavior* 923; J.J. Kish-Gephart et al., above n. 6, p. 21; J.C. Wimbush and J.M. Shepard, 'Toward An Understanding of Ethical Climate: Its Relationship to Ethical Behavior and Supervisory Influence' (1994) 13 *Journal of Business Ethics* 637, 638. See generally L. Mather, 'How and Why do Lawyers Misbehave? Lawyers, Discipline and Collegial Control' in S.L. Cummings (ed), *The Paradox*

and reinforce appropriate behaviour.[96] Such leaders establish a positive ethical climate by treating others fairly and respectfully, maintaining and communicating high ethical standards, accepting responsibility for their errors, upholding a focus on ethics in the face of business concerns, valuing input and feedback, and holding others accountable.[97]

This sort of ethical leadership has been shown to have important effects on ethics throughout an organisation.[98] Individual ethics are influenced by social and organisational norms.[99] Modelling ethical behaviour within legal workplaces signals that ethics are valued and demonstrates how to practise in an ethical manner.[100] Communicating openly about ethics sets the stage for better decision-making processes and openness about mistakes[101] and is associated with more ethical conduct.[102] The behaviour of leadership and the priorities this behaviour manifests can influence the

---

of Professionalism: Lawyers and the Possibility of Justice, Cambridge University Press, New York 2011, pp. 109–31; E. Lazega, *The Collegial Phenomenon: The Social Mechanisms of Cooperation Among Peers in a Corporate Law Partnership*, Oxford University Press, Oxford 2001. See also M.C. Regan, 'Moral Intuitions and Organizational Culture' (2007) 51 *Saint Louis University Law Journal* 941.

96 M.E. Brown et al., 'Ethical Leadership: A Social Learning Perspective for Construct Development and Testing' (2005) 97 *Organizational Behavior and Human Decision Processes* 117, 120.

97 See e.g., L.K. Treviño et al., 'A Qualitative Investigation of Perceived Executive Ethical Leadership: Perceptions From Inside and Outside the Executive Suite' (2003) 56 *Human Relations* 5; G.R. Weaver et al., '"Somebody I Look Up To:" Ethical Role Models in Organizations' (2005) 34 *Organizational Dynamics* 313, 316.

98 J.J. Kish-Gephart et al. above n. 6 (meta-analysis finding that a strong ethical climate, including strong ethical role models, is associated with less unethical behaviour). D.M. Mayer et al., 'How Low Does Ethical Leadership Flow? Test of a Trickle-Down Model' (2009) 108 *Organizational Behavior and Human Decision Processes* 1. M.J. Neubert et al., 'The Virtuous Influence of Ethical Leadership Behavior: Evidence From the Field' (2009) 90 *Journal of Business Ethics* 157. M. Schminke et al., 'The Effect of Leader Moral Development on Ethical Climate and Employee Attitudes' (2005) 97 *Organizational Behavior and Human Decision Processes* 135; J.C. Wimbush and J.M. Shepard, above n. 95, p. 642.

99 See, e.g., L. Levin, 'The Ethical World of Solo and Small Law Firm Practitioners' (2005) 41 *Houston Law Review* 309; L.K. Treviño et al., 'Managing Ethics and Legal Compliance: What Works and What Hurts' (1999) 41 *California Management Review* 131; G.R. Weaver et al., above n. 97, p. 316.

100 See, e.g., L.K. Treviño and S.A. Youngblood, 'Bad Apples in Bad Barrels: A Causal Analysis of Ethical Decision-Making Behavior' (1990) 75 *Journal of Applied Psychology* 378.

101 L.K. Treviño et al., above n. 99.

102 L.K. Treviño et al., above n. 6, p. 967.

ways in which decisions are construed.[103] And ethical climates that are principled in their emphasis on concern for clients, justice, and the social consequences of unethical behaviour tend to be associated with more ethical behaviour.[104]

Ethical leadership and an ethical workplace culture also have implications for wellbeing. As a general matter, employees are more satisfied when they work in an ethical environment.[105] Ethical leadership has been associated with a variety of positive outcomes including increased engagement in work, decreased emotional exhaustion, and greater feelings of equity, accountability, and belonging.[106] A recent meta-analysis found that ethical leadership was positively associated with job satisfaction, organisational commitment, job engagement, and psychological wellbeing, and negatively associated with work stress.[107] And the institutionalisation of an ethical environment is positively associated with both job and life satisfaction, as well as organisational commitment.[108]

5. CONCLUSION

The structure of, changes to, and pressures involved in modern legal practice create conditions that contribute to dissatisfaction and compromised wellbeing among attorneys. In addition, the nature of

---

103 See C. Moore, D.M. Mayer, F.F.T. Chiang, C.D. Crossley, M.J. Karlesky and T.A. Birtch, 'Leaders Matter Morally: The Role of Ethical Leadership in Shaping Employee Moral Cognition and Misconduct' (2019) 104 *Journal of Applied Psychology* 123.

104 J.J. Kish-Gephart et al., above n. 6, pp. 12–13. G.R. Weaver and L.K. Trevino, 'Compliance and Values Oriented Ethics Programs: Influence on Employees' Attitudes and Behavior' (1999), 9 *Business Ethics Quarterly* 315.

105 See, e.g., H.C. Koh and E.H.Y. Boo, 'The Link Between Organizational Ethics and Job Satisfaction' (2001) *29 Journal of Business Ethics* 309; S.J. Vitell and D.L. Davis, 'The Relationship Between Ethics and Job Satisfaction: An Empirical Investigation' (1990) 9 *Journal of Business Ethics* 489.

106 See, e.g., A. Chughtai et al., 'Linking Ethical Leadership to Employee Well-Being: The Role of Trust in Supervisor' (2015) 128 *Journal of Business Ethics* 653; R.R. Sims and W.I. Sauser, Jr., above n. 22.

107 A. Bedi et al., 'A Meta-Analytic Review of Ethical Leadership Outcomes and Moderators' (2016) 139 *Journal of Business Ethics* 517.

108 D. Lee, G.B. Yu, M.J. Sirgy et al., 'The Effects of Explicit and Implicit Ethics Institutionalization on Employee Life Satisfaction and Happiness: The Mediating Effects of Employee Experiences in Work Life and Moderating Effect of Work-Family Life Conflict' (2018) 147 *Journal of Business Ethics* 855, 864.

contemporary lawyering can compound the psychological tendencies that play a role in unethical decision-making and behaviour. Given the interplay between wellbeing and ethics – with ethics influencing wellbeing, wellbeing influencing ethics, and a variety of factors common to lawyers and legal practice with implications for both – it behoves those concerned with improving either aspect of the profession to pay attention to these connections. Doing so will help construct a broader and more nuanced understanding of the issues, expand the channels by which either or both problems might be addressed, and draw attention to the wider range of consequences that might follow from improvements in either domain.

CHAPTER 8

IS 'UBERISATION' THE PATH TO LAWYER WELLBEING?

Margaret THORNTON*

1. Introduction 177
2. The Psychological Distress of Lawyers 180
3. Uber Lawyering 184
4. Flexible and Autonomous 187
5. The Debit Side of NewLaw 190
   5.1. Always Connected 190
   5.2. Ageism 193
6. Conclusion 197

1. INTRODUCTION

The struggle to effect a balance between work and 'life' on the part of lawyers chafing under the constraints of billable hours and the long-hours culture has resulted in high levels of stress and dissatisfaction in traditional legal practice.[1] This has contributed to the haemorrhage of lawyers,

---

* Thanks to Janet Chan for hosting the *Wellbeing in a Changing World* Workshop, UNSW Law, 15 November 2018. Thanks also to HARRY MCLAURIN for research assistance and the Australian Research Council (ARC) for financial assistance (DP120104785).

1 E.g., LAW COUNCIL OF AUSTRALIA, 'National Attrition and Re-engagement Study (NARS)', Law Council of Australia, Canberra 2014; MARGARET THORNTON, 'Work/Life or Work/Work: Corporate Legal Practice in the Twenty-first Century' (2016) 23 *International Journal of the Legal Profession* 13; MARGARET THORNTON, 'Squeezing the Life out of Lawyers: Legal Practice in the Market Embrace' (2016) 25 *Griffith Law Review* 471.

particularly women, which encouraged me to consider whether alternative ways of lawyering might better contribute to lawyer wellbeing.[2]

The introduction of flexible work policies for employees was a response to the feminisation of labour in the late twentieth century.[3] Despite their entry into full-time employment, women were nevertheless still expected to take responsibility for the preponderance of housework, childcare and elder care. The introduction of flexible work policies coincided with the neoliberal turn, which emphasised profit maximisation and promotion of the self through entrepreneurialism,[4] a theme on which Foucault in particular elaborates.[5] Indeed, competition became a central plank of Australian government policy under the Keating Government in the mid-1990s, as illustrated by the passage of the Competition Policy Reform Act 1995 (Cth).[6] A cluster of significant reforms that took place around the millennial turn hastened this imperative. Most notably, these reforms included the incorporation of legal practices,[7] listing on the stock exchange,[8] and the amalgamation of the leading Australian national firms with elite London-based firms.[9] Not only did these reforms emphasise the new mantra of 'law as business'[10] that had begun to animate private practice, but they also assisted in transforming legal practice into

---

2 The author obtained an extension to the ARC (DP 120104785) funding, see above n.*, to carry out interviews with NewLaw lawyers in 2018. For detailed analysis, see Margaret Thornton, 'Towards the Uberisation of Legal Practice' (2019) 1 *Law, Technology and Humans* 46: doi.org/10.5204/lthj.v1i1.1277.

3 Michael Hardt and Antonio Negri, *Commonwealth*, Harvard University Press, Cambridge MA 2009.

4 E.g., Colin Crouch, 'Putting Neoliberalism in its Place' (2014) 1 *Perspectives on Politics* 202; Loic Wacquant, *Punishing the Poor: The Neoliberal Government of Social Security*, Duke University Press, Durham NC 2009; David Harvey, *A Brief History of Neoliberalism*, Oxford University Press, Oxford 2005.

5 Michel Foucault, *The Birth of Biopolitics: Lectures at the Collège de France, 1978–1979*, Michel Senellart (ed), Graham Burchell (trans.), Palgrave Macmillan, New York 2008.

6 The findings and recommendations of the Hilmer Report were central. See Independent Committee of Inquiry into Competition Policy in Australia, *National Competition Policy*, Australian Government Publishing Service, Canberra 1993.

7 Steve Mark and Tahlia Gordon, 'Innovations in Regulation: Responding to a Changing Legal Services Market' (2009) 22 *Georgetown Journal of Legal Ethics* 501.

8 Andrew Grech and Kirsten Morrison, 'Slater & Gordon: The Listing Experience' (2009) 2 *Georgetown Journal of Legal Ethics* 535.

9 Margaret Thornton, 'Hypercompetitiveness or a Balanced Life? Gendered Discourses in the Globalisation of Australian Law Firms' (2014) 17 *Legal Ethics* 153.

10 Joanne Bagust, 'The Legal Profession and the Business of Law' (2013) 35 *Sydney Law Review* 27.

a lucrative legal services 'industry' that irrevocably altered the norms of legal work.

Historically, an employed lawyer or associate in the typical law firm could expect to become an equity partner after a few years, but the bureaucratised character of the new global mega-firms meant that the chances of partnership became increasingly remote. Nevertheless, the idea of a partnership as the ultimate prize continued to be dangled before associates, encouraging them to work ever harder and longer. The long-hours culture became the norm as associates represented the crucial source of profitability for their firms, which was effected through billable hours.[11]

The introduction of flexible work was intended to counteract the high rate of attrition of women lawyers,[12] as the long-hours culture disproportionately affected them. However, the commitment of law firms to flexible work was somewhat ambivalent in light of the privileging of competition policy. It did not alter the construction of the 'ideal worker' as one who devoted [him]self unconditionally to work with no time off for child-bearing or -rearing.[13] Indeed, those who worked flexibly continued to be stigmatised (men even more than women),[14] as it was assumed that those who did not prioritise work over life were not serious about their careers. For the lawyers who did not leave, the relentlessness of billable hours compelled them to catch up at home, thereby causing the dissolution of the boundary between work and home to compound their stress levels.[15]

The pressure to meet billable hours targets also meant that working relationships were increasingly marked by harassment and bullying, which further impacted adversely on lawyer wellbeing.[16] Indeed, it has been shown that a key contributor to workplace stress and depression is

11 Iain Campbell and Sara Charlesworth, 'Salaried Lawyers and Billable Hours: A New Perspective from the Sociology of Work' (2012) 19 *International Journal of the Legal Profession* 89.

12 NARS, above n. 1.

13 Joan Williams, *Unbending Gender: Why Family and Work Conflict and What to Do About it*, Oxford University Press, Oxford 2000, p. 1.

14 E.g., Scott Coltrane, Elizabeth C Miller, Tracy DeHaan and Lauren Stewart, 'Fathers and the Flexibility Stigma' (2013) 69 *Journal of Social Issues* 279; Margaret Thornton and Joanne Bagust, 'The Gender Trap: Flexible Work in Corporate Legal Practice' (2007) 45 *Osgoode Hall Law Journal* 773.

15 Margaret Thornton, 'The Flexible Cyborg: Work-Life Balance in Legal Practice' (2016) 38 *Sydney Law Review* 1.

16 Joanne Bagust, 'The Culture of Bullying in Australian Corporate Law Firms' (2014) 17 *Legal Ethics* 177; Paula Baron, 'The Elephant in the Room? Lawyer Wellbeing and the Impact of Unethical Behaviours' (2015) 41 *Australian Feminist Law Journal* 87.

disempowerment,[17] while autonomy and control enhance wellbeing.[18] It has also been observed that lawyers have lost control over the goals and social purpose of the work in which they engage as a result of the increasing managerialism and bureaucratisation of law firms, a factor that has been exacerbated by the technology of billable hours.[19] Time-billing practices are frequently criticised, not only because of their adverse impact on lawyer wellbeing, but also because they reward inefficiency.[20] Law societies have nevertheless been reluctant to critique billable hours, which favour the most powerful of their members – the equity partners in traditional firms.[21]

In the past, the dissatisfied refugees from corporate law firms might have gone to a smaller firm, the public sector or in-house positions, but NewLaw as a 'disruptive innovation'[22] is an attractive alternative. In this chapter, particular attention is paid to flexibility and autonomy, the distinctive characteristics of NewLaw. Before this, however, is a brief overview of the wellbeing literature, which supports the finding that the absence of flexibility and autonomy in law firms exercises a detrimental impact on the health of lawyers.

2. THE PSYCHOLOGICAL DISTRESS OF LAWYERS

Albeit somewhat surprising in view of their relatively high incomes, lawyers have been shown to have higher rates of depression and suicide than the general population and a propensity to engage in negative behaviours,

---

17 Lonnie Golden, Julia R. Henly and Susan Lambert, 'Work Schedule Flexibility: A Contributor to Happiness?' (2013) 4 *Journal of Social Research & Policy* 107.

18 E.g., William Davies, *The Happiness Industry: How the Government and Big Business Sold Us Well-Being*, Verso, London 2015, p. 250.

19 Cf. Colin James, 'Legal Practice on Time: The Ethical Risk and Inefficiency of the Six-minute Unit' (2017) 42 *Alternative Law Journal* 61, 62.

20 NARS, above n. 1; Victorian Equal Opportunity and Human Rights Commission, *Changing the Rules: The Experience of Female Lawyers in Victoria*, Victorian Equal Opportunity and Human Rights Commission, Melbourne 2012.

21 E.g., Campbell and Charlesworth, 'Salaried Lawyers and Billable Hours'; Tim Batdorf, 'The Billable Hour and Lawyer Wellness' (2011) 90 *Michigan Bar Journal* 48.

22 Clayton M. Christensen, *The Innovator's Dilemma: The Revolutionary Book that Will Change the Way you do Business*, revised ed., Collins Business Essentials, New York 2003.

such as over-indulgence in alcohol[23] and eating disorders.[24] The two main stressors are overwork and work/life conflict, although these stressors are conventionally suppressed because of the benefits associated with high social standing.[25] Krieger and Sheldon nevertheless found that American lawyers in private firms who had the highest pay and occupied the most prestigious positions were less happy than lawyers who occupied the less coveted public service positions.[26] Their study found that increasing firm size and income were correlated with decreasing autonomy, motivation and wellbeing.[27] Koltai et al. recognised that while large organisations provide higher wages, benefits and prestige, their lawyers tended to have less autonomy.[28] Koltai et al. found that the long hours worked in large firms represented a proxy for quality and quantity of productivity – variables that are difficult to measure, but which encourage lawyers to overwork and clock up 'heroic' billable hours.[29] In the Australia-wide survey conducted for 'Balancing Law and Life' in 2013–14 (n = 424),[30] 61 per cent of respondents worked more than 50 hours per week and 20 per cent more than 60 hours per week, some of whom claimed to work as many as 100 hours per week.[31] Of the interviewees (n = 54, 24 men and 30 women), the women invariably reported dissatisfaction with the absence of flexibility, although this was only occasionally noted by the men.

---

23 E.g., *Mental Health and Wellness: Destigmatizing the Discussion and Promoting Solutions* (2018) 92 *The Florida Bar Journal* (Special Issue). One US study involving 13,000 lawyers in 19 States established that 21–36 per cent of currently practising lawyers qualified as problem drinkers. See Patrick Krill, 'What Do the Statistics About Lawyer Alcohol Use and Mental Health Problems *Really Mean?* (2018) 92 *The Florida Bar Journal* 10.

24 Natalie K. Skead, Shane L. Rogers and Jerome Doraisamy, 'Looking beyond the Mirror: Psychological Distress; Disordered Eating, Weight and Shape Concerns; and Maladaptive Eating Habits in Lawyers and Law Students' (2018) 61 *International Journal of Law and Psychiatry* 90.

25 Jonathan Koltai, Scott Schieman and Ronit Dinovitzer, 'The Status-Health Paradox: Organizational Context, Stress Exposure, and Well-being in the Legal Profession' (2018) 59 *Journal of Health and Social Behavior* 20.

26 Lawrence S. Krieger and Kennon M. Sheldon, 'What Makes Lawyers Happy? A Data-Driven Prescription to Redefine Professional Success' (2015) 83 *George Washington Law Review* 554.

27 Ibid. 615.

28 Koltai et al., above, n. 25, p. 33.

29 Ibid. 23.

30 ARC, DP120104785, above n.*.

31 Thornton, 'Work/Life', above n. 1, p. 21.

The causes of stress are uncertain, although Davies argues that the primary trigger for the stress 'epidemic' is social, political and economic rather than neural or behavioural.[32] While the post-millennial reforms referred to appear to have contributed to an increase in lawyer distress, there is a dearth of data from the late twentieth century with which a comparison can be effected to support this author's hypothesis that there is a direct correlation between the neoliberalisation of the legal profession and the increase in stress.

In 2006, James noted an increase in stress in a study of New South Wales solicitors.[33] He found that 35 per cent reported that their current job had been significantly more stressful in the previous 12 months.[34] Unsurprisingly, respondents reported low job satisfaction, with 81 per cent claiming that their work was '"highly demanding", not because of the nature of the work, but because of the high billing targets and long hours'.[35] James also found that globalisation had caused Australian firms to become more Americanised and competitive, with stricter billing expectations than had formerly been the case.[36]

James' study was followed by *Courting the Blues*, an influential study involving more than 2,000 legal practitioners and law students, which was conducted under the auspices of the Brain and Mind Institute at the University of Sydney.[37] The survey found that lawyers exhibited higher levels of psychological distress than comparable members of the wider community.[38] *Courting the Blues* and the work of the Tristan Jepson Foundation sparked widespread interest in the issue of psychological distress and depression among lawyers, giving rise to a virtual industry of organisations and individuals offering advice as to how to create a culture of wellness.[39] A substantial academic literature also emerged

---

32 Davies, above n. 18.

33 Colin James, 'Lawyer Dissatisfaction, Emotional Intelligence and Clinical Legal Education' (2008) 18 *Legal Education Review* 123.

34 Ibid. 129.

35 Ibid. 130.

36 Ibid. 124.

37 Norm Kelk, Georgina Luscombe, Sharon Medow and Ian Hickie, *Courting the Blues: Attitudes towards Depression in Australian Law Students and Lawyers*, Brain and Mind Research Institute, University of Sydney, Sydney 2009. See also, Beaton Consulting and beyondblue National Depression Initiative (2007) *Annual Professions Survey* <http://www.judicialcollege.vic.edu.au/sites/default/files/2007%20-%20Beyond%20Blue%20-%20Annual%20Professions%20Survey.pdf>.

38 Kelk et al., *Courting the Blues*, above n. 37, p. 42.

39 E.g., Christine Parker, 'The "Moral Panic" over Psychological Wellbeing in the Legal Profession: A Personal or Political Ethical Response' (2014) 37 *University of*

attesting to the marked rates of depression, substance abuse and suicide in the profession.[40] While a causal link between neoliberalism and stress can be hypothesised, this cannot be unequivocally established, although supported by the broader socio-political critical literature. Like Davies,[41] Schrecker and Bambra argue that stress is one of the 'epidemics' generated by the precarity of work within neoliberalism.[42] Bullying, sexual harassment and incivility also appear to have increased during the early years of the new millennium or, like stress, these behaviours have become more visible following adverse publicity,[43] a phenomenon known as the 'perception paradox'.[44]

A major American study involving more than 50,000 workers across 11 companies found a high level of tolerance for incivility on the part of the more productive workers,[45] which comports with the emphasis on profit maximisation associated with the neoliberal turn. While a national report commissioned by the Law Council of Australia (NARS) was not prepared to attribute responsibility directly to law firms, it did find that 24 per cent of women reported sexual harassment (compared with eight per cent of men),

---

New South Wales Law Journal 1103; Suzanne Poynton, Janet Chan, Melissa Vogt, Anne Grunsett and Jasmine Bruce, 'Assessing the Effectiveness of Wellbeing Initiatives for Lawyers and Support Staff' (2018) 41 *University of New South Wales Law Journal* 584.

40 E.g., Kieran Pender, *Us Too? Bullying and Sexual Harassment in the Legal Profession*, Legal Policy & Research Unit, International Bar Association, London 2019; Paula Baron, 'Sleight of Hand: Lawyer Distress and the Attribution of Responsibility' (2014) 23 *Griffith Law Review* 261; Adele J. Bergin and Nerina L. Jimmieson, 'Australian Lawyer Well-being: Workplace Demands, Resources and the Impact of Time-billing Targets' (2014) 21 *Psychiatry, Psychology and Law* 127; Janet Chan, 'Conceptualising Legal Culture and Lawyering Stress' (2014) 21 *International Journal of the Legal Profession* 213; Maryam Omari and Megan Paull, '"Shut Up and Bill": Workplace Bullying Challenges for the Legal Profession' (2013) 20 *International Journal of the Legal Profession* 141; Janet Chan, Suzanne Poynton and Jasmine Bruce, 'Lawyering Stress and Work Culture: An Australian Study' (2014) 37 *University of New South Wales Law Journal* 1062.

41 Davies, above n. 18.

42 Ted Schrecker and Clare Bambra, *How Politics Makes Us Sick: Neoliberal Epidemics*, Palgrave Macmillan, London 2015.

43 E.g. Baron, above, n. 16; Bagust, above, n. 16; NARS, above n. 1; Suzanne Le Mire and Rosemary Owens, 'A Propitious Moment? Workplace Bullying and Regulation of the Legal Profession' (2014) 37 *UNSW Law Journal* 1030; Omari and Paull, above n. 40; Victorian Equal Opportunity and Human Rights Commission, above n. 20.

44 This is associated with higher reported rates of bullying and sexual harassment in jurisdictions regarded as more progressive in addressing such issues. See Pender, above n. 40, p. 23.

45 E.g. Michael Housman and Dylan Minor, *Toxic Workers*, Working Paper 16-057, Harvard Business School <http://www.hbs.edu/faculty/Pages/item.aspx?num=50046>.

while an extraordinarily high 50 per cent of women reporting bullying (compared with 38 per cent of men).[46] In addition, there were high levels of gender discrimination more generally.[47] Once again, however, no data is available for the twentieth century with which to effect a comparison. Indeed, only one formal complaint of sex discrimination in legal practice appears to have proceeded to hearing in the twentieth century,[48] although no data is available regarding the number of complaints lodged.

Unlike the American Bar Association, the Australian Law Council has not commissioned a study on the wellbeing of Australian lawyers, and law societies have generally skirted around the possibility that billable hours and the long-hours culture are fundamental stressors,[49] although they are willing to provide individual counselling addressing mental health and substance abuse. For the most part, lawyers as neoliberal subjects are expected to be resilient and to assume responsibility for managing stress at work themselves.[50] They are encouraged to pay particular attention to their physical wellbeing by ensuring adequate sleep, a balanced diet, regular exercise and a limited alcohol intake,[51] while paying attention to their mental wellbeing, including meditation, mindfulness and self-reflection.[52] The individualised focus leaves conveniently untouched the hypercompetitive norms that prevail in traditional legal practice.[53] Little attention has been paid to whether different ways of practising law might be more conducive to wellbeing. With this idea in mind, this chapter now turns to a consideration of 'NewLaw'.

3. UBER LAWYERING

NewLaw does not have a precise denotation but encompasses multiple ways of practising law based on digitalisation and flexibility. NewLaw has

---

46 NARS, above n. 1, p. 32.

47 Ibid.

48 *Hickie v. Hunt & Hunt* (1998) EOC ¶92-137 [1998] HREOCA 8.

49 THORNTON, 'Squeezing', above n. 1, p. 482.

50 HARVEY, above, n. 4, p. 65.

51 E.g., COLIN JAMES, 'Resilient Lawyers: Maximizing Well-Being in Legal Education and Practice' in RACHAEL FIELD, JAMES DUFFY and COLIN JAMES (eds), *Promoting Law Student and Lawyer Well-Being in Australia and Beyond*, Routledge, London 2016, pp. 108–31.

52 KRIEGER and SHELDON, above, n. 26.

53 Cf. CHAN et al., above n. 40.

been described by Eric Chin as a business model in which labour arbitrage (taking advantage of a price difference between two or more markets) is used in the delivery of [legal] services; entities include 'legal process outsourcing firms, lawyer secondment firms and fixed fees service firms that leverage on demand lawyers'.[54] While the feminisation of work was a catalyst for flexible work, flexibility was also deployed as a tool of neoliberal management to overcome the rigidities of Fordism.[55] This signalled a move away from full-time permanent work to casualisation, which meant that workers were employed only when needed.

Flexibility was given a further boost by the gig economy.[56] People who had lost their jobs because of the global financial crisis (GFC) of 2008–09 were prepared to undertake short-term 'gigs' for various employers. As well as appealing to employers, 'gigging' legitimated the ability of workers to adapt their hours of work to accommodate family or other responsibilities.

Advances in technology are the key to the changing norms underpinning NewLaw. The portability of the technology and storage on the cloud enable lawyers to log on from anywhere at any time. 'The office' is no longer central and may be dispensed with altogether; if needed, a co-working space can be rented cheaply. Work flows, document creation and work triage are all likely to be automated, with paper files and face-to-face meetings no longer necessary. The technology facilitates the flexibility that individual lawyers have sought for so long.

Principals and managers of law firms have quite different positions from employed lawyers or independent contractors. The focus of Lachlan McKnight, for example, the CEO of LegalVision, is on capital investment, technology and customer service rather than the opportunities afforded to lawyers to work in new ways.[57] From his perspective, there is little

54 Josef. Legal Bot, 'Interview with Eric Chin, the Man who coined the Phrase "NewLaw"', no date <https://joseflegal.com/blog/interview-with-eric-chin-the-man-who-coined-the-phrase-newlaw.>.

55 David Harvey, *The Condition of Postmodernity: An Enquiry into the Origins of Cultural Change*, Blackwell Press, Oxford 1990, p. 147.

56 The gig economy entails the fragmentation of traditional employment relationship into 'short term, intermittent work for multiple engagers ("gigs")'. See Emily Hong, 'Making it Work: A Closer Look at the Gig Economy', *New American Weekly*, 01.10.2015 <https://www.newamerica.org/weekly/94/making-it-work-a-closer-look-at-the-gig-economy/>.

57 Lachlan McKnight, 'Observations on NewLaw in Australia in 2018', *Lawyers Weekly*, 28.12.2018 <https://www.lawyersweekly.com.au/newlaw/24712-observations-on-newlaw-in-australia-in-2018>. *LegalVision*'s website emphasises the casual lifestyle lawyers can experience if they join the firm, including working 'from the beach' or 'from France' <https://legalvision.com.au/>.

difference between NewLaw and traditional law. Nevertheless, NewLaw has reacted strongly against time billing, one of the major criticisms of traditional legal practice, and generally replaced it with fixed-fee billing. NewLaw has also done away with the expectation that lawyers will work 24/7 to meet targets as well as the somewhat demeaning construction of them as mere units of productivity. A more equitable distribution of profits is favoured, which necessarily scores highly in terms of wellness. Keystone Law, for example, which is listed on the London Stock Exchange, allows lawyers to work remotely and retain 75 per cent of their billings.[58]

Very little academic commentary on NewLaw is presently available because the field is new and dynamic.[59] To remedy the lacuna in knowledge about NewLaw, this author conducted interviews with 38 NewLaw lawyers (30 in Australia and eight in England, by way of comparison) in order to acquire a better understanding of NewLaw practices. In approaching potential interviewees, law societies and websites assisted. Ethics approval was obtained to record and transcribe the interviews (Australian National University Ethics Protocol 2017/597) and the data was anonymised.

NewLaw firms may engage lawyers on a full-time, part-time or casual basis, while the employee relationship is dispensed with altogether in the case of independent contractors. One principal had 12 people working for her, all on different bases: some working *in situ* and some remotely. A common practice was for a firm to engage a nucleus of permanent staff, supplemented by independent contractors as needed. Independent contractors are the paradigmatic Uber lawyers who can work anywhere at any time, provided that they are 'connected'.

NewLaw firms invariably eschew the competitive and hierarchical structures associated with traditional law firms, favouring an egalitarian approach that is more conducive to wellbeing. The nomenclature is also more egalitarian, with 'practice leaders' replacing 'partners', for example. However, one London-based firm bestowed the term 'Partner' on all its lawyers – more than 200 of them, even though the lawyers worked as independent contractors, as it was felt that 'Partner' carried more weight with clients.

---

58 John Hyde, 'Listed Firm Boosts Profits as Job Applicants Spurn "Traditional" Partnerships', *The Law Society Gazette*, 25.09.2018 <https://www.lawgazette.co.uk/practice/listed-firm-boosts-profits-as-job-applicants-spurn-traditional-partnerships/5067681.article>.

59 An exception is Vicki Waye, Martie-Louise Verreyne and Jane Knowler, 'Innovation in the Australian Legal Profession' (2017) 25 *International Journal of the Legal Profession* 213.

To enhance their sense of satisfaction with legal work, some lawyers have created firms that deal with conventional legal problems in an innovative way, such as effecting divorce without litigation, or by setting up on-line platforms to facilitate the cheap and expeditious resolution of legal problems. The role of the lawyer then becomes what one Australian interviewee termed 'marketising creativity'. The pleasure derived from legal work was enhanced by its variety, which contrasted with the 'daily grind' of going to the same office in the city every day and doing more or less the same thing:

> I just feel like we have such limited time on earth and to give 50 of those precious hours to … the corporate monster; it's just not worth it to me. Life is too short. (Employed Lawyer, Australia, Male, 24 September 2018)

4. FLEXIBLE AND AUTONOMOUS

Flexibility and autonomy are the concepts that lie at the heart of both NewLaw and wellbeing. The conjunction of flexibility and autonomy allows lawyers to choose not only their assignments, but also where they work and how much they work. Flexibility and autonomy are thereby imbricated with the increasing feminisation and technologisation of NewLaw, particularly in the way that the demands of work and family are reconciled:

> Whilst I work fulltime [*in situ*], I can choose the hours that I work. So, I can start early, finish early, work the morning, have a break in the afternoon so I can do the school run and then log back on in the evening or cut it anyway I like. I can also work … at home, and that helps me to be around for my kids at the times when they need me because they're needy little people … I'm not interested in doing a job that means I don't see them … It definitely means that I can fit in work around my life rather than the other way around … I've chosen to stop work at 2:30 to go and pick the kids up, and then I'll finish something if it needs to be finished at night or get up early to do it before they wake up. (State Manager, Australia, Female, 25 September 2018)

> I'll go and pick up my daughter at three o'clock and then I'm having a meeting with one of my team members at the park from 3.00 'til 5.00 so that my daughter can play in the park, my six-month-old can sit next to us, and we can discuss some of the projects that she's working on. (Principal, Australia, Female, 9 October 2018)

Once a woman lawyer is 'on the books', the focus is on producing high-quality work, not on where, when or how long they work. Some women with young children, who were juggling day-care and school pick-ups, as well as work, might work as little as 10 hours per week and not at all during school holidays:

> And when I talk about lifestyle I mean it's just a bit more relaxed, so we drop the children off at school and then we start work and if we want to go to sports day, we go to sports day; we do not ask for time off. We don't work [school] holidays; we just add the work time back on. We just use our initiative to get the work done … V. had her child seriously ill recently and she just took six weeks working from home but it was a given; there was no negotiating about it. (Principal, UK, Female, 26 June 2018)

Women were grateful to be able to continue working without a break in their careers and were adamant that they would not return to a conventional nine-to-five way of working:

> Most of my friends that I know outside of work who have had their families don't have [their work] anymore and I find that really sad for them and they are frustrated because they're not in a position to go back to work … Lots of firms now have more flexible working, but it's not remote … I don't think I would have taken that leap if I hadn't had the children … But of those that have done it, I don't know of anybody that has said they would go back to work in the traditional way. (Partner, UK, Female, 18 June 2018)

The sense of vulnerability experienced by those in the more parlous 'Uberised' positions has encouraged increasing numbers of women to establish their own firms. One woman who had experience in both a top-tier corporate law firm and in-house became a director/principal, describing herself as a 'contracted, outsourced, in-house legal', putting her young son into day-care three days a week and working in the evenings. She worked for a number of companies virtually, visiting them maybe once a quarter. Practising as a sole practitioner maximises autonomy even though it involves a degree of stress arising from the financial outlay.

Women principals of NewLaw firms often make a point of incorporating flexibility into their firms when they set them up:

> And I've got two [contractors] at [beachside] who're never in the city, but they do fantastic financial services and corporate work for us and they have incredible lives at [beachside] – beach-walking and yoga and then a little bit of work in the middle <laughs>. Wonderful! … The key is to choose people who all work well together and we're loyal to each other, so we've become this

> tight network of women who just support each other … 'I will commit, but not contractually, to trying to give you ten hours per week and, during school holidays, you don't have to work'. (Principal, Australia, Female, 3 March 2018)

Uberisation also allowed fathers to play a more active role in child-care by working at home without the stigma associated with flexible work in traditional firms.[60] The role of masculinity in law firms, particularly large firms, nevertheless remains an ambiguous one, as Richard Collier argues.[61] The traditional construction that is central to legal professionalism involves an absent father but this representation is increasingly challenged by the contemporary rhetoric of gender equality and the perception of the 'good dad'.[62] Although the NewLaw fathers were prepared to contribute to caring in a way that their own fathers had not, they were generally not the primary carers of young children:

> I'd say, 95 per cent of nights I'm home by 5:30 to do the kids' bed routine and all that kind of stuff, and then often I log on after that to keep things going but you've got a lot of flexibility in terms of when you do the work. (Manager, Australia, Male, 2 March 2018)
>
> I had many conversations with dads who [were] saying, 'I need to work a day [a week] from home as my wife will be going to work on this day as she's coming … back into the workforce'. Their part is consulting during that period to give them greater flexibility as a family unit. (Head, Australia, Female, 16 April 2018)

Engaging in activities outside of work is widely recognised as a means of securing a balance in one's life.[63] Hence, the flexibility that is central to NewLaw is not only about caring for young children, for it also allows lawyers to pursue interests in the arts, sport and volunteering, all of which helped to keep them 'fresh and passionate about their work', as the head of the subsidiary of a corporate firm noted. Working 24/7 in a traditional

---

60 Thornton, 'Work/Life', above n. 1, p. 32.

61 Richard Collier, 'Fatherhood, Gender and the Making of Professional Identity in Large Law Firms: Bringing Men into the Frame' (2019) 15(1) *International Journal of Law in Context* 68: doi.10.1017/S1744552318000162.

62 Ibid.

63 E.g., Jerome Doraisamy, *The Wellness Doctrines for Law Students and Young Lawyers*, Xoum Publishing, QVB Post Office, NSW 2015, pp. 156 ff.

firm precluded any possibility of forming a normal relationship, which was rued by one lawyer who had recently departed to become a consultant:

> Work always got in the way. So even though I'm 46 now, I'm still not married with children, and that's all down to having being married to the job for a decade. (Partner, UK, male, 25 June 2018)

What was consistently underscored by the NewLaw interviewees was that they were happy with the manner of working. Happiness is a key attribute of wellbeing,[64] albeit one rarely heard in the context of traditional legal practice:

> I think if you're happy and you're enjoying your job, you'll give more because you want to give more. If you feel that you're being taken advantage of and squeezed for every inch of your life, then you're gonna leave at five o'clock on the dot and it's gonna be an 'up yours' attitude, isn't it? … So, yeah – and I want [my employees] to stay with me for a long time, so I'll look after them and hopefully they'll look after me. (Partner, UK, Female, 2 July 2018)

A survey of 4,500 workers in the United States revealed that flexibility exerted a greater impact on worker satisfaction and happiness than total number of hours worked or income earned.[65] In the case of NewLaw, it was apparent that this was the case whether the lawyer was a sole practitioner with additional responsibilities,[66] a principal/director, a casual employee or an independent contractor.

5. THE DEBIT SIDE OF NEWLAW

5.1. ALWAYS CONNECTED

In light of the very positive support by interviewees for NewLaw, one must ask: Is it too good to be true? 'Always being connected' undoubtedly has negative overtones for professional workers that cannot be ignored. Ter Hoeven and van Zoonen identify three paradoxes associated with flexible work: the 'telecommunicating paradox', the 'connectivity paradox'

64 Krieger and Sheldon, above n. 26.
65 Golden et al., above n. 17.
66 Cf. Chan et al., above n. 40, pp. 1092–93.

and the 'autonomy paradox'.[67] The ramifications of each of these will be considered in turn.

The first, the 'telecommunicating paradox', acknowledges that flexible work enhances work/life balance but negatively affects work relationships. The paradox arises from being isolated from colleagues by working remotely. While the occasional interviewee preferred to work in the firm office rather than at home, most interviewees were happy to work remotely and rely on email as the primary means of communication. Networking groups exist in some areas, which break down the isolation for both sole practitioners and independent contractors, enabling them to share information, as well as being a useful source of referrals. Some NewLaw firms surveyed organised regular meetings of lawyers working remotely and others hosted social gatherings to keep their lawyers 'feeling loved and happy'. The telecommunicating paradox therefore does not seem to exert a deleterious impact on lawyers involved in NewLaw.

The persistence of email can give rise to ter Hoeven and van Zoonen's second paradox – the 'connectivity paradox',[68] which relates to the fact that while the technology provides more freedom and control over work, it reduces the ability to disengage and adds to work intensification. Commentators have long recognised that human beings cannot work 24/7 without time for recovery.[69] This was a frequent source of grievance for the corporate lawyers who were interviewed for the Balancing Law and Life project, as they were expected to respond to phone calls and emails even when on an (unpaid) flexi-day at home. One interviewee was told to keep her mobile phone turned on by her pillow at night in case she needed to respond to a call from another time zone. In contrast, NewLaw interviewees were of the view that emails did not have to be answered at all hours of the night and made a point of 'pushing back' on client expectations.[70] If clients were informed at the outset that their lawyers did not answer calls after hours, this was generally accepted. It is therefore possible to resist work

67 Claartje L. ter Hoeven and Ward van Zoonen, 'Flexible Work Designs and Employee Well-being: Examining the Effects of Resources and Demands' (2015) 30 *New Technology, Work and Employment* 237.

68 Ibid.

69 E.g,. Hannah Arendt, *The Human Condition*, University of Chicago Press, Chicago 1958, p. 71.

70 Cf. Joan C. Williams, Aaron Platt and Jessica Lee, *Disruptive Innovation: New Models of Legal Practice*, University of California Hasting College of Law, Legal Studies Research Paper Series, 2015, p. 5.

intensification if the hyper-competitiveness that has come to be associated with global legal practice is rejected. One UK firm embraced the Japanese philosophy of Kaizen that is built upon collaboration and constant improvement, which the firm extended to working collaboratively rather than competitively with other firms.

Ter Hoeven and van Zoonen's third paradox, the 'autonomy paradox' posits that the more freedom and autonomy employees have, the more intensely they work.[71] This was attested to by lawyers who were principals of NewLaw firms, who worked hard to ensure the success of their business:

> All the pressure is self-imposed <laughs>. So I manage it … I don't have an employer. It's basically me … So, it's all my responsibility now … I'm juggling as a working mum <laughs> … So, yes, I mean since starting up my own business – understanding the financing, the accounting, how much I put aside for superannuation, for tax, planning all those things, which I think I could've taken for granted when I was an employee … Yes <laughs> … it is probably the dilemma for women like me where we have gone to university, we have got a profession, and I don't want to give that all up. (Principal, Australia, Female, 26 September 2018)

The autonomy paradox is doubly complicated for lawyer/mothers who seek more help from their male partners. They love their children and want to spend time with them when they are small, but they also love their work and do not want to give it up. The stress they face in juggling work and family is compounded by the deep-seated cultural antipathy towards men who participate in the everyday care of children:

> When my son was born I went back to teaching because I had contractually committed to that 18 months prior. My son was four months. When I wanted to set up my own practice, there was a conversation in my husband's workplace of surprise around, 'Oh, your wife wants to go and work?' which sort of <laughs> made my blood boil a bit, actually <laughs> … he was a full-time worker and travelling up to [the city] and there was this kind of surprise that I'm going out and starting my practice and teaching and he might be needed to pick up my son from day care one day a week. He needed some flexibility, which he's had to really fight hard for. So, that was my first-hand experience of – it doesn't get better for me unless it gets better for the man. (Principal, Australia, Female, 26 September 2018)

71 Ter Hoeven and van Zoonen, above n. 67, p. 240.

The stress for women associated with juggling the different components of their lives was offset by the sense of satisfaction they derived from their work. A comparable degree of balance was very difficult if not impossible to achieve in full-time permanent work *in situ* in a traditional firm.[72]

The paradoxes identified by ter Hoeven and van Zoonen therefore do not appear to pose an insuperable problem for lawyers working remotely. In contrast, the issue of ageism is more problematic.

5.2. AGEISM

There has been a marked proliferation of law graduates in both Australia and the UK because of the commodification of higher education.[73] At the same time, there has been something of a decline in the demand by traditional law firms for young lawyers.[74] Practices such as offshoring and nearshoring, as well as the rapid growth in artificial intelligence (AI) have contributed to this decline. It is notable that in the Australian 2017 Urbis *National Profile of Solicitors*, the youngest age cohort (24 or younger) was shown to have decreased by 14.9 per cent between 2014 and 2016, the strongest decrease compared with other age brackets.[75] At the same time, the increase in the numbers of law graduates has exacerbated the competition for places and there is some evidence of exploitation, such

---

72 Ibid. 241.

73 In the 30 years, 1989–2019, the number of Australian law schools increased from 12 to 40, with 7,583 students graduating with a basic law degree (an LLB or a JD) in 2015, Council of Australian Law Deans, *Data regarding Law School Graduate Numbers and Outcomes*, 2015 <https://cald.asn.au/wp-content/uploads/2017/11/Factsheet-Law_Students_in_Australia.pdf>. In the UK in 1970, there were 29 institutions offering law degrees, whereas there were 122 in 2019. This has inevitably led to an explosion in the number of law graduates, with an annual figure of approximately 16,000 in 2016. See Law Society, *Trends in the Solicitors' Profession: Annual Statistics Report 2017*, The Law Society, London 2018 <https://www.womeninthelawuk.com/wp-content/uploads/2018/11/TLS-ASR-2017-final.pdf>.

74 Bill Potts, a Director of the Law Council of Australia suggested that the proportion of graduates practising law had fallen from 50 to 20 per cent because of computerisation and a correlative reduction in staff numbers. See Charmaine Kane, 'Law Council of Australia raises Concerns about Uberisation of Profession by Technology', *ABC Gold Coast*, Business News, 28.09.2018 <http://www.abc.net.au/news/2018-09-28/law-council-of-australia-raises-concerns-about-uberisation/10306298>.

75 Urbis Pty. Ltd., *National Profile of Solicitors 2016* (Report prepared for the Law Society of NSW), 2017, p. 9 <https://www.lawsociety.com.au/sites/default/files/2018-04/NATIONAL%20PROFILE%20OF%20SOLICITORS%202016.compressed.pdf>.

as engaging young lawyers as unpaid interns who then hope to receive an offer of employment.[76] Similarly, it has been claimed that students are being expected to work extraordinary hours despite deterioration in their mental health.[77]

The problems of discrimination involving young lawyers may be compounded in the case of NewLaw as the key criteria of autonomy and control are correlated with seniority and experience. If a lawyer is going to work remotely, either as an employee or an independent contractor, that person needs to have at least five years' Post-Qualified Experience (PQE). Some firms prefer lawyers who have 10 years' PQE and have had in-house and possibly also corporate experience.[78] In addition, there needs to be a bond of loyalty, usually built up over time, so that a firm can be confident that a lawyer may be trusted to work remotely:

> The principal who I went to university with and I are very close friends … We worked together on bigger matters, so we know exactly our strengths and weaknesses. He has more experience than me broadly speaking as a commercial lawyer but I have more experience than him in [my specialty]; so we fill gaps for each other. We've worked together enough that we really know how each other works. So he has a lot of trust in me. (Employed Lawyer, Australia, Male, 24 September 2018)

Trust, however, occludes the inherent ageism associated with NewLaw that renders independent and remote practice difficult for young people. This is despite the fact that NewLaw firms may emphasise youthism, depicting the work as exciting and fast-moving, such as working for groovy 'start-ups'.[79] Nevertheless, the prerequisites of seniority and experience are not arbitrary or unreasonable, as junior lawyers without an unrestricted

---

76 Mardi Grivas, 'Legal Education Issues are Highlighting Vulnerability of Students', *Lawyers Weekly*, 1.10.2018 <https://www.lawyersweekly.com.au/opinion/24156-legal-education-issues-are-highlighting-vulnerability-of-students>.

77 Ibid.

78 Keystone Law, with more than 250 lawyers who work remotely, took on 31 new recruits in the first six months of 2018 with an average age of 46. See John Hyde, 'Listed Firm Boosts Profits as Job Applicants Spurn "Traditional" Partnerships', *The Law Society Gazette*, 25.09.2018 <https://www.lawgazette.co.uk/practice/listed-firm-boosts-profits-as-job-applicants-spurn-traditional-partnerships/5067681.article>.

79 E.g., LegalVision, above n. 57.

practising certificate are not equipped to offer advice in complex matters in an unsupervised capacity:

> We don't have time or the appetite to train a lawyer … We want them to come to us when they've had that training … as our business grows, we'll be able to do that more and it's something we definitely want to do. But I guess at least for a little while, there's probably gonna be limited opportunities for junior lawyers to do a lot of the work – certainly most of the secondment work. (State Manager, Australia, Female, 25 September 2018)

Some law firms nevertheless employ young lawyers to engage in a form of triage, although this work is increasingly being assigned to paralegals:

> They are essentially a call centre/sales team, and what they do is they use their legal knowledge when speaking to clients to help them identify issues and see whether it's something that we can actually help with. They then scope up the project, put forward a quote, and the business either agrees to work with us or they don't. So that team is about 20–22 people, most of them will eventually make their way into the legal team. (HR Manager, Australia, Female, 18 April 2018)

While there is some provision for succession planning in the larger firms, many NewLaw firms are very small and do not have the capacity to embark on training.[80] Millennials are commonly marginalised and consigned to the gig economy unless fortunate enough to secure a training placement in a traditional law firm. Both traditional and NewLaw firms engage young lawyers as independent contractors who call in a couple of days per week or work with 'start-up' clients on secondment. This work, which includes 'search and discovery' and 'due diligence', is largely routine and does not satisfy the need for breadth of training and oversight that would train young lawyers to act independently. Such work may be a form of 'gigging' that is economical for law firms because it entails no overheads. As 'gigging' precludes a regular income, it may compound the stress experienced by young lawyers.[81] In contrast, financial insecurity is unlikely to be a problem

---

80 Cf. Jan L. Jacobowitz, Katie M. Lachter and Gabriella Morello, 'Cultural Evolution or Revolution? The Millennial's Growing Impact on Professionalism and the Practice of Law' (2016) 23 *The Professional Lawyer* (ABA) 20.

81 Young people are already vulnerable to the onset of mental illness. See Kelk et al, above n. 37, p. 37.

for senior experienced lawyers who are not only in demand and have their own clients, but are likely to possess sound financial resources, including superannuation as a result of years of well-paid employment.

The neoliberalisation of corporate practice would seem to have exacerbated the unwillingness to train graduates out of fear that it could affect a firm's profit margins. There is undoubtedly an element of altruism in training the next generation of lawyers, which may be beyond the capacity of either a small NewLaw firm or an individual lawyer:

> If for example, I was running my own practice ... I probably wouldn't take on anyone – ever. I would just work independently because that gives me complete freedom, and if I have too much work, I'll just refer it to my contacts. That works well for me because I'm not trying to build a business; I'm not trying to make more money ... I like supervision but it's very difficult when I have such minimal time and it takes three years to add value ... three years of good commercial law mentoring to be able to start being profitable. I can't afford three years of wages. (Employed Lawyer, Australia, Male, 24 September 2018)

In Krill's large-scale study on the prevalence of substance abuse and poor mental health in the American legal profession, younger lawyers were found to be the most troubled and at-risk group in terms of depression, anxiety and stress.[82] In the UK also, increasing levels of stress, anxiety and poor mental health have been documented among young lawyers.[83] The lack of adequate provision for generational renewal raises significant questions for the future wellbeing of young lawyers.

Lawyers have expressed concern about the possibility of being made redundant by AI.[84] However, if jobs disappear, the most vulnerable are likely to be the least experienced; that is, the junior lawyers engaged in routine work, work that is already being digitalised. Unless the issue of generational renewal is specifically addressed, young lawyers face being reduced to the status of a new precariat.[85]

---

82 Krill, above, n. 23, p. 10.

83 Richard Collier, 'Anxiety and Wellbeing Amongst Junior Lawyers: A Research Study', Presentation at 'Mind your Head', *Anxiety UK*, London, 2019; Junior Lawyers Division, The Law Society, *Resilience and Wellbeing Survey 2019*, The Law Society, London 2019. <http://communities.lawsociety.org.uk/Uploads/b/y/k/resilience-wellbeing-survey-report-2019.pdf>.

84 LexisNexis, '2018 Legal Technology Survey Highlights: Overview & Analysis', *Legal Frontiers from AI to Ethics*, LexisNexis, 2018.

85 Hilary Sommerlad, 'The New "Professionalism" in England and Wales: Talent, Diversity, and a Legal Precariat' in Spencer Headworth, Robert L. Nelson,

Some interviewees initially thought that NewLaw would attract mainly women seeking to accommodate family responsibilities, but its gender composition appears to be mixed. Although precise data are not available because of the volatility of NewLaw, it is apparent that the flexibility of NewLaw is very attractive to senior men in traditional firms who are tired of working 24/7 and are keen to strike out on their own. Nevertheless, as approximately 65 per cent of graduates in both Australia and the UK are female, the imbalance could become more acute over time, with an increasing proportion of young women lawyers working in automated platforms in the gig economy. Decreasing training opportunities could therefore mean that young women lawyers face being disproportionately represented in future statistics on stress and depression in the legal profession.

6. CONCLUSION

The post-Millennial evidence reveals that lawyers in traditional legal practice evince high levels of depression and mental illness while, in contrast, NewLaw suggests that lawyers experience a high level of satisfaction because they are able to work flexibly and autonomously. It is notable that none of the lawyers in NewLaw firms who were interviewed mentioned stress or depression, other than in the context of past experience in a traditional law firm. Those working remotely believed that they were able to effect a balance between the demands of work, family life and leisure activities, thereby significantly boosting their happiness and wellbeing.[86]

It is apparent that NewLaw practice represents a 'disruptive innovation',[87] aided by rapid technological change that is already exercising an impact on traditional law firm practice. Flexible work, fixed fee billing and remote working, are beginning to be implemented by traditional firms to staunch the haemorrhage of experienced lawyers (and their clients). There are so many variations in the types of NewLaw firms found in both England and Australia that generalisations about meaningful distinctions could not be made, especially as the Internet knows no jurisdictional boundary.

Ronit Dinovitzer and David B. Wilkins (eds), *Diversity in Practice: Race, Gender, and Class in Legal and Professional Careers*, Cambridge University Press, Cambridge 2016, pp. 236–60.

86 Cf. Krieger and Sheldon, above n. 26, p. 621.

87 Christensen, above n. 22.

It is undeniable that technological innovation is contributing to the greater flexibility of work generally,[88] but the creativity and agility of NewLaw, as well as its disregard for orthodoxy, gives it an edge over traditional law firms. The centrality of autonomy and flexibility to NewLaw are imbuing legal practice with an unprecedented sense of wellbeing that will necessarily entail revising the conclusions of many of the studies that found high levels of lawyer distress a decade or more ago. In contrast, while the future of NewLaw looks very promising on the surface, the caveat relates to the unresolved issues pertaining to the proliferation of *recent* law graduates who are increasingly likely to find themselves consigned to precarious gigs on the fringes of the profession.

---

88 Ter Hoeven and van Zoonen, above n. 67.

CHAPTER 9

DO LAW FIRM STRUCTURES MATTER?

Incorporated Legal Practices and the Health and Wellbeing of Lawyers

Tahlia Gordon

1. Introduction 200
2. The Unhealthy and Un-Well Profession: Legal Practitioners in Crisis 203
3. The Demands of Practising in the Traditional Law Firm Partnership Structure 205
   3.1. The Billable Hour and Billing Targets 209
   3.2. The Demands of Clients 213
4. Law Firm Practice Structures: A New Look but a Different Feel? . . . 218
   4.1. Benefits of Incorporation for the Health and Wellbeing of Lawyers 221
      4.1.1. Access to External Capital 222
      4.1.2. Limited Liability 226
      4.1.3. Improve Staff Recruitment, Retention and Succession Planning 227
      4.1.4. One-Stop Shopping 229
      4.1.5. Improved Management Structures 230
   4.2. Costs of Incorporation for the Health and Wellbeing of Lawyers 232
      4.2.1. Threat to the Professional and Ethical Obligations of Lawyers 232
      4.2.2. Increased Commercialisation and Loss of Collegiality 234
5. Conclusion 236

1. INTRODUCTION

On 24 August 2018 mega-law firm King & Wood Mallesons received an 'Improvement Notice' from the health and safety regulator in Victoria, in relation to 'the management of employee fatigue in high pressure situations.'[1] The Improvement Notice was prompted by a complaint that legal practitioners in the firm's Melbourne office had been subject to gruelling working conditions as a result of tight deadlines imposed by the Royal Commission into Banking and Finance in Australia. The Improvement Notice is believed to be the first of its kind in Australia in relation to a law firm. Minds Count (formerly the Tristan Jepson Memorial Foundation) described the Notice as a 'watershed moment for the legal profession in Australia' and tweeted as follows:

> The genuine health-risks of excessive work pressure and stress in legal workplaces should be well understood. Depression, anxiety, alcoholism and suicide are all well-established as potential outcomes. The risks are real, and the consequences can be devastating.[2]

The health and wellbeing of legal practitioners in Australia has attracted considerable academic and media attention over the past few decades.[3]

---

1 Sarah Thompson, Jemima Whyte and David Marin-Guzman, 'King & Wood Mallesons investigated for overworking employees', *The Australian Financial Review*, 11 October 2018, https://www.afr.com/business/king--wood-mallesons-investigated-for-overworking-employees-20181010-h16hei.

2 Jerome Doraisamy, 'WorkSafe attention on KWM a "watershed" moment', *Lawyers Weekly*, 17 October 2018, https://www.lawyersweekly.com.au/biglaw/24266-worksafe-attention-on-kwm-a-watershed-moment.

3 See for example, Jill Margo, 'Young lawyer outs depression that is endemic in legal profession', *The Australian Financial Review (online)*, 29 September 2015, https://www.afr.com/lifestyle/health/mens-health/young-lawyer-outs-depression-that-is-endemic-in-legal-profession-20150927-gjw3bu; Thomas Oriti, 'Lawyers need more mental health support, advocates say', *ABC News*, 17 May 2017, http://www.abc.net.au/news/2017-05-16/lawyers-need-more-mental-health-support/8529916; Sarah Whyte, 'Tired, hungry and stressed out: What life is like for many Australian lawyers', *ABC News*, 1 February 2018, http://www.abc.net.au/news/2018-02-01/stressed-lawyers-are-suffering-from-eating-disorders:-study/9375696; Jerome Doraisamy, 'Unethical firm climate breeding unhealthier lawyer', Lawyers Weekly, 1 March 2018; https://www.lawyersweekly.com.au/biglaw/22820-unethical-firm-climate-breeding-unhealthier-lawyers; Emma Ryan, 'Why are lawyers, and other professionals, so depressed?', *Lawyers Weekly*, 6 September 2018, https://www.lawyersweekly.com.au/biglaw/23967-why-are-lawyers-and-other-professionals-depressed.

Research studies indicate that the extent to which Australian legal practitioners suffer from depression and mental illness as a result of their work, as compared to the general population, is alarming.[4] Recent law graduates and young legal practitioners are at most risk of suffering ill health as a result of practising law. The stress of lawyering on recent graduates and young legal practitioners is so immense that an unprecedented number of young legal practitioners have left the profession.[5] The discourse in relation to mental health and wellbeing in the legal profession identifies a number of causal factors that are said to contribute to higher rates of depression and lower levels of wellbeing in legal practitioners.[6] These factors include particular personality traits[7] such as perfectionism, pessimism and anxiety as well as particular workplace demands typical of the traditional law firm partnership structure.[8]

The impact of workplace demands, particularly as a legal practitioner practising in a traditional law firm partnership structure, is immense. The law firm partnership structure is a breeding ground for discontent. Workplace demands such as the billable hour and billable hour targets as well as unreasonable and demanding clients are negatively impacting the

4 Beaton Consulting, 'Annual Professions Survey' (Research Summary, Beyondblue, April 2007) 2–3; Norm Kelk et al., *Courting the Blues: Attitudes towards depression in Australian law students and lawyers* (Report, Brain and Mind Research Institute, University of Sydney, January 2009); Adele J. Bergin and Nerina L. Jimmieson, 'Australian Lawyer Well-Being: Workplace Demands, Resources and the Impact of Time-Billing Targets' (2014) 21 *Psychiatry, Psychology and Law* 427; Janet Chan, Suzanne Poynton and Jasmine Bruce, 'Lawyering Stress and Work Culture: An Australian Study' (2014) 37 *UNSW Law Journal* 1062.

5 Law Council of Australia, *National Attrition and Re-engagement Study* (2014), 5, https://www.lawcouncil.asn.au/policy-agenda/advancing-the-profession/equal-opportunities-in-the-law/national-report-on-attrition-and-re-engagement.

6 Christine Parker and David Ruschena, 'The Pressures of Billable Hours: Lessons From a Survey of Billing Practices Inside Law Firms' (2011) 9(2) *University of St. Thomas Law Journal* 619; Christopher Kendall, *Report on Psychological Distress and Depression in the Legal Profession* (Report, Council of the Law Society of Western Australia, March 2011) 12.

7 See for example, Martin Seligman, Paul Verkuil and Terry Kang, 'Why Lawyers Are Unhappy' (2001) 23 *Cardozo Law Review* 33; Susan Daicoff, 'Lawyer, Know Thyself: A Review of Empirical Research on Attorney Attributes Bearing on Professionalism' (1997) 46 *American University Law Review* 1337; Patrick J. Schiltz, 'On Being a Happy, Healthy, and Ethical Member of an Unhappy, Unhealthy, and Unethical Profession' (1999) 52 *Vanderbilt Law Review* 871; Judy Allen and Paula Baron, 'Buttercup Goes to Law School: Student Wellbeing in Stressed Law Schools' (2004) 29 *Alternative Law Journal* 285.

8 Bergin and Jimmieson, above n. 4, 428–29.

professional and personal lives of Australian legal practitioners. Research conducted on the impact of the workplace on the health and wellbeing of legal practitioners identifies several changes that could be implemented to improve the incidence of stress, depression and mental illness.[9] These include structural and cultural improvements to the workplace such as (i) better systems for managing workloads, client demands and expectations, as well as billing practices; (ii) supporting a healthy and positive work-life balance and (iii) ensuring that working relationships are respectful and collaborative.[10]

This chapter reflects upon these suggestions and considers whether a change in the structure of law firms would improve the health and wellbeing of legal practitioners. In doing so this chapter will specifically focus on whether the incorporation of law firms and the ability of persons that are not legal practitioners ('non-lawyers') to own or invest in law firms as a result of incorporation would have any impact on the health and wellbeing of legal practitioners. This chapter will do so by exploring the benefits and costs that are alleged to flow from non-lawyers being able to own or invest in law firms and the effect of those alleged benefits and costs on the health and wellbeing of legal practitioners. This is the first time that such an exploration has been conducted.

This chapter is organised as follows. Section 2 will commence by outlining the incidence of ill-health and wellbeing in the Australian legal profession. Section 3 will outline two prominent causal factors leading to the incidence of ill-health and wellbeing in the Australian legal profession – time-billing targets and demanding clients. Section 4 will commence with a discussion about the legislative framework in relation to the incorporation of law firms. This section will then explore the key difference between ILPs and traditional law firms – non-lawyer ownership. This section will discuss the alleged benefits and costs that are said to flow from law firms incorporating and having non-lawyer owners or investors. The chapter will then conclude with a discussion about the importance of implementing health and wellbeing initiatives that sustainable and are more than mere 'band-aid' solutions.

---

9 See for example, Dr. Christopher Kendall, *Report on Psychological Distress and Depression in the Legal Profession*, The Law Society of Western Australia, March 2011; Chan et al., above n. 4, 1101.

10 Chan, above n. 4, 1101.

2. THE UNHEALTHY AND UN-WELL PROFESSION: LEGAL PRACTITIONERS IN CRISIS

According to a study conducted in 2007 by *beyondblue* in conjunction with Beaton Consulting, which examined the prevalence of depression and non-prescription drug use among professionals (those working in financial, legal, architectural and similar industries), professionals were found to experience more moderate-to-severe symptoms of depression than the general population.[11] The research study also found that legal practitioners, in particular, were more likely than their colleagues in other professions to use alcohol and other drugs to cope with their depression.

The findings from the 2007 study were analogous to a second study conducted in 2009 by the Brain and Mind Research Institute of Australia (BMRI) in conjunction with the Tristan Jepson Memorial Foundation.[12] The BMRI study, which involved 924 solicitors and 756 barristers, as well as 741 final year law students from 13 Australian Universities, revealed that legal practitioners and law students experience higher levels of psychological distress and risk of depression compared with Australian community norms and other tertiary student groups.[13] The BMRI study further revealed that the attitudes and behaviours of the study's respondents imply a reluctance to seek help for mental health issues because of the stigma attached to mental health and the likelihood of discrimination by employers.[14]

More recent studies such as that by Bergin and Jimmieson[15] and Chan, Poynton and Bruce, both published in 2014; and Skead, Rogers and Doraisamy,[16] published in 2018, reveal similar findings. Bergin and Jimmieson's study, which comprised an online questionnaire completed by 384 legal practitioner respondents working full-time, reported that 37% of respondents experienced moderate to extremely severe depressive symptoms; 31% of respondents experienced moderate to extremely severe

11 Beaton Consulting, above n. 4, 2–3.
12 Kelk et al, above n. 4.
13 Ibid. at 37.
14 Ibid. at 39.
15 Bergin and Jimmieson, above n. 4.
16 Natalie K. Stead, Shane L. Rogers and Jerome Doraisamy, 'Looking beyond the mirror: Psychological distress, disordered eating, weight and shape concerns; and maladaptive eating habits in lawyers and law students', (2018) *International Journal of Law and Psychiatry*, 12 September 2018.

anxiety symptoms; and, 49% of respondents experienced moderate to extremely severe stress symptoms.[17] Chan et al.'s study, which comprised a survey completed by 965 legal practitioners and 30 telephone interviews, revealed that depression, anxiety and stress within the legal profession is considerably high.[18] The respondents in Chan et al.'s study were twice as likely to report moderate-to-severe symptoms of depression compared with respondents in the 2007 *beyondblue* and Beaton Consulting study.[19] Skead, Rogers and Doraisamy's study of 428 law students and 148 legal practitioners revealed that the respondents reported higher levels of depression than the general population for psychological distress. Skead et al.'s study also revealed that both legal practitioners and law students were more concerned about their weight and shape than the general population and were more inclined to restrain themselves from eating.[20] The authors attributed this finding to a variety of factors including the adversarial nature of the practice of law, unrealistic expectations of themselves, pessimism as well as the stressful and time-poor environment in which legal practitioners work.[21]

The research conducted in Australia on health and wellbeing in the legal profession reflects research that has been conducted in other common law jurisdictions.[22] In the United States a recent study conducted by the Hazelden Betty Ford Foundation and the American Bar Association Commission on Lawyer Assistance Programs revealed substantial and hazardous levels of problem drinking and high rates of depression and anxiety symptoms in the U.S. legal profession.[23] The study, which compared over 12,800 legal practitioners across the United States with other professionals, found that

---

17 Ibid. at 437.

18 Thirty two% of respondents reported that they experienced moderate to extremely severe symptoms of depression, 28% of respondents reported that they experienced anxiety, and 26% of respondents reported that they experienced stress. Chan, Poynton and Bruce, above n. 4, 1080.

19 Ibid. at 1081.

20 Stead et al., above n. 16, 9.

21 Ibid.

22 See for example, G.A.H. Benjamin et al., 'The Prevalence of Depression, Alcohol Abuse, and Cocaine Abuse Amongst United States Lawyers' (1990) 13 *International Journal of Law and Psychiatry* 233; Connie J. Beck, Bruce D. Sales and G.A.H. Benjamin, 'Lawyer Distress: Alcohol Related Concerns among a Sample of Practicing Lawyers' (1995) 10 *Journal of Law and Health* 1.

23 Patrick R. Krill, Ryan Johnson and Linda Albert, 'The Prevalence of Substance Use and Other Mental Health Concerns Among American Attorneys' (2016) *The Journal of Addiction Medicine* 46.

alcohol use disorders and mental health issues are far more prevalent amongst these respondents than other professional populations. According to the study more than a fifth of the respondents consume alcohol at levels consistent with 'problem drinking' and respondents in the first 10 years of their careers have the highest incidence of problem drinking. The study further revealed that 28 per cent of the respondents struggle with some level of depression and 19 per cent show symptoms of anxiety.[24] It was the first major study in 25 years to quantify the prevalence of substance abuse among legal practitioners in the United States.

In the United Kingdom statistics published by the Health and Safety Executive – the independent regulator for work-related health and safety in Great Britain – in 2017 on work-related stress, depression or anxiety, place 'legal professionals' fourth in the list of the most stressful jobs in the UK.[25] Research conducted by Keystone Law, a law firm in England and Wales provides some further details about the health and wellbeing of the legal profession.[26] According to Keystone Law just under 70 per cent of the legal practitioners they surveyed agreed that their job is more stressful than other professions. The unrelenting, competitive nature of the practice of law and the demands of the workplace appear to be integrally related to the demise in health and wellbeing in the legal profession.

3. THE DEMANDS OF PRACTISING IN THE TRADITIONAL LAW FIRM PARTNERSHIP STRUCTURE

Historically, legal practitioners in Australia who sought to establish a law firm had a limited number of choices available when choosing the structure of the firm. Law firms could either be structured as partnerships where lawyers could work together with other lawyers; or law firms could be structured as sole practitioners. Legal practitioners were not permitted

---

24 Ibid.

25 Health and Safety Executive, *Work-related Stress, Depression or Anxiety Statistics in Great Britain 2017*, p. 6, http://www.hse.gov.uk/statistics/causdis/stress/stress.pdf.

26 The results were based on a survey of 300 legal professionals from the top 50–100 law firms across the UK. Keystone Law, *Lawyers and the Pursuit of Happiness*, 2016, p. 5, https://www.keystonelaw.co.uk/application/files/5714/7626/1331/Lawyer_Happiness_Survey_HR.pdf.

to form a partnership and share fees with non-lawyers and non-lawyers were not allowed to own or invest in law firms.[27] The restrictions were premised on the belief that a partnership between legal practitioners and non-lawyers would threaten the independence of the legal profession.[28] The sole practitioner structure was the dominant structure in the early years of the legal profession in Australia.[29] However, in the latter part of the twentieth century the law firm partnership assumed greater popularity.[30] The popularity of the law firm partnership continues today.

The traditional law firm partnership is 'a voluntary association of legal practitioners – and only legal practitioners – who agree to share the risks and rewards of a common venture.'[31] Pursuant to this structure, every partner 'owns' the firm and the profits of the firm are shared by all of the owners until the partner leaves the firm.[32] The traditional law firm partnership structure is characterised by a horizontal management structure. Therefore, as 'owners' of the firm, partners are directly involved in the management of the firm and decisions regarding the firm are made by all of the partners in the firm. In this traditional partnership structure, partners rely on associates to assist in the provision of legal services.[33] Associates who perform well are identified as potential partners and provided with an opportunity to join the partnership.[34] Whilst this structure had historically worked effectively, changes have placed inordinate pressure on the efficacy of the traditional law firm partnership structure.

Over the past few decades there has been a considerable increase in competition in the practice of law in Australia.[35] Reasons for the increase in

---

27 New South Wales Attorney-General's Department, *National Competition Policy Review of the Legal Profession Act 1987: Final Report* (Sydney, 1998), para. 10.3.

28 The Honourable Jeff Shaw, *Legal Profession Amendment (Incorporated Legal Practices) Bill*, Second Reading, 23 June 2000.

29 Stan Ross, 'Prospects for structural and economic integration of the Australian legal profession' (1997) 4 *International Journal of the Legal Profession*, 267, 282.

30 S. Roach Anleu, 'The Legal Profession in the United States and Australia' (1992) 19 *Work and Occupations* 184, 189–90; Oliver Mendelsohn and Matthew Lippman, 'The Emergence of the Corporate Law Firm in Australia' (1979) 3 *UNSW Law Journal* 78, 84.

31 Milton C. Regan Jr, 'Lawyers, Symbols, and Money: Outside Investment in Law Firms' (2008) 27 *Penn State International Law Review* 407, 416.

32 Johnathon T. Molot, 'What's Wrong with Law Firms? A Corporate Finance Solution to Law Firm Short-Termism' (2014) 88 *Southern California Law Review* 1, 4.

33 Marc Galanter and Thomas Palay, *Tournament of Lawyers: The Transformation of the Big Law Firm* (University of Chicago Press, 1991).

34 Mendelsohn and Lippman, above n. 30, 91.

35 Chief Justice T.F. Bathurst, 'Commercialisation of Legal Practice: Conflict Ab Initio; Conflict De Futuro' (Paper presented at the Commonwealth Law Association

competition are manifold. Firstly, the number of national and international law firms in Australia has grown considerably,[36] as has the size of corporate law firms as a result of mergers.[37] Secondly, the large accounting firms have entered the legal marketplace offering legal services to clients in addition to the accounting services they traditionally provide.[38] Third, corporate clients dissatisfied with the fees charged by law firms are establishing legal teams in-house to save costs.[39] Fourth, law firms are investing in technology to streamline and automate time-consuming and repetitive legal tasks and are today encouraging their employees to become more tech-literate and learn new skills such as coding.[40] Fifth, there has been an influx of new entrants to the market such as online legal service providers offering low-cost legal documents to small and medium size enterprises (SME) and individual 'mum and dad' consumers.[41] Sixth, the advent of legal information websites such as *AustLII* has enabled the information asymmetry that once existed between legal practitioners and the general public to be ameliorated.[42] The impact of these disruptive factors on law firm partnerships in Australia is prodigious.

Law firms are competing for clients who seek value for money, and are competing for the most talented legal practitioners to service those clients. There has been a significant decrease in work for firms of all sizes from

---

Regional Conference, Sydney, 21 April 2012), http://www.austlii.edu.au/au/journals/NSWJSchol/2012/22.pdf. (2012) 21 *Journal of the Commonwealth Lawyer* 35.

36 Stan Ross, 'Prospects for structural and economic integration of the Australian legal profession' (1997) 4 *International Journal of the Legal Profession*, 267, 268–69, 282–83.

37 Mendelsohn and Lippman, above n. 30; Anleu, above n. 30, 190; Thompson Reuters, *State of the Legal Market: Australia – 2018*, Melbourne Law School, Thompson Reuters, http://images.connect.thomsonreuters.com.au/Web/TRLegalAU/%7B4f3b4839-db77-4dd4-9d5b-a63df5679da2%7D_australia-state-of-the-legal-market-2018_thomson-reuters-australia.pdf.

38 Agnes King, 'Big four accounting firms push into legal services', *The Australian Financial Review (online)*, 21 July 2015, https://www.afr.com/business/accounting/afr8acclawyers-vs-accountants-20150617-ghq715.

39 Joanne Bagust, 'The Legal Profession and the Business of Law' (2013) 35 *Sydney Law Review* 27, 42; Vicki Waye, Martie-Louise Verreynne and Jane Knowler, 'Innovation in the Australian legal profession' (2018) 25(2) *International Journal of the Legal Profession* 213, 216.

40 Law Society of New South Wales, *Future of Law and Innovation in the Profession*, 2017, Law Society of New South Wales, 31, https://www.lawsociety.com.au/sites/default/files/2018-03/1272952.pdf.

41 Ibid.

42 Graham Greenleaf, Technology and the Professions (2017) 40 *UNSW Law Journal* 302, 308–9.

corporate clients.[43] Law firms are consequently turning to technology[44] and outsourcing back-office tasks such as IT, finance and marketing as well as e-discovery, to ensure their clients receive greater value for money and greater price certainty.[45] Recent research on innovation in the legal profession found that a substantial number of law firms had adopted innovation strategies to effectively compete with other law firms and entities providing legal services.[46] Such strategies include implementing new pricing models, changing operational processes, improving managerial and organisational processes and implementing new cost-saving technologies.[47] However, innovation is being stymied because law firms are experiencing difficulties accessing funds to innovate.

Although overall revenue and gross profitability have remained constant, net profit per equity partner has decreased[48] as has the gap between partner earnings.[49] Furthermore, the number of equity partnerships on offer has decreased.[50] As a result of the dwindling offers of equity partnerships, law firms have moved away from the traditional lockstep partnership structure (where partners move through a number of ascending steps of remuneration, irrespective of performance, until

43 Mahlab, *Mahlab Report 2017* (Private Practice, Mahlab Recruitment, 2017) 1, http://www.mahlab.com.au/files/editor_upload/File/Mahlab-Reports/Mahlab-Report-2017-Private.pdf.

44 Macquarie Bank, 'An industry in transition 2017 Legal Benchmarking Results' (2017, Macquarie Bank), 1, 12, http://www.macquarie.com/dafiles/Internet/mgl/au/docs/noindex/macquarie-2017-legal-benchmarking-full-results.pdf#?toggle=success&scroll=request-form.

45 Commonwealth Bank of Australia, Commbank Legal Market Pulse (2017, Commonwealth Bank of Australia), pp. 1, 13, 19, https://www.commbank.com.au/content/dam/commbank/corporate/pds/commbank-legal-market-pulse-Aug-2017.pdf; Macquarie Bank, An industry in transition 2017 Legal Benchmarking Results' (2017, Macquarie Bank), pp. 1, 34, http://www.macquarie.com/dafiles/Internet/mgl/au/docs/noindex/macquarie-2017-legal-benchmarking-full-results.pdf#?toggle=success&scroll=request-form.

46 Martie-Louise Verreynne and Jane Knowler, 'Innovation in the Australian legal profession' (2017) *International Journal of the Legal Profession* 1, 12.

47 Ibid. at 18.

48 Commonwealth Bank of Australia, above n.45, p. 9.

49 Crowe Horwath, 'Stepping Up the Numbers, Financial Performance Benchmarking Study 2017', Crowe Horwath and the Australian Legal Practice Management Association, 1, https://www.crowehorwath.com.au/wp-content/uploads/ALPMA_BenchmarkingReport_2017-FINAL.pdf.

50 Marianna Papadakis, 'Law firms shrink partner numbers as clients cut back', *The Australian Financial review* (online), 23 June 2016, https://www.afr.com/business/legal/law-firms-shrink-partner-numbers-as-clients-cut-back-20160620-gpnvdm; Mahlab, above n. 43.

full parity is achieved with other partners) to a more meritocratic system that is focused on performance, placing pressure on legal practitioners to perform above their peers.

Competition has additionally resulted in a slower path to equity partnership. Unlike years ago, when legal practitioners in their late 20s could expect to become partners, young legal practitioners are having to wait another decade to be offered partnership.[51] The slow path to equity partnership is leading solicitors and senior associates to explore in-house work or a change in career outside the law.[52] The implications of this predicament are dire for legal practitioners. The ramifications of such exigencies are concerning. Workplace demands such as the billable hour and billable-hours targets place undue pressure and stress on legal practitioners and have been found to lead to low levels of health and wellbeing in the legal profession. The demands of clients further exacerbate this demise. The remainder of this section will consider the impact of these workplace demands on the health and wellbeing of legal practitioners.

3.1. THE BILLABLE HOUR AND BILLING TARGETS

The billable hour was historically used as a mechanism for charging clients.[53] Whilst a useful tool for charging clients and indeed encouraged by management consultants to increase profitability,[54] billable hours are also commonly used by law firms as a tool for managing and controlling their employees.[55] Today, billable hour targets set by law firms are closely

---

51 Lara Bullock, 'Becoming an equity partner was once the ultimate aim of many lawyers. But times are changing and so are lawyers goals', *Lawyers Weekly*, 20 June 2016, https://www.lawyersweekly.com.au/features/18813-holy-grail.

52 Mahlab, above n 43, 9.

53 Legal Fees Review Panel (2004) *Lawyer's costs and the time billing*, unpublished Discussion Paper, Sydney. See also Iain Campbell et al., *'The Elephant in the Room': Working-Time Patterns of Solicitors in Private Practice in Melbourne' Working Paper No. 43*, 2008, Centre for Employment and Labour Relations Law, The University of Melbourne, for a detailed discussion of the way in which billable hour targets are used by law firms.

54 David Blades, 'Lawyers, Billable Hours and Professionalism' (2013) 40 *Brief, The Law Society of Western Australia*, 1, 19, https://www.lawsocietywa.asn.au/wp-content/uploads/2015/09/Brief-October-2013.pdf.

55 Iain Campbell et al., above n. 53, 25. See also The Honourable Justice Tom Bathurst, 'Commercialisation of Legal Practice: Conflict Ab Initio; Conflict De Futuro', paper delivered to the Commonwealth Law Association Regional

linked to employee performance. In Australia, the billable hour target for legal practitioners is between six to seven billable hours per day.[56] A failure to meet billable targets can lead to sanctions such as dismissal, whilst success in meeting billable targets can lead to pay rises, bonuses and promotions to partnership.[57]

Use of the billable hour as a management tool has been met with considerable concern. The expectation that legal practitioners attain billable targets can cause legal practitioners to suffer from inordinate stress.[58] The former Chief Justice of Western Australia, Wayne Martin, has for example, identified several negative effects of hourly billing targets on lawyers.[59] According to the Chief Justice, hourly time-billing targets, inter alia, discourage efficiency or innovation; encourage time-sheet padding; distort performance assessment; discourage collegiality; reduce quality of life and force legal practitioners to work long hours alienating them from their family and their community.[60] The effects identified by the Chief Justice are supported by empirical research. Bergin and Jimmieson's research, for example, reveals that legal practitioners with high billing targets (over six hours per day) experienced greater workplace demands than legal practitioners with low-to-moderate billing targets (fewer than six hours per day) and/or legal practitioners with no billing targets.[61] Bergin and Jimmieson's study further revealed that legal practitioners that had high billing targets experienced more time pressure, viewed profit as a being a fundamental demand, were more competitive and experienced more role ambiguity and conflict and as a result experienced more anxiety symptoms, more stress, greater work–life imbalance, and more job dissatisfaction compared with others.[62]

Conference, 21 April 2012 at 7; The Honourable Justice Virginia Bell A.C., 'Putting the Guidelines to Work' (Speech delivered at the Tristan Jepson Memorial Foundation Annual Lecture, 23 October 2014), 14–15, http://www.hcourt.gov.au/assets/publications/speeches/current-justices/bellj/bellj23oct2014.pdf.

56 Lucille Keen, 'Billable hours to always hold a place in law firms', *The Australian Financial Review*, 23 June 2016, https://www.afr.com/business/legal/billable-hours-to-always-hold-a-place-in-law-firms-20160622-gppsrq.

57 Susan S. Fortney, 'The Billable Hours Derby: Empirical Data on the Problems and Pressure Points' (2005) 33 *Fordham Urban Law Journal* 171, 172.

58 Lisa G. Lerman, 'The Slippery Slope from Ambition to Greed to Dishonesty: Lawyers, Money, and Professional Integrity' (2002) 30 *Hofstra Law Review* 879, 881.

59 The Honourable Wayne Martin, 'Billable Hours – past their use-by date', 17 May 2010, Perth Press Club, https://www.supremecourt.wa.gov.au/_files/Perth_Press_Club_Law_Week_20100517.pdf.

60 Ibid. at 12–19.

61 Bergin and Jimmieson, above n. 4, 437.

62 Ibid.

The impact of using billable hour targets to manage performance can also lead to legal practitioners inflating their time sheets to demonstrate that they are working effectively and efficiently.[63] According to Lerman, instances of 'bill padding' are not uncommon.[64] Parker and Ruschena's research study of 324 legal practitioners and 25 law firms in Queensland, Australia, found that 23% of the lawyers had observed instances of 'padding' bills for work not actually performed.[65] Further, a sizeable proportion of lawyers (34%) reported concerns about the billing practices of other legal practitioners in their firm.[66] In 11 of the 25 firms, more than 20% of the lawyers reported that they had actually observed instances of bill padding and in five of the firms more than 40% of the lawyers said they had observed bill padding.[67] When questioned about how they handled these observations or concerns, the lawyers reported various responses including doing nothing (7%); discussing the matter with a supervisor (14%); discussing the matter with another lawyer (11%); and discussing the matter with the lawyer in question (9%).[68] The lawyers reported that whilst some of the firms had measures in place to respond to complaints about unethical billing practices, few firms had proactive measures such as policies or processes in place to monitor or review such practices.[69]

The pressure faced by lawyers in having to meet billable hour targets was clearly illustrated in the case of Carol Foreman, a former family law partner at the Australian law firm Clayton Utz.[70] Foreman was severely disciplined for forging a time sheet that was to be submitted to the Family Court in a costs matter against her client. According to Foreman, she forged the time sheet to support her evidence that she had provided her client

63 John Briton, 'Ethics in the Real World' (2006) Office of the Legal Services Commissioner, Queensland, p. 4, https://www.lsc.qld.gov.au/__data/assets/pdf_file/0014/106223/ethics-in-the-real-world.pdf; Chief Justice James Spigelman, 'Opening of Law Term Dinner, 2004', 2 February 2004, available at: http://www.lawlink.nsw.gov.au/lawlink/supreme_court/ll_sc.nsf/pages/SCO_speech_020204; Susan Saab Fortney, 'Soul for Sale: An Empirical Study of Satisfaction, Law Firm Culture, and the Effects of Billable Hour Requirements' (2000) 69 *University of Missouri-Kansas City Law Review* 239.

64 Lisa Lerman, 'A Double Standard for Lawyer Dishonesty: Billing Fraud Versus Misappropriation' (2006) 34 *Hofstra Law Review* 847, 882.

65 Christine Parker and David Ruschena, 'The Pressures of Billable Hours: Lessons from a Survey of Billing Practices Inside Law Firms' (2011) 9 *University of St. Thomas Law Journal* 619, 640.

66 Ibid.

67 Ibid.

68 Ibid. at 641.

69 Ibid. at 650–51.

70 *Law Society of NSW v. Foreman* (1994) 34 NSWLR 408.

with a written costs agreement. Foreman argued that she faced inordinate pressure from the firm to generate profits and that without the forged time sheet the firm would not have been able to recover the fees and therefore she would not have met her billing target.

The focus on billable hours and billing targets may also have an additional impact on the health and wellbeing of junior lawyers. Billable targets discourage senior lawyers from training junior lawyers because clients cannot be billed for the time senior lawyers take to train junior lawyers. Senior lawyers who are focused on achieving billing targets may be failing to fulfil their training obligations to junior lawyers.[71] As one lawyer has stated:

> if you go to ask someone for help they're either going to put time on your client's account, compounding that [time pressure], or they're giving away their time to you, so there's a culture where you are not encouraged to cooperate … It was like an environment where you weren't allowed to talk to any of your colleagues unless you want them to be putting down their billable hours at the same time.[72]

Inadequate training, support and guidance of young lawyers can lead to anxiety and stress. Research on the experiences of young lawyers indicates that 'a workplace environment that builds competence promotes resilience and insulates new lawyers against psychological distress.'[73]

The extent to which young lawyers suffer as a result of workplace demands was illustrated in a 1999 report on the retention of legal practitioners by the Law Society of Western Australia in conjunction with the Women Lawyers of Western Australia.[74] That report, which comprised an exit survey of 47 lawyers who had left the profession after five years of practice, detailed the experiences of the lawyers. The majority of the lawyers interviewed reported that they felt like they had worked in

---

71 Kate Allman, 'Bloody Terrifying: The Modern Law Graduate Experience' (2018) 46 *Law Society Journal* 33, 34.

72 Law Council of Australia, *National Attrition and Re-engagement Study* (NARS) (2014), 26, https://www.lawcouncil.asn.au/policy-agenda/advancing-the-profession/equal-opportunities-in-the-law/national-report-on-attrition-and-re-engagement.

73 Tony Foley, Vivien Holmes, Stephen Tang and Margie Rowe, 'Helping junior lawyers thrive' (2015) 89 *Law Institute Journal* 44, 46.

74 The Law Society of Western Australia and Women Lawyers of Western Australia, *Report on the Retention of Legal Practitioners: Final Report* (1999).

'sweat-shop conditions' and as a consequence had suffered physically and mentally from such conditions. The lawyers reported symptoms such as exhaustion, stomach ulcers, broken sleep, crying, loss of confidence and self-worth, irritability and depression.

3.2. THE DEMANDS OF CLIENTS

In addition to the billable hour, the demands of clients can lead to un-wellness and ill-health in lawyers. Bergin and Jimmieson's research revealed that more than 40 per cent of respondents experienced high levels of emotional demands as a result of acting for clients.[75] A large percentage of respondents further reported that they experienced moderate levels of emotional demands as a result of acting for clients.[76] According to a research conducted by Keystone Law, 77 per cent of lawyers stated that client demands caused workplace stress.[77]

The demise of a lawyer's health may be caused by multiple client-related factors. A lawyer acting for a client in a matter that the lawyer finds morally reprehensible or ethically objectionable may, for example, result in the lawyer suffering from stress or mental ill-health. Similarly, a lawyer who acts for a client that has committed grave acts of violence or depravity may suffer from so acting.[78] Unreasonable demands and expectations by clients can also lead to un-wellness and ill-health in lawyers. Clients who are consumed by their own emotional and personal dilemmas may be angry and hostile, vengeful, obsessed or emotionally needy and dependent. Clients who demonstrate any of these character traits may compromise their ability to act with reason and make decisions that are in their own best interests. For example, the angry or hostile client may not be able to articulate rational instructions that are in his or her best interests. Similarly, the client that is emotionally needy or dependent may be unable to make decision that is in their best interests. Barnett, Hayes, Large and Nielssen capture the implications of demanding clients as follows:

> [I]n family law, lawyers may be faced with acting on an apparently disturbed client's instructions that appear contrary to the best interests of the children

---

75 Bergin and Jimmieson, above n. 4, 434.
76 Ibid.
77 Keystone Law, above n. 26, 6.
78 Abbe Smith, 'Defending the Unpopular Down Under' (2006) 30(2) *Melbourne University Law Review* 495.

> of the relationship. In criminal law, some lawyers may face psychological and ethical difficulties in appearing for clients who may have committed serious crimes. Across the spectrum of professional practice, clients may be aggressive or unpleasant or, at the other extreme, very pleasant, attractive, vulnerable or sometimes seductive. Lawyers involved in a professional relationship may have strong personal feelings about their clients, either positive or negative, which consciously or unconsciously, may influence their professional responsibilities.[79]

Lawyers may also suffer poor health and wellbeing as a result of clients who are mentally ill. Barnett et al. argue that lawyers who have clients who are mentally ill may themselves be affected through counter-transference which may interfere with their ability to perform their professional duty.[80]

As stated above, a demanding client that instructs a lawyer to act unethically or illegally can affect a lawyer's health and wellbeing. A lawyer is bound to follow the lawful, proper and competent instructions of their client.[81] A lawyer is therefore entitled to refuse to act for a client that instructs them to act contrarily to the professional and ethical obligations to which the lawyer must comply. Whilst lawyers are required to abstain from acting for a client that instructs them to act unethically, a lawyer may not always do so, particularly where the client is a large corporation and/or the lawyer or legal team working for the client is encouraged by the firm to continue acting. Pressure exerted by clients to act in a manner that is contrary to the professional and ethical obligations of a lawyer can be confronting. As one lawyer has stated:

> There are some large corporate clients who we don't think have the same ethics as the professionally trained lawyers in this firm have and that can be very difficult, particularly when they are either running a transaction or they are your direct client and they are trying to get you to do things that ethically you don't agree with. So they're just pushing the deal so hard and there may be some borderline as to how ethical it is, but there are some who will just say: 'I don't care, do it.' So they do come up, they do. They are not infrequent either.[82]

Several high-profile cases illustrate the impact of unethical demands by clients on lawyer conduct. In the *McCabe* litigation, for example the

79 Barnet et al., above n. 79, 64.
80 Ibid. at, 67.
81 *Australian Solicitors Conduct Rules 2015*, r 8.
82 Interview with Female Partner (Melbourne, 6 October 2005) in Bagust, above n. 39, 50.

lawyers assisted their client British American Tobacco by providing advice on how to destroy relevant documents.[83] The lawyers in the *McCabe* case not only allegedly provided such advice, they additionally were alleged to have assisted their client in hiding the fact that the documents had been destroyed and they allegedly assisted their client in delaying the litigation against the plaintiff who was dying of cancer.[84] If such an allegation were made out the lawyers would have breached their duty to the Court and the administration of justice.[85] In the *Australian Wheat Board (AWB)* case the lawyers for AWB condoned the conduct of the AWB in obtaining kickbacks and indeed facilitated its continuation. In the *James Hardie* case the lawyers participated in a scheme to move the James Hardie company offshore and into a separate legal entity in order to avoid paying out any more than a set amount of damages to asbestos victims of its former subsidiary companies.[86]

The influence of workplace demands arising from the traditional law firm partnership structure on the professional and personal lives of lawyers is profound. In traditional law firms, billing targets, the demands of clients and the desire to please supervisors and partners to ensure promotion to partnership shape how individual lawyers morally and ethically act.[87] Granfield and Koenig submit that lawyers are extremely influenced by the culture and values of their workplace.[88] Rhode states that this may be because lawyers who work in law firms today are not 'independent moral agents' but are rather employees with 'circumscribed responsibility, organizational loyalty, and attenuated client contact.'[89] Parker et al. suggest

83 *McCabe v. British American Tobacco Australia Ltd* [2002] VSC 73. The case was overturned on appeal: *British American Tobacco Australia Services Ltd v. Cowell* (2002) 7 VR 524.

84 Camille Cameron, 'Hired Guns and Smoking Guns: McCabe v British American Tobacco Australia Ltd' (2002) 25 *University of New South Wales Law Journal* 768.

85 'It is a well-established principle that lawyers as officers of the Court owe a duty to the Court and the administration of justice and that duty is paramount': *Giannarelli v. Wraith* (1988) 165 CLR 543.

86 Suzanne Le Mire, 'The Case Study: James Hardie and its Implications for the Teaching of Ethics' in Bronwyn Naylor and Ross Hyams (eds), *Innovation in Clinical Legal Education: Educating Lawyers for the Future* (Legal Service Bulletin Cooperative, 2007) 25.

87 Galanter and Palay, above n. 33.

88 Robert Granfield and Thomas Koenig, '"It's Hard to be a Human Being and a Lawyer": Young Attorneys and the Confrontation with Ethical Ambiguity in Legal Practice' (2003) 105 *West Virginia Law Review* 495.

89 Deborah L. Rhode, 'Ethical Perspectives on Legal Practice' (1984) 37 *Stanford Law Review* 589, 590–91.

that law firms 'frame' the conduct of their employees: (i) by limiting the capacity of individual lawyers to 'see' ethical issues; (ii) by constraining or creating options for individual lawyers to make ethical judgments and act on them; and (iii) by creating and magnifying incentives for lawyers to act unethically.[90] The culture of working in teams and working on different aspects of a larger project is said to contribute to individual lawyer conduct being framed in this manner.[91] This situation is said to be exacerbated by role ambiguity and role conflict.[92]

The implications of such a loss of autonomy and failure to 'see' ethical issues can be dire. Research conducted by Moore, Buckingham and Diesfeld in relation to cases brought before the Disciplinary Tribunal in New Zealand from 2009–2013 identifies a correlation between lawyers suffering from depression, anxiety and substance abuse and being disciplined for misconduct.[93] According to the study, 21 of the 74 decisions heard in the Disciplinary Tribunal involved impaired lawyers. The main types of impairment were depression and/or anxiety, substance misuse, and stress.[94]

A growing awareness of the extent to which lawyers are unwell and unhealthy has led many law firms to implement improvements, particularly in relation to work-life balance.[95] These improvements have included

> raising awareness of, and reducing stigma related to, mental health and wellbeing issues; … equipping students and lawyers with the skills and resilience necessary to manage stressors and ensure their wellbeing; and … identifying and addressing underlying structural or cultural issues contributing to the problem, such as billable target pressures, inflexible working arrangements, inadequate management systems, and a lack of response to bullying and harassment.[96]

---

90 Christine Parker et al., 'The Ethical Infrastructure of Legal Practice in Larger Law Firms' (2008) 31 *UNSW Law Journal* 163.

91 Ibid. at 166–67.

92 Ibid. at 429.

93 Jennifer Moore, Donna Buckingham and Kate Diesfeld, 'Disciplinary Tribunal Cases Involving New Zealand Lawyers with Physical or Mental Impairment, 2009–2013' (2015) 22 *Psychiatry, Psychology and Law* 649.

94 Ibid. at 662.

95 Margaret Thornton, 'Work/life or work/work? Corporate legal practice in the twenty-first century' (2016) 23 *International Journal of the Legal Profession* 13, 22–24. See also Chapter 5 in this volume.

96 Suzanne Poynton, Janet Chan, Melissa Vogt, Anne Grunseit and Jasmine Bruce, 'Assessing the Effectiveness of Wellbeing Initiatives for Lawyers And Support Staff' (2018) 41(2) *UNSW Law Journal* 584, 589.

The initiatives have however been questioned as to their effectiveness.

Work/life balance initiatives have been seen as no more than a band aid solution because they do not address the underlying competitive culture of the practice of law.[97] A recent research study by Poynton, Chan, Vogt, Grunseit and Bruce on the effectiveness of health and wellbeing programmes in a public sector organisation revealed that whilst there is high awareness of initiatives in relation to health and wellbeing, the initiatives are not necessarily accessed by staff.[98] Those that did access health and wellbeing initiatives tended to access family and community services leave; flexible working practices; regular staff meetings; and workshops on building resilience and demystifying mental illness.[99] The reasons offered as to why initiatives were not attended included heavy workloads and lack of time available to attend.[100] In addition, there was some concern about the stigma of attending mental health and wellbeing initiatives.[101]

A number of changes can be implemented to reduce the incidence of stress, depression and mental illness. Chan et al., for example, suggest that a lawyer's health and wellbeing can be improved by structural and cultural improvements to the workplace, such as: (i) better systems for managing workloads, client demands and expectations as well as billing practices; (ii) supporting a healthy and positive work–life balance; and (iii) ensuring that working relationships are respectful and collaborative.[102] Keystone Law suggest the following changes to improve the work of lawyers – more flexible work hours; lower billing targets; better management; more support; lighter workload, better remuneration; better collaboration; better benefits; and an opportunity to work remotely.[103] When asked about how health and wellbeing initiatives could be improved in the research by Poynton et al., participants stated that 'fundamental structural changes to the organisation and its culture' were required. The remainder of this chapter considers whether changing the structure of law firms through incorporation may better improve the health and wellbeing of lawyers.

---

97 Opinion, 'After working in a corporate law firm for only a couple of months, I began to develop extreme feelings of anxiety', *Lawyers Weekly*, 8 May 2013, https://www.lawyersweekly.com.au/opinion/11158 fter working in a corporate law firm for only-a.

98 Poynton et al., above n. 96, 603.

99 Ibid. at 603–4.

100 Ibid. at 604.

101 Ibid. at 605.

102 Chan et al., above n. 18, 1101.

103 Keystone Law, above n. 26, 7.

4. LAW FIRM PRACTICE STRUCTURES: A NEW LOOK BUT A DIFFERENT FEEL?

Today, unlike most other common law jurisdictions, law firms in Australia can choose to adopt traditional or non-traditional practice structures. Law firms can, for example, practise in traditional law firm structures as sole practitioners or partnerships. Alternatively, law firms can practise in non-traditional law firm structures such as incorporated legal practices (ILPs).[104] An ILP is a corporation or a company that can provide legal services as well as non-legal services which can be provided by an officer or employee that is not an Australian legal practitioner.[105] In New South Wales and Victoria, law firms can also practise as unincorporated legal practices (ULPs). A ULP is a partnership or unincorporated group that can provide legal services as well as non-legal services which can be provided by an officer or employee that is not an Australian legal practitioner.[106]

New South Wales was the first jurisdiction in Australia to allow law firms to incorporate in 2001. The enactment of legislation permitting law firm incorporation was significant. It was designed to allow law firms to incorporate and expand and compete with other occupational businesses and become 'the legal hub for the provision of legal services in the Australia-Pacific region.'[107] The legislation permitted law firms to conduct a multi-disciplinary partnership[108] and additionally permitted non-lawyers to share fees with the lawyers in the law firm.[109] Not long after the legislation was enacted in NSW, similar legislation permitting law firm incorporation was enacted in the other States and Territories in Australia.

The 2001 legislation set out a range of distinct requirements for law firms wishing to incorporate. Law firms were required to give notice to the Law Society of NSW that they intended to engage in legal practice as an ILP. Law firms were required to register as a company with the Australian Securities and Investments Commission, the regulator of companies in

---

104 Legal Profession Act 2006 (ACT) pt 2.6; Legal Practitioners Act 2006 (NT) pt 2.6; Legal Profession Act 2004 (Vic) pt 2.7; Legal Practice Act 2003 (WA) pt 6; Legal Profession Act 2007 (Qld) pt 2.7: Legal Profession Act 2007 (Tas) pt 2.5; Legal Practitioners Act 1981 (SA), sch 1.

105 Section 6, Legal Profession Uniform Law.

106 Ibid.

107 The Honourable J.M. Samios, Legal Profession Amendment (Incorporated Legal Practices) Bill, Second Reading, 12 October 2000, Legislative Council Hansard.

108 Legal Profession Act 2004 (NSW), section 135(1).

109 Ibid. section 151.

Australia; and, appoint at least lawyer as a 'legal practitioner director' who was to be responsible for the management of the legal services provided by the ILP.[110] In addition, the 2001 legislation required that the legal practitioner director 'implement and maintain appropriate management systems to enable the provision of legal services in accordance with the professional obligations of solicitors and the other obligations.'[111] A failure to implement and maintain appropriate management systems constituted professional misconduct and could result in a legal practitioner director losing his or her practising certificate.[112]

Pursuant to the requirement that ILPs implement and maintain appropriate management systems, ILPs had to develop a management system that addressed 10 elements of good practice. These elements included as follows:

1. Competent work practices to avoid negligence;
2. Effective, timely, and courteous communication;
3. Timely delivery, review and follow up of legal services to avoid instances of delay;
4. Acceptable processes for liens and file transfers;
5. Shared understanding and appropriate documentation from commencement through to termination of retainer, covering costs disclosure, billing practices, and termination of retainer;
6. Timely identification and resolution of conflicts of interest;
7. Records management which minimises the likelihood of loss or destruction of correspondence and documents;
8. Undertakings to be given with authority, monitoring of compliance and timely compliance with notices, orders, rulings, directions or other requirements of regulatory authorities such as the NSW OLSC, Law Society of NSW, courts, or costs assessors;
9. Supervision of the practice and staff; and
10. Trust Account requirements.

ILPs were required to self-assess the management systems they had developed and implemented against the 10 objectives and send a report of the self-assessment to the legal regulator, the Office of the Legal Services Commissioner (OLSC).

110 Ibid. section 140.
111 Ibid. section 140(3).
112 Ibid. section 140(5).

The obligation imposed on ILPs to implement and maintain appropriate management systems ceased in 2015 with the enactment of the Legal Profession Uniform Law (LPUL).[113] Under the LPUL, the implementation and maintenance of appropriate management systems is only required where a 'management systems direction' has been given.[114] A 'management systems direction' can be given to any law firm, not just ILPs. However, notwithstanding this amendment, the OLSC, in effect expects that all law firms have 'appropriate management systems' frameworks in place so that they comply with the regulatory framework.[115]

The ILP and ULP structure has been embraced by law firms in Australia but particularly in NSW.[116] Statistics from the Law Society of NSW, the professional association for the legal profession in NSW, reveal that as at June 2018 there were more than 4,000 ILPs in NSW, comprising over 39 per cent of the legal services market, and over 120 ULPs.[117] Data from the Law Society of NSW further indicated of the 33,000 legal practitioners that hold a practising certificate in NSW, 7,400 of those practise in ILPs and 2,272 practise in ULPs.[118] ULPs registered in NSW include many of the large law firms such as Ashurst Australia, Clayton Utz, Gilbert + Tobin, Herbert Smith Freehills and K. & L. Gates, as well as professional service firms such as Ernst & Young and PriceWaterhouseCoopers. Over the past 16 years since incorporation was first permitted in NSW, three law firms,

---

113 Office of the Legal Services Commissioner, *Practice Management*, http://www.olsc.nsw.gov.au/Pages/lsc_practice_management/lsc_practice_management.aspx. See Justine Rogers, Dimity Kingsford-Smith and John Chellew, 'The Large Professional Services Firm: A New Force in the Regulative Bargain' (2017) 40(1) *UNSW Law Journal* 218, 251–53 for a discussion of why the obligation no longer exists.

114 *Legal Profession Uniform Law* (NSW), section 257.

115 Office of the Legal Services Commissioner, above n. 113.

116 In Victoria, for example, as at 31 August 2018, there were 1,791 ILPs and 31 ULPs of the 9,625 entities registered. Victorian Legal Services Commissioner and Board, *Lawyer Statistics*, http://lsbc.vic.gov.au/?page_id=287. In Queensland, as at 30 June 2018 there were 1182 ILPs as compared with 2222 law firms and 17 multi-disciplinary partnerships (MDPs) registered representing approximately 53.97% of all law firms operating within Queensland. Legal Services Commission, Annual Report 2017–2018, 7, https://www.lsc.qld.gov.au/__data/assets/pdf_file/0011/581897/legal-services-commission-annual-report-2017-18.pdf.

117 Statistics provided by the Law Society of New South Wales as at August 2018. On file with the author.

118 The Law Society of Nsw, *Practising Solicitor Statistics June 2018*, https://www.lawsociety.com.au/sites/default/files/2018-7/201806%20Practising%20Solicitor%20Statistics%20-%20Jun%202018.pdf.

Integrated Legal Holdings, Slater and Gordon and Shine Lawyers have publicly listed on the Australian Stock Exchange.

In the years since Australia liberalised law firm practice structures, only one other jurisdiction outside Australia (England and Wales) has permitted non-lawyers to own or invest in law firms. In 2007 England and Wales enacted legislation permitting law firms to adopt a new structure known as an 'alternative business structure' (ABS).[119] The introduction of the legislation in England and Wales was, similarly to Australia, a direct response to concerns about anti-competitive restrictions in relation to the practice of law.[120]

4.1. BENEFITS OF INCORPORATION FOR THE HEALTH AND WELLBEING OF LAWYERS

The legislative framework governing ILPs and ULPs provides structural flexibility for law firms. Law firms can be partly or wholly owned by passive investors; law firms can access external capital by issuing stock in the firm to non-lawyer investors; law firms can operate as multi-disciplinary practices and share fees with non-lawyers; and, law firms can be owned by non-lawyers who work in the firm and assist lawyers in providing the legal services (such as managing the firm). Similarly, the ABS model in England and Wales permits three different types of firm:

> a model similar to a traditional law firm or legal disciplinary practice but with involvement of one or more non-lawyer managers, without external ownership, and providing solicitor type services only;
>
> the 'co-op law' model where there is complete or partial external ownership operated through a separate entity;

---

119 Legal Services Act 2007, c. 29, ss. 71–111 (UK). For a detailed discussion of the history of developments leading to the 2007 legislation and the aftermath of its enactment see Paul D. Paton, 'Multidisciplinary Practice Redux: Globalization, Core Values, and Reviving the MDP Debate in America' (2010) 78 *Fordham Law Review* 2193, 2232–40; John Flood, 'Will There Be Fallout from Clementi? The Repercussions for the Legal Profession after the Legal Services Act 2007' (2012) *Michigan State Law Review* 537.

120 In 2001 the Office of Fair Trading (OFT) conducted an examination into competition within the professions in the United Kingdom and recommended that the conveyancing and probate markets be liberalised to remove lawyer monopoly and MDPs should be permitted. See Office of Fair Trading, *Competition in Professions: A Report* (2001, London, Office of Fair Trading).

'a multidisciplinary practice' (MDP), where combinations of services from one entity, such as financial services and legal services offered through a single body.[121]

In addition to structural flexibility, multiple benefits are alleged to flow from having non-lawyer owners or investors in a law firm. These benefits include: (i) greater access to external capital, (ii) limited liability; (iii) improved staff retention models; (iv) one-stop shopping for clients; and (v) improved management structures. The alleged benefits and their possible effect on the health and wellbeing of lawyers are discussed in detail below.

4.1.1. Access to External Capital

In the traditional partnership structure, law firms are prohibited from obtaining external capital. Law firm partnerships must therefore rely on the funds they raise internally through the individual equity contributions of partners and the income generated by the partnership itself. The desire of equity partners to fund the firm for future growth is, however, decreasing because the equity provided by the partners cannot be realised until the firm makes a profit. Equity partners are therefore unable to recover any of the equity they provide to the firm until years later. Additional funds can be obtained externally through capital contributions or debt finance; however, there are implications in relying on these external measures to raise capital. Firms raising funds through capital contributions from partners require very substantial contributions, which partners may be unable to provide.[122] Moreover, firms obtaining capital through debt financing will incur considerable expense because debt financing is expensive.

A law firm that obtains debt financing must not only pay back the principal loan but also any interest on the loan. History has shown that a downturn in the economy can make the repayment of the loan difficult.[123] When the credit markets collapsed in 2008, for example, firms in the United States struggled to obtain payment from some of their larger clients. Without their clients' money many law firms were unable to repay the loans

---

121 The Law Society of England and Wales, 'Setting up a practice: Regulatory requirements', 2 December 2019, https://www.lawsociety.org.uk/support-services/advice/practice-notes/setting-up-a-practice-regulatory-requirements/.

122 Tyler Cobb, 'Note, Have Your Cake and Eat It Too! Appropriately Harnessing the Advantages of Nonlawyer Ownership' (2012) 54 *Arizona Law Review* 765, 776.

123 Ibid. at 777.

they had taken out from the banks. Consequently, many firms defaulted on their bank loans. Those firms that did not default and were able to repay the loans struggled to compensate their partners and associates, leading many of those partners and associates to exit the firm.[124] Moreover, even where a bank loan can be obtained, the loan may not cover funding for certain expenditure such as technology.

The implications of limited access to funds for traditional law firm partnership structures can negatively affect the viability of law firms and the provision of legal services, and may therefore place inordinate pressure on staff. Insufficient funding may prohibit law firms from effectively competing with other law firms and entities offering legal services who have unrestricted access to such capital. Law firms that are prohibited from accessing external capital may be unable to invest in technology and innovate to provide more efficient standardised, systematised and commoditised legal services.[125] In addition, law firms with restricted access to capital may not be able to invest in knowledge management systems as well as training programmes for their lawyers in the same manner as other firms that have access to unrestricted capital. Insufficient funding may also prohibit law firms from expanding their geographical reach. Law firms in Australia have cited restrictions on accessing external finance as one of the major barriers to innovation. According to research conducted by Wayne et al., law firms in Australia with traditional partnership structures identified access to finance, as well as the high cost of innovation projects and access to skilled staff, as barriers to implementing innovation.[126]

Law firms that have non-lawyer owners or investors, unlike traditional law firms, can however obtain external capital through private or public offerings to accelerate their growth and compete more effectively with other businesses which have unrestricted access to external capital.[127] The benefits of such access are multiple. Firms with access to unrestricted capital could expand into new geographical areas or into new practice areas.[128] Firms considering closing their doors could keep their doors

124 Ibid.

125 Richard Susskind, *The End of Lawyers? Rethinking The Nature of Legal Services*, Oxford University Press, 2008, 270.

126 Waye, Verreynne and Knowler, above n. 39, 19.

127 See Richard Vincent, 'What are the Commercial and Corporate Law Effects of Incorporating Legal Practices?' (July 2002) *Law Society Journal* 48; Steve Mark and Tahlia Gordon, 'Innovations in Regulation – Responding to a Changing Legal Services Market', (2005) 22 *Georgetown Journal of Legal Ethics* 501, 529–31.

128 Edward S. Adams, 'Rethinking the Law Firm Organizational Form and Capitalization Structure' (2013) 78 *Missouri Law Review* 777, 809.

open with unrestricted access to capital if they have a strong client base.[129] Unrestricted capital could additionally allow firms to experiment with the way they deliver legal services.[130]

The benefits of unrestricted access to external capital would not only benefit the law firm itself, but also clients of such firms. A law firm that expands into new geographical areas could enable clients to have greater access to legal services.[131] A law firm that invests external capital in technology could also provide greater benefits to clients if that technology enabled faster and more cost-effective legal services. Slater and Gordon, for example, have described the impact of being able to access external capital in the following manner:

> regulatory changes permitting us to become a publicly listed company have allowed us to access additional external capital (at lower cost) and in turn this has enabled us to expend in terms of the breadth of practice areas, the geographical reach of services and choice of service models for clients. By reducing the overall cost of capital and utilising capital markets to gain greater access to capital we have been able to employ more significant economies of scale and thereby create greater depth of specialist expertise and offer consistently high service standards with lower delivery costs.[132]

Moreover, unrestricted access to external capital may allow firms to take on contingency cases in jurisdictions where contingency fee cases are permitted and may alleviate the current problems faced by law firms who face resistance when borrowing from banks to fund such cases.[133] The ability of law firms to take on more contingency fee cases may also result in greater access to legal services.[134] Law firms may be able to take on

---

129 Cobb, above n. 122, 776.

130 Richard Devlin and Ora Morison, 'Access to Justice and the Ethics and Politics of Alternative Business Structures' (2012) 91 *Canadian Bar Review* 483, 494.

131 Gillian K. Hadfield, 'The Cost of Law: Promoting Access to Justice through the (Un)corporate Practice of Law' (2014) 38 *International Review of Law and Economics* 43.

132 Slater and Gordon, 'Submission to the American Bar Association Commission on the Future of Legal Services', 29 December 2014, 1, 1.

133 Although noting that the legislative framework in Australia does not permit firms to take contingency fees, but see Molot, above n.32.

134 Bret A. Beldt, 'The Inevitable Change of America's Archaic Limitations on Public Ownership of Law Firms' (2008) 33 *The Journal of the Legal Profession* 117, 129.

risky cases because some of the risk would be passed off to the investors of the firm.[135]

The impact of access to external investment may positively influence work practices of lawyers and lead to improved lawyer health and wellbeing. Access to external capital may enable law firms to invest in technology, resulting in law firms focusing less on the billable hour as a means of generating profit. Law firms may focus more on other alternative forms of billing such as fixed fee agreements that guarantee greater fee certainty.[136] Slater and Gordon report, for example, that access to external capital has allowed them to provide conditional fee funding to their client 'on an unprecedented basis' as well as fixed fees in family law matters.[137] Slater and Gordon state in relation to conditional fees as follows:

> Our relatively low cost of capital provides an enormous benefit to clients who would otherwise not be able to afford access to the legal system after suffering a personal injury ... 'No Win No Fee' arrangements have played a critical and effective role in ensuring that people suffering serious personal or financial injuries, many of whom have lost or have diminished livelihoods, are nevertheless able to pursue their rights to compensation.[138]

In relation to fixed fees, Slater and Gordon state:

> Our development of a 'fixed fee' arrangement for family law services was a response to research regarding client needs and expectations. This research confirmed that uncertainty regarding legal costs substantially increases client anxiety in what is already a stressful period in their lives. The fear of legal costs escalating also inhibits individuals from seeking legal advice at all, and is no doubt partly responsible for the escalation of self-represented litigants in our Court system. The fear of uncertain and unaffordable legal costs is diminished by the 'fixed fee' arrangements.[139]

---

135 Thomas Markle, 'A Call to Partner with Outside Capital: The Non-Lawyer Investment Approach Must Be Updated' (2013) 45 *Arizona State Law Journal*, 1251, 1263–64.

136 Nick Jarrett-Kerr, 'Alternative Business Structures – The Long Pregnancy' (2011) 11 *Legal Information Management* 82, 84.

137 Slater and Gordon, above n. 132, 3–4.

138 Ibid. at 1, 3.

139 Ibid. at 4.

In addition, access to external capital may enable law firms to invest in enhancing the firm's infrastructure. Firms with unlimited access to funds may be able to invest in technology; marketing; knowledge management systems as well as training programmes for current and new lawyers.[140] In doing so, firms would be able to provide greater support systems for their staff and perhaps foster greater collegiality. The changes facilitated by access to external capital may enable a more sustainable solution to improving the health and wellbeing of lawyers.

4.1.2. Limited Liability

In traditional law firm partnerships, individual lawyers retain individual unlimited liability, but the liability of each partner is joint and several.[141] That is, all of the partners in the firm are responsible for misconduct in the firm that may arise from fraud, fiduciary breaches or malpractice. The purpose of entrusting all partners with joint and several liability is to ensure that the partners continuously monitor each other's conduct as well as the conduct of all of the staff within the law firm and the quality of legal services provided by the firm.[142] As Fortney states:

> [I]mposing liability deters harmful conduct by encouraging precautions in the delivery of professional services. First, the risk of individual tort liability discourages individual lawyers from engaging in tortious activity. Second, the risk of enterprise liability should motivate the firm managers to monitor individual lawyers. Finally, the risk of facing vicarious liability for the acts of one's partners encourages partners to devote time and resources to monitoring and risk management activities that promise to reduce their personal liability exposure.[143]

The impact of this responsibility has, however, created a claims minefield, particular for larger firms where there are many hundreds of partners.[144]

---

140 Thomas R. Andrews, 'Nonlawyers in the Business of Law: Does the One Who Has the Gold Really Make the Rules?' (1989) 40 *Hastings Law Journal* 577, 630.

141 Partnership Act 1892 (NSW), section 9.

142 Ian Ramsay, 'Should Law Firms Be Permitted to Incorporate?' (1994) 10 *Australian Journal of Law and Society* 245, 246, 253.

143 Susan S. Fortney, 'Tales of Two Regimes for Regulating Limited Liability Law Firms in the US and Australia: Client Protection and Risk Management Lessons' (2008) 11 *Legal Ethics* 230, 235.

144 Christine Parker, 'Law Firms Incorporated: How Incorporation Could and Should Make Firms More Ethically Responsible' (2004) 23 *The University of Queensland Law Journal* 347, 350.

Moreover, unlimited liability also places inordinate stress on lawyers. As Romly, Talley and Savych write:

> Adverse judgments or settlements against a professional firm might be so costly as to put the firm out of business, and the costs of resolving disputes alone can seriously impact a firm's bottom line. Moreover, professional errors and omissions ('malpractice') represent a unique and significant source of liability exposure for professional services firms.[145]

In ILPs and ULPs, the liability of each lawyer is limited. Lawyers cannot be jointly and severally liable for the conduct of the partners in the firm.[146] Lawyers therefore are only liable for their own professional conduct as well as their investment in shares in the firm and any liability they carry as officers of the firm. Pursuant to this arrangement, creditors of the firm only have access to the business assets of the firm and not the firm's personal assets of former partners or former shareholders.[147]

The limitation of liability as a result of incorporation may have a positive impact on the health and wellbeing of lawyers. Lawyers may be less likely to be worried about the possibility of a claim being brought against them and feel less obligated to monitor the conduct of colleagues. The absence of worry about possible claims and responsibility for monitoring other colleagues may allow lawyers to spend more time on their work and therefore alleviate the stress caused by unlimited liability. However, limited liability may also have the opposite effect. Limited liability may cause lawyers who are unable to disassociate themselves from monitoring the conduct of employees, additional stress.

4.1.3. *Improve Staff Recruitment, Retention and Succession Planning*

In the traditional law firm, the path to partnership for a young lawyer has become extremely long. The law firm hierarchy prevents young lawyers from becoming partners until certain promotions are, if ever, achieved.

---

145 John A. Romly, Eric Talley and Bogdan Savych, 'Do the Owners of Small Law Firms Benefit from Limited Liability?', Kauffman-RAND Center for Entrepreneurship Public Policy, September 2007, 1, 1, https://www.rand.org/content/dam/rand/pubs/working_papers/2007/RAND_WR403.pdf.

146 Vincent, above n. 127, 50.

147 Philip King, 'Legal Practice: Should your Firm Incorporate?' (March 2001) 39(2) *Law Society Journal* 44, 45.

As a result, lawyers today see their work as no more than a paid job.[148] Additionally, lawyers are not well remunerated compared to employees of companies. They have no stock options and there are no opportunities to invest in deals. Partners in the traditional law firm structure fare no better. In a law firm, the partners do not reap benefits from the gross annual revenues in the firm as other executives do in companies.[149] An offer from a private equity or hedge fund to leave the law firm is therefore enticing to a partner because the fund will traditionally offer stock options as part of the salary package. In addition, partners are at a disadvantage because they have to keep a substantial amount of personal capital locked up in the firm and the capital that is held receives little or no interest.[150] Lastly, the taxation obligations imposed on lawyers as income earners are much more onerous when compared to other employees of companies.[151] This leaves lawyers at a competitive disadvantage. As a result, lawyers today have very little loyalty to their firms and will move to a law firm that offers them a better salary package.[152]

Law firms with non-lawyer owners or investors may not suffer the same fate. Unlike traditional law firm partnerships, law firms with non-lawyer owners or investors can recruit young lawyers and offer them ownership of the firm gradually through the purchase of shares.[153] The ability to offer young lawyers shares at an early stage in their career may incentivise those lawyers to stay with the firm rather than leave. Law firms could then avoid having to spend money on recruiting new lawyers to fill vacancies. Lawyers who are offered stock options may also deliver superior legal services because they would know that if they offered a better service the stock in the firm would increase and so would their stock.[154]

In relation to retention, firms with non-lawyer owners or investors can offer their current lawyers certainty in that the equity they build up throughout the time that they work at the firm will not vanish as soon

---

148 Ross, above n. 36, 268.

149 Bruce MacEwen, Milton C. Regan, Jr. and Larry Ribstein, 'Law Firms, Ethics, and Equity Capital: A Conversation' (2008) 21 *Georgetown Journal of Legal Ethics*, 61, 65.

150 Ibid.

151 Ibid.

152 Heather A. Miller, 'Note, Don't Just Check "Yes" or "No": The Need For Broader Consideration of Outside Investment in the Law' (2010) *University of Illinois Law Review* 311, 323.

153 Anne Susskind, 'Incorporation is Here, Now, Says Carter New CEO' (June 2008) *Law Society Journal* 18, 19.

154 Beldt, above n. 134, 130.

as they leave the firm.[155] Rather, the lawyer will continue to own part of the law firm until the lawyer decides to sell that equity back to the firm.[156] In addition, ILPs and ULPs can offer their staff better training and professional development programmes. As stated above, access to unrestricted capital would allow a firm to invest in innovative educational and training programmes for their staff. Offering such programmes may assist law firms in recruiting lawyers and retaining the existing lawyers by marketing their educational and training offerings.

4.1.4. *One-Stop Shopping*

In the traditional law firm partnership, firms are unable to provide clients with services other than legal services because of the prohibition on sharing fees with non-lawyers. Traditional law firms cannot integrate the legal service they offer with other non-legal services unless those non-legal services are provided by lawyers. The restriction on sharing fees with non-lawyers has prohibited law firms from effectively competing with the large professional service firms who originally offered accounting services but today offer clients other professional services.

Firms with non-lawyer owners or investors can offer their clients one-stop shopping so that clients can obtain all of the services they require in one place rather than having to go to multiple providers in different locations. Clients can obtain legal and non-legal services within the one firm. So, for example, a client could see his or her lawyer and at the same time see an accountant, a real estate agent, or an architect.[157] Moreover, personal injury firms could for example, employ an in-house doctor who could assist the lawyers on cases where expert evidence by a doctor is required or the doctor could simply assist the law firm in determining whether the case has merit.[158]

One-stop shopping may positively influence the health and wellbeing of lawyers. One-stop shopping could enable greater convenience and non-duplication of expenses for clients. One-stop shopping may allow lawyers to amend their billing frameworks and move away from the tyranny of the billable hour. Firms offering one-stop shopping may be able to offer their

---

155 Molot, above n. 32, 11–12.

156 Vincent, above n. 127, 50.

157 Devlin, above n. 130, 494.

158 Barron Dickinson, 'Non-Lawyer Ownership of Law Firms in Florida: Issues with Corporate Governance' (2017) 16 *Florida State University Business Review* 99, 112.

clients composite billing options that change according to the capability of clients to pay. The use of alternative billing options may relieve some of the stress imposed on lawyers as a result of billable hours and billable hour targets.

The ability of lawyers to work with non-lawyers in one entity instead of in multiple entities may additionally enable greater coordination and teamwork and thereby improve the health and wellbeing of lawyers.[159] One-stop shopping may alleviate the stress placed on lawyers as a result of demanding clients. In a law firm that offers multiple services, lawyers who act for clients suffering from psychological distress may be able to work with a psychologist in assisting the client. Moreover, the psychologist may be able to assist lawyers in developing effective strategies for dealing with demanding clients. One-stop shopping may also foster greater collegiality between service providers. Lastly, one-stop shopping may improve the quality of legal services provided because every service provider would be motivated to ensure that the brand they are selling is of exceptional quality.[160]

4.1.5. *Improved Management Structures*

In the traditional law firm, the management structure is typically horizontal. Pursuant to this structure, partners are involved at every level in the management of the firm. The horizontal management structure can, however, prove challenging, particularly for law firms that have multiple offices in multiple locations. The coordination of partners meeting can be difficult and can stymie decisions being made in a timely manner. To alleviate this situation and to seek further management expertise some law firms have employed non-lawyer managers to manage the firm. A number of firms have appointed top-tier managers. Traditional law firms who employ top-tier non-lawyer professionals in managerial positions cannot, however, remunerate those employees with stock options because of the prohibition on sharing fees. There is therefore little attraction for top-tier non-lawyer professionals to join a traditional law firm partnership, particularly because it is common for companies to include a considerable

159 John S. Dzienkowski and Robert J. Peroni, 'Multidisciplinary Practice and the American Legal Profession: A Market Approach to Regulating the Delivery of Legal Services in the Twenty-First Century' (2000) 69 *Fordham Law Review* 83, 118.

160 Noel Semple, 'Access to Justice: Is Legal Services Regulation Blocking the Path?' (2013) 20 *The International Journal of the Legal Profession* 267, 276.

stock option in an executive's remuneration package.[161] Consequently, traditional law firms are at a distinct disadvantage when trying to compete with other companies in hiring top-tier professionals. The only way in which law firms can actually compete is by offering alternative remuneration packages that are comparable with ownership interests. Such remuneration packages are, however, costly as they often comprise very high salaries.[162]

Firms with non-lawyer owners or investors can, however, remunerate these non-lawyer professionals by offering them an ownership interest in the law firm. In doing so, law firms will be able to compete with other companies that offer stock options. The firm may not only benefit from the specialised services provided by top-tier non-lawyer professionals but also from increased production and stronger supervision and monitoring that the non-lawyer professionals could provide. The engagement of top-tier professionals could provide significant benefits for a law firm. The employment of such persons may assist in the firm being better managed. Non-lawyers may be able to provide a different insight to those within the profession and suggest changes to management structures and processes that may be innovative and unique. A fresh perspective from non-lawyers may also bring new service delivery ideas that law firms may adopt to attract or retain new clients.[163] As Richard Susskind states, 'Just as librarians did not invent Google, lawyers may not create tomorrow's innovations in legal practice.'[164]

The impact of improved management structures may have a positive influence on the health and wellbeing of lawyers. Under the corporate structure not every partner has to be involved in the management of the firm. Partners who do not wish to have a managerial role can relinquish that role. Partners who chose not to join as part of the management team would therefore have more time to devote to generating revenue for the firm. For those partners that take on management roles, the demands of that role may be eased by having other persons such as non-lawyers on the management team with specific managerial expertise.

In addition, the health and wellbeing of lawyers may be improved because law firms with non-lawyer owners or investors would be required

161 Matthew Bish, 'Revising Model Rule 5.4: Adopting a Regulatory Scheme that Permits Nonlawyer Ownership and Management of Law Firms' (2009) 48 *Washburn Law Journal* 669, 686.
162 Ibid. at 687.
163 Susskind, above n. 125, 173.
164 Bish, above n. 161, 686.

to be more accountable.[165] Unlike the traditional law firm partnership structure where transparency lies in the hands of the top echelons, incorporation imposes greater disclosure requirements and therefore greater transparency.[166] For Adams, the disclosure obligations imposed on corporate structures would bring great benefits to clients, employees, shareholders and creditors and the general community, including increased accountability and financial transparency.[167] The corporate disclosure obligations may also prevent the sudden collapse of law firms, as firms would be required to publicly watch their debt.[168]

4.2. COSTS OF INCORPORATION FOR THE HEALTH AND WELLBEING OF LAWYERS

Whilst there may be considerable benefits arising from changing law firm structures to allow non-lawyer ownership or investment that may have a positive influence on the health and wellbeing of lawyers, there are also considerable costs. Opponents argue that non-lawyer law firm ownership or investment poses a threat to the ethical and professional obligations of lawyers and negatively impinges on the culture of collegiality within law firms. The following section outlines these costs in more detail and considers their impact on the health and wellbeing of lawyers.

4.2.1. Threat to the Professional and Ethical Obligations of Lawyers

The greatest concern of non-lawyers owning or investing in law firms is the impact of non-lawyers on the professional and ethical obligations of lawyers. Scholars have expressed some concern that if non-lawyers are involved in the delivery of legal services the ethical and professional obligations with which lawyers must comply will be under threat from being upheld.[169] This concern is premised on the fact that non-lawyers are not subject to, and do

---

165 Adams, above n. 128, 790.

166 Ibid.

167 Ibid. at 811–15.

168 Ibid. at 813.

169 James W. Jones and Bayliss Manning, 'Getting at the Root of Core Values: A "Radical" Proposal to Extend the Model Rules to Changing Forms of Legal Practices' (2000) 84 *Minnesota Law Review* 1159, 1186–89.

not understand, the core ethical and professional obligations of lawyers.[170] It is argued that as a result of this lack of understanding, non-lawyers will force lawyers to abandon their ethical and professional obligations.[171]

Opponents of non-lawyers owning or investing in law firms argue that the absence of professional and ethical obligations for non-lawyers, their lack of understanding about the ethical and professional obligations and market pressure to attain profit will: impact the lawyer's duty of confidentiality, force lawyers to disclose client confidential information and destroy legal professional privilege.[172] Opponents also argue that the imposition of non-lawyers in law firms will create unresolvable conflicts of interests and result in lawyers practising to the share price rather than their duty to the Court.[173] The impact of this pressure by non-lawyer owners on lawyers' health and wellbeing could be immense.

A number of scholars, however, reject the assumption that non-lawyer ownership or investment in law firms would threaten the professional and ethical obligations of lawyers. Dzienkowski and Peroni, for example, reject the claim that non-lawyers pose a threat to the core values of the legal profession on the premise that there is no empirical evidence to support the proposition that lawyers working in non-lawyer-owned law firms will be any less likely to meet their ethical duties than lawyers working in traditional law firms.[174] Moreover, according to Andrews, no evidence exists to suggest that non-lawyers have the ability to overpower lawyers into making unethical decisions[175] and there is no evidence to suggest that there would be any harm if the prohibition against non-lawyer ownership were removed.[176]

Jones and Manning also reject the concerns regarding core values and argue, for example, that the presumption that non-lawyers are unethical

---

170 James R. Debuse, 'Note, Opening at $25 1/2 is Big Firm U.S.A.: Why America May Eventually Have a Publicly Traded Law Firm, and Why Law Firms Can Succeed Without Going Public' (2008) 34 *The Journal of Corporation Law* 317, 336.

171 Cindy Alberts Carson, 'Under New Mismanagement: The Problem of Non-Lawyer Equity Partnership in Law Firms' (1994) 7 *Georgetown Journal of Legal Ethics* 593, 612; Andrews, above n. 140, 601–2.

172 Carson, above n. 171, 622.

173 MacEwen et al., above n. 149, 10; Bish, above n. 161, 694–97; Carson, above n. 171, 618.

174 Recognising, that lawyers in many traditional law firms face ethical dilemmas. See Dzienkowski and Peroni, above n. 159, 139.

175 Andrews, above n. 140, 607.

176 Ibid. at 621.

and will compromise the duty of confidentiality is unwarranted.[177] Jones and Manning note that non-lawyer professionals are required to maintain confidentiality, and most comply with that obligation every day.[178] Adams and Matheson also reject the contention that the core values and ethics of the legal profession will be eroded by non-lawyer interference because any breach of confidentiality would ultimately detrimental to the reputation of the firm.[179]

For Andrews, the contention that the professional and ethical obligations of lawyers will be compromised because of non-lawyer law firm ownership is 'furphy'.[180] According to Andrews, the professional and ethical obligations of lawyers are already at risk of being compromised in traditional law firm partnership structure.[181] Andrews submits that the supervisory structures in law firms where partners are responsible for managing associates are just as dangerous as having non-lawyer involvement because partners, like non-lawyers, are motivated by profit.[182] Similarly, Parker argues that the traditional law firm structure breeds unethical conduct, particularly as a result of the impact of billable hour targets.[183]

4.2.2. *Increased Commercialisation and Loss of Collegiality*

Commentators have expressed concern that the ability of non-lawyers to own or invest in law firms will result in a distorted and commercialised legal services market that is dominated by 'mega law firms' who are owned by large retail corporations or accounting firms.[184] This concern, colloquially referred to as 'the fear of Sears' argument (Sears being a Department Store

---

177 Jones and Manning, above n. 169, 1202.

178 Ibid.

179 Edward S. Adams and John H. Matheson, 'Law Firms on the Big Board?: A Proposal for Nonlawyer Investment in Law Firms' (1998) 86 *California Law Review* 1, 16.

180 A furphy is Australian slang for an erroneous or improbable story that is claimed to be factual. Furphies are supposedly 'heard' from reputable sources, sometimes second-hand or third-hand, and widely believed until discounted.

181 Andrews, above n. 140, 606.

182 Ibid.

183 Parker, above n. 144, 360–61.

184 Bernard Sharfman, 'Note, Modifying Model Rule 5.4 to Allow for Minority Ownership of Law Firms by Nonlawyers' (2000) 13 *Georgetown Journal of Legal Ethics* 477, 479, 481; Andrews, above n. 140, 595.

in the United States) assumes that that large multinational corporations provide legal services and thereby force the smaller firms to close their doors or be bought out by the corporations.[185] Commentators such as Carson are concerned about the impact of corporations engaging in legal practice and argue that non-lawyer ownership of law firms will lead to a commercialised legal marketplace that will 'denigrate the profession into a business.'[186]

Non-lawyers owning or investing in law firms may negatively impact the culture of law firms. Scholars have suggested that the influence of non-lawyers will result in greater managerialism and that as a consequence the levels of collegiality that are traditionally experienced by the legal profession will no longer be attainable. Parker for example, writes:

> The management structure of ILP will break down trust, loyalty and collegial respect between practitioners. Colleagues will no longer feel responsible for assisting each other. Nor will they have the incentive of avoiding vicarious liability to encourage them to monitor each other's work. The working environment in ILPs will be more competitive, and less amenable to collegial identification, discussion and resolution of ethical and other problematic issues in the provision of client services. More junior lawyers will not be encouraged to think for themselves but simply to follow instructions from above, while more senior lawyers' ethical sensibilities will be over-ridden by the profit-making purpose of the firm.[187]

Whilst incorporation may pose such as risk, one could also argue that the traditional partnership today carries the same risk of favouring managerialism over collegiality. Ross, for example, has discussed the loss of collegiality in the modern law firm partnership as follows:

> The disadvantage for many working in large firms is that they have become more bureaucratic with those at the top becoming organisers and paper pushers. There has also been a loss of community and autonomy as the firms rapidly increased during the last 35 years … within this structure there is still collegiality but it is restricted in its operations.[188]

185 Adams and Matheson, above n. 179, 10, 14–15.
186 Carson, above n. 171, 605–6.
187 Parker, above n. 183, 355–56.
188 Ross, above n. 36, 268.

Roach Anleu similarly writes in her discussions of the practice of law in Australia and the United States:

> In sum, in both the United States and Australia, more lawyers work in bureaucratic organizations than previously. This suggests that lawyers have less control over the types of work they perform, have little contact with clients, and experience less autonomy performing tasks, developing policy and managing time.[189]

It could therefore be argued that the imposition of non-lawyers in the ownership and management of law firms could negatively impact the health and wellbeing of lawyers. It could be argued that non-lawyers may impose further bureaucratic and industrialised forms of management styles that could cause undue stress for non-lawyers who are more accustomed to working autonomously.

5. CONCLUSION

Over the past few decades a plethora of stories have appeared in published articles, journals, research studies and reports about the diminution in the health and wellbeing of Australian lawyers vis-à-vis the practice of law in the twenty-first century. In response to those stories, the professional associations, regulators of the legal profession, Minds Count and law firms have recommended a variety of initiatives that have been aimed at assisting lawyers to mentally and physically cope with the changing and demanding landscape of legal practice. The initiatives have focused on, inter alia: giving those that are suffering from poor health and wellbeing a voice to articulate their stories; moving away from the billable hour as a charging mechanism; and embracing and implementing reforms that support a healthy work environment and a positive work-life balance. These reforms have primarily focused on the cultural norms of legal practice.

This chapter considers whether reforms that address the structural anomalies of legal practice could have a positive impact on the health and wellbeing of lawyers. In particular, this chapter considers whether allowing law firms to change their practice structure from that of the traditional partnership model to a model in which non-lawyers are able to own or

[189] Anleu, above n. 30, 191.

invest in a law firm would increase the health and wellbeing of lawyers. In doing so, this chapter looks at the alleged benefits and costs that flow from changing the ownership structure of a law firm to allow non-lawyers to own or invest in the firm and the effect of the alleged benefits and costs on the health and wellbeing of lawyers.

The benefits that are alleged to flow from non-lawyers owning or investing in law firms, such as access to external capital and limited liability, seem to suggest that non-lawyer law firm ownership or investment is likely to have a positive impact on the health and wellbeing of lawyers. Conversely, the costs of non-lawyer ownership, such as threats to the professional and ethical obligations of lawyers and the impact of bureaucratisation, suggest that the health and wellbeing of lawyers could be adversely impacted. The determination of the impact of changes in law firm structures on the health and wellbeing of lawyers cannot, however, be realised until research is undertaken in this area.

CHAPTER 10

ARTIFICIAL INTELLIGENCE AND LAWYER WELLBEING

Felicity Bell, Justine Rogers and Michael Legg*

1. Introduction 239
2. Definitions and Current Situation 242
3. Indicators of Wellbeing within a Wider Context 243
   3.1. The Profession as a Calling 244
   3.2. ... or the Profession as Market Control. 246
   3.3. The Profession as a Business 248
4. What does Artificial Intelligence Mean for Wellbeing?. 250
   4.1. Employment Effects: Efficiency and Precarity 251
   4.2. Expertise, Authenticity and Autonomy. 257
   4.3. Change, Fragmentation and Professional Community. 261
5. Concluding Remarks 264

1. INTRODUCTION

This chapter investigates what Artificial Intelligence (AI) means for the wellbeing of lawyers. Lawyers' wellness is a central topic of academic and professional discussion, particularly after several studies found lawyers to be especially prone to psychological distress.[1] Meanwhile, the use of

* This research was undertaken with the support of the Law Society of New South Wales Future of Law and Innovation in the Profession (FLIP) Research Stream at UNSW Law.

1 Two main surveys that are used to establish the poor mental health of Australian lawyers and law students are: Beaton Consulting, 'Annual Professions Survey', Research Summary, BeyondBlue, April 2007; and N. Kelk et al., *Courting the Blues: Attitudes towards Depression in Australian Law Students and Lawyers*, Report, Brain and Mind Research Institute, University of Sydney, January 2009.

AI in legal service-related activities is rapidly increasing, as measured by the growth in 'LegalTech',[2] and a flurry of practice-oriented and academic commentary. The effects of automation have been debated for decades, but only with recent improvements in AI has automation been capable of impacting professional work such as the fields of medicine and law. In terms of the impact of AI in general, there is some consensus that particular jobs within occupations, or tasks within jobs, are susceptible to automation; but rarely is an entire occupation automatable.[3] In this vein, recent work on how AI will affect law or legal services refers to the augmentation of lawyers by AI,[4] rather than the automation of law (and replacement of lawyers) per se. The use of AI in legal services is often discussed in relation to other kinds of change, whether they be technological, structural or economic. In this way, as in this chapter, AI is a symbol for change, as it is emblematic of the most extreme form of technological change.[5] However, our concern is what AI, as a shortcut for change, then means for wellbeing.

The rosiest views of what AI means for legal practice focus on its capacity to eliminate or reduce 'grunt work', freeing lawyers to engage only in higher-level, more interesting and self-directed activities. The pessimistic forecast is that AI is likely to intensify an already highly-competitive legal services market: the jobs of those in the most precarious positions (junior lawyers and paralegals) are most threatened by automation, while more senior lawyers will face continuous pressure to cut costs, adapt

2 For expansive lists of legal technology companies and applications, see, e.g., Angel, *All Companies* <https://angel.co/companies?markets%5b%5d=legal+tech>; CodeX TechIndex, *Discover Legal Technology*, Stanford Law School <https://techindex.law.stanford.edu/>.

3 See, eg, M. Chui, J. Manyika and M. Miremadi, 'Four Fundamentals of Workplace Automation', *McKinsey Quarterly* (online), November 2015, <https://www.mckinsey.com/business-functions/digital-mckinsey/our-insights/four-fundamentals-of-workplace-automation>; E. Brynjolfsson and A. McAfee, *The Second Machine Age: Work, Progress, and Prosperity in a Time of Brilliant Technologies*, W.W. Norton, New York 2014; C.B. Frey and M.A. Osborne, *The Future of Employment: How Susceptible are Jobs to Computerisation?*, Working Paper, Oxford Martin School, 2013, <https://www.oxfordmartin.ox.ac.uk/downloads/academic/The_Future_of_Employment.pdf>.

4 B. Alarie, A. Niblett and A. Yoon, 'How Artificial Intelligence Will Affect the Practice of Law' (2018) 68(Suppl. 1) *University of Toronto Law Journal* 106; A. Yoon, 'The Post-Modern Lawyer: Technology and the Democratization of Legal Representation' (2018) 68(Suppl. 1) *University of Toronto Law Journal* 456.

5 See, eg, F. Pasquale and G. Cashwell, 'Four Futures of Legal Automation' (2015) 63 *University of California LA Discourse* 26.

to new technology and see their work steadily eroded. As discussed in this chapter, AI has implications for the employment environment; for the construction of lawyers' expertise and their autonomy in both work and regulation; and even for the ideal of professional service and access to justice. AI is a significant, perhaps fundamental, change, and research indicates that lawyers, in whatever context they work, are as a group especially ill-equipped to deal with change compared to other occupational groups. They typically possess psychological qualities that mean that change can adversely affect their wellbeing: they are highly sceptical (doubt others' motivations), pessimistic, and rigid in their thinking and work styles.[6] Even before AI is integrated widely into legal practice, it would be reasonable to predict that most lawyers will find its advance difficult and distressing.

This chapter positions wellbeing within the wider, changing nature of professionalism so that it, and any effects of AI, are seen at the collective, sociological level as well as the individual and psychological levels.[7] To this end, the authors describe two foundational conceptions of legal professionalism and the critiques made of them: the traditional model of the profession as a calling (labelled by its detractors as a monopolistic form of market control); and the commercialistic 'profession as a business' model (arguably, symptomatic of a dynamic, yet fragmenting profession). The authors consider how these contrasting models variously support and undermine lawyers' wellbeing, and then further how AI will impact them, and therefore wellbeing. Thus, this chapter examines how AI will change lawyers' work, and the associated pros and cons for lawyers' wellbeing. It illustrates how these impacts and their possibilities vary across the profession, according to practice context, with each meaning different things for professionalism.

---

6 L. Richard, 'The Lawyer Personality: Why Lawyers are Skeptical' (16 November 2015) American Bar Association <http://www.abalcc.org/2015/11/16/the-lawyer-personality-why-lawyers-are-skeptical>. M.E.P. Seligman, P.R. Verkuil and T.H. Kang, 'Why Lawyers Are Unhappy' (2001) 23(1) *Cardozo Law Review* 33, 40–41; J. Foster et al., 'Understanding Lawyers: Why We Do the Things We Do: Results from the Hogan Assessment Project of Lawyer Personality', White Paper, Hogan Assessment Systems and Hildebrandt Baker Robbins, 2010.

7 For a discussion of the importance of showing both the political as well as the personal dimensions of wellbeing, see C. Parker, 'The Moral Panic over Psychological Wellbeing in the Legal Profession: A Personal or Political Ethical Response' (2014) 37(3) *UNSW Law Journal* 1103.

2. DEFINITIONS AND CURRENT SITUATION

'Artificial intelligence' has no unitary meaning,[8] but encompasses computer software which can be pre-programmed to follow logical rules, and hence engage in a simple reasoning or decision-making process, and that which can, by undertaking sophisticated analysis of data, generate a 'model' and apply it to new data – in other words, can 'learn' independently.[9] Arising primarily from advances in machine learning, a number of legal applications of AI have been developed.[10] These can be broken down into time-saving applications – such as automated review and automated drafting of documents, and so-called 'expertise automation' or automation of advice-giving[11] – but also what might be referred to as augmenting applications, including legal research tools and predictive analytics.[12] In short, the former applications promise to take away some tedious and mechanistic work, such as review of documents; while the latter may equip lawyers to do their work better or to a higher standard. At present, however, AI can only supplement defined aspects of what lawyers do.

Despite this, the diverse uses of AI within legal practice predict diverse impacts across a diverse profession.[13] Firstly, the applications of AI are varied. While some practitioners may use similar technology its use can be for quite distinct tasks and occur in different contexts – such as that used to review many documents and that used to review individual documents. Moreover, a range of products has been developed and with different intended consumers in mind – some designed for use by lawyers, others for use by clients themselves.[14] Secondly, the legal profession is diverse in terms of what it does: different areas of practice, clients, sectors and

---

8 See M. Mills, 'Artificial Intelligence in Law: The State of Play 2016', Report, Thomson Reuters, 2016.

9 K.D. Ashley, *Artificial Intelligence and Legal Analytics: New Tools for Law Practice in the Digital Age*, Cambridge University Press, Cambridge 2017, p. 234.

10 P. Lippe and D.M. Katz, '10 Predictions about how IBM's Watson will Impact the Legal Profession' (2 October 2014) *ABA Journal* 'Legal Rebels' <http://www.abajournal.com/legalrebels/article/10_predictions_about_how_ibms_watson_will_impact/>.

11 J. Bennett et al., *Current State of Automated Legal Advice Tools – Discussion Paper 1*, Networked Society Institute, University of Melbourne, 2018.

12 For diagrammatic depiction of existing legal AI applications, see Neota Logic, *AI in Law* (19 April 2018) <https://www.neotalogic.com/2018/04/19/ai-in-law/>.

13 D. Remus and F. Levy, 'Can Robots Be Lawyers? Computers, Lawyers, and the Practice of Law' (2017) 30(3) *Georgetown Journal of Legal Ethics* 501.

14 See, eg, CodeX TechIndex, above n. 2.

practice structures mean that legal work itself is heterogeneous. A sole practitioner practising primarily in criminal law has little in common, in terms of day-to-day work, with a lawyer doing corporate work at a large international firm. Yet both will likely be impacted by AI. The criminal lawyer may be expected to consult a database which uses past decisions to predict the likely length of a client's sentence or whether bail should be granted. The corporate lawyer, meanwhile, may find that clients are turning to AI to conduct work such as contract review themselves; or are no longer willing to pay for lawyers to perform tasks which can readily be automated, such as review of documents for discovery or due diligence. Thus, as others have noted, AI's impacts on the profession are, and will be, variable[15] – but all lawyers will come to feel its effects in some form. The implications of this for the wellbeing of lawyers are considered in the following sections.

3. INDICATORS OF WELLBEING WITHIN A WIDER CONTEXT

In order to analyse AI for its potential to support or threaten lawyer wellbeing, it is necessary to set out some of the recognised causes and indicators of lawyer distress. Wellbeing is a challenging phenomenon for study since it is dynamic and multifaceted. According to the American legal profession's National Task Force for Lawyer Wellbeing, wellbeing is

> a continuous process whereby lawyers seek to thrive in each of the following areas: emotional health, occupational pursuits, creative or intellectual endeavours, sense of spirituality or greater purpose in life, physical health, and social connections with others. Lawyer wellbeing is part of a lawyer's ethical duty of competence. It includes lawyers' ability to make healthy, positive work/life choices to ensure not only quality of life within their families and communities, but also to help them make responsible decisions for their clients.[16]

---

15 Remus and Levy, above n. 13; T. Rostain, 'Robots versus Lawyers: A User-Centered Approach' (2017) 30(3) *Georgetown Journal of Legal Ethics* 559.

16 National Taskforce on Lawyer Well-Being, *Creating a Movement To Improve Well-Being in the Legal Profession*, 2017, p. 9. The National Task Force is a collaborative initiative, comprising a number of entities from American legal professional associations, that aims to 'create a movement towards improving the health and wellbeing of the legal profession': American Bar Association, *National Task Force on Lawyer Well Being* <https://www.americanbar.org/groups/professional_responsibility/task_force_lawyer_wellbeing/>.

To arrive at this definition, the National Task Force consulted other prominent wellbeing definitions and social science research, which emphasise that 'wellbeing is not limited to: (1) an absence of illness, (2) feeling happy all the time, or (3) intra-individual processes – context matters'.[17]

There are not yet any reported studies of the psychiatric impacts of AI for individuals.[18] Further, even then, such a research approach can risk individualising the problem of mental distress. Therefore, this chapter picks up the last dimension highlighted by the National Task Force, the contextual features, to situate wellbeing within the wider context of the changing nature of legal professionalism. As noted in the Introduction, the chapter sets out two main models of professionalism in relation to some of the key indicators of wellbeing, which are then used to analyse different components of AI. These models are referred to as 'the profession as a calling', and 'the profession as a business'. These are archetypes that illustrate the broad picture for lawyers, and represent what is likely already supporting, or not supporting, their wellbeing. Section 4 then turns to how AI might fit into (and change) this picture.

3.1. THE PROFESSION AS A CALLING

The profession as a calling was the steady template for professionalism up until the last 40 years. Under this model, lawyers are 'guaranteed' wellbeing because it supports many of their fundamental needs, which are then associated with psychological thriving. The hallmark of law as a calling is autonomy, in which lawyers are, to a significant extent, free from the competitive and financial pressures, regulatory intervention, and interpersonal dictates that characterise other, non-professional work. Professional work is then marked out by individualism, independence and 'professional judgement' (a special blend comprising the intellect, skill,

---

17 National Taskforce on Lawyer Well-Being, above n. 16, p. 10. See discussion of the term in M. Thornton, 'Squeezing the Life Out of Lawyers: Legal Practice in the Market Embrace' (2016) 25(4) *Griffith Law Review* 471; R. Collier, 'Wellbeing in the Legal Profession: Reflections on Recent Developments (Or, what do we talk about, when we talk about wellbeing?)' (2016) 23(1) *International Journal of the Legal Profession* 41.

18 This study would be difficult, as it would require isolating the effects of AI as distinct from accompanying or coincident work changes and from other existing conditions (including lawyers' documented propensity to psychological illness).

creativity, intuition and interpersonal nous of the practitioner). Autonomy, or the freedom to make one's own choices and for that activity to support an integrated sense of self,[19] correlates highly to wellbeing; some see it as the premier wellbeing condition.[20]

In wellbeing terms, lawyers' 'relatedness', or meaningful, caring and secure connection to others, is also salient.[21] Professionals tend to work for and with people, their clients or patients. Professional expertise seeks to address – and define[22] – the most important social problems, including for lawyers, our legal rights and entitlements. Under this model, then, professionals have a strong sense of their own relevance, inclusion and social status. Professionals' affiliation with their peers and overall community is, or was, equally strong. This connection then supports their competence, or their engagement in optimal challenges and mastery.[23]

With autonomy and relatedness, competence is the third main driver of wellbeing.[24] Through the traditional apprenticeship model, enforced and later continued by strict organisational and professional hierarchies, professionals learn how to be a professional over a long period of time, step up through the ranks in a controlled, predictable way, and enjoy the benefits of being an insider in which a whole network of expertise is available to them once they have 'passed the threshold'.[25]

The ethos of this community is a moral one: for the benefits of a monopoly or quasi-monopoly and limited competition with both their peers and outsiders (or other occupations), the professional commits to serving the interests of the client/patient above themselves, and to

---

19 E.L. Deci and R.M. Ryan, 'The "What" and "Why" of Goal Pursuits: Human Needs and the Self Determination of Behavior' (2000) 11(4) *Psychological Inquiry* 227, 231.

20 K.M. Sheldon, G. Williams and T.E. Joiner, *Self-Determination Theory in the Clinic: Motivating Physical and Mental Health*, Yale University Press, New Haven CT 2003, p. 19; L.S. Krieger, 'The Most Ethical of People, the Least Ethical of People: Proposing Self-Determination Theory to Measure Professional Character Formation' (2011) 8 *University of St. Thomas Law Journal* 168, 174.

21 Deci and Ryan, above n. 19, 231, 252.

22 P.S.C. Lewis, 'Introduction' in R.L. Abel and P.S.C. Lewis (eds), *The Common Law World*, University of California Press, Berkeley 1988.

23 Deci and Ryan, above n. 19, 252.

24 Deci and Ryan, above n. 19.

25 Taken from the anthropological 'rites of passage' framework. For an analysis of these processes, see J. Rogers, 'Feeling Bad and Being Elite: A Comparative Analysis of the Anxieties and Uncertainties of Aspiring Barristers' (2014) 13(1) *Comparative Sociology* 30.

protecting and advancing professional expertise and institutions.[26] For lawyers, this is embodied in their ultimate fidelity to the law and the administration of justice and the duty to serve the client's interests. Being a professional is a vocation, a calling, and a lifelong career. These associate clearly with the stability, strong social group and meaningful purpose conditions of wellbeing.

3.2. … OR THE PROFESSION AS MARKET CONTROL

The traditional model of professionalism as a special, moral community was impugned by scholars from the late 1970s for taking the professions' self-definitions and claims of integrity at face value.[27] Had it been their focus, these writers would likely have seen wellbeing conditions for professionals as typically grounded in economic advantage, prestige, and idealised identities, rather than altruistic service. These conditions are, they argued, created and continued by state-sanctioned monopolies and the professions' own 'market control' strategies.[28] The main strategies are uniform systems of training and admission, and testing for and cultivating knowledge that is objective, erudite and respectable.[29] Practical manifestations of the monopoly included rights of appearance[30] and other measures such as the split profession, advertising restriction and controls on non-lawyer involvement in legal service provision.[31] These allowed professions to control their jurisdictions, maintain high barriers to entry, and keep their expertise 'pure' or free from other forms of expertise and non-professional forms of work. It also enabled the maintenance of intellectually interesting and meaningful work, largely unrestrained by administrative and bureaucratic demands.

---

26 For a more fulsome discussion of this model, see J. Rogers, D. Kingsford Smith, and J. Chellew, 'The Large Professional Service Firm: A New Force in the Regulative Bargain' (2017) 40(1) *UNSW Law Journal* 218, 223–28.

27 Again, for more fulsome discussion, see ibid. 228–30.

28 R.L. Abel, 'The Decline of Professionalism?' (1986) 49(1) *Modern Law Review* 1, 15–16.

29 M. Sarfatti Larson, 'Professionalism: Rise and Fall' (1979) 9 *International Journal of Health Services* 607, 608.

30 R.L. Abel, 'Comparative Sociology of Legal Professions: An Exploratory Essay' (1985) 10(1) *American Bar Foundation Research Journal* 1, 28–29.

31 Ibid, 30–32; R.L. Abel, 'The Transformation of the American Legal Profession' (1986) 20 *Law & Society Review* 7, 9; R.L. Abel, 'Lawyer Self-Regulation and the Public Interest: A Reflection' (2017) 20(1) *Legal Ethics* 115, 118–19.

Regarding the 'purity' notion, the literature holds that lawyers especially esteem that which is professionally 'pure' or expressing and supporting unadulterated legal knowledge. A 'true' (and prestigious) lawyer is someone who applies and develops core, abstract legal knowledge and, as a corollary, is able to exclude 'non-legal' tasks from their work.[32] It is only when high status clients demand non-legal work or, for this chapter, new technologies, that it becomes – reluctantly – esteemed.[33]

These regulatory and conventional strategies also meant that once professionals had successfully traversed the prolonged and difficult stages of entry, their progression and social and financial rewards were, as mentioned, largely steady and assured. They were then given the context for civil, even congenial relationships with professional colleagues. Clients did not question the mastery and competence of professionals. The market control critique highlighted the domination of professionals, including lawyers, over those clients and patients who trusted them.[34] While such power imbalances may not seem to indicate healthy 'relatedness' or to support wellbeing, self-efficacy (or trusting one's ability to perform well) and pleasure in being effective, are associated with positive motivation.[35]

As will be outlined shortly, most of these arrangements and conditions have either been dismantled or eroded by political, regulatory and social changes. Some writers do not see the incompatibility or necessary tension within the model of the profession as a calling. For them, the protections engendered by market control allow professionals to get on with altruistic service and (in terms of wellbeing) to experience the sense of community and connection that supports psychological thriving.[36]

Finally, having set up this first model, the profession as a calling (or market control) as in some respects assuring wellbeing, it also contains elements that are the precise opposite, namely that are psychologically corrosive. Traditional professional structures also involve, and/or have

---

32 R.L. Sandefur, 'Work and Honor in the Law: Prestige and the Division of Lawyers' Labor' (2001) 66(3) *American Sociological Review* 382, 338.

33 Ibid.

34 One of the most influential 'power' critiques comes from E. Freidson, *Professional Powers: A Study of the Institutionalization of Formal Knowledge*, University of Chicago Press, Chicago IL 1986.

35 Deci and Ryan, above n. 19, 253.

36 J. Evetts, 'Professionalism Beyond the Nation-State: International Systems of Professional Regulation in Europe' (1998) 18(11)–(12) *International Journal of Sociology and Social Policy* 47; and T.C. Halliday, *Beyond Monopoly: Lawyers, State Crises and Professional Empowerment*, University of Chicago Press, Chicago IL 1987.

historically involved, exclusionary, elitist and discriminatory practices.[37] The prolonged and intense training and rituals of socialisation that marked out professional entry have been shown to cause anxiety and stress (and, in some cases, self-harm and suicide).[38] Professional work itself, while high on autonomy, is typically solitary and involves high workload, strict timeframes, high stakes for the patient or client (and therefore risks of discipline and liability for the practitioner), high emotional labour and associated risks of secondary trauma and burnout, and intense peer review in a context in which reputation is the main social currency.[39]

3.3. THE PROFESSION AS A BUSINESS

The upheaval of the professions over the past 40 years by government, academics and the media (and other forces, including technological and demographic) has been well-documented.[40] In the political rearrangement,

---

37 H. Sommerlad, 'Women Solicitors in a Fractured Profession: Intersections of Gender and Professionalism in England and Wales' (2002) 9(3) *International Journal of the Legal Profession* 213; H. Sommerlad, '"What are you doing here? You should be working in a hair salon or something": Outsider Status and Professional Socialization in the Solicitors' Profession' (2008) 2(1) *Web Journal of Current Legal Issues* 1; A. Francis and H. Sommerlad, 'Access to Legal Work Experience and its Role in the (Re)Production of Legal Professional Identity' (2009) 16(1) *International Journal of the Legal Profession* 63.

38 Rogers, 'Feeling Bad and Being Elite', above n. 25; S.M. Willcock et al., 'Burnout and Psychiatric Morbidity in New Medical Graduates' (2004) 181 *Medical Journal of Australia* 357; P. Schattner, S. Davidson and N. Serry, 'Doctors' Health and Wellbeing: Taking Up the Challenge in Australia' (2004) 181 *Medical Journal of Australia* 348; A.L. Markwell and Z. Wainer, 'The Health and Wellbeing of Junior Doctors: Insights from a National Survey' (2009) 191(8) *Medical Journal of Australia* 441.

39 L.C. Harris, 'The Emotional Labour of Barristers: An Exploration of Emotional Labour by Status Professionals' (2002) 39(4) *Journal of Management Studies* 553; A.P. Levin and S. Greisberg, 'Vicarious Trauma in Attorneys' (2003) 24(1) *Pace Law Review* 245; L. Caplan, 'Stress, Compassion Fatigue and Burnout: Occupational Hazards of Practicing Law' (2012) 45(3) *Maryland Bar Journal* 54; B. Glesner Fines and C. Madsen, 'Caring Too Little, Caring Too Much: Competence and the Family Law Attorney' (2007) 75(4) *University of Missouri-Kansas City Law Review* 965; P.L. Vrklevski and J. Franklin, 'Vicarious Trauma: The Impact on Solicitors of Exposure to Traumatic Material' (2008) 14(1) *Traumatology* 106.

40 J. Evetts, 'New Professionalism and New Public Management: Changes, Continuities and Consequences' (2009) 8(2) *Comparative Sociology* 247; R.L. Abel, *English Lawyers Between Market and State: The Politics of Professionalism*, Oxford University Press on Demand, 2003; R. Greenwood, R. Suddaby and C.R. Hinings, 'Theorizing Change: The Role of Professional Associations in the Transformation of Institutionalized Fields' (2002) 45(1) *Academy of Management Journal* 58.

the professions' monopolies were weakened and their self-regulatory powers were either taken away or supplemented by government bodies. The professions were subjected to twin movements of consumer protection and national (and international) competition reform.[41]

On the one hand, competition reform, the latter, might be seen as enhancing professional autonomy by allowing practitioners greater choice about how to run their practices, including across jurisdictions. Likewise, consumer protection could be seen as positive for professional competence and connectedness, by both redressing a power imbalance between professional and 'consumer' and improving access to professional services. This programme would seem to be advancing better – more transparent, dignified and ethical – relationships: relationships that are more likely to support the practitioner's wellbeing. The consumer movement can be positioned alongside wider reforms to the professions to make them more modern and meritocratic and for presumably many aspiring and practising professionals, less exclusive and stressful: to end discrimination, improve admission and training processes by making them more transparent and skills-based, and less subject to informal, hidden tests and rituals.

However, of the two, the competition agenda has been more vigorously pursued by government and professional leaders.[42] Competition would seem to threaten lawyers' wellbeing by adding pressure, increasing the need to prove oneself, and by stripping away community values to be replaced with more aggressively for-profit orientations. This context requires individual practitioners to be driven by more sharply extrinsic motivations, motivations that are negatively correlated to or not associated with wellbeing.[43] The pursuit of money is generally a 'need substitute' for not being able to pursue what is naturally interesting, enjoyable and optimally challenging. This more commercialistic focus would suggest greater scope for ethical 'blind-spots' and misconduct. It would also seem to make the public custodian role both less expected and less practical (because more time is needed to compete, and charging no-fees or reduced fees makes practice financially unsustainable). This is detrimental because being able to express and enact one's ethical values is associated with wellbeing. Further, to signal the discussion below, in some areas, consumer protection might be experienced by lawyers as consumer demands.

41 For a summary of these changes as they related to the legal profession in Australia, see Rogers, Kingsford Smith and Chellew, above n. 26, 236–46.

42 Ibid. 258.

43 Ryan and Deci, above n. 19, 249, citing E.L. Deci, *The Psychology of Self-Determination*, Lexington Books, Lexington MA 1980.

Within a wider competitive environment, clients, armed with information technology, can come to the legal practitioner with their own ideas, ready to test the lawyer's expertise. Clients might also 'shop around' or ask for only certain parts of the work to be done (unbundling). In other words, in some contexts, the relationship has perhaps over-corrected too far in favour of the client.

Finally, at the same time as their environments are being de-regulated, lawyers also face extensive regulation in the form of practice and conduct rules and consumer protection legislation. Some of these are protective, as per the model above – for example, only 'qualified entities' (lawyers or legal practices) can practise law[44] – however this regulation represents less autonomy over the nature and conditions of lawyers' work. Lawyers also face increasing external control in their workplaces in the form of performance measurement. This challenge to autonomy might be especially felt by lawyers who, as a group, value autonomy more so than other occupational groups[45] and regard managerialism as a form of 'de-skilling'[46] or in wellbeing terms, a threat to their competence. A professional's community is now less centred in the profession as a whole, and more in their workplace, practice area and the industries or communities of their most powerful clients. These affiliations are more diffuse, and some are global.

4. WHAT DOES ARTIFICIAL INTELLIGENCE MEAN FOR WELLBEING?

This section uses the two models of professionalism just described as a lens through which to examine the impacts of artificial intelligence on

---

44 Legal Profession Uniform Law 2014 (NSW) s. 10.

45 D.L. Rhode, 'What Lawyers Lack: Leadership' (2011) 9 *University of St. Thomas Law Journal* 471; Foster et al., above n. 6; L. Richard, 'Herding Cats: The Lawyer Personality Revealed' (2002) 29(11) *Report to Legal Management* 2.

46 For analyses of managerialism in law: H. Sommerlad, 'Managerialism and the Legal Profession: A New Professional Paradigm' (1995) 2(2)–(3) *International Journal of the Legal Profession* 159; D. Muzio and J. Flood, 'Entrepreneurship, Managerialism and Professionalism in Action: The Case of the Legal Profession in England and Wales' in M. Reihlen and A. Werr (eds), *Handbook of Research on Entrepreneurship in Professional Services*, Edward Elgar, Cheltenham 2012, p. 369. For other professions see: A. Kolsaker, 'Academic Professionalism in the Managerialist Era: A Study of English Universities' (2008) 33(5) *Studies in Higher Education* 513; H. Busher and R. Saran, 'Deskilling a Profession: Professionalism Deprofessionalisation and the New Managerialism' in H. Busher and R. Saran (eds), *Managing Teachers as Professionals in Schools*, Routledge, London 2013.

the legal profession and on lawyers' wellbeing. AI may support wellbeing by enhancing those aspects of professionalism that are associated with wellbeing, such as engagement in meaningful work and serving the community. Yet it may also inflame existing pressure points or stressors in the professional paradigms by heightening harmful elements: increasing competitive tensions in an already hyper-competitive occupation; potentially threatening the loss of lawyers' monopoly on legal work (where that monopoly still exists); and with associated loss of prestige and sense of purpose.

A further possibility is that the integration of AI with the practice of law will bring about a more fundamental transformation of professionalism. It has been observed that with technological change some professions will disappear, some will grow, and new ones will be created.[47] Two formulations which may impact wellbeing are worthy of consideration. The first is whether the legal profession will expand to include a much larger range of legal-related occupations. The second, which is the opposing perspective, is whether the legal profession will contract as the definition of legal work becomes more confined. The third option – that the legal profession would cease to exist – is not discussed, as there would be no lawyers for whom wellbeing would be of concern.

4.1. EMPLOYMENT EFFECTS: EFFICIENCY AND PRECARITY

As the previous section indicates, the most immediate and obvious impact on lawyers' wellbeing stemming from AI is the change it will wreak on the employment landscape. As noted in the Introduction, there is disagreement as to what proportion of occupations are automatable.[48] Previously, it was thought that 'low-skill, low-wage activities on the front line' were the most at risk from automation,[49] but developments in AI have placed professionalised occupations at risk too. A 2015 report by global consultants McKinsey found that 'a significant percentage of the activities

47 M. Bruckner, M. LaFleur and I. Pitterle, *The Impact of the Technological Revolution on Labour Markets and Income Distribution*, United Nations Department of Economic & Social Affairs, 2017, p. 26 <https://www.un.org/development/desa/dpad/wp-content/uploads/sites/45/publication/2017_Aug_Frontier-Issues-1.pdf>.

48 See, e.g., the references cited above, n. 3.

49 Chui, Manyika and Miremadi, above n. 3.

performed by even those in the highest-paid occupations (for example, financial planners, physicians, and senior executives) can be automated by adapting current technology'.[50] The realisation that lawyers' work was also susceptible to automation has generated headlines at turns alarmist and hopeful.[51] In the most extreme prognosis, lawyers' market power and economic prospects are decreased due to AI performing work previously done by lawyers.[52]

Job loss or being unable to find a job significantly compromises individuals' wellbeing.[53] Insecurity of employment increases hostility and competition between lawyers, even those who are colleagues,[54] as each lawyer tries to monopolise work and clients even if this results in overwork. Yet predictions of a wholesale 'robot lawyer' takeover have given way to speculation about precisely how much of lawyers' work might be at risk, though there is little consensus. McKinsey Global estimated that 23 per cent of a lawyer's tasks can be performed by AI;[55] while commentator and LegalTech company founder Michael Mills suggests up to 10 per cent.[56] American academics Remus and Levy found that some tasks conducted

---

50 Ibid.

51 T. Davenport, 'Let's Automate All the Lawyers?', *The Wall Street Journal* (online), 25 March 2015 <https://blogs.wsj.com/cio/2015/03/25/lets-automate-all-the-lawyers/>; J. Naughton, 'Come Friendly Robots and Take Our Dullest Jobs', *The Guardian* (online), 16 July 2017 <https://www.theguardian.com/commentisfree/2017/jul/16/come-friendly-robots-and-take-our-dullest-jobs-automation>; J. MacKenzie, 'It is Time Lawyers Embraced, Not Resisted, the Robot Revolution', *The Times* (online), 8 June 2017 <https://www.thetimes.co.uk/article/it-is-time-lawyers-embraced-not-resisted-the-robot-revolution-msmn389hz>; L. Walcutt, '"Robot Lawyer" Gives A Voice to Underserved Communities', *Forbes* (online), 30 November 2016 <https://www.forbes.com/sites/levelup/2016/11/30/robot-lawyer-gives-a-voice-to-underserved-communities/#27632c3b4831>.

52 J.O. McGinnis and R.G. Pearce, 'The Great Disruption: How Machine Intelligence Will Transform the Role of Lawyers in the Delivery of Legal Services' (2014) 82(6) *Fordham Law Review* 3041; see also Working Party No. 2 on Competition and Regulation, Organisation for Economic Co-operation and Development, *Protecting and Promoting Competition in Response to 'Disruptive' Innovations in Legal Services: Issues Paper by the Secretariat*, 61st meeting, DAF/COMP/WP2(2016)1, 13 June 2016 ('*OECD Issues Paper*').

53 See, e.g., discussion and literature cited in N. Balmer et al., 'Worried Sick: The Experience of Debt Problems and their Relationship with Health, Illness and Disability' (2005) 5(1) *Social Policy and Society* 39.

54 S. Robbins, 'From Big Law to Legal Education: The Trickle Down Effect of the Recession' (2014) 27(3) *Georgetown Journal of Legal Ethics* 841.

55 J. Manyika et al., 'Harnessing Automation for a Future that Works', Report, McKinsey Global Institute, 2017 <https://www.mckinsey.com/featured-insights/digital-disruption/harnessing-automation-for-a-future-that-works>.

56 Mills, above n. 8.

by lawyers are more susceptible to automation than others.[57] AI's impacts on wellbeing will be complex, as the use of AI in law has the potential to variously support and undermine each of the models of professionalism outlined above, in turn producing differential effects on lawyers' wellbeing.

While job loss is still credible, the lens has re-focused on the more nuanced ways that AI will change (and indeed is already changing) lawyers' work.[58] As described above, traditionally, a profession was a vocation rather than a job, and lifelong service to the profession was the norm. Under the 'profession as a calling' model, the stability and social cohesion that flow from this promote wellbeing. As we also illustrated, this paradigm has been destabilised by the State's rejection of the professional monopoly and the infusion of competition principles.[59] Perhaps a profession's central, enduring quality is its ability to face and control the conditions of change. However, context is critical. For example, several writers have demonstrated how different parts of the profession came out of the drastic set of political changes just outlined, differently. In terms that signal something broad about the possibility for wellbeing of their members, Hanlon has listed the 'winners' and 'losers' in this rearrangement: for large professional organisations of accountants and management consultants, actuaries, engineers, and also corporate lawyers, this resulted in a dramatic widening of their markets.[60] Large Australian law firms as a sector were quick to accept the demands of competition policy.[61] Some of the 'losers' were lawyers in conveyancing, probate and legal aid.[62]

---

57 Remus and Levy, above n. 13.

58 See, e.g., Pasquale and Cashwell, above n. 5; see also K. Crawford and M. Whittaker, *The AI Now Report – The Social and Economic Implications of Artificial Intelligence Technologies in the Near-Term*, 22 September 2016, p. 10 <https://ainowinstitute.org/AI_Now_2016_Report.pdf>.

59 A. Paterson, *Lawyers and the Public Good: Democracy in Action*, Cambridge University Press, Cambridge 2012, p. 17 ('[legal] professionalism … is now in terminal decline'); Abel, above n. 40; R. Moorhead, A. Paterson and A. Sherr, 'Contesting Professionalism: Legal Aid and Non-lawyers in England and Wales' (2003) 37(4) *Law & Society Review* 765; J. Webb, 'The Dynamics of Professionalism: The Moral Economy of English Legal Practice and Some Lessons from New Zealand' (2008) 16 *Waikato Law Review* 21; J. Flood, 'The Re-Landscaping of the Legal Profession: Large Law Firms and Professional Re-Regulation' (2011) 59(4) *Current Sociology* 507; Canadian Bar Association, *Reports: Face the Future with Curiosity, Confidence, Creativity*, CBA Legal Futures Initiative <https://www.cba.org/CBA-Legal-Futures-Initiative/Reports>.

60 G. Hanlon, *Lawyers, the State and the Market: Professionalism Revisited*, Macmillan Press, London 1999, pp. 32–37.

61 E. Shinnick, F. Bruinsma and C. Parker, 'Aspects of Regulatory Reform in the Legal Profession: Australia, Ireland and the Netherlands' (2003) 10 *International Journal of the Legal Profession* 237, 258.

62 Hanlon, above n. 60, pp. 32–37.

In relation to the profession as a calling, therefore, AI would seem to be damaging to lawyers' wellbeing by further eroding many of the benefits associated with this model. AI implies precarity of work and an associated diminution in prestige, as well as making further inroads into the traditional monopoly. Yet, as discussed below at Section 4.3, AI may also subvert some of the negative aspects of this model for wellbeing, namely the profession's hierarchies around entry and ascendancy.

On one view, AI is more closely aligned with a business-oriented model of professionalism, as it promotes efficiencies and furthers competition. Further, AI seems likely to make further inroads into lawyers' monopoly on legal services and lead to greater use of 'unbundling'. Particularly in the United States, online services utilising AI have been seeking to undercut lawyers' offerings for many years, and the number of such providers continues to grow.[63] Under a business-focused model, using AI for increased efficiency of legal service delivery is the primary means by which lawyers' wellbeing will be enhanced.[64] Thus it is argued that firstly, lawyers can garner material rewards both by capitalising on the efficiencies available through AI and through increased demand for their services.[65] Secondly, it is claimed that lawyers will be able to 'do more with less', with smaller firms in particular able to increase their competitiveness. For example, through the use of document automation technologies, small firms can increase the range of areas of law in which they practise. Third, the number of jobs is not finite and there will be opportunities for entirely new legal roles connected to AI and the management of new entrants to legal services. One retort to predictions of job losses stemming from AI is that whole new fields of legal problems are likely to emerge, including increased regulation around the use of AI itself in many contexts.[66] Thus, this optimistic outlook sees the legal profession moving beyond the existing current forms of legal practice.

---

63 See, e.g., B.H. Barton, *Glass Half Full: The Decline and Rebirth of the Legal Profession*, Oxford University Press, Oxford 2015; Pasquale and Cashwell, above n. 5.

64 R. Susskind, *Tomorrow's Lawyers: An Introduction to Your Future*, Oxford University Press, Oxford, 2nd ed., 2017.

65 See, e.g., J. Becker, *4 Ways that Law Firms Benefit from Legal Analytics*, LexisNexis <https://www.lexisnexis.com/pdf/legal-analytics/Legalanalyticwhitepaper.pdf>, discussing a survey of leaders of the 200 highest grossing United States law firms, which included findings that 'Legal Analytics' (defined to mean 'tools and/or capabilities powered by artificial intelligence technology') helped firms attract clients not only by providing technology-enhanced services, but by deploying analytics to 'prove' to clients that the firm is the right choice.

66 D.M. Katz, 'Make Law Better – the Legal Innovation Agenda in Vectors and Phases', Speech delivered at the Law Society of New South Wales Future of Law and Innovation in the Profession Conference, Sydney, 14 September 2018.

At present the legal profession may be conceived of as including private practice (varying from sole practitioners through to national and global law firms), in-house corporate lawyers, in-house government lawyers and not-for-profit lawyers, such as those working in the community legal sector. New law-related occupations which are the direct or indirect result of AI and the legal products it capacitates may include:

- knowledge management counsel,
- legal solutions architects,
- legal data scientists,
- legal project managers, and
- commoditised legal service assistants.[67]

Some commentators predict these careers will come to substantially outnumber traditional lawyer roles.[68] Growth in the legal profession may therefore come from an expansion of the current conception of what a lawyer is. For example, the legal solution architect who designs legal tools for both lawyers and clients using AI, as well as other technologies and design principles, may be seen as a lawyer. So, too, the legal project manager who applies project management tools to allow for the scoping, scheduling and costing of legal work, accompanied by resourcing, managing and monitoring with a view to delivering that legal work in an efficient and effective manner. Just as the legal profession has brought in-house lawyers within the fold, these new roles may become a part of a new concept of the legal profession. This scenario is buttressed by law-related occupations already being part of law firm personnel.

On the other hand, AI has the potential to exacerbate those aspects of a commercialised legal sector that are most detrimental to lawyers' wellbeing, such as hyper-competitiveness. Law graduates are apparently in oversupply in the US (and similar assertions have been made in Australia and the UK);[69] graduates therefore already compete for limited numbers

---

67 M. Legg, 'UNSW Law Mini-Curriculum Review Report on Technology and the Law School Curriculum' [2017] *University of New South Wales Faculty of Law Research Series* 90, p. 6.

68 Susskind, above n. 64, ch. 13.

69 B. Tamanaha, *Failing Law Schools*, University of Chicago Press, Chicago IL 2012; Barton, above n 63; E. Tadros and K. Walsh, 'Too Many Law Graduates and Not Enough Jobs', *Australian Financial Review* (online), 22 October 2015 <https://www.afr.com/business/legal/too-many-law-graduates-and-not-enough-jobs-20151020-gkdbyx>; but contrast with A. Patrick, 'Junior Lawyer Shortage Drives Freehills to

of jobs which may become ever-more scarce. For those who *do* enter the profession, there are implications for the quality of work they will be assigned and therefore for their training and career path. Large corporate clients have already made headlines by rejecting a business model which saw junior lawyers billed out at high rates incommensurate with their levels of experience.[70] Next, they may complain that routinised work, done by junior lawyers or paralegals, could be performed by AI.[71] Changes may go beyond juniors: an American report on mid-level associates found that around 14 per cent named 'artificial intelligence' as a threat to their current role.[72]

AI will undoubtedly change how work is undertaken and with it the quantity and quality of work for the legal profession. These effects are unlikely to be evenly distributed. For the 'winners', wellbeing support might be found in interesting work, high status and high salaries; although, wellbeing is less assured or less straightforward as a by-product of extrinsic motivations such as money. Rather, extrinsic motivations need to be supported and synthesised with other values and motivations such as autonomy.[73] For Hanlon's 'losers', a sense of being special and valued in society is harder to find. Indeed, research has documented the low self-esteem and demoralisation of legal aid lawyers.[74] Without the guarantees of 'bread and butter' work for lawyers, such as conveyancing, wills, debt recovery and so on, there is reduced financial reward and stability. In addition, feelings of efficacy and mastery, critical to wellbeing, would appear

New Zealand', *Australian Financial Review* (online), 20 September 2018 <https://www.afr.com/business/legal/juniors-lawyer-shortage-drives-freehills-to-new-zealand-20180919-h15m8b>.

70 *OECD Issues Paper*, above n. 52, pp. 9, 19, citing McGinnis and Pearce, above n. 52.

71 D. Kravets, 'Law Firm Bosses Envision Watson-Type Computers Replacing Young Lawyers', 26 October 2015, *Ars Technica* <http://arstechnica.com/tech-policy/2015/10/law-firm-bosses-envision-watson-type-computers-replacing-young-lawyers/>. This is not dissimilar to the impact of outsourcing, in that those in lower-wage occupations tend to be most affected: M.C. Regan Jr and P.T. Heenan, 'Supply Chains and Porous Boundaries: The Disaggregation of Legal Services' (2010) 78(5) *Fordham Law Review* 2137, 2185, citing A. Davis-Blake and J.P. Broschak, 'Outsourcing and the Changing Nature of Work' (2009) 35 *Annual Review of Sociology* 321.

72 R. Strom, weekly email newsletter 'The Law Firm Disrupted', 30 August 2018, citing *The American Lawyer*, 'The 2018 Midlevel Associates Survey', 26 August 2018 <https://www.law.com/americanlawyer/2018/08/26/the-2018-midlevel-associates-survey/>.

73 Deci and Ryan, above n. 19, p. 239.

74 See, eg, H. Sommerlad, '"I've Lost the Plot": An Everyday Story of the "Political" Legal Aid Lawyer' (2001) 28(3) *Journal of Law and Society* 335.

to be sporadic in the context of budget cuts and other resource problems. However, predicting the winners and losers is not straightforward and much may depend on a confluence of factors such as regulation and the legal profession's adoption or rejection of AI.

4.2. EXPERTISE, AUTHENTICITY AND AUTONOMY

As discussed in Section 3, the specialised knowledge and expertise of lawyers is the cornerstone of professionalism: this justifies exclusionary practices and self-regulation, while supporting esteem and self-worth once acceptance into the profession has been achieved. Time-saving applications of AI may enhance lawyers' engagement in higher-level work by 'freeing' them from menial and run-of-the-mill tasks, which AI will instead perform.[75] These AI applications are particularly relevant for lawyers in large firms, who may otherwise spend time doing tasks which do not demand especial expertise such as document review. In discovery, for example, a senior lawyer is still needed to 'train' AI software to conduct the document review and make higher-level decisions; but the bulk of the review function can be done by machine.[76] By hiving off some tasks to an automated system, arguably lawyers can return to something closer to the traditional professional ideal of meaningful, bespoke work as opposed to a commercialised 'factory' or production line.[77] In smaller firms, software can produce first drafts of documents such as simple contracts, wills, and so on,[78] leaving lawyers to focus on substantive issues in the terms themselves, negotiation, and explanation to the client. In these examples, AI plays the role of the legal secretary, paralegal or junior solicitor who reviews documents or produces the initial draft; while the expert solicitor fulfils

75 N. Ramanujam and A. Agnello, 'The Shifting Frontiers of Law: Access to Justice and Underemployment in the Legal Profession' (2017) 54(4) *Osgoode Hall Law Journal* 1091, 1108.

76 J. Didday, 'Informed Buyers of E-Discovery: Why General Counsel Must Become Tech Savvy' (2013) 5 *Hastings Science & Technology Law Journal* 281, 306.

77 G.K. Hadfield, *Rules for a Flat World: Why Humans Invented Law and How to Reinvent It for a Complex Global Economy*, Oxford University Press, Oxford 2016; Barton, above n. 63.

78 See, eg, K.D. Betts and K.R. Jaep, 'The Dawn of Fully Automated Contract Drafting: Machine Learning Breathes New Life into a Decades-Old Promise' (2017) 15 *Duke Law & Technology Review* 216; G.J. Clark, 'Internet Wars: The Bar Against the Websites' (2013) 13 *Journal of High Technology Law* 247.

the same function as previously, focused on client relations, substantive law and challenging issues.[79]

As well as the benefits of expertise, the traditional model of professionalism supports wellbeing by venerating individualism and independence, particularly the concept of professional wisdom. The blend of life experience, knowledge of the social world and ethical imperatives renders this relatively immune from automation. Thus AI may increase the value placed on those human qualities needed for legal practice which cannot presently (and may never) be effectively automated.[80] This might include the qualities necessary to conduct the higher-level work described above: human discretion; judgement; 'evaluation and flair';[81] creativity; and empathy.[82] In other words, AI may actually enhance the importance and hence value (in a broad sense) of these traditional professional indicia, thus supporting wellbeing under the 'profession as a calling' model.

The counterargument is that the use of AI in legal services, rather than facilitating meaningful work for lawyers, is part of a wider loss of skills and de-professionalisation, with negative implications for wellbeing. As Pasquale and Cashwell observe, fewer lawyers overall might mean 'their clout would also fade, starting a self-reinforcing cycle of diminishing influence'.[83] These authors posit that the use of AI could further exacerbate inequalities within the profession: 'Those at the bottom of the profession would continue to be replaced by machines; those at the top would find software complementing their expertise and connections, extending their reach and power'.[84] As well as actual loss of work, there is a threatening or 'reminding' aspect to the automation of some parts of work – lawyers are reminded that the work they do can be undertaken by AI. This causes both

79 Frey and Osborne, above n. 3, 41.

80 M. Legg, 'Embrace robotic disruption but don't lose your human skills', *The Australian* (online), 16 June 2017 <http://www.law.unsw.edu.au/news/2017/06/embrace-robotic-disruption-don%E2%80%99t-lose-your-human-skills>; S.V. Schoonmaker IV, 'Withstanding Disruptive Innovation: How Attorneys Will Adapt and Survive Impending Challenges from Automation and Nontraditional Legal Services Providers' (2017) 51(2) *Family Law Quarterly* 133.

81 B. Simpson, 'Algorithms or Advocacy: Does the Legal Profession Have a Future in a Digital World?' (2016) 25(1) *Information & Communications Technology Law* 50, 51.

82 C. Westaby and E. Jones, 'Empathy: An Essential Element of Legal Practice or "Never the twain shall meet"?' (2018) 25(1) *International Journal of the Legal Profession* 107.

83 Pasquale and Cashwell, above n. 5, p. 36.

84 Ibid. 35.

a crisis in terms of meaningfulness and expertise, and a looming sense of precarity or impermanence.

Though entry may be strictly controlled, within the profession the combination of mentorship, connection to colleagues and shared expertise promotes wellbeing. This may be perceived as threatened by AI – firstly as the training of young lawyers is rendered uncertain without basic work available as a learning tool. Historically, lawyers honed their craft through years of practice, being supervised or mentored by more senior members of the profession.[85] This has already been eroded through the growth of practical legal training courses and decline of the apprenticeship model. Along with document review and drafting of agreements, even drafting memos or letters is possible for AI software.[86] It is unclear how training of junior lawyers will be affected as AI further diminishes the work available to them.[87] Susskind has asked: 'If the basic legal work, upon which young lawyers used to cut their teeth, is to be undertaken by others, how does a young lawyer take the early steps towards becoming an expert?'[88] Secondly, it is uncertain what impact this will have on the inculcation of professional values, but it seems likely to have a negative impact, leading to further fragmentation.

On the other hand, the rise of AI in legal services brings the possibility that new kinds of knowledge and a new skillset will be required of lawyers. This skillset may be considered to include three categories. First is the ability to effectively use AI and the technology solutions it spawns. This includes understanding what the technology does and whether it is 'fit-for-purpose' in relation to the client's requirements. Those requirements may also be informed by the client's collaborators and adversaries, or third parties such as courts or regulators. Secondly, lawyers need to be able to

---

85 See, e.g., G. Gasteen, 'National Competency Standards: Are They the Answer for Legal Education and Training' (1995) 13(1) *Journal of Professional Legal Education* 1, 6–7; J. Giddings and M. McNamara, 'Preparing Future Generations of Lawyers for Legal Practice: What's Supervision Got to Do with It?' (2014) 37(3) *UNSW Law Journal* 1226, 1230.

86 See, e.g., the capabilities of 'ROSS', an 'advanced legal research tool that harnesses the power of artificial intelligence': Ross, *AI Meets Legal Research* <https://rossintelligence.com/>.

87 Susskind, above n. 64; Strom, above n. 73; C. Merritt, 'Days of All Hands on Tech: Interview with Michael Legg', *The Australian*, 2 November 2018, p. 25.

88 Susskind, above n. 64, p. 167.

comprehend and interrogate the output of AI systems, which will require statistical literacy and quantitative skills. Thirdly, lawyers will need the capacity to incorporate the various technology solutions, whether they be document review, document creation or predictive analytics, into the larger legal service offering which requires project management skills.[89] While antithetical to the traditional professional model, which emphasises the time-honoured nature of legal knowledge, under a more dynamic, business-oriented model this could be viewed as a positive. Younger lawyers, and those entering the profession in the future, may be better placed to adapt to the changes required.[90]

The future lawyer would utilise a mixed skill set drawing from a range of disciplines. The effect of this may be less shared values and a loss of identity as lawyers' training, operational context and influences vary much more than today; the professional calling and its associated benefits for wellbeing may be reduced or lost. Equally, the profession as a form of market control may be lost as the lawyer role moves even closer to that of a business. Traditional lawyers may morph into a legal consultant-type role where they bring knowledge of substantive law to a multi-disciplinary team of legal solutions architects, data scientists and project managers.[91] The lawyer would have skills in coding, statistics and project management though only to the extent necessary to work with other disciplines. However, multi-skilled lawyers may find themselves in greater demand and more employable.

---

89 M. Legg, 'New Skills for New Lawyers: Responding to Technology and Practice Developments' in K. Lindgren, F. Kunc and M. Coper (eds), *The Future of Australian Legal Education*, LawBook Co., Sydney 2018, p. 373.

90 See Lippe and Katz, above n. 10. Students currently in school or university have grown up surrounded by technology. 'Information and Communication Technology (ICT) is "one of seven general capabilities … taught throughout [Australian] students' pre-university schooling", and the Australian Curriculum Assessment and Reporting Authority's "Digital Technologies curriculum" requires Year 10 students to apply complex technological knowledge, showing understanding of privacy and security requirements including for data use, online collaboration and sharing and protocol development, management of digital projects, and design of user experiences and algorithms': Legg, above n. 67, p. 7. To this may be added that even online games such as Minecraft and Fortnite allow for online collaboration, making online interactions increasingly commonplace: see, e.g., N. Wynarczyk, 'Fortnite "designed to be addictive" for kids', *New York Post* (online), 13 June 2018 <https://nypost.com/2018/06/13/fortnite-designed-to-be-addictive-for-kids/>.

91 E. Ryan, 'Law firms to shift more into consultancy model', *Lawyers Weekly* (online), 26 September 2017 <https://www.lawyersweekly.com.au/biglaw/21956-law-firms-to-shift-more-into-consultancy-model>.

4.3. CHANGE, FRAGMENTATION AND PROFESSIONAL COMMUNITY

Finally, the authors turn to consider how the nature of the professional community and affiliation has changed and will undergo further change. The 'profession as a calling' paradigm espouses the special status and prestige of the profession of law; as explained in Section 3, while psychologically beneficial, there are also stressors associated with the traditionally elitist and discriminatory aspects of restricted membership. The profession as a business model also has negative associations with hierarchical and competitive fragmentation into different groups: lawyers are in competition with one another; with non-professionals such as those offering cheaper or unbundled legal services; with non-lawyer professionals, such as the 'big four' accounting firms, who offer legal services;[92] and even with clients who may turn to outsourcing or insourcing their legal work.[93] Thus, there is more intense intra-professional competition.[94] While scholars and professional leaders might be interested in the status differences and fragments across the profession as a whole, practitioners and firms themselves are concerned with competitive pressures from those in their practice area who are competing for the same types of clients.[95] The rise of AI and the automation of legal advice, dispute resolution and document creation may further increase competition and fragmentation. Legal work which was solely the province of lawyers, due to both required knowledge and regulation, can now be performed by various versions of AI, causing a further reduction in the legal profession's role and monopoly. Other changes, including for instance, the mobility of professionals as employees, would seem to compound other pressures (such as billable hours, securing

92 A. King and K. Walsh, 'Big Four Accounting Firms Push into Legal Services', *Australian Financial Review* (online), 21 July 2015 <https://www.afr.com/business/accounting/afr8acclawyers-vs-accountants-20150617-ghq715>.

93 G. Marchant, 'Artificial Intelligence and the Future of Legal Practice' (2017) *SciTech Lawyer* 20, <https://www.americanbar.org/content/dam/aba/administrative/litigation/materials/2017-2018/2018-sac/written-materials/artificial-intelligence-and-the-future.pdf>, M. Legg and F. Bell, 'Insourcing – Implications for In-House Counsel and Private Practice Lawyers' (2018) 45 *Law Society of New South Wales Journal* 70.

94 J. Webb, 'Turf Wars and Market Control: Competition and Complexity in the Market for Legal Services' (2004) 11(1)–(2) *International Journal of the Legal Profession* 81.

95 As shown in the empirical findings of D. Hartstein and J. Rogers, 'Professional Associations as Regulators: An Interview Study of the Law Society of New South Wales' (2019) 2(1)–(2) *Legal Ethics* 49, 63–64.

new work, and so on). There is evidence to suggest that firms and seniors now devote less time to mentoring and training.[96] Lawyers may work in specialist teams which act as silos and can fragment them from peers and from the overall matter.[97] Further, there might be multiple generations within one firm – generations whose abilities to manage change, and therefore stay well, vary. One paradoxical phenomenon that might be occurring is that those perhaps the best equipped to master change – and the most invested in it – are the most junior, who also have the least decision-making latitude or autonomy to respond.

It may, however, be possible for AI to subvert some of these latent professional hierarchies by levelling the field and creating new meritocratic entry paths to the profession, or new avenues to success within it.[98] The path to professional success has become more varied, with alternative legal service providers, also known as 'New Law', other AI-enabled legal practices, and legal technology companies arriving. The law student who does not fit into the traditional legal mould can still pursue a legal career, possibly as a disruptor reimaging legal services with the aid of AI. The legal profession may on the whole become less elitist and more responsive to, and engaged with, client interests. This greater connection to a 'broader church' of lawyers and clients may improve wellbeing.

AI may also lead to a shift in the status of different occupations within law: authors such as Semple have, for example, argued that 'personal plight' lawyers – such as those working in criminal law or family law – will be relatively advantaged by developments in AI as their work is less

---

96 American Bar Association Commission on Billable Hours, *ABA Commission on Billable Hours Report*, American Bar Association, 2002, p. 5; Giddings and McNamara, above n. 86.

97 To understand how the large law firm context can and does impact on ethical behaviour, see C. Parker et al., 'The Ethical Infrastructure of Legal Practice in Larger Law Firms: Values, Policy and Behaviour' (2008) 31(1) *University of New South Wales Law Journal* 158.

98 For example, lawyers and start-ups are recognising the potential of technology to improve competitiveness in small- and medium-sized practices. See, e.g., N. Black, *Today's Tech: A Litigation Attorney Uses Technology to Level the Playing Field*, 6 August 2015, Above the Law <https://abovethelaw.com/2015/08/todays-tech-a-litigation-attorney-uses-technology-to-level-the-playing-field/>; Attorney IO, 'Bay Area Startup Wants to Replace Lawyers with AI to Level the Playing Field', 21 February 2018, *Cision PR Newswire* <https://www.prnewswire.com/news-releases/bay-area-startup-wants-to-replace-lawyers-with-ai-to-level-the-playing-field-300601908.html>; J. Unger, 'How Technology and Automation Enable Lawyers to Deliver Personalized Service', *Forbes* (Online), 16 November 2016 <https://www.forbes.com/sites/forbeslegalcouncil/2016/11/16/how-technology-and-automation-enable-lawyers-to-deliver-personalized-service/#3ca10be15a6a>.

susceptible to automation[99] than those, for example, working in corporate legal services. This is because personal plight lawyering relies more heavily on non-legal aspects such as those mentioned in the previous section, like emotional intelligence and empathy; and involves individualised situations – such as the threat of criminal conviction or an unfavourable separation agreement – which are usually of crucial importance to those involved. Ironically, lucrative large-scale transactional work such as mergers and acquisitions, generally considered high-status legal work, is increasingly vulnerable to automation with developments in natural language processing and machine learning. Susskind has commented that 'this concept of "high-end work" is something of a myth – even in the world's largest deals and disputes there are substantial components of work that can be routinized'.[100] Accordingly one existing legal hierarchy may be upended by AI. On the other hand, small or mid-sized firms may lose some dependable straightforward work such as the drafting of simple documents.

As discussed in the preceding section, a sense of community among lawyers facilitates wellbeing: the same can be said of meaningful connection to society generally. A hallmark of professionalism is a devotion to serving the public good; having a greater or higher purpose beyond commercial aims. Yet the legal profession's commitment to facilitating access to justice for legally under-served communities has frequently been questioned. Particularly in the US, the suggestion of numerous commentators has been that the traditional mode of lawyer offerings has failed to increase access[101] and legal services continue to be unaffordable for many.[102] Similar complaints are made in Australia, though in more muted fashion.[103]

---

99 N. Semple, 'Personal Plight Legal Practice and Tomorrow's Lawyers' (2014) 39(1) *Journal of the Legal Profession* 25; Rostain, above n. 15.

100 Susskind, above n. 64, p. 61.

101 See, e.g., G.K. Hadfield and D.L. Rhode, 'How to Regulate Legal Services to Promote Access, Innovation, and the Quality of Lawyering' (2016) 67(5) *Hastings Law Journal* 1191; B.H. Barton and S. Bibas, *Rebooting Justice: More Technology, Fewer Lawyers, and the Future of Law* (Encounter Books, 2017); L. Moxley, 'Zooming Past the Monopoly: A Consumer Rights Approach to Reforming the Lawyer's Monopoly and Improving Access to Justice' (2015) 9(2) *Harvard Law and Policy Review* 553.

102 See, e.g., Commission on the Future of Legal Services, American Bar Association, *Report on the Future of Legal Services in the United States* (2016) pp. 11–18.

103 Australian cuts to legal aid funding may be the greater concern: see, e.g., M.A. Noone and S. Tomsen, *Lawyers in Conflict: Australian Lawyers and Legal Aid* (Federation Press, 2006); J. Giddings and M.A. Noone, 'Australian Community Legal Centres Move into the Twenty-First Century' (2004) 11(3) *International Journal of the Legal Profession* 257.

Lawyers do provide many hours of pro bono representation[104] and legally-aided work; however, legal services remain too expensive for many persons with legal needs.[105] It is claimed that AI offers another means to expand the reach of legal services through efficiencies and affordability. One author explains: 'Expert systems … may not solve every legal problem, but they can help address simple, recurring legal problems at scale. Indeed, one-to-many software tools may be one of the only scalable ways to address the access-to-justice problem.'[106] Meanwhile, time-saving applications such as automated drafting may also enable lawyers to offer more affordable services and therefore increase accessibility. Increasing affordability and increasing the number of people with access to legal advice and assistance would have a positive impact in terms of the traditional professional model. At the same time, however, there is threat to the professional monopoly from external sources which utilise AI to mimic lawyer offerings while undercutting price. This impacts negatively on the profession's credentials in terms of the public good, as it implies that lawyers have failed to provide access to justice and outsiders are therefore using technology to do what the profession could (or would) not.

5. CONCLUDING REMARKS

Lawyers' wellbeing is a complex phenomenon which can be examined from a multitude of different perspectives. Here, taking a perspective based in the literature of the professions, this chapter outlined the two key and contrasting models of legal professionalism and how each variously supports and detracts from wellbeing. It then examined the potential implications of AI and its particular impacts on these professional models.

As demonstrated in Section 4, AI may exaggerate some of the key elements of each model. That is, it may paradoxically strengthen the traditional model of the profession as a calling, as lawyers retain those tasks which are both the most complex, and that require human qualities such as empathy – thereby continuing to play the role of trusted advisor.

---

104 E.g., Australian Pro Bono Centre, *National Pro Bono Target* <https://www.probonocentre.org.au/provide-pro-bono/target/>.

105 C. Coumarelos et al., *Legal Australia-Wide Survey: Legal Need in Australia* (Law and Justice Foundation of NSW, 2012).

106 E. Walters, 'Read/Write: Artificial Intelligence Libraries' (2017) 22(1) *AALL Spectrum* 21, 22; see also D. Luban, 'Optimism, Skepticism and Access to Justice' (2016) 3(3) *Texas A & M Law Review* 499, 500.

Yet AI may also increase competition, further diminish lawyers' exclusivity when it comes to legal work, and thereby engender greater insecurity. AI may change the field so that different blends of 'winners' and 'losers' emerge – new types of legal practice, the advantaging of smaller firms, or greater job security concentrated in 'low-status' branches of the profession.

There is also the possibility that AI will wreak more fundamental change upon the profession: that the profession will either expand and diversify more than ever before; or will become essentially a small and segregated specialisation: what Pasquale and Cashwell describe as a 'vestigial' legal services sector.[107] In terms of the fragmentation of roles, Susskind argued in *Tomorrow's Lawyers* that a small group of elite law firms would retain their elite status and that small or mid-sized firms with specialised expertise would survive and even thrive; but was pessimistic about the outlook for many small 'high street' firms.[108] Susskind predicts that 'two kinds of traditional lawyer' will retain their roles into the future: the expert trusted advisor; and what he terms the 'enhanced practitioner', who makes use of technology to assist experts but does not provide a bespoke service – a kind of over-qualified legal assistant.[109] In a similar vein, McGinnis and Pearce have also argued that two kinds of lawyer will be the 'winners' from the impacts of AI – successful, expert lawyers will become even more so, while other lawyers who use technology strategically can improve and broaden their offerings by serving an 'expanding market of legal services'.[110]

What seems clear is that AI will have a widening effect, which is neither categorically positive nor negative for wellbeing, but seems likely to exacerbate the fragmentation of the profession. Thus, lawyers' wellbeing may be improved as AI enhances the value of human professional skills which it cannot replicate; many more options for different legal roles are created; and efficiencies may lead to greater material returns. At the same time, however, fewer traditional and meaningful legal roles may be supported, and the number of competitors for automatable work will increase, diminishing wellbeing by further damaging the security of the traditional professional monopoly.

Overall, what does this all mean for lawyer wellbeing? AI will undoubtedly change the practice of law and most likely give rise to greater diversity in the way in which law is practised. Some of those practices will

---

107 Pasquale and Cashwell, above n. 5.

108 Susskind, above n. 64, pp. 63–64.

109 Ibid., pp. 133–34.

110 McGinnis and Pearce, above n. 52, 3042.

be closer to the model of traditional professionalism (an example may be barristers or advocates), others will be very much the profession as business as they seek to sell commoditised legal offerings to individuals and businesses (for example, LegalTech). Indeed, as raised above, there will be a question as to whether these offerings remain solely within the purview of the legal profession, or come to be offered by others. There is also likely to be a middle ground composed of the large/global law firm and the hypothesised 'lawyer as business consultant' who will seek to have a foot in each camp. There will be a desire to draw on, and project, professionalism, but also the capacity to structure and operate legal practices in the most advantageous manner. There is also a question as to what suburban or 'high street' firms will look like in the future, as well as the form that the 'people's lawyer' will take. They may be the new franchise or be subsumed in the local supermarket (the so-called 'Tesco lawyer'). But they may also, through connection to the local community and reliance on traditional professional characteristics, such as trust and independence, associated with law as a calling, mark out a niche practice.

Wellbeing for the individual lawyer will depend on that individual having the ability to choose the type of work and way of working that they find satisfying. The ability to choose will in turn depend on education and a skillset that is strong on law but also on technology and 'soft' skills such as collaboration, adaptability and empathy. It is a skillset that is likely to require continual refinement and updating – lifelong learning. Admission to legal practice will not alone guarantee wellbeing as it no longer carries the security which was once offered. Wellbeing will be attained by preserving those desirable characteristics of the profession as a calling, such as competence, autonomy and relatedness, while accepting that AI will bring further competition and deregulation.

CHAPTER 11

LAWYERS' FEE ARRANGEMENTS AND THEIR WELLBEING

Michael LEGG and Justine ROGERS*

1. Introduction 268
2. The Billable Hour and AFAs: The State of Play 270
3. Fees and Wellbeing 275
   3.1. Relatedness, Autonomy and Competence 275
      3.1.1. Lawyers' 'Relatedness' 276
      3.1.2. Motivation 278
   3.2. Lawyers' Motivations 280
   3.3. Contextual Wellbeing Factors 282
4. Billable Hours 284
   4.1. Relatedness 285
   4.2. Autonomy 288
   4.3. Competence 289
   4.4. Motivation 290
5. Alternative Fee Arrangements 292
   5.1. Contingency Fee and Reverse Contingency Fee 292
      5.1.1. Relatedness 294
      5.1.2. Autonomy 295
      5.1.3. Competence 296
      5.1.4. Motivation 296
   5.2. Fixed Fee 298
      5.2.1. Relatedness 298
      5.2.2. Autonomy 300

* This research was undertaken with the support of the Law Society of NSW Future of Law and Innovation in the Profession (FLIP) Research Stream and with the research assistance of Sharon Mo and Deborah Hartstein.

5.2.3. Competence 300
5.2.4. Motivation 301
5.2.5. Variants on Fixed-Fee Arrangements 302
5.3. Value-Based Billing 303
5.3.1. Relatedness 304
5.3.2. Autonomy 304
5.3.3. Competence 305
5.3.4. Motivation 305
6. Conclusion 306

1. INTRODUCTION

Typically, methods of charging are examined through the lens of professional ethics and/or economics: what is permitted by the conduct and practice rules, and who 'wins' and 'loses' between the lawyer and client depending on the form of charging employed. This chapter investigates lawyers' billing methods for their relationship to lawyers' wellbeing – or lack of wellbeing.

A growing research base has established that the wellbeing of lawyers is generally poor.[1] Meanwhile, lawyers' charging methods have been singled out as 'the lifeblood of the legal profession, crucial to the livelihood of the majority of lawyers'.[2] To date, there has been little discussion on the connection between the two. As the sole exception, the billable hour has been identified as a significant causal or correlative factor in lawyer

1 See, e.g. Beaton Consulting, *Annual Professions Survey: Research Summary*, BeyondBlue, April 2007. <https://www.liv.asn.au/PDF/LIJ/LIJ-June-2007/2007professionsurvey.aspx>; N. Kelk et al., *Courting the Blues: Attitudes Towards Depression in Australian Law Students and Lawyers*, Brain and Mind Research Institute, University of Sydney, January 2009 <https://www.lsc.qld.gov.au/__data/assets/pdf_file/0003/106698/courting-the-blues.pdf>; S. Medlow, N. Kelk and I. Hickie, 'Depression and the Law: Experiences of Australian Barristers and Solicitors' (2011) 33(4) *Sydney Law Review* 771, 771–99. Some studies explain why there are high rates of mental distress or despondency among lawyers and their effects: M.E.P. Seligman, P.R. Verkuil and T.H. Kang, 'Why Lawyers are Unhappy' (2001) 10(1) *Deakin Law Review* 49, 49–66; J. Hagan and F. Kay, 'Even Lawyers Get the Blues: Gender, Depression, and Job Satisfaction in Legal Practice' (2007) 41(1) *Law & Society Review* 51, 51–78; P.T. Pulliam, 'Lawyer Depression: Taking a Closer Look at First-Time Ethics Offenders' (2008) 32 *Journal of the Legal Profession* 289, 289–315.

2 G.E. Dal Pont, *Law of Costs*, 4th ed., LexisNexis, Chatswood 2018, pp. 1–2.

distress, or at least in their declining work conditions.[3] Time-based billing involves charging the client by reference to the time taken to complete the work required, multiplied by each lawyer's hourly rate.[4] The billable hour is impugned because of its role in performance review, especially in large law firms, representing an intense form of management and audit.

Largely in response to client demands and expectations, there has been increasing adoption of Alternative Fee Arrangements (AFAs). Alternatives to the billable hour are not strictly new, as other forms of billing such as scales of fees, fixed fees and contingency fees have a long history – but for at least the past 40 years the billable hour, with its use of timesheets and six-minute increments, has been the dominant form of fee arrangement. This chapter considers whether this move towards AFAs, including value-based billing, signals a positive change for the wellness of lawyers, or whether AFAs have their own implications for lawyer distress. As part of this analysis, the authors consider whether the wellbeing critique of billable hours is a fair one.

The analysis of fee arrangements is framed in terms of two core drivers for wellbeing: motivation-support and our relationships with others. As explained below, the wellbeing literature shows that people are more likely to thrive, or at least learn and work in an engaged way, when their own, internalised motivations are supported. They are also more likely to experience wellness when they are part of good relationships, or relationships that are dignified, trusting, meaningful and productive in their contexts, meaning here, the law firm or workplace organisation and the wider legal profession. It is argued in this chapter that fee arrangements reflect and reinforce relationships between lawyers and their clients and colleagues, including senior lawyers such as partners and principals, occurring within working environments.

---

3 P.J. Schiltz, 'On Being a Happy, Healthy, and Ethical Member of an Unhappy, Unhealthy, and Unethical Profession' (1999) 52(4) *Vanderbilt Law Review* 871, 871–951; C. James, 'Lawyer Dissatisfaction, Emotional Intelligence and Clinical Education' (2008) 18(1)–(2) *Legal Education Review* 123, 130, 136; I. Campbell and S. Charlesworth, 'Salaried Lawyers and Billable Hours: A New Perspective From the Sociology of Work' (2012) 19(1) *International Journal of the Legal Profession* 89, 89–122.

4 R. Quick, D. Garnsworthy and E. Harris, *Quick on Costs*, Thomson Reuters Online, Sydney 2018, paras. [170.550], [170.580]; M. Friston, *Friston on Costs*, 3rd ed., Oxford University Press, Oxford 2018, pp. 1319–20. Time-based billing is effectively costs-plus pricing where the price is calculated by way of the cost of providing the services (labour and overheads) plus a mark-up or profit.

The chapter is structured as follows. In Section 2 the authors provide a short history of billable hours and AFAs to demonstrate their origins and current usage, and establish the relevance of our analysis. Section 3 sets out the theoretical framework and concepts which are then used to examine fee arrangements from a wellness perspective; how they might support or harm lawyer wellbeing. Section 4 analyses the billable hour and Section 5 turns to the main types of AFAs: contingency fees, fixed fees (including capped fees and collared fees) and value-based fees. Sections 4 and 5 consider, more specifically, how these arrangements support lawyers' work motivations and what types of relationships each of them seems to indicate and cultivate within organisations. In the process, a framework is built for starting to assess fee arrangements for their impacts on lawyers' wellbeing.

2. THE BILLABLE HOUR AND AFAs: THE STATE OF PLAY

Legal fees have historically been charged in a number of ways, including scales or schedules of fees, task-based billing and annual retainers.[5] However, as mentioned, the target of the critical wellness literature is time-based billing. Arising in the 1950s, time-based billing was driven by several factors. Corporate clients and the management and accounting tools that dominated senior management thinking in those institutions were an important influence. The inhouse legal department was required to adopt the same business principles that applied to the rest of the business to the purchase of legal services.[6] The timesheet, as such one accounting tool, made its way into law firms in order to meet client expectations by matching their practices. But it was also actively adopted by law firms. As legal matters became more complicated, lawyers found themselves needing to work longer for the same standard or fixed fee.[7] In 1958, an American

5 H. Leblebici, 'Your Income' in L. Empson (ed), *Managing the Modern Law Firm – New Challenges, New Perspectives*, Oxford University Press, Oxford 2007, pp. 121–26; M. Trotter, *Profit and the Practice of Law*, University of Georgia Press, Athens GA 1997, pp. 150–54.

6 H.M. Kritzer, 'Lawyers' Fees and the Holy Grail: Where Should Clients Search for Value?' (1994) 77(4) *Judicature* 186, 187; H. Leblebici, above n. 5, p. 128; J.H. Choi, 'In Defense of the Billable Hour: A Monitoring Theory of Law Firm Fees' (2018) 70 *South Carolina Law Review* 297, 314–16.

7 F. Strong, 'History and Origin of the Billable Hour' (22 June 2015) *LexisNexis Business of Law Blog* <http://businessoflawblog.com/2015/06/history-origin-billable-hour/>.

Bar Association (ABA) committee published a pamphlet called *The 1958 Lawyer and His 1938 Dollar*. The pamphlet lamented the economic plight of lawyers and their failure to keep pace with the earnings of other professions. The pamphlet argued that by pursuing the high ideal of 'devotion to public interest', lawyers were failing as 'businessmen'. Time-based billing was the answer.[8] In 1972 it was reported that '[t]he lawyer who records time is consistently a higher earner than the non-timekeeper'.[9]

While time-based billing may have originally been a means to an end (the transparent recording of time to allow internal law firm monitoring of lawyer workload), it rapidly became the end itself, as law firms became about selling lawyer time, with budgets and rewards linked to the time billed.[10] Indeed, the billable hour became 'a mindset and a way of life' that shaped the business model for the law firm.[11]

The billable hour way of life was then disrupted by the 2008 global financial crisis. Corporate clients sought to cut costs, including their spend on legal services. Increased competitive pressures beset law firms, who were now asked to bid for work and put forward innovative methods of charging.[12] These innovative methods of charging have been termed Alternative Fee Agreements or AFAs. The rise of AFAs is frequently linked, then, to corporate dissatisfaction with high legal costs.[13]

---

8 N. Kuckes, 'The Short, Unhappy History of How Lawyers Bill Their Clients' (September/October 2002) *Legal Affairs* <http://www.legalaffairs.org/issues/September-October-2002/review_kuckes_sepoct2002.msp>.

9 M. Miller, 'A Systemic Approach to Time Control' in American Bar Association and Canadian Bar Association (eds), *Law Office Efficiency*, American Bar Association, Chicago IL 1972, p. 157. See also G. Munneke, *Law Practice Management in a Nutshell*, Thomson, St Paul MN 2003, p. 88.

10 W. Ross, *The Honest Hour: The Ethics of Time-Based Billing by Attorneys*, Carolina Academic Press, Durham 1996, p. 21.

11 R. Susskind, *Tomorrow's Lawyers*, Oxford University Press, Oxford 2017, p. 17.

12 See generally L. Ribstein, 'The Death of Big Law' (2010) *Wisconsin Law Review* 749, 770; P. Woldow and D. Richardson, 'Adopting Legal Project Management: Why LPM Is Here to Stay and the Law Firm Manager's Role in Its Evolution' (2011) 30(4) *Legal Management* 33, 33–39.

13 See, e.g. C. Ho, 'Law Firms Look for Alternatives to the Billable Hour' (15 April 2012) *The Washington Post* <https://www.washingtonpost.com/business/economy/law-firms-look-for-alternatives-to-the-billable-hour/2012/04/15/gIQAeyW9JT_story.html?noredirect=on&utm_term=.393339eea2f7>; L. McMullan Abramson, 'Is the Billable Hour Obsolete?' (15 October 2015) *The Atlantic* <https://www.theatlantic.com/business/archive/2015/10/billable-hours/410611/>. High costs continue to be a concern, and the need for in-house legal departments to control external legal costs has persisted: Thomson Reuters and Acritas, *2018 State of Corporate Law Departments*, 2018, p. 8.

An AFA is a fee arrangement that is not based on hours multiplied by rates. AFAs include contingency or success fees, fixed-fee arrangements, and value-based billing. The last includes methods tied to the results of the work, or the value of those results to the client. Strictly speaking, AFAs are not discounts on hourly rates, blended rates or progressive discounts, although many commentators and legal practitioners treat them as AFAs.[14]

AFAs have grown in popularity in some areas, but still account for only a minority of all fee arrangements. The American Bar Association reported in July 2015 that AFAs had increased from five per cent of total revenue at the world's largest firms in 2008–09 to around 22 per cent in 2015.[15] In Australia, the 'Macquarie Bank 2017 Legal Benchmarking' survey found that billable hours continue to be the billing method of choice across every practice area, except property and estate law where fixed fees prevail.[16] However, value-based billing has been adopted to a limited extent, and 33 per cent of firms surveyed said billable hours would not be their primary billing method in the next 12 months.[17] Pricing methods by practice area are shown in Figure 1, below.[18] Norton Rose Fulbright's 2017 'Litigation Trends Survey' of more than 300 corporate counsel representing US-based organisations found that 37 per cent of respondents were going to increase their use of AFAs.[19] A similar figure was reported in 2018.[20] The survey also found fixed fees and capped fees were the most widely used type of AFA; these findings are shown

---

14 R. Quick, D. Garnsworthy and E. Harris, above n. 4, para. [170.550]. A discount on hourly rates is a reduction, usually by a percentage, of the standard hourly rate charged by a law firm. A blended rate is an hourly rate but devised through averaging the hourly rates of lawyers at different levels of seniority. Progressive discounts are reductions in the hourly rate charged after a certain level of fees has been charged.

15 'Making Alternative Fee Arrangements Work For Any Size Law Firm' (29 June 2015) *Your ABA* <https://www.americanbar.org/news/abanews/publications/youraba/2015/july-2015/making-alternative-fee-arrangements-work-for-any-size-law-firm/>.

16 Macquarie Bank, *An Industry in Transition – 2017 Legal Benchmarking Results*, Macquarie Bank, 2017, pp. 16–17.

17 ibid., p. 16.

18 ibid.

19 Norton Rose Fulbright, *2017 Litigation Trends Annual Survey – Perspectives from Corporate Counsel*, Norton Rose Fulbright, October 2017, p. 20.

20 Norton Rose Fulbright, *2018 Litigation Trends Annual Survey – Perspectives from Corporate Counsel*, Norton Rose Fulbright, November 2018, p. 13.

in Figure 2. A blended rate, where a single rate for each hour of work done by any lawyer irrespective of their experience or seniority, was also popular, though effectively still a use of hourly billing.[21] Performance/rewards billing, which is the use of bonuses for successful outcomes, is also employed in combination with other fee arrangements. Contingency fees were found to be used less than other arrangements, but that is not unexpected in a survey of corporate counsel, as the contingency fee is typically used for plaintiff-side litigation.[22] In 2018, despite a 95 per cent satisfaction level with AFAs, 70 per cent of work was still conducted under an hourly rate.[23] In this way, while AFAs are becoming more common, time-based billing is by no means dead. Time-based billing remains central, then, to our discussion on wellbeing.

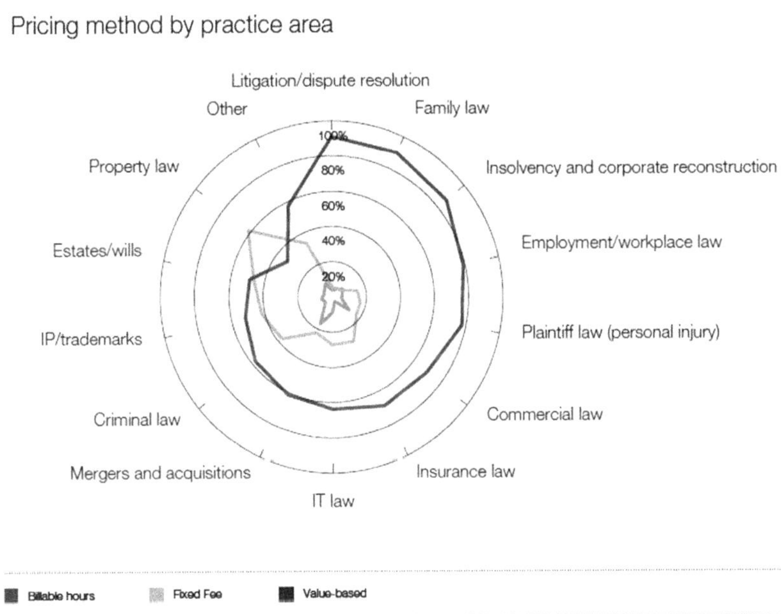

Figure 1. Macquarie Bank 2017 Legal Benchmarking Results

[21] Norton Rose Fulbright, *2017 Litigation Trends Annual Survey – Perspectives from Corporate Counsel*, Norton Rose Fulbright, October 2017, p. 21.

[22] ibid., pp. 20–21.

[23] Norton Rose Fulbright, *2018 Litigation Trends Annual Survey – Perspectives from Corporate Counsel*, Norton Rose Fulbright, November 2018, pp. 2, 13.

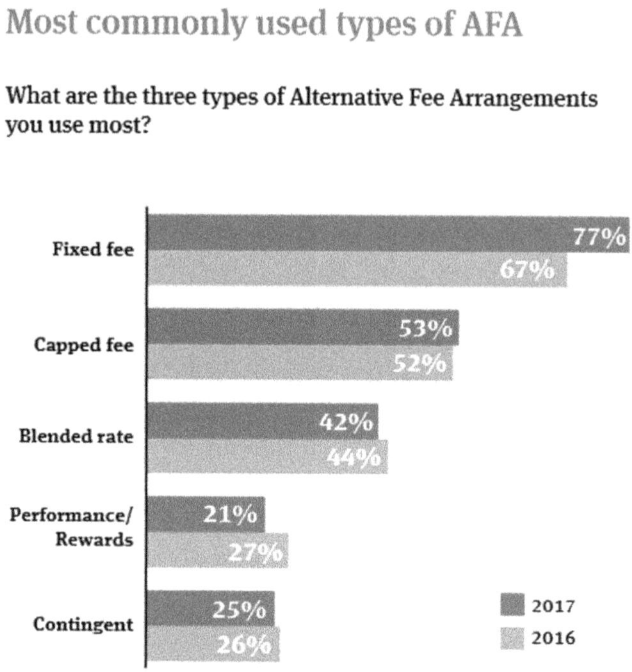

Figure 2. Norton Rose Fulbright Litigation Trends Survey 2017

This chapter also focuses on three types of AFA, as flagged: contingency fees (a very different proposition to time-based billing that has a long history amongst plaintiff lawyers in some jurisdictions[24]); fixed fees (the most popular AFA as shown above); and value-based fees (more an approach to fee setting than a fee arrangement, as discussed below, but also an approach that is being widely advocated for).[25] As raised in the introduction, there is no substantive research linking each fee arrangement and its workings to wellbeing. The next section maps out the theoretical constructs with which to start to single out the things one might look for in a fee arrangement, as indicating likely wellbeing support (or not) for lawyers. In doing so, it presents a systematic approach to assessing the effects of various fee arrangements on lawyers' wellbeing.

[24] W. Emons and C. Fluet, 'Why Plaintiffs' Attorneys Use Contingent and Defense Attorneys Fixed Fee Contracts' (2016) 47 *International Review of Law and Economics* 16, 16–23.

[25] W. Ross, above n. 10, p. 236; R. Quick, D. Garnsworthy and E. Harris, above n. 4, [170.670].

3. FEES AND WELLBEING

Drawing on the theoretical background below, the authors propose four (overlapping) aspects or dimensions of wellbeing that may be helped or hindered by a given fee arrangement: *Relatedness*; *Autonomy*; *Competence* and *Motivation*. This section examines what is known from the literature about lawyers' 'relatedness' or significant working relationships and their driving motivations. In Sections 4 and 5 that follow, these elements are applied to lawyers' different fee arrangements, allowing a picture of the connections between billing and wellbeing to emerge.

3.1. RELATEDNESS, AUTONOMY AND COMPETENCE

Self-determination theory (SDT), from psychology, provides a useful foundation for examining lawyer wellbeing and their billing methods. SDT is a theory of motivation that was initially developed by psychologist-scholars Deci and Ryan[26] and has since been extensively applied and expanded.[27] SDT focuses on analysing people's 'inherent growth tendencies and innate psychological needs' that form the basis of their drives to activity and their wellbeing.[28] These innate needs are: autonomy (a sense of control and authenticity); competence (feelings of mastery over tasks and activities); and relatedness (feeling included or affiliated with others).[29] SDT posits and has demonstrated that when an environment and activities promote these individual basic needs, a person is more likely to be engaged in their learning and work in a sustained and healthy way.[30]

Autonomy has been shown empirically to be the premier need, since only feelings of relatedness and competence that result from autonomous or self-driven, self-endorsed behaviour will lead to optimal engagement

26 E.L. Deci and R.M. Ryan, 'The "What" and "Why" of Goal Pursuits: Human Needs and the Self-Determination of Behavior' (2000) 11(4) *Psychological Inquiry* 227, 227–68.

27 See, e.g. M. Hartnett, *Motivation in Online Education*, Springer, 2016, p. 20.

28 E.L. Deci and R.M. Ryan, 'Self-Determination Theory and the Facilitation of Intrinsic Motivation, Social Development, and Well-Being' (2000) 55(1) *American Psychologist* 68, 68.

29 ibid.

30 ibid., 76. See generally E.L. Deci and R.M. Ryan, 'The Importance of Universal Psychological Needs for Understanding Motivation in the Workplace' in M. Gagné (ed), *Oxford Handbook of Work Engagement, Motivation, and Self-Determination Theory*, Oxford University Press, New York 2014, pp. 13–32.

and wellbeing.[31] However, as this chapter is looking at fee structures that shape and reflect relationships with others, the authors' interest is in whether they produce more or less positive – dignified (respectful, autonomy-supportive, fair, trusting), productive, and meaningful – relationships for lawyers. Relatedness is therefore positioned as the 'super driver' of self-determination and wellbeing in this context, and this section examines the scope for autonomy, competence (or mastery) and meaning *within* lawyers' relationships as defined by their fee arrangements.

Relatedness can be easily linked to both autonomy and competence. Autonomy is relational in the context of costs: autonomy is constrained by pressure from others, power imbalances, and the question of who controls the relationship embodied in the fee arrangement. In certain contexts, autonomy is defined as something closer to ethics, authenticity and integrity or being 'true to oneself',[32] which in this relational sense would be expressed as: 'Can I enact my personal and professional values within this fee relationship?'. Relatedness also links to mastery and efficiency: productivity is shaped by pressure from clients and colleagues, by the relationship elements of managerialism, performance review and auditing, and by the question of who controls what is being rewarded.

3.1.1. Lawyers' 'Relatedness'

Of the many relationships inherent in the lawyer's role, perhaps the most significant in the fees' context is the lawyer-client relationship. There is rich philosophical and sociological discussion on how to best characterise this relationship, with one strand discussing the extent to which this relationship is a moral one, and another debating who, lawyer or client, has more power over the other. In the first discussion, lawyers' billing methods reflect pure market economics and risk allocation; they involve for lawyers a duty to adhere to and *respect* laws regarding fair and reasonable billing; and may

---

31 E.L. Deci and R.M. Ryan, above n. 26, 243, citing R.M. Ryan, 'Agency and Organization: Intrinsic Motivation, Autonomy and the Self in Psychological Development' in J. Jacobs (ed), *Nebraska Symposium on Motivation: Developmental Perspectives on Motivation*, vol. 40, University of Nebraska Press, Lincoln NE 1993, pp. 1–56.

32 J.G. La Guardia, 'Developing Who I Am: A Self-determination Theory Approach to the Establishment of Healthy Identities' (2009) 44(2) *Educational Psychologist* 90, 97, citing R.D. Laing, *Self and Others*, 2nd ed., Tavistock Publications, London 1969, p. 127. See also L.S. Krieger, 'The Most Ethical of People, the Least Ethical of People: Proposing Self-Determination Theory to Measure Professional Character Formation' (2010) 8 *University of St. Thomas Law Journal* 168, 174.

entail a moral obligation to tailor them to the client's means and needs.[33] In the second, sociological discussion, billing typically represents a means by which lawyers can and do exploit clients.[34] However, challenging this idea, at least in certain contexts: the change to AFAs is seen as the outcome of a reversal, in which corporate clients are able to dominate lawyers and their firms, or at least have a far greater say in billing.[35] Proponents of AFAs see 'true' AFAs, by contrast, as creating a win/win relationship, in which risks, efficiencies and rewards are fairly allocated and where the focus is on longer-term relationships.[36]

Meanwhile, most writing on relationships between lawyers and their colleagues (in their firms as well as in court) has emphasised threats in the forms of bullying, incivility, discrimination, intense managerialism and overwork.[37] Some have discussed the negative impacts poor collegial

---

33 S.L. Pepper, 'The Lawyer's Amoral Ethical Role: A Defense, A Problem, and Some Possibilities' (1986) 11(4) *Law & Social Inquiry (American Bar Association Research Journal)* 613, 613–34; C. Fried, 'The Lawyer as Friend: The Moral Foundations of the Lawyer-Client Relation' (1976) 85(8) *The Yale Law Journal* 1060, 1060–89; W.B. Wendel, *Lawyers and Fidelity to Law*, Princeton University Press, Princeton NJ 2010, p. 3; L. Shaffer, 'Legal Ethics and the Good Client' (1987) 36(2) *Catholic University Law Review* 319, 319–30.

34 R.L. Abel, 'Toward a Political Economy of Lawyers' (1981) *Wisconsin Law Review* 1117, 1117–87; E. Freidson, *Professional Dominance: The Social Structure of Medical Care*, Aldine Press, Chicago IL 1970.

35 J. Bagust, 'The Legal Profession and the Business of Law' (2013) 35(1) *Sydney Law Review* 27, 27–52.

36 R. Bayley, 'Balancing the Risks and Rewards of Alternative Fees' (2010) 36(6) *Law Practice Magazine* 32, 32.

37 Victorian Equal Opportunity and Human Rights Committee, *Changing The Rules: The Experiences of Female Lawyers in Victoria*, Victorian Equal Opportunity and Human Rights Commission, Melbourne 2012 <https://humanrightscommission.vic.gov.au/home/our-resources-and-publications/reports/item/487-changing-the-rules-the-experiences-of-female-lawyers-in-victoria>; Urbis, *National Attrition and Re-Engagement Study (NARS) Report*, Law Council of Australia, 2014 <https://www.lawcouncil.asn.au/policy-agenda/advancing-the-profession/equal-opportunities-in-the-law/national-report-on-attrition-and-re-engagement>; J. Whealing, 'The Unhappy Rule of Law' (3 October 2013) *Lawyers Weekly* <https://www.lawyersweekly.com.au/news/14764-the-unhappy-rule-of-law>; P. Baron, 'The Elephant in the Room? Lawyer Wellbeing and the Impact of Unethical Behaviours' (2015) 41(1) *Australian Feminist Law Journal* 87, 87–119; K.A. Nagorney, 'A Noble Profession – A Discussion of Civility Among Lawyers' (1998) 12(4) *Georgetown Journal of Legal Ethics* 815, 815–27; R. Reis, 'Best Practice: "You Fat, Ugly Git!": ... and Other Grounds of Complaint' (2016) 239 *Ethos: Official Publication of the Law Society of the Australian Capital Territory* 30, 30–35; P. McMurdo, 'Civility and Professional Courtesy', Queensland Law Society Symposium, 21 March 2014 <http://www.austlii.edu.au/au/journals/QldJSchol/2014/22.pdf>; L.P. Vrklevski and J. Franklin, 'Vicarious trauma: The impact on solicitors of exposure to traumatic material' (2008)

relationships have on the wellbeing of lawyers.[38] In Sections 4 and 5 below, the aspects of fee arrangements that might affect both lawyers' client and non-client 'relatedness' are discussed for their potential effects on lawyers' wellbeing. *Autonomy* and *Competence*, SDT's two other innate needs, are also explicitly addressed.

3.1.2. *Motivation*

The second central tenet of SDT is that motivation varies along a continuum from intrinsic motivation (doing something because it is enjoyable, optimally challenging, supports personal growth or community), to extrinsic motivation (doing something because it leads to or avoids a separate outcome) and amotivation (the state of lacking an intention to act).[39] Extrinsic motivation can be classed into four categories with varying degrees of regulation or external control, and therefore varying degrees of internationalisation of the behaviour according with one's own reason for acting. These categories are: external regulation (compliance, obtain external rewards and avoid punishments); introjected regulation (self-control, ego-involvement such as pride, internal rewards and punishments through guilt, shame and false self-ascriptions); identified regulation (personal importance, conscious valuing); and, at the 'least controlled' or most self-determined end of the extrinsic motivation part of the continuum, integrated regulation (congruence, awareness, synthesis with self).[40]

The discussion in Sections 4 and 5 below applies these concepts of regulation and the classes of motivation they engender to analyse fee arrangements and their incentives, and the authors provide a sense

14(1) *Traumatology* 106–18; H. Sommerlad, '"I've Lost the Plot": An Everyday Story of Legal Aid Lawyers' (2001) 28(3) *Journal of Law & Society* 335, 335–60; S.S. Fortney, 'Soul For Sale: An Empirical Study of Associate Satisfaction, Law Firm Culture, and the Effects of Billable Hour Requirements' (2000) 69(2) *University of Missouri-Kansas Law Review* 239, 239–309.

38 See, e.g. P. Baron, above n. 37, particularly pp. 107–10.

39 K.C. Chen and S.J. Jang, 'Motivation in Online Learning: Testing a Model of Self-Determination Theory' (2010) 26(4) *Computers in Human Behavior* 741, 741–52. At the far end of the motivation spectrum, lawyers can be amotivated or intend not to act, or not to engage in a fee relationship with a client. It's possible that this would occur where fee arrangements are too onerous, controlling, unfair, and without possibility for a dignified relationship with the client or employer. However, this chapter looks at fee arrangements that are entered into, rather than those that are avoided or abandoned.

40 E.L. Deci and R.M. Ryan, above n. 28, 72.

of how this concept fits that analysis here. At the most 'regulated' end, fee arrangements that relate to extrinsic motivations might reflect the simple desire for money and status of the lawyer, perhaps even greed and competitiveness; the dominance of the client and the looming threat that they could find another lawyer or firm for work; the management requirements and supervision of the employer; any professional regulations and/or any institutional procedural requirements that govern the relationship and the costs structure. Nonetheless, even where these relationships are beset by outside objectives and controls, the lawyer's motivations can be more nuanced, along a spectrum more or less proximate to intrinsic motivation, as discussed above. When applied to the fee context, the spectrum includes: introjected regulation (for example, the pay arrangement demonstrates oneself as worthy in relation to the lawyer's peers, seniors or client); identified regulation (whereby the outside demands – meeting performance review targets, striving for financial gain, pleasing and retaining the client, etc. – are consciously understood by the individual and accepted as personally meaningful); and integrated regulation (where the lawyer's personal need for payment, even, say, payment contingent on success, is an assimilated part of the lawyer's story about themselves as a lawyer with certain values and beliefs).

To give an indication of some of the analysis below, unless it is pro bono work, it does not seem possible to talk of a fee arrangement as supportive of or indicating *purely* intrinsic motivations (interesting, meaningful, altruistic work) since something is still being done for another end (primarily, payment, or probable payment in the case of no-win, no-fee arrangements, for example). Even pro bono work might in fact be an external requirement of the law firm. Indeed, all formal work relationships are to some degree externally regulated; the employee pursues work activity for external ends (for money and what can be done with money outside work, to avoid losing their reputation and/or job), not simply for personal satisfaction or enjoyment derived from the work, nor for the client relationship itself. Further, in the case of law, the client pursues legal services for particular ends, and where the lawyer-client relationship must meet certain contractual requirements. In other words, unless the fee arrangement has no bearing on or expresses nothing of the nature of lawyers' working lives, intrinsic motivations can only exist in conjunction with other motivations, and motivation by fee arrangement is therefore more properly classified as one of the four forms of extrinsic motivation outlined above, from the most externally controlled end right through to the most self-determined form of external motivation.

All of these motivations exist as drivers for participating in learning and in work,[41] but pursuits driven by intrinsic motivation, or at least extrinsic motivation that is meaningful to and coherent for individuals ('identified regulation' or 'integrated regulation'), are those associated with better outcomes.[42] They lead to greater persistence, performance and health.[43] This is because there is harmony between the person's identity and values and what they are doing, which, even if externally set, is internalised as important.[44] Monetary reward, pursuit of fame or status, deadlines or targets, evaluation and surveillance all undermine a person's intrinsic motivation; the motivation is replaced by outside control, even if they are rewards.[45] To connect the two strands, intrinsic and more self-determined extrinsic motivations yield direct need satisfaction (autonomy, competence and relatedness). Extrinsic motivations – wealth, fame, self-image – are less likely to yield *direct* need satisfaction.[46] To come from the other side, if the conditions and practices of work support someone's autonomy and competence, and at least if their sense of belonging and connection is secure, their intrinsic motivation is enhanced, which, as mentioned, supports learning, performance and wellbeing.[47]

3.2. LAWYERS' MOTIVATIONS

Turning to what is known about lawyers' motivations,[48] there is some evidence that suggests lawyers are especially driven by 'quality' – high-quality cases, high-quality clients and high-quality colleagues,

---

41 M. Gagné and E.L. Deci, 'Self-Determination Theory and Work Motivation' (2005) 26(4) *Journal of Organizational Behavior* 331, 331–62.
42 E.L. Deci and R.M. Ryan, above n. 26, particularly pp. 235–41.
43 ibid., 241.
44 ibid., 236, 239.
45 ibid., 233–34.
46 ibid., 244, 246.
47 ibid., 233–35.
48 For an overview of the many surveys on lawyers' satisfaction with their legal careers, see generally J.M. Organ, 'What Do We Know About the Satisfaction/Dissatisfaction of Lawyers? A Meta-Analysis of Research on Lawyer Satisfaction and Well-Being' (2011) 8 *University of St. Thomas Law Journal* 225, 225–74. Results of lawyer job satisfaction surveys are not consistent, likely at least in part because they employ different sampling techniques and different measures to gauge satisfaction. See, e.g. J.P. Heinz, K.E. Hull and A.A. Harter, 'Lawyers and Their Discontents: Findings from a Survey of the Chicago Bar' (1999) 74(3) *Indiana Law Journal* 735, 735–36; J. Monahan and J. Swanson, 'Lawyers at Mid-Career: A 20-Year Longitudinal Study

or 'the three Cs' – perhaps even more than money.[49] Indeed, a study of 'top' Canadian lawyers found that elite corporate litigators, one of the sub-groups, were driven by self-actualisation, mastery, peer recognition, winning, and making a contribution, not money or power.[50] Salomon conducted an interview study of 25 managing partners, consultants to law firms, people that coach lawyers, and others with experience in the UK and European legal industry. He found that the main driver for partners, for example, is the intellectual challenge of each matter, and the fear of losing profitability is only a relative one, linked to quality:

> Partners would not care much if all top firms experience a profit decrease of about the same magnitude, but if their firm would have a larger profit decrease than market average, they would care because they would see this as a sign of quality loss recognised by the market.

However, other interviewees reported that lawyers are very money-driven.[51] Either way, these motivations include external ones: money, status and peer recognition. Further, law students are known, as a group, to be highly extrinsically motivated when compared to the general university population.[52] There is also research to show that, like other occupational groups, the intrinsic motivations of lawyers can be 'crowded out' in practice by the demands of everyday living.[53]

Sheldon and Krieger's body of research focuses on lawyers' motivations, professionalism and their wellbeing. Surveying several thousand lawyers, their studies of lawyer wellbeing show that public service lawyers are

---

of Job and Life Satisfaction' (2009) 6(3) *Journal of Empirical Legal Studies* 451, 452–55, 470 (reporting positive findings of lawyer career satisfaction, and contrasting them with other reports of high lawyer discontent).

49 J. Foster et al., *Understanding Lawyers: Why We Do the Things We Do. Results from the Hogan Assessment Project of Lawyer Personality*, White Paper, Hogan Assessment Systems and Hildebrandt Baker Robbins, 2010, p. 8.

50 S.S. Daicoff, 'Expanding the Lawyer's Toolkit of Skills and Competencies: Synthesizing Leadership, Professionalism, Emotional Intelligence, Conflict Resolution, and Comprehensive Law' (2012) 52(3) *Santa Clara Law Review* 795, 820, discussing I.E. Taylor, 'Canada's Top 25 Corporate Litigators' (July 2002) *Lexpert Magazine*.

51 M. Salomon, *Lawyer Personality and Resistance to Change*, Masters' Thesis, INSEAD, 2014, pp. 54–55.

52 M. Tani and P. Vines, 'Law Students' Attitudes to Education: Pointers to Depression in the Legal Academy and the Profession?' (2009) 19(1)-(2) *Legal Education Review* 3, 3–40.

53 K.M. Sheldon and L.S. Krieger, 'Walking the Talk: Value Importance, Value Enactment, and Well-Being' (2014) 38(5) *Motivation and Emotion* 609, 611, citing B.S. Frey, *Happiness: a Revolution in Economics*, The MIT Press, Cambridge MA 2008.

typically happier than large law firm lawyers, despite the better university results and higher pay of the second group.[54] They explain this finding as a function of lawyers' satisfaction of their fundamental needs (including authenticity).[55] Healthier lawyers also professed more internally-motivated reasons for work: self-improvement, enjoyment, interest and community values as distinct from affluence, power or recognition.[56] Among healthier junior lawyers, their supervision provided some scope for autonomy.[57] A finding that is important to the next section, one of the significant negative predictors of wellbeing was the billable hour: its presence and the number of billable hours required.[58] Besides this work, there appears to very little writing on how lawyers' motivations, and then their wellbeing, are supported by billing methods. *Motivation* therefore forms a significant part of the authors analyses of fee arrangements in Sections 4 and 5.

3.3. CONTEXTUAL WELLBEING FACTORS

As a final dimension, fee arrangements and their meanings for lawyers' wellbeing are shaped by the wider context in which they are embedded. Indeed, the fee arrangement and the context are likely to be in a reflexive relationship, with each affecting the other. Context involves relational elements, as mentioned: who is in charge of the fee arrangements; lawyer status and how they are paid (as well as their demographic profile and extra-work commitments); and the client's importance. But also: workflow/work arrangements; organisation (structure and culture); practice area (hence the contrasting findings between public service and corporate lawyers above); and environmental pressures. Certain contexts better allow for lawyers' fee arrangements to be, or feel, more self-determined or less externally controlling.

To understand how a fee method and its relational elements and wellbeing impacts are influenced by contextual variables, it is useful to

---

54 L.S. Krieger and K.M. Sheldon, 'What Makes Lawyers Happy? A Data-Driven Prescription to Redefine Professional Success' (2015) 83(2) *George Washington Law Review* 554, 554–627; K.M. Sheldon and L.S. Krieger, 'Service Job Lawyers Are Happier Than Money Job Lawyers, Despite Their Lower Income' (2013) 9(3) *Journal of Positive Psychology* 219, 219–26.

55 L.S. Krieger and K.M. Sheldon, 'What Makes Lawyers Happy?', above n. 54, 617–19.

56 ibid., 617–18.

57 ibid., 618.

58 ibid., 619.

consider how legal work may be undertaken in practice and the weight given to developing or preserving relationships. To achieve an outcome, whether that be drafting an agreement or resolving a dispute, the lawyer responsible for the matter, usually a partner, must determine the steps that will be taken.[59] These steps may be more or less to the benefit of the partner (and the firm), the client, and the other lawyers working on the matter. For example, a law firm partner may choose to have junior lawyers manually reviewing documents, or they may use technology. The concern for law firm partners is that when they achieve efficiencies such that a task be completed more quickly, it can reduce income if they bill by the hour.[60] If a task previously took six hours and with investment in technology it can now be done in one hour, then billing by the hour sees the loss of five hours of revenue. However, a different approach may occur under a fixed fee. If the lawyer previously charged $500/hour then technology could be seen as reducing the firm revenue from $3000 to $500. Under a fixed fee, meanwhile, the lawyer may be able to charge $1000 for the task. This allows the lawyer to make a greater return on the hour of effort; they have five more hours that can be devoted to other revenue-generating activities, but also reduce the cost to the client.[61] The fee method creates incentives in this example. However, the law firm partner does not have to respond in the way set out above. The lawyer using the billable hour may focus on relationships and can choose to employ technology so as to reduce costs for the client and lessen the burden on the junior lawyers.

Indeed, the experience of a billing method, and whether it is autonomy-supportive or not, is likely to vary depending on the lawyer's role. Within a firm, the fee arrangement may directly link to partner profitability and there can be a sense of control over the choice of billing method, or the way in which work is undertaken under a particular billing method, subject to client and competitive pressures. However, for the junior lawyer fee arrangements are more distant. They impact work demands, but not necessarily remuneration, leading to less control.[62] Moreover, lawyers

---

59 D. Curtis and J. Resnik, 'Teaching Billing: Metrics of Value in Law Firms and Law Schools' (2002) 54(6) *Stanford Law Review* 1409, 1413–14.

60 W. Ross, above n. 10, pp. 69–70, quoting a law firm partner as observing 'if this associate stays up all night I get rich, but if he does the job in seconds and goes home with his family, I do not.' A. Krikorian, 'Billing Outside the Box' (2014) 27(3) *Georgetown Journal of Legal Ethics* 655, 633.

61 W. Ross, above n. 10, pp. 70–71.

62 D. Curtis and J. Resnik, above n. 59, 1412–13.

doing more routine commercial work are likely to come under greater fee pressure from the client than the lawyer undertaking bespoke work using in-demand legal skills, or the lawyer acting primarily for unsophisticated individuals.

Turning to wider organisational and practice area variables, and echoing the findings in Figure 1 above, Big Law is typically thought of as a billable hour business, while New Law or alternative law firms are seen as being more likely to use AFAs.[63] A law firm culture may promote and reward long hours and commitment to the firm because the firm uses time-based billing. Equally, time-based billing may give rise to a culture of long hours. Moreover, a firm's profitability and past billing practices will inform its culture and attitudes toward alternative billing arrangements.[64] The profitable firm may see no need to change. Within the current wider context of intense competition and declining work conditions, the struggling firm may be more open to different forms of billing. Innovative firms that have adopted novel forms of practice are likely to embrace AFAs. Finally, regarding practice area, contingency fees are usually the province of the plaintiff's lawyer while defence lawyers use hourly rates or fixed fees.

Having set up what is known about lawyers' relationships and motivations and the many variables of legal practice, the authors now use the wellbeing theoretical frameworks and concepts to examine how lawyers' fee arrangements support their wellbeing: the extent to which each arrangement appears to support positive relationships (or 'relatedness') and motivations for lawyers, including by promoting autonomy and competence. Although this chapter engages in a comparison between billing methods, it is worth emphasising that the task to change billing methods to better support lawyers' wellbeing is up against the varied forces of context just outlined.

4. BILLABLE HOURS

As shown in Section 2, a combination of factors saw the use of time-based billing significantly increase. Below, this section outlines elements of time-based billing that may support or hinder lawyers' wellbeing.

---

63 B.H. Barton, 'A Glass Half Full Look at the Changes in the American Legal Market' (2014) 38 *International Review of Law and Economics* 29, 29–42.

64 J. Molot, 'Purism and Pragmatism in the Legal Profession' (2018) 31(1) *Georgetown Journal of Legal Ethics* 1, 25.

4.1. RELATEDNESS

Of all fee arrangements, the billable hour might have the most pervasive influence over the lawyer's relationships with others. In terms of lawyer-client relationships, in the billable hour's favour is that a client can see the tasks undertaken, how much time was spent, who did the work and the hourly rate used. This provides for transparency in assessing the work undertaken by the lawyer.[65] Transparency is a positive counterweight to the power and information imbalances between the lawyer and client, and can be regarded as part of healthy relatedness. By contrast, value-billing, which is examined below, for instance, has been identified as opaque and therefore easily abused.[66] Time-based billing can also be an effective way to deal with a matter that has numerous variables and an unclear progression,[67] whereas AFAs may create the risk that a fair fee cannot be calculated in advance; this transparency and relative certainty might again improve the lawyer-client relationship.

However, as a strong critical literature has discussed, time-based billing can also undermine client relationships and incentivise unethical behaviour among lawyers. As explained in the theoretical discussion, ethics and authenticity are associated with wellbeing. More specifically, time-based billing can create a perverse incentive to prolong and complicate matters to generate greater billable hours.[68] As one legal regulator put it, time-costing makes it

> physically impossible to provide personalized customer service. To the contrary, the temptation, and worse than that, the common practice ... is to mask such

---

65 H. Leblebici, above n. 5, p. 127; Productivity Commission, *Access to Justice Arrangements – Inquiry Report*, vol. 1, no. 72, 5 September 2014, p. 613; G.E. Dal Pont, above n. 2, p. 57; J.H. Choi, above n. 6, pp. 297–318, particularly pp. 299–302, 304.

66 A. Woolley, 'Evaluating Value: A Historical Case Study of the Capacity of Alternative Billing Methods to Reform Unethical Hourly Billing' (2005) 12(3) *International Journal of the Legal Profession* 339, 339–66, particularly pp. 344–53.

67 Norton Rose Fulbright, above n. 19, p. 20.

68 R. Susskind, above n. 11, p. 17. See also M. Kirby, 'Billable Hours in a Nobel Calling?: Ethics and the Australian Legal Profession' (1996) 21(6) *Alternative Law Journal* 257, 259; S. Mark, 'Analysing Alternatives to Time-Based Billing and the Australian Legal Market', Paper presented on Finance Essentials for Practice Management, Sydney, 18 July 2007, pp. 2–3 <http://www.olsc.nsw.gov.au/Documents/analysing_alternatives_to_time-based_billing_july_2007.pdf>. Cf C. Parker and D. Ruschena, 'The Pressures of Billable Hours: Lessons From a Survey of Billing

> inhumane pressure by inflating time sheets, undertaking unnecessary work, exaggerating the need to review everything during discovery, undertaking overzealous due diligence processes and other practices readers will be familiar with. In other words, we cheat and lie to make ends meet. We act dishonestly as a matter of course ... Everyone does it.[69]

Of course, the charging of fees in the lawyer-client relationship is subject to numerous protections, including costs agreements, mandatory disclosures such as costs estimates and updates, requirements that costs be fair, reasonable and proportionate as well as a facility for the client to obtain an independent review of the lawyer's bill.[70] Nonetheless, excessive hours are likely to be billed to the client and paid, particularly if the client is unsophisticated or does not have the time to scrutinise invoices. Even where this is not the case, clients might *assume* that they are being charged for unnecessary, inefficient work, which strains the relationship with the lawyer. By extension, given its transparency, they might try to dispute it. Indeed, dissatisfied clients can easily become 'difficult', take their business elsewhere, or complain to the firm or the professional bodies.[71] Auditing by clients increases anxiety and adds to managerial surveillance.[72]

Further, as Sheldon and Krieger found in their research, time-based billing may have other, non-client relational effects that negatively predict lawyer wellbeing.[73] Time-based billing can negatively impact on the wellbeing of lawyers by diminishing the quality of their relationships with seniors and colleagues, by increasing anxiety about outside expectations of colleagues, both formal (e.g. billing targets, as discussed below) and

---

Practices Inside Law Firms' (2012) 9(2) *University of St. Thomas Law Journal* 619, 619–63, who analyse ethical pressures in detail, and argue that the pressures that drive unethical practices, such as a desire to maximise profits, cannot be attributed to the billing system and are likely to survive under alternative methods of billing.

69 J. Briton, 'Ethics in the Real World', Speech, Queensland Law Society, 2006, p. 5 <https://www.lsc.qld.gov.au/__data/assets/pdf_file/0014/106223/ethics-in-the-real-world.pdf>, citing a former partner of a large firm quoted in issue 266 of the *Lawyer's Weekly*, 11 November 2005.

70 See, for the New South Wales and Victoria example, the Legal Profession Uniform Law Part 4.3: Legal Profession Uniform Law 2015 (Vic); Legal Profession Uniform Law 2015 (NSW).

71 See M.E.P. Seligman, P.R. Verkuil and T.H. Kang, above n. 1, 53 discussing the link between 'unhappy lawyers', poor productivity/representation, and client complaints.

72 M. Thornton, 'Squeezing the Life Out of Lawyers: Legal Practice in the Market Embrace' (2016) 25(4) *Griffith Law Review* 471, 477.

73 L.S. Krieger and K.M. Sheldon, 'What Makes Lawyers Happy?', above n. 54, 596, 615.

informal (e.g. staying at work late). The constant pressure from supervisors[74] leads to insecurity.[75] Among peers, billable hours adds to a competitive environment, and a culture in which lawyers make assumptions about other lawyers' abilities and value on the basis of their billable hours.[76] Indeed, the billable hour is associated with, and reinforces, the pyramidic business structure in law firms in which the owner or partner sits at the top, with employed lawyers below them – all billing by the hour. The more lawyers at the base of the pyramid, with billable targets are multiples of their salary, the more profitable the law firm[77] – and the more these intra-firm relational elements are reinforced.

Some commentators go further still, arguing that the billable hour is strongly negative from a relational standpoint – a form of management bullying, and a source of inappropriate behaviour:[78] 'the routine subjugation of employees by organizational practices may in itself be seen to constitute bullying'.[79] This approach might support unethical management practices such as 'shifting the goalposts' and 'placing unrealistic deadlines and unreasonable demands on employees'.[80] As Omari puts it, 'there is a fine line between managerial prerogative; operational efficiency; performance driven cultures; competitive work environments and workplace bullying'.[81]

---

74 M. Omari and M. Paull, '"Shut Up and Bill": Workplace Bullying Challenges for the Legal Profession' (2003) 20(2) *International Journal of the Legal Profession* 141, 150.

75 M. Thornton, 'Squeezing the Life Out of Lawyers', above n. 72, 477.

76 J. Briton, above n. 69, pp. 6–7. See also p. 8 citing Kirby J in *Law Society of New South Wales v. Foreman* (1994) 34 NSWLR 408, 422 who stated that the charges 'were rendered not by Ms Foreman but by her firm' and that her conduct was 'influenced by a system of time-charging and budget requirements within the firm that were not of her individual making.'

77 R. Susskind, above n. 11, pp. 17–18. See also L. Keen, 'Billable Hours to Always Hold a Place in Law Firms' (23 June 2016), *The Australian Financial Review* <https://www.afr.com/business/legal/billable-hours-to-always-hold-a-place-in-law-firms-20160623-gppsrq>, noting that the average number of fee earners per partner in Australia is 3.5 and the highest is 7.9.

78 M. Omari and M. Paull, above n. 74, 141–60; P. Baron, above n. 37, 113–14. See also C. Parker and D. Ruschena, above n. 68, 641–44.

79 A.P.D. Liefooghe and K. Mac Davey, 'Accounts of Workplace Bullying: The Role of the Organization' (2001) 10(4) *European Journal of Work and Organizational Psychology* 375, 378.

80 J. Bagust, 'The Culture of Bullying in Australian Corporate Law Firms' (2014) 17(2) *Legal Ethics* 177, 197.

81 M. Omari, *Towards Dignity and Respect at Work: An Exploration of Work Behaviours in a Professional Environment*, Edith Cowan University, Perth 2010, p. 9.

4.2. AUTONOMY

Time-based billing reduces individual autonomy or work–life balance.[82] Recording hours can take away from time spent doing inherently interesting work. Even where lawyers continue to exercise autonomy within their job, it forms a paradox, with intense constraint and overwork.[83] Then, as another threat to autonomy, putting a price on time can instigate impatience during unpaid time and in so doing impair people's ability to enjoy happiness from pleasurable experiences.[84]

Diminished hours are also often erroneously conflated with diminished performance and a lack of commitment.[85] Indeed, some say this billing method, measuring the worth of individual lawyers in direct proportion to their generation of revenue, supports the 'ideal worker' type: the unencumbered worker who 'steadily works full-time hours, leaves caring responsibilities at the office or factory door, and stands ready and available, often at short notice, for additional hours at the behest of the employer.'[86] It dissuades employers from allowing flexible workplace practices,[87] such as part-time roles, and working from home, and so directly hinders individual autonomy, especially working mothers or those with caring responsibilities.[88] Indeed, a 2002 American Bar Association guide to law firm associates on how to make partner provided the following advice:

> Part of working hard and working the requisite number of billable hours will mean having a flexible schedule. You will sometimes need to work early

---

82 C. James, 'Legal Practice on Time: The Ethical Risk and Inefficiency of the Six-Minute Unit' (2017) 42(1) *Alternative Law Journal* 61, 61.

83 I. Campbell and S. Charlesworth, above n. 3, particularly pp. 113–14.

84 S.E. DeVoe and J. House, 'Time, Money, and Happiness: How Does Putting a Price on Time Affect Our Ability to Smell the Roses?' (2011) 48(2) *Journal of Experimental Social Psychology* 466, 466–74.

85 M. Thornton and J. Bagust, 'The Gender Trap: Flexible Work in Corporate Legal Practice' (2007) 45(4) *Osgoode Hall Law Journal* 773, 790; H. Sommerlad, 'Women Solicitors in a Fractured Profession: Intersections of Gender and Professionalism in England and Wales' (2002) 9(3) *International Journal of the Legal Profession* 213, 222–23.

86 I. Campbell, S. Charlesworth and J. Malone, 'Part-time of What? Job Quality and Part-Time Employment in the Legal Profession in Australia' (2011) 48(2) *Journal of Sociology* 149, 161. See also J. Williams, 'The Politics of Time in the Legal Profession' (2007) 4(3) *University of St. Thomas Law Journal*, 379–404.

87 Note that flexible practices are dissolving the boundary between work and life altogether, and can be therefore sources of work distress.

88 M. Thornton, 'The Flexible Cyborg: Work-Life Balance in Legal Practice' (2016) 38(4) *Sydney Law Review* 1, 1–21; M. Thornton and J. Bagust, above n. 85, 773–811.

> mornings, late evenings, and weekends. ... When extra effort is required, work with a smile. Do not complain. Do not be a martyr. All this off-hours activity will be particularly difficult for the primary caregiver of young children or older relatives. You must develop a backup system in the event you cannot get home or pick up children at day care as scheduled. ... Without backup arrangements, you will never get the hours you need to succeed.[89]

4.3. COMPETENCE

In certain applications, time-based billing can be applied to support lawyers' personal and professional growth and development. For example, time-based billing can be used to account for work that involves more intrinsic elements, such as client relations, professional development, innovation management, or pro bono work. Firms can provide billable hour credits to encourage lawyer participation.[90] By equating desirable activities with billable work, time-based billing can ameliorate unhealthy or anti-social behaviour that a focus only on paid work may create, and promote the development of positive counters to those behaviours. The recording of time also allows for a lawyer's capacity to undertake work, or lack thereof, to be monitored. A lawyer who is billing large numbers of hours can signal that their workload needs to be shared, that leave needs to be taken, or at least that the firm should acknowledge the contribution.[91] This readjustment is a form of mastery-support.

However, the billable hour may also undermine the workings of 'mastery' in wellbeing, since it is no longer simply expertise that is being tested for. Moreover, with an intense focus on financial results, the gradual, secure development of lawyers' mastery is less likely, since there is less focus on supervision, mentoring and training.[92] There would seem to be

89 J. Sapp, *Making Partner – A Guide for Law Firm Associates*, 3rd ed., American Bar Association, 2002, pp. 31–32.

90 J. Keuning and A. Rainhart, 'The Law Firm Operations Team: Collaborative Agent of Change in A Changing Profession' (2018) 44(1) *Mitchell Hamline Law Review* 41, 54.

91 H. Vogel, *Corporate Law Department Practice*, Prentice-Hall, Englewood-Cliffs 1972, pp. 100–101. There is anecdotal evidence of some firms giving lawyers additional leave, paying for lunches/dinners or weekends away for the lawyer and their spouse/partner.

92 See, e.g. C. James, 'Lawyer Dissatisfaction' above n. 3, 132, 136; P.J. Schiltz, above n. 3, 927–28.

less time for professional development, such as publication of articles, presentation at meetings, and participation in training, networking and professional associations.[93] Further, billable hours penalise the efficient and productive lawyer who is able to complete a matter in less time than their slower counterpart and, to link back to the client relationship dangers discussed above, the number of hours it takes to complete a task does not then necessarily correlate to the value of that particular task to the client.[94] There is, then 'no incentive for partners to manage work flows or the billing of clients efficiently.'[95] In short, there is a 'distinct potential to result in overcharging'.[96]

Mastery of other, less traditionally 'professional', skills may also suffer. Billable hours might diminish the value of interpersonal skills and connection. Unless their associated labour is made to count as 'billable', qualities such as 'customer service attitude, customer retention rates, creativity, and innovation, willingness to delegate, mentoring and teaching skills, and practice development activities are all diminished in value because of the emphasis placed upon production of billable hours.'[97] This constrains authenticity too.

4.4. MOTIVATION

As a positive in terms of motivation, time-based billing gives rise to extrinsic demands that are clear, that are clearly linked to a goal, and where the link between work and reward is transparent. The lawyer knows what is expected of them and if they meet what is a largely objective measure, they will be rewarded with remuneration and promotion. Success can be measured, and therefore feels more within their control than when it is based on tacit criteria – and added control is also positive for autonomy. These circumstances might provide some comfort for a lawyer who may be toiling away without direct contact with a supervising partner or, in the case of a partner, a managing partner or remuneration committee.

---

93 L.L. Cooney, 'Walking the Legal Tightrope: Solutions for Achieving a Balanced Life in Law' (2010) 47(2) *San Diego Law Review* 421, 435.

94 S. Mark, above n. 68, p. 3.

95 M. Thornton, 'Work/Life or Work/Work? Corporate Legal Practice in the Twenty-First Century' (2016) 23(1) *International Journal of the Legal Profession* 13, 22.

96 *Law Society of New South Wales v. Foreman* (1991) 24 NSWLR 238, 422 (Kirby J).

97 C. Kendall, *Report on Psychological Distress and Depression in the Legal Profession*, Council of the Law Society of Western Australia, March 2011, p. 13.

The lawyer's contribution and value to the firm is made more tangible. This has the potential to support positive relationships.

Nonetheless, as mentioned above, the billable hour is typically used as a form of management or performance review; a 'powerful tool for monitoring and controlling the work of employees'.[98] It supports a range of extrinsic motivations for the lawyer, then: compliance, surveillance, rewards, salary, bonuses, promotion by and the general esteem of superiors, colleagues' regard, and related internal regulations, via pride, shame and guilt.

The billable hour's clearest manifestation as a motivational driver is as a billing target, which if set too high (or too narrowly) can adversely affect wellbeing. Lawyers with high billing targets (and therefore a high degree of extrinsic or introjected motivation) will experience greater workplace demands and greater strain, giving rise to a poor work/life balance, than lawyers with low-to-moderate billing targets or no billing targets.[99] With these motivations as a firm's background, lawyers' relatedness and autonomy may also suffer. Studies have found that high billers experience more time pressure and view their workplace as having greater emphasis on profits and being more competitive. They experience more role stress in the form of ambiguity and conflict, less control over their work, and are less able to work with, and help, people who needed their assistance. They experience, then, less social value in their work, greater anxiety, and more job dissatisfaction.[100] Finally, these types of motivations have negative consequences for competence (including that which thrives on relationships, such as in all types of informal training and mentoring), as well as for the other aspects of wellbeing discussed above. As the American Bar Association's (2002) Commission on Billable Hours put it:

> [T]he increased need for billable hours has caused the pace of law practice to become frenetic and has had a negative effect on mentoring, associate

---

98 I. Campbell and S. Charlesworth, above n. 3, p. 109, documenting how time-based-billing is not just used to bill clients but to control and monitor lawyers which through the setting of targets and various rewards/sanctions such as bonuses, promotion can create not just an unethical profession but an unhappy profession.

99 L. Keen, above n. 77, noting that on average Australian firms set billable targets at 6.5 hours per day, but some firms set targets of 7.5 hours or 7 hours a day. See also V. Marrero, 'The Cost of Rules, The Rule of Costs' (2018) 40(1) *Cardozo Law Review* 293, 306–7 reporting an annual budget of 2000 hours in 2010 in larger US law firms.

100 See, e.g. I. Campbell and S. Charlesworth, above n. 3, pp. 89–122, particularly pp. 106–7. See also the focus on targets in A.J. Bergin and N.L. Jimmieson, 'Australian Lawyer Well-Being: Workplace Demands, Resources and the Impact of Time-Billing Targets' (2014) 21(3) *Psychiatry, Psychology and Law* 427, 435–37.

> training and collegiality. Lawyers no longer are being recognized primarily for the quality of their work and their talent. As a result, the quality of law firm cultures are in decline and the pressure for hours makes it impossible for many lawyers to achieve balance in their lives.[101]
>
> [Billable hour targets] shift the focus of the new lawyer's work from doing the job and deriving satisfaction from that endeavor to a preoccupation, even an obsession, with logging the number of hours required for retention, promotion, and bonuses.[102]

The implications of billable hours for lawyer wellbeing are given in the concluding discussion. The next section considers what AFAs might mean for lawyer wellbeing.

5. ALTERNATIVE FEE ARRANGEMENTS

As least in theory, AFAs have the potential to express and cultivate mutually-beneficial relationships in which both the lawyer's and the client's interests are met. In this section, three types of AFAs and their variants are defined and analysed according to the same factors as applied above.

5.1. CONTINGENCY FEE AND REVERSE CONTINGENCY FEE

One of the most well-known forms of AFA is a contingency fee arrangement whereby the client only pays the law firm if it achieves a successful outcome, such as a settlement or judgment in the client's favour. The fee is a percentage of the settlement or judgment achieved.[103] Contingency fees are widely employed in the United States.[104] In England and Wales,

---

101 American Bar Association, *ABA Commission on Billable Hours Report 2001–2002*, p. 5 (citation omitted).

102 ibid., p. 43.

103 'Alternative Fee Arrangements: A Primer' (August 2013) *ABA News*; D. Van Puymbrouck and J. Kurtzman, 'The Rise of Alternative Fee Arrangements' (11 December 2013) *Corporate Counsel E-Newsletter* <http://apps.americanbar.org/litigation/committees/corporate/articles/fall2013-121113-rise-alternative-fee-arrangements.html>.

104 American Bar Association, *Model Rules of Professional Conduct*, rule 1.5(c); L. Brickman, *Lawyer Barons: What Their Contingency Fees Really Cost America*, Cambridge University Press, New York 2011.

since 2013, damages-based agreements (DBAs) have been permitted for contentious work (i.e. litigation or arbitration proceedings).[105] In Australia, contingency fees calculated by reference to the recovery sum are illegal in all jurisdictions.[106] The Australian and Victorian law reform commissions have recommended that legal practitioners should be permitted to charge contingency fees subject to exceptions and regulation.[107] Meanwhile, Australia *does* permit conditional billing, also called speculative fee agreements or no win-no-fee agreements, where the lawyer's fee only becomes payable to the lawyer if a successful outcome is achieved.[108] Conditional billing may also be combined with an uplift fee agreement where the lawyer takes his or her usual fee plus an agreed amount or percentage of this usual fee, the uplift, if the action succeeds.[109] The payment to the lawyer is usually calculated through time-based billing.

A variation on the above, a 'reverse contingency fee', can also be used in defendant cases. When used with a defendant, the client and law firm agree

---

105 Section 45 of the Legal Aid, Sentencing and Punishment of Offenders Act 2012 (LASPO) amended section 58AA of the Courts and Legal Services Act 1990 to permit DBAs.

106 Legal Profession Act 2006 (ACT) s. 285; Legal Profession Uniform Law 2015 (NSW) s 183; Legal Profession Act (NT) s. 320; Legal Profession Act 2007 (QLD) s. 325; Legal Practitioners Act 1981 (SA) sch. 3 s. 27; Legal Profession Act 2007 (TAS) s. 309; Legal Profession Uniform Law 2015 (Vic) s. 183; Legal Profession Act 2008 (WA) s. 285. See also *Bolitho v Banksia Securities Limited (No. 4)* [2014] VSC 582, [50].

107 Australian Law Reform Commission, *Integrity, Fairness and Efficiency – An Inquiry into Class Action Proceedings and Third-Party Litigation Funders*, Report No. 134 2018, recommendation 17, p. 205 (for use in class actions only); Victorian Law Reform Commission, *Access to Justice – Litigation Funding and Group Proceedings*, March 2018, recommendation 7, p. 63.

108 Conditional fee agreements are dealt with Legal Profession Act 2006 (ACT) s. 283(3); Legal Profession Uniform Law 2015 (NSW) s. 181; Legal Profession Act (NT) s. 318(3); Legal Profession Act 2007 (QLD) s. 323(3); Legal Practitioners Act 1981 (SA) sch. 3 s. 25; Legal Profession Act 2007 (TAS) s. 307(3); Legal Profession Uniform Law 2015 (Vic) s. 181; Legal Profession Act 2008 (WA) s. 283.

109 Uplift fees are permitted by Legal Profession Act 2006 (ACT) s. 261; Legal Profession Uniform Law 2015 (NSW) s. 182; Legal Profession Act (NT) s. 295(1); Legal Profession Act 2007 (QLD) s. 302; Legal Practitioners Act 1981 (SA) sch 3 s 25; Legal Profession Act 2007 (TAS) s. 283; Legal Profession Uniform Law 2015 (Vic) s. 182; Legal Profession Act 2008 (WA) s. 252. Uplift fees must not exceed 25% (excluding disbursements) of the legal fees otherwise payable: Legal Profession Act 2006 (ACT) s. 284(4)(b); Legal Profession Uniform Law 2015 (NSW) s. 182(2); Legal Profession Act (QLD) s. 324(4); Legal Practitioners Act 1981 (SA) sch. 3 s. 26(4); Legal Profession Act 2007 (TAS) s. 308(4)(b); Legal Profession Uniform Law 2015 (Vic) s 182(2); Legal Profession Act 2008 (WA) s. 284(4)(b).

upon an expected damages amount.[110] If the damages are equal to or lower than that amount, then the firm receives a fee, which grows in proportion to the extent that the damages are under budget.[111] For example, the fee may be structured so that the agreed damages amount is $10 million and the law firm receives 25 per cent of the difference between the agreed damages amount and the amount the defendant has to pay. If the defendant is found liable to pay $8 million then the law firm receives 25 per cent of $2 million or $500,000. The reverse contingency may be used in conjunction with a fixed fee (discussed below).

5.1.1. Relatedness

The contingency fee can promote relatedness or affiliation with others, namely the client, as they work together to achieve the client's goals. This might reflect broader, inherently relationship-oriented motivations for becoming a lawyer and practising in a particular area of law: to help others or contribute to the community. These humanitarian motivations were identified among public service lawyers in Sheldon and Krieger's research.[112] Likewise, the conditional fee can also promote the lawyer's altruistic motivation as no fee is charged unless a successful outcome is achieved. This suggests that it may be the lawyer's willingness to charge the client only if there is a recovery that is the important component of the fee arrangement – an aspect that may reduce the power imbalance and improve the lawyer-client relationship overall.

However, contingency fees may create a temptation for the lawyer to prefer their own interests, including financial wellbeing, over the interests of clients. Indeed, professional obligations identify a range of potential conflicts between the duty to the client and the lawyer's own interest. This has been recognised in a conditional billing context when a client refused

---

110 The difficulty with a reverse contingency is being able to reach agreement on what a claim is worth without access to all of the relevant information. The pleadings will outline the claim but without access to documents and witnesses it may be difficult to arrive at an accurate assessment of the claim at the time the lawyer is to be retained.

111 D. Van Puymbrouck and J. Kurtzman, above n. 103; T. Fulkerson and E. Gibson, 'Alternative Fee Arrangements in Commercial Litigation' (2015) 52 *Houston Lawyer* 10, 11–12.

112 See generally K.M. Sheldon and L.S. Krieger, 'Service Job Lawyers Are Happier', above n. 54, 219–26; L.S. Krieger and K.M. Sheldon, 'What Makes Lawyers Happy?' above n. 54, 554–627.

to accept a settlement offer that the lawyer advised should be accepted. The conflict was explained as follows:

> In a 'No Win – No Charge' retainer when solicitors' livelihoods and incomes are bound up with and dependent upon the client taking a particular step in litigation, it seems to me that the capacity to provide the client with objective advice about taking that step is compromised. The greater the amount of fees to be lost the greater the prospect of compromise.[113]

The lawyer may encourage the use of a contingency fee even though there is no contingency or risk – liability is clear – so as to increase the fee.[114] The lawyer may charge a fee that is higher than warranted by the work/risk to be undertaken.[115] They may seek to settle early before significant effort is required and/or to avoid the risk of losing at trial and their efforts producing no fee.[116] The lawyer may stir up litigation, even when not in the client's interest, to create a dispute from which a fee can be earned.[117] Conditional billing or a contingency fee 'by no means requires or justifies a relaxation of the standards of professional conduct on the part of lawyers'.[118] However, the prospect of a large contingency fee or avoiding no fee has the capacity to undermine the lawyer's duty to the client. Moreover, these practices threaten the lawyer's relationship with their client, their personal and professional integrity, and, as a result, their wellbeing.[119]

5.1.2. Autonomy

Yet, by breaking the link between hours worked and the fee earned, the contingency-fee lawyer may have greater freedom as to how they pursue the matter to accomplish the end goal of a successful case, promoting their

113 *Spence v. Gerard Malouf and Partners Pty Ltd* [2010] NSWSC 764, [110]. See also *Re Robb* (1996) 134 FLR 294.

114 M. Legg, 'Contingency Fees – Antidote or Poison for Australian Civil Justice?' (2015) 39(3) *Australian Bar Review* 244, 260.

115 ibid., 253–57.

116 ibid., 260.

117 ibid., 258 discussing concerns about champerty. Note that Legg also suggests, however, that contingency fees encourage the screening out of unmeritorious cases: at 251–53.

118 *Re Robb* (1996) 134 FLR 294, 315.

119 For a discussion of the relationships between our fundamental psychological needs, ethics and professionalism, and wellbeing see L.S. Krieger, above n. 32, 168–93.

autonomy. More specifically, the lawyer must decide the broad strategy of the case: what claims to plead, what discovery to seek, what evidence to lead, what arguments to make. Lawyers billing based on time must make the same decisions; however, as discussed, there is also the temptation to increase the time taken rather than simply seeking to obtain the best outcome. For example, the lawyer charging by the hour has an incentive to seek broad discovery while the lawyer working on a contingency basis (provided that they can avoid the moral hazards discussed above) needs only the discovery necessary to win the case. As illustrated, research has shown the positive connection between (autonomously) abiding by professional ethics and wellbeing.[120]

5.1.3. Competence

Contingency fees are inherently geared toward rewarding competence. The principal argument in favour of contingency fees is that they provide the citizen's 'key to the courthouse', or access to justice[121] and, by being directly linked to the result achieved, contingency fees align the lawyer's and client's interests in seeking to maximise recovery. If the case is unsuccessful then neither the client nor the lawyer makes a recovery. The client is not liable to their lawyer for legal costs incurred. The lawyer has an incentive to do their best – to develop and deploy the greatest mastery possible in each case – to achieve a successful outcome; otherwise they receive no reward.[122]

5.1.4. Motivation

The access to justice objective of the contingency fee and the alignment between lawyer and client interests discussed above can also promote

---

120 See Section 3.2 of this chapter. See also L.S. Krieger, above n. 32, 188–89.

121 See, e.g. P. Corboy, 'Contingency Fees: The Individual's Key to the Courthouse Door' (Summer 1976) 2(4) *Litigation* 27, 27–36; S. Landsman, 'The History of Contingency and the Contingency of History' (1998) 47(2) *DePaul Law Review* 261, 262 stating that a fundamental goal of the contingency-fee system is 'to guarantee that both rich and poor will have access to the courts and will be assured an opportunity to avail themselves of the assistance of counsel.'

122 R. Birnholz, 'The Validity and Propriety of Contingent Fee Controls' (1990) 37(5) *University of California Los Angeles Law Review* 949, 954. The contingency fee can be contrasted with time-based billing in this regard. Time-based billing operates so that the client pays based on the time spent by the lawyer on the matter regardless of the outcome of the proceedings. Even if the client loses, the lawyer may win as their bill must still be paid.

lawyer wellbeing by supporting a strong intrinsic motivation that can easily be assimilated with other, extrinsic motivations (including fee recovery); the lawyer is providing tangible assistance to people who otherwise would be unable to pursue their legal rights. The lawyer's ability to facilitate and further a client's cause can be extremely fulfilling, and the contingency arrangement may promote identified or integrated regulation – especially when the client's cause has broader social ramifications.[123]

However, a range of concerns tempers this hopeful view of contingency fees. The contingency fee can support the lawyer's extrinsic motivation where that motivation is to make money, or seek financial status. Being able to earn a living is not unimportant and is related to the satisfaction of personal needs; however, contingency fees may be particularly prone to extrinsic motivations where moral risks, as discussed above, are present.

Moreover, the contingency fee can pit at least two extrinsic motivations against each other: the desire for financial reward and to meet professional requirements. The latter must prevail, at least from an external perspective, but this can create discomfort and distress from the lawyer's. Undertaking a great deal of work for a client, which means being unable to pursue other opportunities, for no reward can leave the lawyer disillusioned and undermine internally-driven motivations such as promoting access to justice. Indeed, in extreme cases the unsuccessful contingency fee agreement can lead to bankruptcy.[124] This highlights that while the contingency fee can promote wellbeing, there is still a need for the lawyer to have certain specialised competencies, in addition to a legal knowledge competency as discussed above. They need to have mastered effective practice management techniques, including having a range of cases to allow for the spreading of risk as some cases will be unsuccessful.

---

123 Lawyers acting on a contingency or conditional fee basis may be included in the category of 'cause lawyers' who pursue social change. However, the overlap is not complete. Contingency or conditional fees can be used to facilitate individual client compensation. Equally, cause lawyers may often act on a pro bono basis or with some other fee arrangement. See A.-M. Marshall and D.C. Hale, 'Cause Lawyering' (2014) 10 *Annual Review of Law and Social Science* 301, 301–20. Marshall and Hale note that 'cause lawyers are motivated by the same complex set of factors that motivate all social action – some combination of rational self-interest, altruism, politics and ideology, reputational concerns, and emotional commitments', at 302.

124 See, e.g. J. Harr, *A Civil Action*, Random House, 1995 recounting the US toxic tort case *Anderson v. Cryovac* 862 F.2d 910 (1st Cir. 1988).

5.2. FIXED FEE

In a fixed-fee arrangement, the firm agrees to represent the client in exchange for a specified fee, regardless of the number of billable hours. The arrangement can be structured so that the law firm earns a flat fee on a task-by-task or stage-by-stage basis within a single matter, or for the totality of a single matter.[125] A retainer is a fixed fee paid on an annual basis to the firm, that allows the client to send as much or as little legal work as it wishes to the firm for that year. Under the related *capped* fee agreement, as detailed below, the client pays on an hourly or task basis, but the law firm agrees that the total bill will not exceed the capped amount. *Collared* fees, also explained below, offer something of a hybrid between capped fees and time-based billing. Fixed-fee arrangements usually cover transactional work such as corporate compliance tasks, asset sale or purchase agreements, employment contracts, and commercial leases, but can also include more routine litigation such as debt recovery matters. The fixed fee is also prevalent in relation to consumers, such as for residential property transactions and wills.

A fixed-fee arrangement is less suited to large complex matters because of the difficulty of predicting the investment needed for such a matter.[126] The uncertainty involved in large matters can be reduced by employing fixed fees on a stage-by-stage basis, as both lawyer and client will gain knowledge about how the matter will play out at each stage. However, the fixed fee may not be able to be applied to all matters.

5.2.1. Relatedness

A fixed-fee arrangement can promote lawyer wellbeing, because it indicates that a long-term lawyer-client relationship is present and that there is an ongoing attempt at a win-win outcome. Fixed fees can encourage firms to complete tasks or resolve cases efficiently to maximise profit margins – an aim aligned with clients' interests, and productive of positive relationships. Further, clients who desire budgeting certainty often find fixed-fee arrangements attractive, and the structure can build trust into the lawyer client relationship. A fixed fee, of whatever sort, is usually most

125 Association of Corporate Counsel and Crowell Moring, *Handbook for Value-Based Billing Engagements*, 2015, p. 3; A. Krikorian, above n. 60, 664.

126 R.E. Litan and S.C. Salop, 'Reforming the Lawyer-Client Relationship Through Alternative Billing Methods' (1994) 77(4) *Judicature* 191, 194–95.

appropriate for repeat or repetitive engagements where both the client and law firm have a similar understanding of the necessary work and the amount it should cost – a basis for a lawyer-client relationship with relatively little power imbalance and relatively high mutual trust and confidence. Where a fixed fee involves undertaking multiple transactions/cases, this can result in more work for the firm overall, thus increasing profits. The high volume can also generate efficiencies, generating savings that are passed on to clients and aligning lawyers' and clients' interests, thus reinforcing positive relationships.

Fixed-fee arrangements may also generate opportunities for improved non-client relationships by incentivising greater teamwork within the firm. Where efficiency is prioritised, all lawyers, including junior lawyers, may be encouraged to find ways to improve the firm's service offering and to communicate their efforts with colleagues and seniors. This shared goal builds relatedness within the firm, and can also support lawyers' identified or integrated regulation, by attaching value to creative work and meaningful contribution.

However, fixed fees may give rise to risk of disputes with clients. First, this form of billing is less clearly defined, making negotiation necessary, and possibly creating opportunities for re-negotiation, which can be stressful.[127] Further, lawyers (having completed a certain amount of work already) may be tempted to ignore a client's need for further interaction or advice – or the client may simply form this impression,[128] in either case damaging the lawyer-client relationship. Finally, while fixed fees provide cost certainty for clients, if matters are resolved quickly clients may end up paying more than if they had paid an hourly rate.[129] The controlled, 'fixed' nature of the pricing might also breed negative client emotions, compounding price resistance (a client's initial reluctance), price anxiety (or 'buyer's remorse', where a client may be unsure whether to continue) and payment resistance (after bills are issued).[130] These emotions may make positive lawyer-client relationships harder to maintain.

---

127 W.G. Ross, 'The Ethics of Hourly Billing by Attorneys' (1991) 44(1) *Rutgers Law Review* 1, 84.

128 H.M. Kritzer, 'Lawyer Fees and Lawyer Behavior in Litigation: What Does the Empirical Literature Really Say?' (2002) 80(7) *Texas Law Review* 1943, 1973–74; J.H. Choi, above n. 6, 302.

129 Association of Corporate Counsel and Crowell Moring, above n. 125, p. 3.

130 Legal Fees Review Panel, *Legal Costs in New South Wales*, December 2005, p. 53, citing R.J. Baker, *Burying the Billable Hour*, Certified Accountants Educational Trust, 2001, pp. 13, 21–24.

5.2.2. *Autonomy*

As well as the firm-wide creativity incentives discussed above, once fees are agreed, there is also scope for greater autonomy for individual lawyers, and incentives for creativity within given tasks. Fixed fees can also allow for greater freedom in staffing decisions, matter management, and the development of forms, technology and systems.[131] However, autonomy and creativity may also be hemmed in by the fixed fee. If a matter requires extra thought or additional effort from the lawyer, such as in trying to obtain an advantage for the client or protect against a risk, the fixed fee may dissuade them from this.

5.2.3. *Competence*

Aside from the benefits associated with creativity in intellectual work, negotiating a fixed fee could in itself support lawyers' professional growth, by requiring a detailed understanding of their practice. For juniors, the autonomy benefits discussed above may be combined with greater responsibility and the development of new skillsets: skillsets required by all lawyers. Fixed fees generate pressure to foresee all contingencies, and fully understand the costs of providing services – or risk losing money on the engagement.[132] The lawyer needs skills, or access to skills, in pricing and costs assessment:

> The ability to successfully move away from the billable hour depends on a firm's ability to disaggregate legal work to find the lowest-rate biller (including identifying, and appropriately outsourcing, commoditized legal work and other services); using analytics to determine the costs of the various unbundled components (requiring a historic practice of collecting critical data); and re-aggregating the work to set a price for the client.[133]

The lawyer also needs to know how the service will be delivered in a profitable manner, requiring new skills, including legal project management. It may also mean adopting technology. A fixed fee enables

---

131 P. Eggenberger, 'License to Bill = License to Kill? Ethical Considerations on Lawyers' Fees (with a View to Switzerland)' (2002) 20(3) *Penn State International Law Review* 505, 523.

132 S. Mark, above n. 68, p. 8.

133 J. Keuning and A. Rainhart, above n. 90, p. 54.

a lawyer to better capture the value generated by innovation, compared to time-based billing where an efficiency gain would mean fewer hours worked and lower profits.[134]

However, particularly for the junior lawyer trained only in black-letter law, the broader required skillset may be daunting. Junior lawyers may find they receive less supervision and training when firms' costs are constrained by pre-negotiated fee arrangements, and competence may suffer from the bottom up.

5.2.4. Motivation

The autonomy and relational benefits discussed above may all be conducive to identified and integrated regulation, approaching intrinsic motivation for lawyers, as they promote the equation of meaningful, helpful, and objectively valuable work with success.

However, if fees are inadequately calculated, and a firm receives insufficient payment to motivate vigilant engagement with its work, quality of service and outcomes may suffer.[135] In that case, a firm may choose to relegate work to junior (hence cheaper) lawyers or pay less attention to the matter – not only endangering the relationship with the client, but entrenching extrinsic, price-oriented motivations in its lawyers. Individual lawyers setting fixed-fee arrangements face similar pressures and the stresses that accompany them; whereas time-based billing at least guarantees a recovery of costs, fixed-fee arrangements risk generating losses, and the preliminary importance of pricing may place heightened emphasis on extrinsic – profit-related – motivations. Further, fixed fees make it easier for clients to put out legal work for bid, and thus bring competitive pressures to bear on legal fees.[136] Fixed-price billing enables 'comparison shopping' and is associated with reduced prices charged for legal services.[137] Lawyers might then feel pressure to maintain a high caseload in order to generate an adequate stream of profits.[138]

---

134 ibid., 55–56.

135 R.E. Litan and S.C. Salop, above n. 126, 194; W. Ross, above n. 10, pp. 240–41; G. Hazard and W.W. Hodes, *Law of Lawyering*, CCH Online, 2015, §9.19; A. Krikorian, above n. 60, 665.

136 R.E. Litan and S.C Salop, above n. 126, 194.

137 V. Waye, M.-L. Verreynne and J. Knowler, 'Innovation in the Australian Legal Profession' (2018) 25(2) *International Journal of the Legal Profession* 213, 230.

138 H.M. Kritzer, above n. 128, 1973.

These competitive pressures and the firm practices that they require might then cause extrinsic motivations to become ingrained at all levels within the firm.

5.2.5. *Variants on Fixed-Fee Arrangements*

Capped fees are similar to fixed fees in that a maximum fee is specified. However, a capped fee usually still employs hourly billing. A capped fee, like a fixed fee, provides the client with cost certainty, which can promote a positive relationship. However, a capped fee may provide less benefit to the firm, other than possibly by securing work that may have been given to another firm. The capped fee does not provide a clear incentive for efficiency, as the lawyer can only bill the hours they work until they hit the cap, such that efficiency gains reduce the fee paid. With a capped fee, unlike a fixed fee, there is no upside for the lawyer. If the fees charged are under the cap, the lawyer is paid for exactly the hours they worked, the same as under time-based billing. They do not reap the reward of being more efficient – and autonomy benefits associated with fixed fees are forgone. Further, if the lawyer incurs costs above the cap, they are not paid for that time.[139] Lawyers have reason to work as much as possible to reach the cap and then work as little as possible to complete the matter, thus pegging motivation to billing, and leaving little room for a sense of the work in itself as meaningful or valuable in the sense of identified or integrated regulation. This arrangement also encourages both overwork and the cutting of corners, both of which negatively impact lawyers' relationships with clients and colleagues.

Some of the negative aspects of fixed or capped fees can be addressed through a 'collared fee' agreement. The firm continues to keep track of the value of time actually spent at agreed hourly rates and compares it with the fixed or capped fee. If the time actually spent goes over the fixed or capped fee by an agreed amount or percentage then the client agrees to pay a portion of the over-run. Similarly, if the actual time spent is below the fixed fee by an agreed amount or percentage then the lawyer agrees to refund or provide a credit for a portion of the difference. The advantage of a collar is that it provides some protection against an incorrectly set fee for the lawyer, and demonstrates goodwill to a client by the lawyer being prepared to share

139 S. Glover, 'Why Capping Hourly Fees is Usually a Bad Idea' (17 March 2017) *The Lawyerist* <https://lawyerist.com/capping-hourly-fees/>.

its efficiency gains.[140] The relational and autonomy benefits of fixed fees are maintained, and some of the motivational and flow-on competence risks discussed above may be avoided. However, the collared fee arrangement is still negotiated and 'set', albeit in a slightly different manner, like the fixed fee, and so the above concerns for wellbeing are likely still to be present.

5.3. VALUE-BASED BILLING

Value-based billing sets fees by reference to the perceived or estimated value of the service to the client. Unlike time-based billing, which is effectively costs-plus pricing, in value-based billing the cost of carrying out the work does not determine the price. Rather, price is determined by the subjective value to the client. This price then determines the costs that can be incurred to deliver the service.[141] The objective of value-based billing is not to cover a law firm's costs and make a profit margin, which is the rationale behind time-based billing. Instead, the aim is to create wealth for the firm (its partners) and its clients. Wealth for the firm comes from selling intellectual capital and the solutions it provides.[142]

Value-based billing does not equate to a particular form of pricing: it could be a fixed fee (on a case-by-case basis or a monthly retainer), and/or could include a contingency or success fee. Fees could still be charged by the hour if that was of value to the client.[143] The aim is to mutually agree a fee method with the client that reflects the value that the law firm creates for the client and is also profitable for the firm. Value-based billing does not mean that the law firm charges a lower fee. On the contrary, if the firm is offering something valuable to the client then it can usually charge more. In some instances, it may charge a lower fee because the client values a low-cost service, but that low-cost service is only offered if it is profitable to the firm. The firm may also decline to provide services that are not profitable.[144]

---

140 Association of Corporate Counsel and Crowell Moring, above n. 125, pp. 7–9.

141 M. Friston, above n. 4, pp. 1321–22.

142 R. Quick, D. Garnsworthy and E. Harris, above n. 4, para. [170.670]; G. Munneke, above n. 9, p. 88, providing the following example: 'If Donald Trump calls me on the phone for advice on whether to sell the Taj Mahal casino, and I tell him yes or no, the three minute call in no way represents the value of my advice'.

143 M. Friston, above n. 4, pp. 1325–26.

144 ibid., p. 1322.

5.3.1. *Relatedness*

Value-based billing supports lawyer wellbeing from a relatedness perspective, because it brings the interests of the firm with those of the client into agreement, setting the foundation for positive lawyer-client relationships. To be able to offer value-based pricing, it is necessary for the lawyer to have a thorough understanding of the scope of the work the client needs and its value to them;[145] the first step in achieving a successful lawyer-client relationship under this arrangement will be to have an in-depth conversation with the client about their needs, goals and expectations. This exercise in listening and understanding promotes inclusion, affiliation and productivity. In addition to the initial discussion, there need to be avenues for ongoing feedback, learning and re-negotiation, which allow for the relationship to continue in a positive way. Open communication is made fundamental to the lawyer's work, meaning both lawyer and client are able – and required – to express their interests and concerns authentically, further improving relatedness.

Potentially negative relationships can be avoided under this arrangement, because a lawyer will have no incentive to agree to undertake work that they cannot complete profitably based on the client's expectations. If the client is the wrong 'fit' for the law firm in terms of pricing and service expectations, their work will not be accepted and future negative effects are avoided.

5.3.2. *Autonomy*

In value-based arrangements, lawyers may be able to exercise autonomy and tailor their services, such as by providing more basic or automated service delivery using technology to fit within the client's view of value. The autonomy afforded by this less rigid and more responsive framework, and the lawyer's ability to define their own role, can then mean that even with many external motivational components, identified and integrated regulation is possible.

---

[145] S. Craft, 'Why Value Pricing is the New Billable Hour' (1 September 2016), *In the Black* <https://www.intheblack.com/articles/2016/09/01/why-value-pricing-is-the-new-billable-hour>.

5.3.3. *Competence*

Similarly to the discussion above regarding fixed fees, value-based pricing necessitates not just obtaining an understanding of what the client values, but also what the lawyer can offer in terms of expertise, range of services and associated costs.[146] The need to gain new skills represents a likely source of concern for the lawyer, as it is another form of expertise to master. Arguably, the need to ascertain and understand value makes it a more difficult skillset to grasp than that required for offering fixed fees. However, once those competences are acquired, the lawyer can internalise and project confidence based on a real understanding as to how they and their firm can deliver on the value proposition to the client. This greater understanding can then support more creative, autonomous approaches to charging. Indeed, to be successful at value-based billing, an innovative approach is critical. At the core of value-based billing is a focus on the outcome or result. The lawyer is assessed on what they achieve, not how much time they spent getting to the conclusion.

5.3.4. *Motivation*

The junior lawyer, though unlikely to be part of winning business and negotiating retainers, is integral to value-based billing. The junior lawyer needs to operate within the parameters negotiated between the law firm and the client. This should mean that they understand what the client values and how the firm aims to provide that value in a profitable manner. It follows that if the junior lawyer knows where they fit into the business relationship then they should be more engaged with their work. This understanding would seem to push their motivational support to the more self-determined end of extrinsic motivation, allowing for personal meanings. Further, value-based billing may make the evaluation of a junior lawyer's performance more qualitative than quantitative, strengthening those effects. A qualitative approach that considers efficiency, effectiveness and innovation – and the interpersonal skills these entail – should foster a more rewarding workplace that recognises employees (and partners) more fully and authentically. Its success here would depend on how the lawyer, whether senior or junior, responds to such a change and how well it is integrated within the rest of the firm's structures and culture.

---

146 M. Friston, above n. 4, p. 1326.

6. CONCLUSION

Lawyers have been identified as typically less psychologically healthy than the general population, and writers have singled out billable hours as one of the factors in their distress. A driving interest in writing this chapter was whether AFAs might signal a positive force for lawyers' wellness, since AFAs are widely presented as the future for legal practice. As such, the authors looked closely at the precise features and workings of the billable hour for its role in lawyers' wellbeing, before analysing the nature of potential effects of several AFAs for comparison, and thus broadening the treatment of legal fees.

One of the challenges of this inquiry was to connect fee arrangements (and their contextual variables) with wellbeing constructs. This analysis relied on the application of two key insights from SDT. First is that activities and environments that offer individuals autonomy, competence and relatedness are more likely to support intrinsic motivations (or more self-determined extrinsic motivations) that then lead to healthier outcomes. Second is that activities and environments that support extrinsic motivations are negatively correlated to wellbeing, while those that support individuals' interest, enjoyment and community connection, or at least extrinsic motivations that are more easily assimilated with other values and beliefs, are positively correlated to wellbeing. With a special focus on relatedness, the discussion then applied these concepts to uncover which aspects of a given fee agreement might support – or hinder – the elements of lawyers' wellbeing. In the process, the study provided a framework for decisions to be made about fee structure that include wellbeing/lack of wellbeing and its related ethics risks.

The authors' analysis revealed that AFAs do not appear to be a panacea for wellbeing and can also have adverse effects on wellbeing. Notwithstanding, the findings do not purport to be definitive statements of the 'right' fee arrangement, or even of the absolute value of each for lawyers' wellbeing. What they have demonstrated is that it is possible to identify the aspects of fee arrangements that may benefit or harm wellbeing, and that analysis and comparison on common terms is possible. The focus on relatedness, autonomy, competence and motivation allowed a nuanced picture to emerge – one that suggests scope for a combination of elements to promote wellbeing while maintaining other work priorities. This study has a number of implications for lawyers' (and their firms') methods of billing:

First, for fees to enhance wellbeing, they need to support good – trusting and fair – relationships. Where fee arrangements are not pursued in good faith, they prevent or diminish good relationships and therefore the wellbeing of the parties involved. Within any kind of billing arrangement, there is potential for misalignment between interests and needs.[147] The temptation for the lawyer to take advantage of incentives that favour them has been highlighted by several studies in the context of the billable hour. However, as demonstrated here, the temptations and scope for exploitation can go both ways, including from client to lawyer.

Indeed, as discussed above, AFAs are, in several respects, products of the increasing power of clients, and may be demanded by in-house counsel, for example, on the basis that they can reduce legal costs. However, for law firms, AFAs might be seen as a means of generating greater profits. When put in these stark terms, it would seem clear that a fee arrangement cannot both reduce costs and increase fees at the same time. There must be a winner and a loser, and if that is the case then there will be tension and regret. This simple win/loss outcome can be avoided if risks, efficiencies and rewards are fairly allocated over a longer-term lawyer-client relationship.[148] For example, an AFA that involves a fixed fee for undertaking multiple cases can result in more work for the firm overall, thus increasing profits. But it can also generate efficiencies which reduce the cost of litigation passed onto the client so that their legal spend is reduced. Where possible, the relationship and the benefits for both parties should be the priority, since it allows the lawyers to get on with productive work that is easier to intrinsically value and therefore from which to derive wellbeing.

Secondly, for fee arrangements to enhance wellbeing, they must continue to foster good client relationships once the fee arrangement has been decided. The positive dimensions of value-based billing – its emphasis on value, communication and feedback – could be more fully adopted in relation to all forms of fee agreement. Indeed, these dimensions appear to make good business sense as well as supporting wellbeing. Open lines of communication about the scope of the work to be undertaken and informed estimates of the price to complete the work build the relationship between client and lawyer. Equally, changes to the scope – whether caused by the client or a third party, such as an opponent in litigation – need to be openly acknowledged and their impact on price discussed. Feedback on

---

147 S. Boulden, 'The Business of Startup Law: Alternative Fee Arrangements and Agency Costs in Entrepreneurial Law' (2013) 11(1) *Journal on Telecommunications and High Technology Law* 279, 304. See also: at p. 285.

148 R. Bayley, above n. 36, p. 32.

how changes were addressed must be available and responded to. However, it must also be accepted that contextual influences, such as firm and client budgets and lines of reporting, will place limits on the individual's ability to accept or reject higher charges.

Thirdly, for fee arrangements to enhance, or at least not detract from, wellbeing, they need to be attached to reasonable billing targets and will ideally include other objectives, such as pro bono, innovation and professional development. As discussed, targets that are set too high or adopt a narrow focus as to what is important can adversely affect wellbeing through time pressure, stress, lack of control and an adverse impact on relationships with colleagues and clients. Significantly for this chapter, the billing target does not have to equate with any particular type of fee agreement; though it is usually associated with the billable hour, lawyers can still have high targets when billing using a contingency fee, fixed fee or value-based fee. AFA lawyers may not record the hours but work just as hard.[149]

Perhaps surprisingly, the billable hour may be the easiest for the lawyer to understand in terms of what they need to do to achieve the billable target (that is, divide the target by the hourly chargeout rate and work the required number of hours). This relates to a fourth and final practical finding: lawyers need training in how to engage with clients and colleagues about fee arrangements, so that they can do it well or at least better understand their position in the arrangement that has been decided and the associated expectations.

To turn back to the scholarly discussion, fee arrangements are, as has been shown, a work practice as well as wider condition, and therefore their potential support for impediment against intrinsic motivation and wellbeing has imprecise boundaries. A fee structure could tell us only something very technical and narrow, or could extend right to all the contextual variables that were outlined and illustrated in the introductory sections, involving lawyer status, law firm structure and culture, and practice area, and including the one just outlined: billing targets. These might be only tangentially related. The varied intertwining of billing method and context in practice means is that it can be difficult to precisely indicate how much billing influences motivation and wellbeing. While economic imperatives, from avoiding personal/business failure through to maximising income/profits, are significant drivers, it

---

149 D.R. Richmond, 'In Defense of the Billable Hour' (2003) 14(2) *Professional Lawyer* 1, 6.

seems likely that the conditions of a lawyer's job swing from providing lawyers with intrinsic motivational support to thwarting such support. Moreover, as indicated throughout this analysis, the power dynamics and wider organisational leadership and culture are also significant factors. A fee agreement alone may be neither good nor bad, but rather it is the way in which it is responded to and monitored – in the law firm culture or work environment – which will be central to the effect it has. Further, if adverse consequences are identified by managers or seniors, steps can be taken to alter the conditions (incentives, opportunities for discussion or re-negotiation, etc.). The question becomes whether the person who creates, or has autonomy over, those conditions – client, law firm, lawyer – is willing to alter those conditions or improve the motivational and behavioural responses to them. In fee agreements, the conditions and related practices will be the result of negotiation between the parties with each typically seeking to obtain a result that best suits them. Usually the party with the power in the relationship will be able to create arrangements that favour them.

Having emphasised the complexities of lawyers' work and the embedded and shifting role of fees, this analysis does yet provide an important piece in explaining and supporting lawyers' wellbeing. To connect the authors' wellbeing discussion to the wider context: while this framework, drawing on SDT, is not a power critique itself, it is valuable because it provides standards by which to test the conditions of work and the relationships involved, including in fee arrangements (lawyer-client) and related rewards/performance review measures (lawyer-employer). As demonstrated, if fee arrangements help support conditions and relationships that support individuals' fundamental needs, they are more likely to foster ethical, productive and psychologically well lawyers.[150]

[150] L.S. Krieger and K.M. Sheldon, 'What Makes Lawyers Happy?', above n. 54, pp. 624–25. See also L.S. Krieger, above n. 32, p. 188. Krieger suggests that there may be no difference between the state of psychologically thriving and being ethical and professional.

PART IV
CONCLUSION

CHAPTER 12

REFLECTIONS ON THE UK EXPERIENCE OF LEGAL ACADEMIC WELLBEING AND THE LEGAL PROFESSIONS

Moving Across Silos

Richard COLLIER

1. Introduction 313
2. From Legal Practice to Law School: A Snapshot of Wellbeing and Mental Health in the UK Legal Community. 315
3. Approaching (Legal) Academic Wellbeing 318
4. From Legal Practice to Law School, or Moving Across Silos: Shared Themes 322
5. The Potential and the Problems of Wellbeing: Identity, Resilience and Responsibility. 326
6. Concluding Remarks 330

1. INTRODUCTION

The UK legal community has in recent years experienced growing concern about the wellbeing and mental health of lawyers. This is an interest reflected across an array of practical and policy initiatives, reports, research studies, articles and books on the topic, as well as substantial media coverage.[1] Much of the wider legal wellness literature in the UK context, as elsewhere, has tended to focus on the areas of legal professional practice and law

[1] This literature is now extensive, the work discussed below conveying just a flavour of the whole.

students within legal education and training.[2] There are tentative signs, however, of a heightened focus within UK legal studies on the wellbeing and mental health of university legal academics (see below).[3] This chapter seeks to connect up this emerging discussion of legal academic wellbeing with the more established wellbeing debates taking place across the UK legal services sector. By unpacking selected themes within a rapidly expanding interdisciplinary literature on academic wellbeing in UK universities, the chapter explores shared concerns and themes, as well as significant points of difference, in how wellbeing is conceptualised across these discrete legal fields.[4]

A closer look at what is shared *across* law schools and the legal professions, it is argued here, can shed considerable light on our understandings of the place and purpose of university legal education itself at the present moment; and how, with regard to wellbeing, specific legal 'communities … act as containers for their own experiences, doubts, joys and frustrations'.[5] In moving 'beyond silos', this chapter suggests, research and theory about learning the law and legal education has much to gain from a closer engagement with the legal wellbeing debates.[6] At the same time, the emergence of wellbeing as a distinctive kind of problem to be addressed by discrete legal communities must be set in the context of structural and cultural changes productive of new ideas of legal professionalism, enmeshed with the law's current 'wellbeing problem' – a development impacting on lawyers, law students and legal academics alike, albeit in different and frequently contradictory ways.

---

2 See further below and generally, for discussion that pre-dates the current explosion of interest, M.K. Miller and B.H. Bornstein (eds), *Stress, Trauma, and Wellbeing in the Legal system*, Oxford, Oxford University Press, 2013.

3 See for example J. Clare Wilson and C. Strevens, 'Perceptions of Psychological Well-being in UK Law Academics' (2018) 52(3) *The Law Teacher* 335–49 available at: https://doi.org/10.1080/03069400.2018.1468004. This study of 185 UK law teachers suggests that changing and increasing expectations on the part of universities, students and academics have had an impact upon the self-perceptions of well-being in law teachers.

4 This discussion focuses primarily on UK university law schools and the academic stage of legal education. It is important to note, however, that providers of vocational legal education are similarly facing growing concerns around wellbeing and mental health amongst law students.

5 S. Tang, 'Valuing persons and communities in doing wellness for law well' in R. Field, J. Duffy and C. James (eds), *Promoting Law Student and Lawyer Wellbeing in Australia and Beyond*, London, Routledge, 2016, p. 20.

6 On the changing nature of this field see W. Twining, 'Rethinking Legal Education' (2018) 52(3) *The Law Teacher* 241–60. See also F. Cownie, *Legal Academics*, Oxford, Hart, 2004.

2. FROM LEGAL PRACTICE TO LAW SCHOOL: A SNAPSHOT OF WELLBEING AND MENTAL HEALTH IN THE UK LEGAL COMMUNITY

Within the UK legal wellbeing debates and the literature of the past five or so years there appears a general acceptance that the research base on law and wellbeing and the development of practical initiatives within both legal practice and law schools have, to date, lagged behind other jurisdictions, notably Australia[7] and the United States.[8] Nonetheless, a growing body of recent work across the UK legal professions is now highlighting the scale of the problems that exist around wellbeing and mental health. This is evident in recent research studies and policy developments by Law Societies,[9] from the work of bodies representing junior lawyers,[10] in the context of the judiciary,[11] at the Bar[12] and on the part of regulators such as the Solicitors Regulation Authority;[13] within the work of transnational corporate law firms,[14] and of legal wellbeing charities such as *Lawcare*,[15] via a range

---

7 The Australian research base on this topic, beyond the scope of this paper, is voluminous. See further, and generally, discussion in Field et al., n. 5 above; *Wellness Network for law*, http://wellnessforlaw.com/.

8 See, for example, the work of the *National Taskforce on Lawyer Wellbeing* (NTLW), at: http://lawyerwellbeing.net/.

9 For example, The Law Society, *Solicitors' Health and Well-being: The Law Society's PC Holders Survey 2014*, London, The Law Society, 2014.

10 The Law Society, *Supporting Resilience and Wellbeing in the Workplace: Guidance for best Practice*, London, The Law Society, 2018; The Law Society *Resilience and Wellbeing Survey Report: Junior Lawyers Division* London, The Law Society, 2019, available at: https://communities.lawsociety.org.uk/Uploads/b/y/k/resilience-wellbeing-survey-report-2019.pdf.

11 See for example Lady Justice Sharp, 'In Sickness and in Health: Judicial Welfare in England and Wales' (2016), available at: https://www.judiciary.uk/wp-content/uploads/2017/04/lj-sharp-judicial-welfare-speech-20161118.pdf.

12 *Positive Wellbeing at the Bar: A Resilience Framework Assessment (RFA) by Positive*, London, Positive, 2015, a report on the data gathered via a resilience framework assessment in 2014/15, available at: https://www.barcouncil.org.uk/media/348371/wellbeing_at_the_bar_report_april_2015__final_.pdf; https://www.wellbeingatthebar.org.uk/.

13 The Solicitor's Regulation Authority (SRA), 'Your Health, Your Career', available at: https://www.sra.org.uk/sra/news/press/wellbeingnewsrelease-2016.page.

14 See, for example, the *Mindful Business Charter* available at: https://home.barclays/content/dam/home-barclays/documents/who-we-are/Mindful%20Business%20Charter%202018.pdf.

15 https://www.lawcare.org.uk/.

of commercial reports on the subject[16] and, increasingly, in relation to debates around emotional competency in law and what it might mean to be 'fit for law'.[17] In each area a strong case can be made that wellbeing is an idea whose time has come in the UK legal professions.[18]

What, however, of UK university law schools? Here there are also signs of a heightened concern around law student wellness. This has been prompted, in no small part, by the sheer numbers of law students self-disclosing a wide range of mental health problems; and, with it, a concern about the consequences of such self-disclosure for the work of law schools themselves.[19] At a practical level in the UK many university law schools are seeking to ratchet up the support offered to their students via the introduction of a host of wellbeing activities and related developments, including the rolling out of various 'wellbeing weeks', wellbeing days and so forth. There is a growing focus in UK legal studies – here drawing on the extensive Australian legal wellness literature and networks – on the nature of the law curriculum and its relation to wellbeing; on 'intentional design' for wellbeing,[20] the place of resilience and emotion within university legal education,[21] the nature of the transition from legal education and training to legal practice[22] and the ethical obligations that providers of legal education have to 'educate for wellbeing'; and a concern, more generally, with how

---

16 For example *The Bellweather Report 2019: Stress in the Legal Professions – Problematic or Inevitable?*, available at: https://www.lexisnexis.co.uk/research-and-reports/stress-in-the-legal-profession-problematic-or-inevitable.html.

17 See *Fit For Law: Emotional Competence and professional Resilience*, an online course produced by The Open University in collaboration with the charity LawCare: https://www.open.edu/openlearncreate/course/view.php?id=3476.

18 Note also the formation in 2016 of a *Legal Professions Wellbeing Taskforce*, spearheaded by the charity Lawcare and The Law Society: M. Fouzder, 'Mental Health Taskforce for Legal Professionals', *The Law Society Gazette*, 16 May 2016: http://www.lawsociety.org.uk/news/stories/legal-professions-wellbeing-taskforce/. Note also A. Lyon, *A Lawyers' Guide to Wellbeing and Managing Stress*, London, Ark, 2016.

19 Exemplifying the growing focus on law students in the media, C. Baksi, 'Help us at hand for students struggling with Mental health' *The Times Brief: Student Law Week* 19 February 2018, available at: https://www.thetimesbrief.co.uk/users/39765-catherine-baksi/posts/30357-help-is-at-hand-for-students-struggling-with-mental-health.

20 Note also *Intentional Education Design for Wellbeing*, Institute for Advanced Legal Studies, 2 May 2019, available at: https://www.sas.ac.uk/events/event/19653.

21 See further below n. 24.

22 Note the work of the *City Mental Health Alliance* (CMHA): http://citymha.org.uk/wp-content/uploads/2018/07/CMHA-Thriving-at-Work-Guide-final-PDF.pdf.

law school teaching practices and cultures can impact in deleterious ways on law students.[23]

A related strand of legal scholarship in the UK, meanwhile, is exploring what contribution an engagement with law and emotion,[24] the principles of positive psychology,[25] insights of self-determination theory and therapeutic jurisprudence can each make to better understanding the management of subjective wellbeing not just within legal professional practice but also, increasingly, in legal education and law schools.[26] This discussion of law student wellbeing is taking place within the context of what has been widely termed the contemporary 'crisis' of wellbeing and mental health within the UK Higher Education sector.[27] Universities have seen the

---

23 See further R. Field and C. Strevens (eds), *Educating for Well-Being in Law: Positive Professional Identities and Practice* (London, Routledge, 2019): Field et al., above n. 5; R. Field, *Promoting law student well-being through the curriculum: Final Report of: Stimulating strategic change in legal education to address high levels of psychological distress in law students* (2014), available at: https://eprints.qut.edu.au/75519/1/Field_R_NTF_report_2014_.pdf.

24 E. Jones, *Emotions in the Law School: Transforming Legal education through the Passions*, London, Routledge, 2019; E. Jones, 'Transforming Legal Education Through Emotions' (2018) 38(3) *Legal Studies* 450–79: L. Bleasdale and S. Humphries, *Undergraduate Resilience Research Project*, Leeds University Institute for Teaching Excellence, Leeds, available at: file:///H:/2018%20Oct/LITEbleasdalehumphreys_fullreport_online.pdf.

25 See, in addition to work cited above, Legal Education Research Network/Institute of Advanced Legal Studies, Positive Psychology Workshop. *Intentional Education Design for Well-being*, 2 May 2019, available at: http://ials.sas.ac.uk/events/event/19653, *Intentional Education Design for Well-being: Transition Pedagogies*, 5 July 2019, City Law School, London.

26 See further Jones, *Emotions in the Law School*, above n. 24: E. Jones, *Therapeutic Jurisprudence: Exploring a New Paradigm*, available at: http://slsablog.co.uk/blog/blog-posts/therapeutic-jurisprudence-exploring-a-new-paradigm (2019); E.L. Deci and R.M. Ryan, 'The "What" and "Why" of Goal Pursuits: Human Needs and the Self-Determination of Behaviour' (2000) 11 *Psychological Inquiry* 227; K.M. Sheldon and L.S. Krieger, 'Understanding the negative effects of legal education on law students: A longitudinal study of self-determination theory' (2007) 33 *Personality and Social Psychology Bulletin* 883; K.M. Sheldon and L.S. Krieger, 'Does legal education of undermining effects on law students? Evaluating changes in motivation, values and wellbeing' (2004) 22 *Behavioural Sciences and the Law* 262.

27 See for example C. Thorley/IPPR, *Not by Degrees: Improving Student Mental Health in the UK's Universities*, London, IPPR, 2017; Office for National Statistics, *Estimating suicide among higher education students, England and Wales: Experimental Statistics* (London, ONS, 2018); Universities UK, *Minding Our Future: Starting a Conversation about the support of student mental health*, London, UKK, 2018,

introduction of a wide range of policy initiatives,[28] beyond the scope of this chapter, including the establishment, in 2018, of a dedicated *University Mental Health Charter.*[29] Addressing student wellbeing, indeed, has been positioned as no less than part of the core function *of* the university.

What, however, of legal academics? How do these issues of lawyer and law student wellbeing, as above, intersect with the organisation of academic labour in ways that raise questions about the 'pressures that threaten to distort [the] mission [of legal education] and undermine the resilience of its academic practitioners'?[30]

3. APPROACHING (LEGAL) ACADEMIC WELLBEING

The *Universities UK* 'Step-Change' Framework to mental health, just one of a host of initiatives addressing wellbeing in the Higher Education sector, provides a place to start. It acknowledges that 'a whole-university approach' to the issue is needed;[31] that the wellbeing of students and those they teach are interlinked in a myriad of ways. As Rachel Field and others have asked, how is it possible to promote law student wellbeing if the staff they encounter are not well equipped and/or competent to do so? (the 'first put on your own oxygen mask' analogy).[32] Yet a now substantial interdisciplinary research base, exploring the emotional and affective consequences of

---

available at: https://www.universitiesuk.ac.uk/minding-our-future; M. Holt and S. Powell, 'Healthy Universities: A guiding framework for universities to examine the distinctive health needs of its own student population' (2017) 137(1) *Perspectives in Public Health* 53–58; E. Southgate, 'Freshers declaring mental health illness up 73% in four years', *The Guardian*, 22 February 2019; Higher Education Policy Institute *The Invisible Problem? Improving Students' Mental Health*, London, EPI, 2016.

28 Universities UK (UUK) 2018; #stepchange: Mental Health in Higher Education, available at: http://www.universitiesuk.ac.uk/stepchange; Student Mental Health Research Network, available at: https://www.smarten.org.uk/; Universities UK/Papyrus (2018) Suicide-Safer Universities, (London, UUK), available at: file:///J:/2018%20Nopvember/To%20print/guidance-for-universities-on-preventing-student-suicides.pdf.

29 https://www.studentminds.org.uk/charter.html.

30 A Workshop on Vulnerability and the Organisation of Academic Labour. A Vulnerability and the Human Condition Initiative Workshop, 25–26 October, Nottingham Trent University, Nottingham.

31 Above n. 28.

32 See F. Bell, J. Rogers and M. Legg, 'Artificial Intelligence and Lawyer Wellbeing', Chapter 10 in this volume.

the marketisation of the Higher Education, suggests that the organised practices, structures and cultures of UK universities are deeply implicated in the current state of mental health of its members.[33] The evidence base highlighting the scale of poor mental health, not only amongst UK university students but also university staff, including academics, is now considerable. The 2019 Higher Education Policy Institute Report *Pressure Vessels: The Epidemic of Poor Mental Health Among Higher Education Staff* is just the most recent of a number of studies and data sets highlighting poor staff wellbeing in the Higher Education sector.[34] There is no reason to think UK legal academics are immune from the processes being described within the critical universities scholarship that has emerged over the past five years or so seeking to explore just what may be going on here.[35]

So what is the problem? The connections between poor wellbeing and the 'neoliberal' marketised university are complex and multi-layered.[36]

---

33 L. Peake and B. Mullings, 'Critical Reflections on Mental and Emotional Distress in the Academy' (2016) 15(2) *ACME: An International Journal for Critical Geographies* 253. See further below.

34 L. Morrish, *Pressure Vessels: The Epidemic of Poor Mental Health Among Higher Education Staff*, Higher Education Policy Institute Report Occasional Paper 20, London 2019. Also 'Higher Education Staff Suffer "Epidemic" of Poor Mental Health', *The Guardian*, 23 May 2019. HEPI Policy Note 13 (May 2019) Measuring Wellbeing in Higher Education, available at: https://www.hepi.ac.uk/2019/05/09/measuring-well-being-in-higher-education/. For just a flavour of other studies see G. Kinman, F. Jones and R. Kinman (2006) 12(1) *Quality in Higher Education* 15–27: Rand Europe (on behalf of the Royal Society and Wellcome Trust) Understanding Mental Health in the Research Environment, available at: https://www.rand.org/randeurope/research/projects/researcher-mental-health.html; G. Kinman and S. Wray, *Work-Related Wellbeing in UK Higher Education – 2014* (London, UCU, 2015), available at: https://www.researchgate.net/publication/319464567_Work-related_wellbeing_in_UK_Higher_Education-2014; G. Kinman, 'Doing More with Less? Work and Wellbeing in Academics' (2014) 4(2) *Somatechnics* 219–35; G. Kinman, 'Pressure Points: A Review of Stresses and Strains on UK Academics' (2001) 21(4) *Educational Psychology* 473–92. See further C. Shaw, 'Overworked and Isolated – work pressure fuels mental illness in academia', *The Guardian*, 8 May 2014, available at: http://www.theguardian.com/higher-education-network/blog/2014/may/08/work-pressure-fuels-academic-mental-illness-guardian-study-health; J. Grove, 'Half of UK academics "suffer stress-linked mental health problems"', 2018, available at: https://www.timeshighereducation.com/news/half-uk-academics-suffer-stress-linked-mental-health-problems; S. Inge, 'University Mental Health: The Weight of Expectations', *Times Higher Education*, 1 March 2018, available at: https://www.timeshighereducation.com/features/university-mental-health-day-weight-expectations.

35 Peake and Mullings, above n. 33.

36 See further in the context of law M. Thornton, *Privatising the Public University: The Case of Law*, Abingdon, Routledge, 2011; M. Thornton (ed), *Through a Glass*

Nonetheless, and at the risk of simplifying a rich and distinctive field of literature, it is possible to discern key and recurring themes. These include, but are not confined to, a concern to interrogate the impact on the subjective wellbeing of university academics of the following:

- an intensification of metricisation and audit, and the proliferation of the multitude of rankings that pervade academic life associated with the rise of the 'Data University';[37]
- the new 'structures of feeling'[38] that have emerged within Higher Education workplace cultures, shaped, in a myriad of ways, by the relentless calculative competitions arising from the new forms of performance management,[39] an increasing 'quantified control'[40] of academics and the transformation of workplace cultures marked by a monetisation of traditional academic values;[41]

Darkly: The Social Sciences Look at the Neoliberal University, Canberra, ANU Press, 2015. Also, generally, H. Radice, 'How We Got Here: UK Higher Education under Neoliberalism' (2013) 12(2) *ACME: An International Journal for Critical Geographies* 407–18.

37 See L. Morrish and The Analogue University, 'Academic Identities in the Managed University: Neoliberalism and Resistance at Newcastle University UK' (2017) 59(2) *Australian Universities Review* 23–35. On the Data University, see C. Knowles and R. Burrows, 'The Impact of Impact' (2014) 18(2) *Etnográfica* 237–54; L.D. Gonzales and A.M. Núñez, 'The Ranking Regime and the Production of Knowledge: Implications for Academia' (2014) 22 (31) *Education Policy Analysis Archives* 1–2; A. Fazackerley, 'Universities' league table obsession triggers mental health crisis fears', *The Guardian*, 12 June 2018.

38 R. Burrows, 'Living with the h-index: Metric assemblages in the contemporary academy' (2012) 60(2) *The Sociological Review* 355–72. See also R. Burrows, 'Ancient cultures of conceit reloaded? A comparative look at the rise of metrics in higher education' (2016), available at: https://blogs.lse.ac.uk/impactofsocialsciences/2016/02/29/ancient-cultures-of-conceit-reloaded/.

39 See further R. Watts, *Public Universities, Managerialism and the Value of Higher Education*, London, Palgrave Macmillan 2017.

40 Knowles and Burrows, above n. 37; D. Lupton, *The Academic Quantified Self*, 2013, available at: https://simplysociology.wordpress.com/2013/10/14/the-academic-quantified-self/.

41 Burrows, above n. 38. See for further discussion J. Chubb, 'Academics fear the value of knowledge for its own sake is diminishing' (2017) *The Conversation*, 19 June 2017, available at: http://theconversation.com/academics-fear-the-value-of-knowledge-for-its-own-sake-is-diminishing-75341; B. Davies and P. Bansel, 'Governmentality and Academic Work: Shaping the hearts and minds of academic workers' (2010) 26(3) *Journal of Curriculum Theorizing* 5–20; J. Pack, *How the Neoliberalization of Academia Leads to Thoughtlessness: Arendt and the Modern University*, Lexington Books, Lanham MD, 2018.

- the emergence of a now commonplace subjective feeling of being always monitored and assessed,[42] a normalisation of long working hours within a culture of 'hyper-performance' in an increasingly 'accelerated academy';[43]
- related to this, the rise of 'impostor syndrome',[44] burnout, fear of 'being found out', of experiences of isolation;[45] and, interlinked to the above, a greater emphasis on the impact, visibility and performance of academic labour, a development bringing about new configurations of social inequalities;[46]
- and, with particular bearing on wellbeing and poor mental health, the longer-term subjective consequences of inhabiting an organisation increasingly focused, at a multitude of levels, on the management of individual and institutional *risks*.[47] Of particular note here is the emergence in recent work of the idea of the *anxious university*, an organisation whose practices and cultures are deeply implicated in the concerns that are now being raised about poor wellbeing.[48]

---

42 See M. Pereira, *Power, Knowledge and Feminist Scholarship: An Ethnography of Academia*, London, Routledge, 2017.

43 See for example M. Carrigan, 'Life in the Accelerated Academy: Anxiety, Thrives, Demands Intensify and Metrics hold the Tangled Web Together', available at: http://blogs.lse.ac.uk/impactofsocialsciences/2015/04/07/life-in-the-accelerated-academy-carrigan/.

44 M. Breeze, 'Impostor syndrome as a public feeling' in Y. Taylor and K. Lahad (eds), *Feeling Academic in the Neoliberal University: Feminist flights, fights and failures*, London, Palgrave Macmillan, 2018, at p. 199. See further below.

45 O. Sibai, B. Figueiredo and M. Christina Ferreira, 'Overworked and isolated: The rising epidemic of loneliness in academia', *The Conversation*, 29 January 2019, available at: https://theconversation.com/overworked-and-isolated-the-rising-epidemic-of-loneliness-in-academia-110009.

46 Knowles and Burrows, above n. 37.

47 The subjective consequences of management performance demands have been of particular concern following the suicides of UK academics; see for example S. Cassidy, 'University Enquiry into Professor Stefan Grimm's death', *The Independent*, 28 November 2014: R. Pells, 'Cardiff plans review after suicide of 'overworked' lecturer', *Times Higher Education*, 8 June 2018.

48 See Moorish, above n. 34: R. Hall, 'Notes on the University as anxiety machine', 10 July 2014, available at: http://www.richard-hall.org/2014/07/10/notes-on-the-university-as-anxiety-machine/. R. Hall and K. Bowles, 'Re-engineering Higher Education: The Subsumption of Academic Labour and the Exploitation of Anxiety' (2016) 28 *Workplace: A Journal for Academic Labour* 30–47, available at: http://ices.library.ubc.ca/index.php/workplace/article/view/186211; L. Berg, E. Huijbens and H.G. Larsen, 'Producing Anxiety in the Neoliberal University' (2016) 60(2) *The Canadian Geographer* 168; H. Staff, 'Andrea Brady on the Anxiety Machine that is Academia', *Poetry Foundation*, 13 July 2018, available at: https://www.poetryfoundation.org/harriet/2018/07/andrea-brady-on-the-anxiety-machine-that-is-academia; Andrea Brady,

An exploration of the 'hidden injuries' of neoliberalism,[49] in short, reveals significant physical and emotional costs of inhabiting cultures productive of hyper-competition, anxiety, shame, fear and uncertainty.[50]

This author has argued elsewhere that it is not possible to extrapolate across the very different fields of legal practice and legal academy.[51] There is no unitary 'wellbeing problem' within law across these diverse sectors. Nonetheless, it will be observed that the wellbeing debates now taking place in the UK legal community are, on closer examination, marked by recurring themes. The above discussion of legal practice may at first sight seem quite distinct from the legal academy; the university far removed from the concerns around billing, deadlines and low autonomy, among many other issues, that have marked the studies of lawyer wellbeing. In seeking to 'connect up' legal practice and the legal academy, however, the following section explores what these debates may share first, in terms of common themes and concerns and, secondly, with regard to how wellbeing is conceptualised.

4. FROM LEGAL PRACTICE TO LAW SCHOOL, OR MOVING ACROSS SILOS: SHARED THEMES

On one level the issues and concerns discussed within recent autobiographical accounts and personal testimonies of contemporary

---

'Part Four: My Story' Anxiety Machine: Mental Health and the Modern University (2018) 'Turning Down the Dial on the Anxiety Machine', available at: https://anxietymachine.wordpress.com/. See generally D. Beer, 'Is neoliberalism making you anxious? Metrics and the production of uncertainty' (2019) *LSE British Politics and Society* blog, available at: http://blogs.lse.ac.uk/politicsandpolicy/55395-2/.

49 R. Gill, 'Breaking the Silence: The Hidden Injuries of the Neoliberal University' in R. Flood and R. Gill (eds), *Secrecy and Silence in the Research Process: Feminist Reflections*, London, Routledge, 2009.

50 In the context of junior lawyers, see R. Collier, *Anxiety and Wellbeing Amongst Junior Lawyers: A Research Study* (2019), available at: https://www.ncl.ac.uk/media/wwwnclacuk/newcastleuniversitylawschool/files/RC%20Briefing%20Digital.pdf. Note also J. Gove, 'Competition drives researchers to counselling – and exit door', 2020, reporting that half of researchers have sought or wanted professional help to deal with anxiety or depression, and blaming competition and targets for creating an aggressive culture of bullying and overwork, available at: https//www.timeshighereducation.com/news/competition-drives-researchers-counselling-and-exit-door.

51 R. Collier, 'Wellbeing in the Legal Profession: reflections on recent developments (or, what do we talk about when we talk about wellbeing?)' (2016) 23(1) *International Journal of the Legal Profession* 41–60.

academic life, work emerging across academic disciplines, including law to a degree, mirrors themes within the literature on lawyer wellbeing. What we have here, for example, is a picture of pervasive and at times significant mental distress in the workplace; of concern about, and desire to challenge, stigma around the disclosure of mental health difficulties;[52] accounts of low personal accomplishment, depersonalisation and a frequent sense of alienation;[53] of some specific emotional and affective reactions to work, including exhaustion, stress, anxiety, unhappiness, overload, insomnia, shame, guilt, feelings of worthlessness, depression and, in some instances, suicidal ideation. In each context the wellness literature seeks to address high levels of workplace stress associated with increasing workload, poor work–life balance[54] and the wellbeing implications of new technologies blurring traditional distinctions between 'work' and 'life'.[55]

With regard to ideas of professional identity, meanwhile, academics, like lawyers, are cast as increasingly entrepreneurial subjects, new kinds

---

52 Note, for example, the involvement of the legal community in the 'Green Ribbon' campaign aimed at challenging mental health stigma in the City of London: http://citymha.org.uk/this-is-me-in-the-city/.

53 See further R. Barcan, *Academic Life and Labour in the New University: Hope and Other Choices* London, Routledge, 2016; Gill, above n. 49; G. Krause, 'We must confront the culture of overwork to tackle academia's mental health crisis', 2018, available at: https://www.timeshighereducation.com/blog/we-must-confront-culture-overwork-tackle-academias-mental-health-crisis; Peake and Mullings, above n. 33; R. Hall, *The Alienated Academic: The Struggle for Autonomy Inside the University*, London, Palgrave Macmillan, 2018; T. Peseta, S. Barrie and J. McLean, 'Academic Life in the Measured University: Pleasures, Paradoxes and Politics' (2017) 36(3) *Higher Education Research and Development* 453–57; A. Brady, 'Bind me – I still can sing', 2018, available at: https://blog.stillpointspaces.com/2018/07/bind-me-i-still-can-sing: L. Mitchell, 'Neoliberalising HE – Part II', 2018, available at: https://seriouslylearned.com/2018/03/16/neoliberalising-he-part-ii/.

54 In addition to work cited above see, for example, *Times Higher Education, Work life balance survey 2018; long hours take their toll on academics* in E. Bothwell, 'Get a life? No time for that' *Times Higher Education*, 8–14 February 2018, 34–47. 8 February 2018, available at: https://www.timeshighereducation.com/features/work-life-balance-survey-2018-long-hours-take-their-toll-academics. In legal practice, see M. Thornton, 'The flexible cyborg: work-life balance in legal practice' (2016) 38(1) *Sydney Law Review* 1; M. Thornton, 'Work/life or work/work? Corporate legal practice in the twenty-first century' (2016) 23(1) *International Journal of the Legal Profession* 13.

55 See J. Wajcman, *Pressed for Time*, Chicago, University of Chicago Press, 2015; J. Crary, *24/7: Late Capitalism and the Ends of Sleep*, London, Verso, 2013; S. Turkle, *Alone Together: Why We Expect More from Technology and Less from Each Other*, New York, Basic Books, 2011. Also M. Reisz, '"Email overload" risks "emotional exhaustion" for academics', 2016, available at: https://www.timeshighereducation.com/news/email-overload-risks-emotional-exhaustion-academics.

of business professionals who have experienced declining professional autonomy and status, inhabiting workplaces marked by cultural and regulatory/performance management imperatives to enact a particular kind of 'enterprising self'.[56] Turning to literature on the cohort attributes of those who enter the law – a theme highly resonant within both the legal academic and legal wellbeing scholarship – it seems that for lawyers, law students and academics the consequences for these 'insecure overachievers' of a toxic mix of regulatory processes can be far-reaching; bound up with institutional and individual complicity in a cultural hyper-identification with work and the resulting long hours, that serves to reproduce cultures of stigma around mental health problems.[57]

An intersectional reading of wellbeing in each field, legal practice and law schools, reveals some further connections; shared concerns, for example, around the increased precarity of many legal workers and the particular difficulties that can face early-career lawyers and legal academics in the context of new forms of classed, raced and gendered professional segmentations within the legal community;[58] how these legal wellbeing

---

56 See V. Hey, 'The Construction of Academic Time: Sub-Contracting Academic Labour in Research' (2001) 16(1) *Journal of Educational Policy* 67–84; M. Pereria, 'Struggling within and beyond the performative university: Articulating activism and work in an "academic without walls"' (2016) 54 *Women's Studies international forum* 100–110, at p. 105.

57 L. Empsom, quoted in R. Fishbein, 'Insecure Overachieving: Yet another thing we can hate ourselves for doing', 2018, available at: https://jezebel.com/insecure-overachieving-yet-another-thing-we-can-hate-ou-1829288055. See further A. Hill, 'Insecure Overachiever? You are Perfect for the Job: How Worrywarts Underpin Professional Service Firms Success', *The Financial Times*, 2 October 2017.

58 See for example, H. Sommerlad, '"A pit to put women in": Professionalism, work intensification, sexualisation and work–life balance in the legal profession in England and Wales' (2016) 23(1) *International Journal of the Legal Profession* 61–82; S. Inge, 'UK Universities rely on casual staff 'for up to half of teaching', *Times Higher Education*, 6 March 2018, available at: https://www.timeshighereducation.com/news/uk-universities-rely-casual-staff-half-teaching; A. McKie, 2020, 'Casualised staff 'dehumanised' in UK universities', available at: https://www.timeshighereducation.com/news/casualised-staff-dehumanised-uk-universities. Note also academic precariat, @acaprecariat: J. Holmwood, 'Early career planning and the management of the self in the neoliberal university' (2015) *The Sociological Review* (blog), available at: https://www.thesociologicalreview.com/blog/early-career-planning-and-the-management-of-the-academic-self-in-the-neo-liberal-university.html; L. Archer, 'The New Neoliberal Subjects? Young/er academics' constructions of professional identity' (2008) 23(3) *Journal of Education Policy* 265–85, DOI: 10.1080/02680930701754047; K. Bhopal, *The Experiences of Black and Minority Ethnic Academics*, London, Routledge, 2015, finding that Black and minority ethnic (BME) academics remain underrepresented, particularly at senior

debates are enmeshed with equality, diversity and inclusion issues, including concerns around discrimination, harassment and violence in what can, for some, be highly toxic workplace cultures.[59] Meshing with key themes in the wider workplace wellbeing literature, at the level of 'what works' and securing practical interventions, within each domain can be seen a shared focus on the pivotal role of management in tackling wellbeing; a concern with the messages that managers radiate and an urgent need for line-manager training in dealing with mental health matters. Law firms and law schools alike reflect the broader 'wellbeing turn' of recent years in the UK in their commitments to 'taking wellbeing seriously'.[60] And at this practical level what we are seeing, in law firms and UK law schools, is a wellbeing agenda focused on some recurring practices; 'wellbeing weeks', 'wellbeing rooms', yoga and tai chi for staff, self-knowledge, spirituality and mindfulness taster sessions; the introduction at an organisational level of online Cognitive Behavioural Therapy provision, of 'digital detox' periods, provision of five-minute massages, a heightened engagement with outside speakers from mental health organisations and the like.

To identify these links is not to negate significant differences between these wellbeing debates as they are currently playing out in the UK in legal practice and law schools. It is to suggest, to follow the remit of the charity *Lawcare*, rather that law schools are *part of* this broader legal community and, in turning to wellbeing, may have much to learn from what is known about the issue in the context of the legal professions. The remainder of this chapter, therefore, suggests that there is something else these discrete parts of the legal community share; what can be termed a new *politics of* wellbeing and the emergence of wellbeing as a particular kind of social problem to be addressed in law – a problem that raises rather different

---

levels in higher education, and are concentrated in new, post-1992 universities; V. Loveday, 'Embodying deficiency through "affective practice": Shame, relationality and the lived experience of social class and gender in higher education' (2016) 50(6) *Sociology* 1140–55; K. Inkle, 'Unreasonable adjustments: The additional unpaid labour of academics with disabilities' (2018) 33(8) *Disability and Society* 1372–76.

59 See in particular International Bar Association (IBA), *Us Too? Bullying and Harassment in the Legal profession*, available at: https://www.ibanet.org/bullying-and-sexual-harassment.aspx.

60 Note, for example, discussion of wellbeing at the *Future of Legal Education and Training Conference*, 28 January 2019. See also *The London Wellbeing for Lawyers Conference*, 17 September 2019, organised by the Wellbeing Work Alliance, available at: https://www.litigationfutures.com/conference/the-london-wellbeing-for-lawyers-conference-17-sept-2019.

questions about the nature of legal professionalism, the 'ideal worker' and the place and purpose of legal education.

5. THE POTENTIAL AND THE PROBLEMS OF WELLBEING: IDENTITY, RESILIENCE AND RESPONSIBILITY

Within both legal practice and law school scholarship wellbeing is a politically contested and open-ended concept. In each domain, for example, wellbeing has become a key part of a set of counter narratives to what are presently seen, within their respective wellbeing literatures, as the dominant ways of working that are harmful to wellbeing. It informs attempts within legal practice to reposition poor lawyer wellbeing as a 'force of change',[61] to develop new ways of working that might challenge traditional work cultures and organisational structures, not least in relation to forms of billing of legal work.[62] In Higher Education, wellbeing has become a central feature of attempts to *resist* the marketised neoliberal university and re-envision what a 'good university' might be.[63] This is a particular theme in recent feminist scholarship exploring challenges facing feminism within a marketised academy.[64] Looking to the 'Five Ways to Wellbeing' that organisations across the UK workforce widely seek to encourage as

---

61 J. Chan, 'Conceptualising Legal Culture and Lawyering Stress' (2014) 21(2) *International Journal of the Legal Profession* 213–32.

62 On the idea of 'new law' see, for example, M. Thornton, 'Liberty Fellow Lecture: The Uberisation of Legal Practice', 30 May 2018, Leeds University, UK, available at: https://allevents.in/leeds/liberty-fellow-lecture-2018-the-uberisation-of-legal-practice-professor-margaret-thornton/1000044590597678 and her 'Uberisation: The Path to Lawyer Wellbeing', Chapter 8 in this volume.

63 R. Connell, *The Good University: What Universities Actually Do and Why it's Time for Radical Change*, London, Zed Books, 2019; Goldsmiths University and College Union, *The Gold Paper* (2016), available at: https://goldsmithsucu.wordpress.com/the-gold-paper/; *Campaign for the Public University*, available at: http://publicuniversity.org.uk; M. Heath and P. Burdon, 'Academic Resistance to the Neoliberal University' (2013) 23(2) *Legal Education Review* 379–401. See also The Analogue University, 'Correlation in the Data University: Understanding and Challenging Targets-based Performance-management in Higher Education' (2019) 18(6) *ACME: An International Journal for Critical Geographies* 1184–1206.

64 See, for example, M. Pereria, '"Feminist theory is proper knowledge but …": The status of feminist scholarship in the academy' (2012) 13(3) *Feminist Theory* 283–303; S. Burton, 'Writing yourself in? The price of playing the (feminist) game in the neoliberal university' in Taylor and Lahad, above n. 44; M. Pereria, above n. 56.

part of organisational wellbeing strategies, addressing wellbeing involves urging academic staff to 'slow down', to take time *away* from work;[65] to be, in the title of Berg and Seeber's 2016 book, a 'slow professor'.[66]

Far from seeing wellbeing as a marginal topic in relation to contemporary legal scholarship, therefore, and in relation to debates within the legal academy and legal professions, from the above perspective it is a topic around which a broad set of concerns relating to structural and cultural changes coalesce; and it is in relation to the new ideas of professionalism associated with these changes that the problem or limits of wellbeing, emerge most clearly.

In what way is this so? In relation to both the legal profession wellness literature and the discussion of wellbeing in law schools and legal education, there is an alternative reading of the legal community's 'wellbeing turn' to be found. This suggests that the dominant wellbeing narrative that has emerged across organisations is politically and conceptually problematic in two interlinked respects: first, in how it tends to individualise the social processes discussed above; and secondly, how it frames responsibility to 'do something' about poor wellbeing in a way that detracts from a consideration of the structures and cultures that are productive of problems in the first place.[67] Taken together this locates the law's wellbeing

---

65 M. O'Neill, 'The Slow University: Work, Time and Wellbeing' (2014) 15(3) *Forum: Qualitative Social Research*, available at: http://www.qualitative-research.net/index.php/fqs/article/view/2223/3692; Y. Hartman and S. Darab, 'A call for slow scholarship: A case study on the intensification of academic life and its implications for policy' (2012) 34(1)–(2) *Review of Education, Pedagogy, and Cultural Studies* 49–60.

66 M. Berg and B. Seeber, *The Slow Professor: Challenging the Culture of Speed in the Academy*, Toronto, University of Toronto Press, 2016. Also A. Mountz et al., 'For Slow Scholarship: A Feminist Politics of Resistance through Collective Action in the Neoliberal University' (2015) 14(4) *ACME: An International E-Journal for Critical Geographies* 1235–59; *Slow Academic* website: https://theslowacademic.com/2018/07/16/which-university-which-self/.

67 See, for example, discussion in M. Thornton, 'The Case of Law Student Wellbeing: A Neoliberal Conundrum' (2016) 58(2) *Australian Universities Review* 42–50; P. Baron, '"Sleight of Hand": Lawyer Distress and the Attribution of Responsibility' (2014) 23(2) *Griffith Law Review* 26; R. Collier, 'Wellbeing in the Legal Profession: Reflections on recent developments (or, what do we talk about when we talk about wellbeing?)' (2016) 23(1) *International Journal of the Legal Profession* 41–60; R. Collier, '"Love Law, Love Life": Neo-Liberalism, Wellbeing and Gender in the Legal Profession – The Case of Law School' (2014) 17(2) *Legal Ethics* 202; C. Parker, 'The "moral panic" over psychological wellbeing in the legal profession: A personal or political ethical response?' (2014) 37(3) *University of New South Wales Law Journal* 1103–41.

problem as enmeshed with a reframing of the 'ideal' (responsible) worker and a model of professional identity *as* a distinctly moral project; one in which the 'good lawyer' and 'good academic' is positioned as an individual who will, or at least should, respond to the realignment of demands (increased workload, insecurity, the fusing of 'private life' and work) by better attending to their own personal wellbeing – by becoming resilient, and so forth.

There are several problems, however, with such an approach. It can easily mask, for example, the longer-term consequences for individuals of working at the level of consistent 'excellence' that such processes bring. This is exemplified by themes within the autobiographical accounts of depression, anxiety and burnout that have become a marked feature of both the legal professional and academic wellbeing literature discussed above.[68] Rather than position resilience as something called upon in the exceptional circumstance, it is positioned as a 'base-line' requirement in ways that reify what continue to be viewed as highly desirable organisational traits. Contra the call to 'take time' from work, the cultural and regulatory pressures to work long hours, to be 'care-less' in terms of caring commitments,[69] to be a suitably entrepreneurial subject and so on continue.[70] What we see in these narratives of poor wellbeing are how individuals who may have developed outwardly adequate coping skills and resources may nonetheless not remain unscathed by these ways of working over a period of time.[71]

---

68 J. Moran, 'The University: A Guide for Depressives', *Times Higher Education*, 1 March 2018, available at: https://www.timeshighereducation.com/features/university-guide-depressives; C. Maslach and M.P. Leiter, *The Truth about Burnout: How Organisations Cause Personal Stress and What to Do about It*, San Francisco, Jossey Bass, 1997; M.P. Leiter and C. Maslach, 'Six areas of work life: A model of the organisational context of burnout' (1999) 21(4) *Journal of Health and Human Services Administration* 472–89.

69 M.P. Moreau and M. Robertson, *Carers and Careers: Career Development and Access to Leadership Among Academic Staff with Caring Responsibilities*, London, Leadership Foundation, 2017.

70 Kinman, 'Pressure points', above n. 34, at p. 488 notes, for example, how 'the changing nature of academic work appears to have led to a considerable increase in job demand with no corresponding increase in resources. Under such conditions, many workers feel they have no alternative but to work long hours – often during evenings and weekends … it appears that employees form the lower grades and women academics may be particularly vulnerable to occupational stressors and strains.'

71 See for example Z. Krupka, 'Corporate resilience training works – but what are we being asked to bear?', 21 March 2016, *The Conversation*, available at: http://theconversation.com/corporate-resilience-training-works-but-what-are-we-being-asked-to-bear-54827; See also P. Baron, 'The Persistence of Distress' in R. Field et al. above n. 5; R. Martin, *This Too Will Pass: Anxiety in a professional World*, London, Trigger Books, 2018;

It is a recognition of broader structural concerns that, in turn, underscore the increasing calls to do something about these *cultures* of law in relation to wellbeing, as evident in the counter-narratives discussed above.

There is another problem. A focus on personal adaptation, in such a way that structural problems become framed as matters best resolved by self-regulation, can merge easily into self-blame and, with it, a furthering of individual distress. Within organisations it can legitimate an 'enactment of ritual', a focus on 'doing the document' rather than introducing substantive change.[72] Across the UK Higher Education sector, revealingly, wellbeing is now being seen as a new locus of metric and audit in which well-meaning goals (improving staff wellbeing) are to be assessed via a host of 'wellbeing league tables', audit games to be played by institutions seeking to ensure value for money and consumer choice.[73] It is an approach that rests on a central assumption that individual personal deficits can be worked on in ways that will improve performance, be it at work or in 'private' life; a development that must itself be framed, this author has argued elsewhere, against the backdrop of a pervasive commodification of 'wellbeing' and the emergence of what Will Davies has termed the new 'happiness industry'.[74] It is important to remember here that the law's wellness turn

---

M.A. Vickers and A. Kouzmin, '"Resilience" in Organisational Actors and Rearticulating "Voice": Towards a humanistic critique of New Public Management' (2001) 3(1) *Public Management Review* 95–119; C. Marlow, 'Is employee resilience training needed in the workplace?', 27 June 2018, available at: https://www.lawsociety.org.uk/news/blog/is-employee-resilience-training-needed-in-the-workplace/.

72 S. Ahmed, '"You end up doing the document rather than doing the doing": Diversity, race equality and the politics of documentation' (2007) 30(4) *Ethnic and Racial Studies* 590–609; See also D.R. Litvin, 'The Business Case for Diversity and the "Iron Cage" in B. Czarniawska and H. Hopkinson (eds), *Casting the Other: The Production and Maintenance of Inequalities in Work Organizations*, London, Routledge 2002, pp. 160–184, cited in L. Ashley and L. Empson, 'Convenient Fictions and Inconvenient Truths: Dilemmas of Diversity at Three Leading Accountancy Firms' (2016) 35 *Critical Perspectives on Accounting* 76–87, available at: file:///J:/2019%20Jan/To%20print/Convenient%20Fictions%20and%20Inconvenient%20Truths_Ashley%20and%20Empson%201.pdf.

73 R. Adams, 'Universities could lose league table positions for diversity failures', *The Guardian*, 1 February 2019, available at: https://www.theguardian.com/education/2019/feb/01/uk-universities-lose-league-table-positions-diversity-failures?CMP=share_btn_tw//; H. Dale-Harris, 'Higher education is about making lives better. That's why we need better well-being metrics and yes, maybe even a well-being league table', available at: https://www.hepi.ac.uk/2019/05/13/higher-education-is-about-making-lives-better-thats-why-we-need-better-well-being-metrics-and-yes-maybe-even-a-well-being-league-table/.

74 W. Davies, *The Happiness Industry: How the Government and Big Business Sold us Wellbeing*, London, Verso, 2015.

in the UK is bound up within a wider wellbeing industry, in which a host of private providers are now selling wellbeing services to the legal community;[75] hence the emergence of new wellbeing technologies engaged in the measurement of wellbeing and inducements to make '"informed" or "strategic" choices about what services and products we consume'.[76] Seen from such a perspective wellbeing has become part of systems that 'enable differentiation … facilitate rankings … demarcate winners from losers'.[77]

6. CONCLUDING REMARKS

> In order to effect … critical change we need to take seriously the quest to engage in conversations that subject the space of the academy to scrutiny and explore the changing culture of knowledge production and its role in creating environments of mental and emotional distress, not least, because no one should go through these experiences alone.[78]

A closer interrogation of recent developments around wellbeing in the UK legal community, this chapter argues, can reveal much about the shifting terrain of legal practice, research and education; and in the case of universities, the particular focus here, what is happening in relation to the 'private life' of the contemporary law school.[79] Manifestation of distress within these wellbeing debates, be it in the context of lawyers, law students or legal academic staff, should not be understood simply in terms of individual pathology, located solely in a medicalised framework, but situated, rather, within a political, economic and cultural context. That context is one in which mental health problems are increasingly acknowledged to have become endemic across societies as a result of new

---

75 Note, for example, H. Neuman Love, *YOGA for Lawyers: Mind Body Techniques to Feel Better All the Time*, Chicago, American Bar Association, 2015; J. Cho and K. Gifford, *THE Anxious Lawyer: An 8-Week Guide to a Joyful and Satisfying Law Practice Through Mindfulness and Meditation* (Ankerwycke, 2016), *The Mindful Lawyer Magazine*, 2017, available on a free download from: http://theanxiouslawyer.com/mindful-magazine/, *The Conscious Lawyer: Serving the Transition to a More Beautiful World*, available at: https://www.theconsciouslawyer.co.uk/.

76 Beer, above n. 48. See also R. Gill and N. Donaghue, 'Resilience, apps and reluctant individualism: Technologies of self in the neoliberal academy' (2016) 54 *Women's Studies International Forum* 91–99, at 91.

77 Ibid.

78 Peake and Mullings, above n. 33, at pp. 276–77.

79 Cownie, above n. 6.

diagnostic categories, a cultural normalisation of illness and an increased awareness of wellbeing issues amongst specific populations (such as, say, university staff and students). This debate about wellbeing, that is, is enmeshed with concerns about the way we live and work now. For Davies the explosion of interest in wellbeing of recent years is aligned to a reframing of feeling as a political force in relation to which individuals, governments and organisations would appear to exist increasingly in a state of constant and heightened alertness, what Davies terms a 'nervous state'.[80] This is the context in which the individualising of wellbeing discussed above occurs, one in which the subjective effects of particular working conditions are being reframed as aspects of personal growth, resilience, hygiene. The individualising of wellbeing and framing of responsibility raises questions about the emotional dimensions of new forms of governance of social life;[81] precisely how in order 'to understand how markets govern, to understand how they discipline us and shape our behaviour, we need to understand how [they] … make us *feel*.'[82]

To recognise wellbeing as a multi-faceted problem[83] in a way that seeks to embed individual biographies within a matrix of culture, politics and history does *not* mean the heightened provision of wellbeing advice and support within the legal community is in any way unhelpful or unwelcome. The introduction of diverse initiatives around self-help, online courses, the establishment of links to talking therapies, curriculum reform, coaching, mindfulness and resilience training, counselling, enhanced professional support and so forth are signs of a significant cultural and political shift around wellbeing in the legal community. It is essential, it is argued here, to move beyond deterministic critiques and develop work that seeks to be of real value to practitioners and policy-makers; to recognise the scale of

---

80 W. Davies, *Nervous States: How Feeling took Over the World*, London, Jonathan Cape, 2018.

81 See for example C. Scharff, 'Life as an Enterprise: Ten Ways through which Neoliberalism is Experienced on an Emotional Level' (2016) *British Politics and Policy Blog*, LSE, available at: http://blogs.lse.ac.uk/politicsandpolicy/the-psychic-life-of-neoliberalism/.

82 Beer, above n. 48. On neoliberalism as a political ideology and a 'social imaginary', a way of thinking about what is valued and valuable in a society see further P.A. Hall and M. Lamont (eds), *Social Resilience in the Neoliberal Era*, Cambridge, Cambridge University Press, 2013.

83 See further I. Bache and L. Reardon, *The Politics and Policy of Wellbeing: Understanding the Rise and Significance of a New Agenda*, Cheltenham, Edward Elgar, 2016 at pp. 5–7; I. Bache and L. Reardon, 'An idea whose time has come? Explaining the rise of well-being in British Politics' (2013) 61(4) *Political Studies* 898–914.

poor wellbeing that does exist in the law community and attend to practical reforms that might address the requirements of both practitioners tasked with driving change and law students and legal academics in building universities as 'flourishing institutions'.[84] Recognising the importance of macro (societal-structural), micro (individual) and meso (organisational) level responses involves a systemic multi-level and integrated approach. To see tackling wellbeing as an ethical issue, as the 'right thing to do', however, raises questions about our understanding of core institutional values,[85] the importance of psychological health at work,[86] and issues of professional identity, resilience and responsibility.[87]

What of the future? There is no reason to think the concerns we are now seeing in the legal profession and legal education and training around wellbeing will soon disappear; that this is another passing fad, a problem that is easily solvable or, indeed, a moral panic in the law whose time will pass. It may be more helpful, this author would suggest, to characterise wellbeing as 'a "wicked problem", one that defies any easy definition or agreed solution' and which itself raises difficult questions about what it may mean to take wellbeing seriously.[88] The very kinds of solutions that are presently being proposed within the UK's law wellness turn – for example, improving work–life balance, reducing stigma, encouraging self-disclosure, dispelling myths about mental health and so on – may each have unintended consequences for legal organisations. What constraints may law firms face in fostering work–life integration for their employees? What are the limits of encouraging employees to 'be mindful' within a culture of financialisation?[89] If law students or legal academic staff self-disclose with mental health problems, what are the implications for

---

84 See F. Vailes, 'Well-being in Education: what is building flourishing institutions was the answer?', September 2019, Bristol Institute for Learning and Teaching (BILT), available at: https://bilt.online/tag/fabienne-vailes/.

85 S. Tang, 'Valuing persons and communities in doing wellness for law well' in Field et al., above n. 5 at p. 20; V. Holmes, 'Values: The Flip Side of the wellbeing Coin' in Strevens and Fields (eds), above n. 23.

86 C. James, 'The Ethics of Wellbeing: Psychological Health as the Vanguard for Sociological Change' in Strevens and Fields (eds), above n. 23.

87 C. Strevens, R. Field and N. Duncan, 'Self-care as a professional virtue for lawyers' in Strevens and Fields (eds), above n. 23.

88 I. Bache, L. Reardon and P. Anand, 'Wellbeing as a wicked problem: Navigating the arguments for the role of government' (2015) 17(3) *Journal of Happiness Studies* 893–912.

89 A point implicitly recognised in the *Mindful Business Charter*, above n. 14.

managers who may be dealing with limited resources (and who are being urged, simultaneously, to look after their own wellbeing)?

This chapter has explored a set of contradictions between workplace cultures and structures that appear to simultaneously fetishise overwork and advocate self-improvement.[90] In this wellbeing debate overwork has become a kind of culturally acceptable self-harming activity.[91] In both legal professional practice and the marketised legal academy, within their respective wellbeing literatures, individual committment to long working hours has become something of a motive force within organisational cultures in which, there is some degree of acceptance, self-care can very easily wither.[92] Many professionals such as lawyers and academics, Blagoev, Empsom and Ortleib suggest, are complicit in such processes, tending to hyper-identify with a particular professional ideal even up to the extent of becoming "corporate clones … unable to recognize how work takes over their lives";[93] and in the case of universities, it has been suggested:

> This is the source of our discomfort … it is not just that we might have some political objections to these value transformations. The root of the issue is that we are fully *implicated* in their enactment.[94]

There is a need to recognise how the pleasures and rewards, financial and psychological, of identification with a particular professional (and, indeed, management) ideal are enmeshed with a set of practices known to be detrimental to wellbeing; practices accepted, research suggests, at least for

---

90 Although see S. Brinkmann, *Stand Firm: Resisting the Self-Improvement Craze*, London, Polity Press, 2017.

91 Hall (2017), above n. 48. See discussion in A. Fazackerley, 'Universities' league table obsession triggers mental health crisis fears', *The Guardian*, 12 June 2018, available at: https://www.theguardian.com/education/2018/jun/12/university-mental-health-league-table-obsession.

92 See, in addition to work cited above, A. Siddiquee, J. Sixsmith, R. Lawthorn and J. Haworth, 'Paid work, life-work and leisure: A study of wellbeing in the context of academic lives in higher education' (2016) 35(1) *Journal of Leisure Studies* 36–45.

93 B. Blagoev, L. Empsom and R. Ortlieb, 'Overwork, Identity and the Autonomy/Control Paradox in Professional Organizations' (2017), available at: https://www.egosnet.org/jart/prj3/egos/main.jart?rel=de&reserve-mode=active&content-id=1499635422149&subtheme_id=1474852915025. See generally on this idea M. Bunting, *Willing Slaves: How the overwork culture is ruling our lives*, London, HarperCollins Publishers, 2005. On academic complicity see Burrows, above n. 38.

94 Burrows, above n. 38.

some of the life course, with the consequences of this 'package deal', and the forms of (gendered) commitment it entails, tending to be revealed at particular times of life transition, vulnerability and personal crisis.[95]

Understandings of the term wellbeing differ not only across legal communities, as we have seen. They can also entail different values and perceptions of the purpose of legal education and research. In the case of university law schools a further tension underscores this wellbeing discourse; a tension between, on the one hand, organisational and individual commitments to the intrinsic rewards and values associated with a liberal legal education 'in its own right', and, on the other, the proliferation of systems of rankings, metrics and so forth increasingly associated with earning capacity and market value.[96] This informs a profound uncertainty around how how 'universities talk the language of "flourishing" whilst "league tables force us into competition" and "our excellence" is itself always comparative'.[97] The voices of law students and lawyers, meanwhile, suggest that the competitive cultures of much of legal practice and education have consequences of subjective wellbeing and that contemporary legal education and training in the UK is itself a highly *anxiety inducing* experience.[98] At the present, notwithstanding the welcome interventions of the law's 'wellbeing turn', it remains the case that the perception of many lawyers, law students and legal academics is one of a disconnect between these organisational commitments to improved wellbeing and the systemic causes of such distress.

---

95 See R. Collier, 'Fatherhood, gender and the making of professional identity in large law firms: Bringing men into the frame' (2019) 15(1) *International Journal of Law in Context* 68.

96 For discussion of the impact of market-based thinking on law schools in North America see for example, R. Tejanti, *Law Mart: Access and for-profit law schools*, Stanford CA, Stanford University Press, 2017.

97 J. Woolf, 'What is the point of higher education if it doesn't lead to greater happiness?', *The Guardian*, 12 February 2019.

98 A theme highlighted in Collier, above n. 50.

INDEX

A

Adversarialism 166–167
Ageism 193–197
Alcohol and drug use 22, 58, 63, 66, 68–72, 79, 162, 164, 184, 203, 205
Alternative Fee Arrangement 16, 25, 269, 271, 292–305
Anxiety 5, 20–21, 25, 31–56, 58, 60, 62, 64–74, 78–80, 108, 117, 161–164, 167–168, 170, 196, 200–201, 204–205, 210, 212, 216, 225, 248, 286, 291, 322–323, 328, 334
  see also Psychological distress
Artificial intelligence (AI) 12–13, 24, 193, 239–266
Automation 240, 242, 251–254, 258, 261, 263
Autonomy 10, 20, 23, 25–26, 35, 37–38, 44, 47, 48, 53, 55–56, 75, 106, 112–113, 135, 140, 143, 148–150, 180–181, 187–188, 191–192, 194, 198, 216, 235–236, 241, 244–245, 248–250, 256–260, 262, 266, 275–280, 282–284, 288–291, 295–296, 300–306, 309, 322, 324

B

Barristers 18, 19, 21, 55, 58, 79, 89–90, 99, 101, 203, 266
Billable hours 7, 22, 55, 91, 94, 106, 118, 167, 177, 179–181, 184, 209–210, 212, 230, 261, 269–270, 272, 282, 284–292, 298, 306
Bullying 22, 77–103, 147, 157, 179, 183–184, 216, 277
  intimidation and aggression 89
Bureaucratisation 24, 106, 114, 116, 180, 237

C

Career satisfaction 64, 68, 71, 73–74
Clients' expectations 166, 191, 270, 304
Competence 5, 14, 25, 35, 37, 49, 140, 156, 163, 171, 212, 243, 245, 247, 249–250, 266, 275–280, 284, 289–291, 296, 300–301, 303, 305–306
Competition 14, 22, 56, 83, 106, 167, 178–179, 193, 206–207, 209, 245, 249, 252–254, 261, 265–266, 284, 320, 322, 334
Consumer 13, 112, 133–134, 142–143, 148, 207, 242, 249–250, 298, 329
Contractualisation 75, 112, 114, 116
Corporatisation 21, 24, 134
Cost cutting 106–107, 114–116, 119–120

D

Databases 11–12
Demand Control Model 60
Depression Anxiety Stress Scales (DASS) 62, 65, 117
Depression 5, 20–21, 31–56, 58–60, 62, 64–68, 70–74, 78–79, 101, 106, 108, 115, 117, 127, 161–165, 179–180, 182–183, 196–197, 200–205, 213, 216–217, 323, 328
  see also Psychological distress
Digital technology 11, 26
Dot com 9, 11

E

Efficiency 10, 12, 19, 24, 26–27, 135, 147, 150, 206, 210–211, 223, 251–257, 264, 276–277, 283, 287, 290, 298–299, 301–303, 305, 307
Effort-reward Imbalance Model 60, 63, 68–72
Ethics 5, 20, 23, 40, 50–52, 136, 155–175, 186, 211, 214, 216, 233–234, 268, 276, 285, 287, 296, 306
Ethics and wellbeing 23, 155–175, 296
Expertise 224, 257–260, 265, 289, 305
Extrinsic reward/motivation 36, 53, 55, 140, 249, 256, 278–280, 297, 302, 305–306

F

Financial issues/pressure 23, 165, 167–172, 244
Flexibility 16, 23, 26, 92, 95, 127, 180–181, 184–185, 187–190, 192, 197–198, 221–222
  Flexible work paradox 107, 128, 142, 179, 185, 189–191, 217
  Flexible work policies 178
    See also Autonomy
  Connectivity 190
  Telecommunicating 190–191
Future of Law and Innovation in the Profession (FLIP) 4, 24

G
Gender 41, 66, 72, 83, 86–87, 92, 141, 184, 189, 197, 334
Gig economy 16–17, 23, 185, 195, 197
Globalisation 3, 8–11, 21, 26, 84, 156, 182
Global law firms 9–11, 18, 26, 255, 266

H
Harassment 21, 77–129, 157, 179, 216, 325
 see also Sexual Harassment
Health and safety regulation 78, 82, 84, 100–102, 200

I
In house lawyers 11, 255
Incorporated Legal Practice (ILP) 15, 199–237
Incorporation 178, 202, 217–218, 220–236
Innovation 4–5, 14, 19–20, 23–24, 26–27, 153–309
Intrinsic motivation 38, 50, 53, 140, 171, 278–282, 297, 301, 306, 308–309

J
Job satisfaction 22–23, 58–59, 64, 85, 90–91, 108, 116, 120–124, 141, 161, 174, 182
Job security 74, 115–116, 118–121, 123–124, 265

K
Knowledge 11, 14, 47–52

L
Law firms 6–12, 14–19, 23–27, 86, 106, 120–124, 179–198, 200–237, 239–309
 Australia 4, 8–12, 14, 17–19, 21–22, 32–75, 77–103, 105–129, 131–151, 164, 177–198, 200–237, 253, 255, 263, 272, 293, 315–316
 Canada 10, 161, 281
 non-lawyer owners of 24, 202, 222–223, 228–237
 profitability 15, 106, 179, 196, 208–209, 281, 283–284, 287, 300, 303–304
 regulatory structure 24, 202
 UK 10, 17–18, 22, 25, 75, 109, 112–114, 132, 136–138, 141–144, 146, 150, 188, 190, 192–193, 196–197, 205, 255, 281, 313–334
 US 6–7, 9–10, 18, 33, 36, 38, 156, 163, 272
Law students 5, 20, 25, 32–56, 58, 131–151, 167, 182, 203–204, 281, 314, 316–317, 324, 330, 332, 334
 age, gender and language 41–42
 focus on marks 38
Law teachers 22–23, 131–151, 246
 administrative burden 22, 143–145, 149–150, 246
 metrics 144–145, 334
Lawyers' ability to cope with demands 61, 71
Lawyers' career paths 256
Lawyers' liability 25, 123, 136, 222, 226–227, 235, 237, 248, 295
Lawyers in private practice 18–19, 75, 90, 92–95, 97, 124, 126, 156, 160
Legal academics 20, 26, 131–151, 313–334
Legal aid lawyers 75, 112–114, 256
Legal fees 7, 267–309
 contingency 25, 224, 269–270, 272–274, 284, 292–298, 303, 308
 fixed 16, 25, 225, 269–270, 274, 283, 298–303
Legal profession 3–5, 13–15, 17–26, 32–33, 47, 56, 68, 77–79, 81–87, 90, 97–103, 106, 111, 123–124, 147, 156, 165–175, 182, 196–197, 200–202, 204–206, 208–209, 220, 233–236, 241–243, 251, 253–257, 261–263, 266, 268–269, 314, 325, 327, 332
 as business 15, 24, 178, 248–250, 266
 as market control 241, 246–248, 260
 attrition and causes 78, 85, 87, 93–97, 179

M
Mental health issues 5, 21, 25, 54, 59–62, 64–74, 78–80, 84–85, 91, 101–102, 115, 145, 161, 163–165, 194, 196, 201, 203, 205, 315–319, 323–325, 330, 332
 see also Anxiety
 see also Stress
 see also Depression
 see also Substance abuse
 see also Suicide
 see also Psychological distress
 see also Wellbeing
Motivation 38, 50, 53, 55–56, 140, 171, 247, 275, 278–282, 290–292, 294, 296–297, 301–302, 305–306, 308–309
 see also Intrinsic motivation
 see also Extrinsic reward/motivation

N
Neoliberalism 22–23, 105–129, 133–134, 136, 139, 150, 183, 322
Neoliberalism and legal education 21–22, 133–135, 139, 150, 183, 322
Neoliberalism and legal practice 21–22, 26, 75, 105–129, 142–146, 148, 150, 178, 182–186, 196, 319–322, 326
Neoliberalism and university management 21–22, 132–136, 139, 142–151, 322, 326

NewLaw 17–18, 23, 180, 184–198
New law firms 14–17
New Public Management 22, 75, 112

O
Organisational Justice Model 60
Overcommitment 21, 64, 67–72
Overwork 26, 93–97, 181, 252, 277, 288, 302, 333

P
Phenomenography 139–140
Positive psychology 317
Precarity 24, 183, 251–257, 259, 324
Professionalism 23–24, 113, 123, 143, 156–159, 161, 163, 165, 171–172, 189, 241, 244, 246, 250–251, 253–254, 257–258, 263–264, 266, 281, 314, 326–327
Psychological distress 33–34, 38, 58, 180–184, 203–204, 212, 230, 239
  Risk factors 21, 78, 84–85, 98, 100–103, 126
  see also Stress
  see also Anxiety
  see also Depression
  see also Mental health issues
Psychosocial injury 83–85
  costs of 79, 84, 97, 202, 322
  risk factors 21, 73, 78, 84–85, 98, 100–103, 126
Public and community sector lawyers 22–23, 107–108, 111–129
  job security 22, 115–116, 118–121, 123–124
  lack of resources 23, 118–119, 122
Public interest lawyers 59
  see also Public and community sector lawyers

R
Relatedness 25, 35, 37, 140, 245, 247, 266, 275–280, 284–287, 291, 294, 298–299, 304, 306
Resilience 32, 74, 101, 107, 111, 124, 126–127, 133, 212, 216–217, 316, 318, 326, 328, 331–332
Responsibility (for wellbeing) 22, 101, 107, 128, 150, 183–184, 326–327, 331–332

S
Salaries 6–7, 123, 231, 256
Self-determination Theory (SDT) 25, 140, 275, 317
Sexual harassment 22, 78, 80–83, 85, 89–90, 98–100, 183
  experience of women lawyers 80–82, 85, 89–90, 98–100, 183
  reasons for under-reporting 82, 98–100
Sharing economy 16, 23
  see also Gig economy
Social connectedness 20, 36–37, 51, 53
Solicitors 18–20, 55, 58, 73, 75, 101, 123, 182, 193, 203, 209, 219, 295, 315
Stress 5, 19–27, 32–75, 77–103, 105–129, 131–151, 162, 164, 174, 177, 179, 182–183, 188, 192–193, 195–197, 200–202, 204–205, 209–210, 212–213, 216–217, 227, 230, 236, 248, 291, 308, 323
  see also Psychological distress
Stressors 19–20, 22–23, 26, 32, 55–56, 74–75, 108, 116–120, 126, 132, 136, 138–139, 150, 161, 181, 184, 216, 251, 261
Substance abuse 5, 78, 161, 163–165, 183–184, 196, 205, 216
Suicide 5, 58, 79, 101, 180, 183, 200, 248

T
Technological change 5, 20–21, 75, 84, 197, 240, 251
Technology 1–17, 20–21, 26–27, 33, 50, 75, 107, 114, 147, 156, 167, 180, 185, 191, 207–208, 223–226, 241–242, 250, 252, 259–260, 262, 264–265, 266, 283, 300, 304, 314
  impact on legal profession 11–14, 16–17, 177–198, 239–266
Therapeutic jurisprudence 317

U
Uberisation of legal practice 16, 24, 177–198
Unincorporated Legal Practice (ULP) 218, 220–221, 227, 229
Universities 22–23, 25, 80, 129, 131–151, 203, 313–334

W
Wellbeing 3, 5, 8, 13, 20, 22–25, 32, 35–39, 45, 55, 58–60, 74, 78–80, 82, 84, 98, 107–108, 111, 115–116, 128, 131–134, 136–138, 142–143, 149–151, 156, 159–163, 165, 167–168, 171–172, 174–175, 178–181, 184, 186–187, 190, 196–198, 200–202, 204–205, 209, 212, 214, 216–217, 222, 225–227, 229–233, 236–237, 241, 243–247, 249–256, 258–260, 262–266, 268–270, 273–286, 289, 291–292, 294–298, 303–304, 306–309, 313–334
  personal adaptation vs structural reform 74, 107, 128–129, 150, 314, 329
Wellbeing initiatives/interventions 22, 74, 108, 124–129, 202, 217, 325, 326
Work deadlines 118, 142, 167, 200, 280, 287, 322

Work hours 5, 7–8, 22–23, 55, 64, 68, 74, 84, 91–94, 97, 106, 114–115, 118, 123–124, 127, 142, 146, 164, 167, 177, 179–182, 184–185, 187–191, 194, 209–210, 212, 217, 230, 261, 264, 272, 282–292, 301–302, 306, 308, 321, 324, 328, 333
Work stress intervention
  primary, secondary and tertiary 126
  see also Wellbeing initiatives/interventions
Working conditions 61, 63, 118, 124, 126, 128, 147, 151, 156, 200, 331
Work-life balance 91, 107–108, 160, 202, 216–217, 236, 323, 332
Workplace culture 60–61, 63–64, 68, 73, 79, 84, 90–97, 174, 320, 325, 333
Workplace demands 79, 201, 209–210, 212, 215, 291
Workplace leadership 24, 89, 101, 147, 150–151, 172–174, 309

ABOUT THE EDITORS

Michael Legg is a Professor at UNSW Law. He is also the Director of the Law Society of New South Wales Future of Law and Innovation in the Profession (FLIP) research stream at UNSW. His research interests are in complex civil litigation (including class actions and regulatory litigation) and the legal profession. He is a member of the Law Society of New South Wales' Future Committee that conducted the Inquiry into the Future of Law and Innovation in the Profession. He was the Chair and author of the UNSW Law School's 2017 technology curriculum review, which examined the ramifications of the impact of technology on the legal profession for legal education. In 2017, he was awarded Academic of the Year at the Lawyers Weekly Australian Law Awards for his innovative teaching of technology and legal practice, especially in relation to litigation and alternative dispute resolution, and engagement with the legal profession.

Prue Vines is Professor, Co-Director of the Private Law Research & Policy Group, and Associate Dean (Education) at UNSW Law and a Fellow of the Australian Academy of Law. She was Director of First Year Studies at UNSW Law from 1996–2019 and in that role created a number of initiatives for the wellbeing of law students and was a founding member of the Tristan Jepson Memorial Foundation, now the Minds Count Foundation, which aims to improve the mental health of legal practitioners. She is a member of the Scientia Education Academy at UNSW. She is the author of a number of articles on wellbeing in legal students and the legal profession and is currently undertaking a study of judicial trauma in a team of law and psychology researchers. She has also been a member of numerous professional accreditation committees.

Janet Chan is Professor and co-leader of the Data Justice Research Network for the Allens Hub for Technology, Law and Innovation at UNSW Law. She is a multidisciplinary scholar in criminology, technology studies and creativity. She is internationally recognised for her contributions to policing research, especially her work on police culture and the use of information technology in policing. Janet has been awarded a number of major research grants, ranging from policing, juvenile justice, restorative justice, creativity, work stress among lawyers, to Big Data analytics for policing and social policy. She is a Fellow of the Academy of Social Sciences in Australia and the joint recipient of the 2015 ANZ Society of Criminology Distinguished Criminologist Award.

www.ingramcontent.com/pod-product-compliance
Ingram Content Group UK Ltd.
Pitfield, Milton Keynes, MK11 3LW, UK
UKHW021845100926
8556IPUK00019B/1069

9 781780 689555